SPOKEN HERE

SPOKEN HERE

TRAVELS AMONG THREATENED LANGUAGES

MARK ABLEY

HOUGHTON MIFFLIN COMPANY

Boston • New York

2003

For information about permission to reproduce selections
from this book, write Permissions, Houghton Mifflin Company,
215 Park Avenue South, New York, NY 10003.

Visit our Web site: www.houghtonmifflinbooks.com.

Library of Congress Cataloging-in-Publication Data

Abley, Mark.

Spoken here : travels among threatened languages / Mark Abley.

p.   cm.

Includes bibliographical references and index.

ISBN 0-618-23649-X

1. Language obsolescence. I. Title.

P40.5.L33A25 2003

417'.7 — dc21   2002192181

Printed in the United States of America

Book design by Robert Overholtzer

QUM 10 9 8 7 6 5 4 3 2 1

The author is grateful for permission to quote from "Marsh Languages,"
from *Morning in the Burned House: New Poems by Margaret Atwood.*
Copyright © 1995 by Margaret Atwood. Reprinted by permission of
Houghton Mifflin Company. All rights reserved; and from "Lie Still,
Sleep Becalmed," by Dylan Thomas, from *The Poems of Dylan Thomas,*
copyright © 1946 by New Directions Publishing Corp. Reprinted by permission of New Directions Publishing Corp.

Portions of this book first appeared, in slightly different form, in *Brick,
Maisonneuve,* and the *Times Literary Supplement.*

This book is for Annie

Hey now, you got me by the tongue
I feel like, there's nowhere I belong.

—David Gray, *Faster, Sooner, Now*

The dark soft languages are being silenced:
Mothertongue Mothertongue Mothertongue
falling one by one back into the moon.

—Margaret Atwood, *Marsh Languages*

O felix peccatum Babel!

—J.R.R. Tolkien, "English and Welsh"

Contents

SPOKEN HERE

Patrick's Language

AN OLD MAN watches a milky ocean roll in to the shore. High above the waterline, two children are skipping barefoot along an otherwise empty beach, its contours defined and guarded by a pair of mangrove swamps. A long, low island nudges the western horizon. This could be an afternoon scene on almost any tropical coast: the heat rising off the sand, a hawk scouring the sky. In fact, the surf is brushing a remote edge of northern Australia — remote, that is, except to the old man's people, the Mati Ke, who may have lived in the area for tens of thousands of years.

One of the children pauses in her game. Among the fragments of driftwood and corrugated iron, the rusted fishing traps and crushed plastic bottles, she has found something different: a shell as long as her forearm. She looks up from the beach to the few scattered houses in the hamlet of Kuy. Then she calls to her grandmother, Mona, who is sitting as usual on a yellow foam mattress. Laid out on a verandah, the mattress gives a view of the sea.

The child uses her grandmother's language, Murrinh-Patha. It's also her own, and the daily language of a few thousand other people in the region. Most of its speakers live an hour's rough ride away, in a town called Wadeye. The trip is possible only in a four-wheel-drive vehicle down a dirt trail that slithers inland through the silver-green bush, passing the corpse of a small airplane and fording the same creek twice before it links up with a gravel road that ends or begins in town.

Somewhere along that trail, as you skirt the treacherous pools of deep red sand or disturb a loud gathering of cockatoos, you pass a border. The border is no less real for its lack of fences, checkpoints, and customs officers. It marks the ancient division between the Murrinh-Patha land that includes the town of Wadeye and the Mati Ke land that includes the small outstation here at Kuy. In Aboriginal Australia, land and language are intimately related. Traditionally, the continent was defined and divided not only by its hills, creeks, and water holes but also by its hundreds of languages. Wadeye grew up in the 1930s as a Catholic mission, and the Mati Ke were one of several peoples who moved off their land and switched over — out of a mixture of respect, convenience, and necessity — to a daily use of Murrinh-Patha. They also learned English, so as to comprehend the noise of authority. At first, nobody realized that the Mati Ke language was slipping away.

From her home above a calm shore of the Timor Sea, Mona gives her granddaughter an encouraging shout. Then she turns to her husband, Patrick Nudjulu, to explain. Unless he is wearing his hearing aid, words are lost on Patrick. But as the old man of Kuy, he likes to know what's going on. Besides, this is his land. Its stories belong to him.

Standing there on his verandah, his beard and flowing hair the color of the snow he has never seen, his skin as dark as wild grapes, Patrick has the gravitas of a biblical patriarch — a tall one, with a sly sense of humor. Some days he doesn't bother to put on a shirt. But if there's any chance that strangers might be present, he always wears long pants and shoes. That way, it won't be obvious that one of his legs is false — the aftermath of leprosy in his youth. A slight film over his eyes betrays the arrival of cataracts. But he can still see down to the beach; he can dream; he can remember.

"I remember *all*," he says in English, his fourth or fifth language. "I was born in my own bush here. Therefore I can't forget." He sips from a tin mug of tea that Mona has brewed up on the open fire pit at the far end of the verandah. "I dream in Mati Ke. See all the past."

And maybe the future, too? "Yeah." The old man is grinning. A few of his teeth are left. "Old future, and new future."

In his dreams, the fruit of the peanut tree whose seeds are eaten raw in the wet season is *mi warzu*. That's the name of the fruit in Mati Ke. But if he mentions the dream to Mona, he reverts to her more powerful language, Murrinh-Patha, and talks about *mi kurl*. The saltwater prawns that his grandchildren find among the mangroves are *a dhan gi* in his own tongue. But to Mona and the grandchildren, they are *ku tha-*

pulinh. The delicious goanna lizard that roams the bush all year is *a wayelh* in Mati Ke. But to speak of it and make himself understood, Patrick has to call the lizard *ku yagurr*.

A wide-eyed boy about a year in age totters over from the mattress where Mona is sitting. Children no more than five or seven years old take turns looking after him, hauling him back to his grandmother for comfort if he falls. Patrick peels a mandarin orange and hands it, chunk by chunk, to the little boy. Conch shell in hand, the boy's sister arrives beaming from the beach. Slumped beside Patrick's bamboo fishing spear farther along the verandah, an older grandchild on the brink of adolescence looks on. He and his mother are visiting from their home in Wadeye. His shirt is army fatigue; his hair displays streaks of blond dye; his gaze is sullen.

Patrick too spent many years in town. His family began to give up the bush when he was a boy. Over the decades, he watched Wadeye evolve from a resting place of hunters and foragers to a sitdown community, dependent on the welfare subsidies that Australia's government, possibly with noble intentions, has chosen to give Aboriginal people. Deprived of the old habits of life, unable to embrace the new, a host of men and women forfeited their pride. Patrick did not. Twelve or fifteen years ago, when the government was promoting the growth of outstations as a way for Aboriginal people to regain a spirit of independence and self-control, he led his wife and some of their extended family away from the frustrations of town and back to his own land, the place he knew by heart. Not that they were returning to the bark-and-bough shelters of his childhood. The government built bungalows at Kuy, and erected a small water tower, and hooked up electricity. Patrick's house has solar panels in its corrugated roof. One of the other houses is equipped with a satellite dish, and the children of the outstation go there to watch TV.

The TV pours a quick, bubbling stream of English into their ears and minds; but primary school and family life take place in Murrinh-Patha. Sometimes Patrick speaks to his grandchildren in Mati Ke, and he claims they understand. Yet whether they grasp more than a few commands, a familiar phrase or two, is open to doubt. They answer him in Murrinh-Patha: the language of their parents, their friends, their doting grandmother. Words in their grandfather's tongue trip haltingly, if at all, off their lips. What Patrick Nudjulu hears only in his dreams is another fluent speaker of Mati Ke.

The lone elder, the half-comprehending family, the stealthy invasion of other languages — this scene is not unique to Kuy, or Australia, or the Southern Hemisphere. It is happening all over the planet, from the snowpeaks of the Himalayas to the humid rivers of West Africa and the shantytowns of great cities in South America. The phenomenon is not new, for languages have always been in flux; languages have always died. No one alive today can hold a conversation in Hittite or Nubian. But the sheer pace of change is unprecedented. On every inhabited continent, languages keep falling silent. New replacements are rare. Linguists believe that about six thousand languages still flow into human ears: the exact total is a matter of debate. By some estimates, a maximum of three thousand are likely to be heard at the century's end, and fewer than six hundred of those appear secure. Within our children's lifetimes, thousands of human languages seem fated to dwindle away.

They are vanishing under similar pressures. A few languages of high prestige — English is the prime but not the sole example — dominate the media and the marketplace, school systems and bureaucracies. Almost anywhere you care to go — the Cayman Islands, the Andaman Islands, the Marshall Islands, the Galápagos Islands — young people are absorbing the same music and watching the same movies, most of them from Hollywood. Local cultures, less forceful, less alluring, are swept aside. At the same time, economic patterns of migration and displacement mean that fewer and fewer small languages still have a vibrant local base, a spoken homeland they can call their own. Cities provide new opportunities; they also blur and erase old identities. A minority language can quickly come to seem a hobby for the old — a quaint refuge from ambition, knowledge, progress. A minority language always depends on popular will. It dies as its voices fade in the midst of PalmPilots, cell phones, and Walkmans. It dies as its remaining speakers find they have less and less to talk about.

The price of that loss is beyond estimation. We have grown used to giving cultural artifacts a dollar figure: so many thousand for a Yeats manuscript, so many million for a Ming porcelain. But a language is more than any artifact. You can't slap a price tag on a language, no matter how small and obscure, any more than you can pin down the financial value of an ivory-billed woodpecker or a bill of rights. Mati Ke lacks the ever burgeoning scientific terminology of English and Japanese, nor does it enjoy a written literature. But like all other human languages, it is a full and rich expression of a way of life, a culture, an identity.

Whether or not it ever makes sense to use the term "primitive society," the phrase "primitive language" is an absurdity.

Mati Ke, for example, arranges all the objects and beings in the world by means of a system of noun classes. You can't speak of an object without also classifying it. There are ten of these classes, and they reveal an enormous amount about how Patrick Nudjulu understands his daily experience. A kind of red-flowering tree, for instance, is *thawurr babarlthang*— *thawurr* being the noun class for trees, wooden items, and long rigid objects. The string made from the inner bark of that tree is *nhanjdji babarlthang*. You use *nhanjdji* in front of a broad range of substances both manufactured, like the bark string, and natural: the wind, the sand, the sun. The tree's edible seeds are *mi babarlthang;* all vegetable foods are prefaced by *mi*. And so on. Weapons go in the same class as lightning. Places go in the same class as times (Mati Ke, you might say, anticipated Einstein by several thousand years). Speech and language deserve a separate noun class of their own. This is how Mati Ke interprets the world.

Murrinh-Patha's vocabulary is very different from Mati Ke's, but the underlying syntax is similar. Its arithmetic stops at the number five. Yet without counting, a fluent speaker of Murrinh-Patha knows thirty-one different pronouns and thirty-five verb classes. The grammar and syntax of Mati Ke and Murrinh-Patha are just as elaborate, just as complex and intellectually demanding, as the grammar and syntax of any well-known European tongue. Being widely spoken does not make a language any better, more intelligent, or more perceptive than a language that has never spread beyond its birthplace. As the literary critic George Steiner once observed, "We have no sound basis on which to argue that extinct languages failed their speakers, that only the most comprehensive or those with the greatest wealth of grammatical means have endured. On the contrary: a number of dead languages are among the most obvious splendours of human intelligence."

In Aboriginal culture, human life and the rest of the natural world are bound together by a system of totems — a child grows up in the knowledge that she belongs to the totem of the bush yam, say, or the female kangaroo. The language reflects and embodies this understanding. In Mati Ke, *nhanjdji marri* is the name for the cycad — an ancient plant whose tall, palmlike fronds are a familiar sight in the northern Australian bush. The cycad's seeds, poisonous straight off the plant, can be made into a kind of flour after prolonged washing; those seeds, being eventually edible, are *mi marri*. But *a* defines the class for animals (and people, if you mean to insult them). So what are we to make of *a marri*? That's the word, it turns out, for a kind of bush cockroach that inhabits dead cycad fronds. The class for higher beings — spirits and also people, if you're referring to them with respect — is expressed by *me*. And *me marri* defines those people whose totems are the cycad and the bush cockroach. Aboriginal languages have fewer words in them than English does. But those words are held and balanced in an intricate web of relationships. Lose the vocabulary, and you lose the relationships too.

Back in town, in a windowless room of the local museum, a ginger-haired, Queensland-born electrician named Mark Crocombe works part time as coordinator of the Wadeye Aboriginal Languages Centre. He spends most of his time on Mati Ke and a few other local languages whose numbers are severely depleted. High above the bark paintings and black-and-white photographs on the museum's walls, a gecko awaits mosquitoes. SLAYER AS GOD reads a piece of graffiti inscribed in neat capital letters outside the front door — TV shows like *Buffy* having permeated most of the human world. Once in a while, when his other jobs allow, Mark Crocombe leaves the office, fetches a camcorder from his house, puts it on the passenger seat of his beat-up minivan, and drives out to Kuy. His aim is to record Patrick speaking Mati Ke.

Thanks to their sporadic efforts, Mati Ke will experience a kind of afterlife: a partial, disembodied future. Elsewhere in Australia and in dozens of other countries, too, anthropologists, linguists, graduate students, tribal insiders, and well-meaning outsiders are hastening to record the voices of elders. Every captured story is a small victory over time. Through the electronic power of CD-ROMs or the slightly older magic of cassette tapes and the printed page, students in decades to come will be able to gain a limited knowledge of a vanished tongue. But a CD-ROM of an extinct language bears an uneasy resemblance to a stuffed dodo. A museum specimen, lovingly preserved, can give scientists all sorts of useful information except, perhaps, what is most essential: how the extinct bird behaved in the wild. Likewise, languages are social creations, constantly being tested and renewed in the mouths of their speakers. They require use, not just study. You can no more restore a vanished language from a scholarly monograph and a software program than you can restore a population of cheetahs from a vial of frozen sperm and a National Geographic film.

Hence the loneliness of Patrick Nudjulu: the gathering silence behind the old man's eyes. Speaking to his wife, his children, and his grandchildren, he employs a language that does not come as naturally to him as breath. The grandchildren jostle around him on the verandah facing the milky sea. But occasionally he brushes them aside, looking out on the water and the powdery beach without saying a word.

The coastal outstation at Kuy was, from my perspective as a North American, the most remote place I would visit between the years 2000 and 2002. Likewise, Mati Ke and Murrinh-Patha were among the most distant languages from my own that I would hear: among the most foreign ways of exercising the mind. Living in Montreal, a city where English, French, and other languages are in daily contact — usually friendly, sometimes bitter — I had seen a good many statistics about language loss. But the statistics told little of the passions and arguments that arise from a language's disappearance. And it was the emotions, not the numbers, that I cared about: the figures of speech, not the figures on a chart. I wasn't sure I could imagine what it meant for men and women to feel the language of their childhood melting away. I wasn't sure how much sense it made for them to fight back.

Eventually I embarked on a series of journeys, investigating the fate of linguistic diversity in places as discrepant as a village in the Canadian Arctic and an island off the Australian coast, a scrub farm in Oklahoma and a medieval city in Provence. In a few of these places, minority languages appear to be settling down into a comfortable oblivion; in others, the speakers of lesser-used languages are battling, not just to preserve a language but to strengthen and extend it. The tongues I heard are by no means a representative sample of the world's endangered languages — working without the help of researchers, secretaries, or graduate students, I did not have the resources to explore countries like Papua New Guinea and Cameroon, where hundreds of small languages survive. Still, I believe that the challenges facing hundreds, even thousands of minority languages are mirrored in these pages.

In Oklahoma, for example, I spent some time among the few remaining speakers of the Yuchi language. Yuchi is what linguists call an isolate: it bears a clear relation to no other living tongue. I wanted to discover what knowledge and understanding may die with Yuchi if it does indeed disappear. In the south of France, I hoped to see whether Provençal — one of the great literary languages of Europe — has a future as well as a past. Meeting speakers of Yiddish in several places would allow me to investigate the fate of a diaspora language. In Wales, the country where my parents were born, I was keen to discover how a Celtic language has, against all odds, remained vibrant beside the homeland of English. And so on.

Wherever I traveled, I tried to listen to the actual speakers of languages under threat — the loyalists of minority cultures. How do people who know their language is endangered bear the weight of such knowledge? I wanted to see how far their defiance could stretch, and how easily resignation could take hold. I wanted to learn what steps can be taken to sustain and strengthen a threatened tongue. Above all, I wanted to test my own hunch that the looming extinction of so many languages marks a decisive moment in human history — a turning away from vocal diversity in favor of what optimists see as a global soul and others as a soulless monoculture. In the end, should anybody care that thousands of languages are at risk?

That's the central question I will attempt to answer in this book. But I have a confession to make. I work as a journalist, poet, and editor; I am not a professional linguist. Indeed, my knowledge of the entire discipline of linguistics is patchy and often cursory. These pages do not touch on constructional homonymity and depth-first parsers; such matters lie beyond my frame of reference. My defense is one of analogy. You don't have to be a theologian to talk of God; you don't have to be a veterinarian to describe cats. Besides, this book is not just about threatened languages but about the people who speak them. I beg the forgiveness of linguists for trespassing on their territory and perpetrating whatever blunders have found a home in these pages — and I would gently remind them that their own voices are unlikely to be heard on the subject unless they speak out in terms that are lucid, intelligible, and free from jargon.

What will we lose if our abundance of languages shrinks to a fraction of what now survives? A speaker of English or Chinese might answer differently from a speaker of Mati Ke. The simplest response, perhaps, is this: we will lose languages that are astonishingly unlike any widespread tongue. Languages employ sounds and organize the mental world in ways that are natural to their speakers but can seem downright weird to other people. Nootka, one of the languages of Vancouver Island, is a case in point. As the linguist Benjamin Lee Whorf once noted, to express the idea "He invites people to a feast" Nootka requires but a single word: *tl'imshya'isita'itlma.* Literally, "Boiling result eating those go to get somebody." Not quite so literally, "He, or somebody, goes to get eaters of cooked food." The Nootka would alter their speech — adding hissing noises or extra consonants for effect — when they were talking to or about children, fat people, short people, left-handed people, circumcised males, lame and hunchbacked people, greedy people (also ravens), and people with eye defects.

Or take Kakardian, also known as Circassian, which arises from that great hotbed of linguistic diversity, the Caucasus Mountains. It boasts forty-eight consonants — more than double the number in English — but two vowels at most. In linguistic circles, a few experts have doubted those vowels' existence, suggesting that the language has *no* regular vowels. Can this be possible? To speak Ubykh, a language that originated in the same region, you'd need to get your tongue around eighty-one consonants. Abkhaz, which also belongs to the northwestern slopes of the Caucasus, had a special "hunting language" spoken by the local nobility on their journeys into the forests. The verbs would stay the same as in everyday Abkhaz. But to ensure good luck in finding and killing animals, hunters were forbidden to call objects by their workaday names. Therefore the hunting language contained an entirely distinct array of nouns, unknown to Abkhaz peasants and tradesmen.

Even more remarkable was an Australian language called Damin, spoken only by initiated men on three small islands in the Gulf of Carpentaria, due south of New Guinea. The daily language used by most of those men was called Lardil. After puberty, boys were circumcised (without anesthetic, of course) and taught Marlda Kangka — a sign language. For a year, it alone enabled them to communicate with anyone who had attended their circumcision. Marlda Kangka was more than just a basic code: its signs allowed a boy to convey information like "Last night I saw my mother's brother and father fighting in the bush." The most succulent food around the islands was the dugong, or sea cow. And Marlda Kangka had separate signs for "large young female dugong," "small female dugong," "old male dugong," and so on.

Marlda Kangka was just the beginning. After a year or more, young men who were brave enough moved on to the second stage of initiation: penile subincision. (Don't ask.) The reward for enduring the pain was a second auxiliary language, Damin. Unlike Marlda Kangka, it was spoken. But like Marlda Kangka — or Klingon or Elvish — Damin was a deliberate invention. Its sound system enforced a contrast with the parent language, Lardil. *M, l, r,* and a few other Lardil consonants were absent from Damin, yet Damin speakers employed eleven sounds not found in Lardil. Four of them were click consonants, otherwise used only in southern and eastern Africa. That's not all. Damin also demanded a "bilabial ejective," an "ingressive lateral fricative," and a "duplicated bilabial trill" (very roughly, *pr-pr,* with a roll for each *r*) — consonants that are found nowhere else in the world. Damin had five types of "phonetic initiation" — five ways for the vocal organs to produce sound — more than any other known language.

Ken Hale, one of the few linguists to study Damin, called it an "intellectual tour de force," for its structure was as amazing as its sound system. The language winnowed pronouns down to their essence. For any set of people including the speaker (that is, for the English terms "I," "me," "we," and "us"), Damin speakers said *n!aa* — ! representing a nasal click. For anyone and everyone else ("you," "they," "them," "he," "she," "him," "her"), Damin speakers said *n!uu.* The language's lexicon was small: just a couple of hundred basic words. But by ingeniously manipulating those words, initiated men could express almost anything they needed to say. Suppose a Damin speaker saw a sandpiper in flight. "Sandpiper" was not in Damin's lexicon. But the watcher could evoke the bird by saying *ngaajpu wiiwi-n wuujpu:* literally, "person-burning creature." The phrase harks back to a creation story in which Sandpiper starts a lethal fire — a familiar tale to all speakers of Damin. Likewise an ax was "honey-affecting wood": a wooden object used to obtain wild honey. Because it imposed this rigorous, semi-abstract vocabulary on the familiar syntax of Lardil, Damin could be learned in a few days. Initiated men would speak it at ceremonial gatherings, but also while searching for food or just sitting around gossiping. Extreme suffering had brought a gift of sacred knowledge.

No ritual initiations have been carried out in the Gulf of Carpentaria for half a century. As a result, Marlda Kangka and Damin are extinct. Their parent language, Lardil, is endangered. Abkhaz continues to be spoken, although its hunting language does not. Nootka survives, barely, as does Kakardian. But the last fluent speaker of Ubykh died in 1992. Multiply this paragraph a few hundred times over. Such is the fate of our languages.

Mati Ke may never have had more than a thousand speakers. For millennia, that was enough. Then, under the accumulated pressures facing Aboriginal people in the late twentieth century, the language collapsed. A 1983 study found it had about thirty fluent speakers left. Now, all evidence suggests, there are three. And one of the three — an old-timer living in Wadeye — might be annoyed to find himself on the list. For Johnny Chula knows his language not as Mati Ke but as "Magati Ge." Words have a different ring when he utters them. His dialect is heavier than Patrick's — the terms are mostly the same, but they arrive with extra syllables, chunkier in the mouth. "Johnny's the only speaker of Magati Ge," Mark Crocombe told me. "But he's too old now to work on the language."

Most of the time, whether on the sandy paths of Kuy or in the streets of some burgeoning city, a language ends with a long sequence of whimpers. Even if the language has just one fluent speaker, that speaker will often keep in touch with some younger men or women who know how to produce a few sentences, or who remember a smattering of words, or who cherish some traditional songs. So it is with Patrick's language. Near the pale waves of the Timor Sea, in lands where Mati Ke and its forerunners were probably spoken before the foundations of Sumer and Babylon were dug — and before the great myth of Babel first entered anyone's mind — not all knowledge of the language will vanish with his generation; Wadeye has a few middle-aged people who can stumble a short distance along the trails of Mati Ke. If the old man speaks with extra care, they can understand some of what he says.

Aloysius Kungul, one of Patrick's nephews, knows more than any of these other partial speakers. "Aloy, he's learning," Patrick insists. "He's learning, bit by bit." But the confidence soon dwindles from his voice. "It's difficult. I talk to him real slow." Aloysius is Mati Ke by inheritance: his totem animals are the masked plover, the mud crab, and the magpie goose, which distinguish the land around Kuy. Meeting him in Wadeye, I found him reluctant to say much about Mati Ke. It was his father's language; therefore, in Aboriginal society, it became his language too. But his father did not pass it on. One day when Aloysius was approaching puberty, he overheard his father speaking Mati Ke. "What's that language?" he asked. "It's ours," his father replied, offhand.

Flash forward a few decades: by Aloysius's own account, "I can hear the language, but I don't speak it, just a bit." He pointed at his own head, where black hair drooped toward his eyes in unruly bangs. "I got it *there*. But it's the speaking." If he were to spend months with his uncle, the speaking would come. But Patrick lives at the outstation, and Aloysius in town. With every succeeding year, his chances of fluency recede.

Which leaves just one other speaker of Mati Ke: an old woman called Agatha Perdjert. "And she's not real good at it," in Mark Crocombe's frank opinion, "because she left the Mati Ke country when she was fifteen." More than half a century has elapsed since Agatha married a Murrinh-Patha man and moved to Wadeye.

The red dirt track between Kuy and Wadeye is rough even in the dry season; in the wet, it can become impassable. A whole section of road is liable to vanish beneath the spillover creek. But on occasion Patrick still makes it into town, riding high in someone else's juddering machine down the straight road past the airstrip. In Wadeye, you might think, he could look up Agatha, so that they'd have a chance to revel in a language now almost unique to them. Maybe after all these years, Agatha has forgotten certain words. The salty billygoat plum that ripens in the rainless months, *mi kulurduk* in Murrinh-Patha: what do you call that fruit in Mati Ke? Maybe Patrick has lost a phrase in a particular song, or Agatha no longer recalls the name of a headland where she camped as a girl . . . Ah yes, the plum is *mi bakulin,* of course.

But this is a fantasy, nothing more. Agatha is Patrick's sister. The culture by which they live prohibits a brother and sister from conversing after puberty. They will never forage for missing words, never share their memories of childhood; any such conversation would be taboo. They must not even pronounce each other's names. When they die, the soul of a language will die with them.

Dreamers

LANGUAGES IN
NORTHERN AUSTRALIA

"CALLED BY THE NATIVES *Kangooroo*," James Cook wrote in his journal in June 1770, his ship pierced by coral along the Great Barrier Reef, its marooned captain facing a new world. This undreamed-of creature, for example, which moved "by hopping or jumping 7 or 8 feet at each hop upon its hind legs only . . . Excepting the head and ears which I thought something like a Hare's, it bears no sort of resemblance to any European animal I ever saw." Once his men had finally repaired *Endeavour* and he'd removed it from the reef, Cook sailed back to London with news of an unknown continent where the fauna and flora seemed bizarre. As proof, he took a stuffed specimen of the hind-leg hopper — the first kangaroo to arrive in Europe, and the first word of any Australian language to make its way into English.

"Kangooroo!" said the penal colonists of Botany Bay, eighteen years later. But the Iora people among whom they landed had no idea what the British were talking about. To them the animal was a *patagarang*. Guugu Yimidhirr — the language Cook had heard far to the north, at what he called Cape Tribulation — was entirely different from the language the Iora spoke. *Patagarang* never made it into English, but the colonists went on asking the Iora and neighboring peoples about the remarkable animals, plants, and landscapes all around them. And in short order *budgerigar, koala, kookaburra, dingo, boomerang, billabong,* and a few dozen other Aboriginal terms were being mouthed by the intruders from the far side of the world.

When those first ships landed near what would become the metropolis of Sydney, the sailors confronted a people who found them peculiar beyond belief. Instead of using bark canoes, the oddly colored newcomers rode enormous vessels on which flat plant material seemed to hang between trees. Instead of carrying wooden spears, the newcomers had long sticks, as hard as stone, that could produce a terrifying noise. Instead of walking naked, they wore bright disguises, even on top of their heads. They also hid their manhood. Were they men at all? The bravest among the Iora began to poke at British breeches, hoping to find out. Finally an embarrassed lieutenant ordered one of his men to extricate his penis and display it to the people who had gathered on the beach. When the sailor complied, the people "made a great shout of admiration." So the British version goes.

The Aboriginal people, it seems safe to say, were struck by what the British possessed. The British were struck by what the Aboriginals lacked. They had no clothes. They had no farms or domestic animals. They used no pottery. They had no permanent houses, no settled communities, no means of preserving food. They appeared to have no religion of any kind. And of course they had no guns; this was convenient, though hardly surprising. Their land was ripe for the taking. Without obvious possessions, they were ready to be dispossessed.

What the Aborigines did have, though, were languages. Estimates of their number have gone as high as six hundred; 270 seems the best current guess. Some of these languages were spoken by fewer than a thousand people. But each of them embodied an elaborate network of rules and laws. In many cases the intricacy of kinship systems matched the intricacy of grammar, so that even within a small society, an individual could not speak to some people at all and could address others only by using a special vocabulary. The Yolngu speakers of Arnhem Land, in the far north, lived by the *Madayin* — a concept that embraces codes, protections, controls, song cycles, trading highways, sacred sites, and much else. The Yolngu carried their laws and their religion in their minds. This does not mean their laws and religion were simple matters. Before the invention of alphabets and printing presses, human beings on every continent were capable of feats of memory that most people today find incomprehensible (the *Iliad* and the *Odyssey*, remember, were composed by illiterates). Each fully initiated Yolngu, intimate with the *Madayin*, possessed a library of unwritten knowledge.

No matter what language they spoke, the Aboriginal peoples had a high degree of social organization and a resolute attachment to a particular stretch of land. The land had been given to them, so they believed, by ancestral beings in the Dreamtime: the dawn of consciousness. The Dreamtime beings often lived in animal form — emus, frogs, opossums, and so on — but they performed recognizable human tasks like camping and fishing, making love and making war. Having arisen from a featureless land, they moved over it, creating its qualities as they went: a creek here, a rock formation there. Before they left the world, they bequeathed to its people the systems of clan and totem, the tools and weapons that would make up the fabric of Aboriginal life. They also bequeathed language: theirs were the words that came before all else, each name a living gift from the ancient past. Australia was not a new world, as Captain Cook imagined; it was an immensely old one.

The stories of the Dreaming cross physical and linguistic boundaries. A tale one clan begins to tell beside a seashore, another clan may finish far inland in a different language. The stories name and explain the landscape, so that patterns of wording and patterns of earth are inextricably linked. But the Dreamtime is not just something that happened once, long ago. It exists in a realm beyond ordinary time. Its beings defined the world. Perhaps they will appear again.

The good nature of the earliest encounters between Aborigines and whites did not last. Very soon it became clear to the indigenous Australians that these firearmed invaders had no intention of leaving. But the Aborigines made little effort to flee the guns, as some indigenous peoples did in the Americas. In Australia they stood their ground. If they tried to escape, they would have to enter someone else's land without permission. They would be abandoning their own — the land that gave their lives meaning, expressed in words that had come down to them from the Dreaming.

Generations after the first shock of contact, much of the land has been transformed beyond recognition, and many of its words have been erased. Guugu Yimidhirr, the source of "kangaroo," may still have a dozen or two speakers. But the languages that first told of koalas and kookaburras are no more. Indeed most of the languages belonging to land now occupied by Australia's major cities — Sydney, Melbourne,

Adelaide, Perth, Brisbane, Canberra — have not been heard for decades. The latest edition of *Ethnologue,* a directory of the world's languages, lists 417 as "nearly extinct." Of these, 138 are in Australia: a third of the total.

Only in the Northern Territory, far from major cities, do a few of the ancestral languages flourish. Traveling in the region, I glimpsed some of the difficulties that face minority languages around the world.

A few miles away from Patrick Nudjulu's house at Kuy, three adults and a dozen children were tramping across sand dunes in the harsh midday heat. "Just a short walk," Gemma Tganbe had said when we got out of the bus — really a small truck, pulling behind it a flatbed platform with benches and wire-mesh sides. And it *was* a short walk through the bush, until we reached the beach. A filament of sand stretched out for miles between the bush and a line of mangrove trees that protruded from the thick dark mud. Beyond the mangroves lay the audible waters of the Timor Sea. Now and then a barefoot child would leave the dunes and dart into the mangroves, searching for crabs, provoking cry after cry from the nameless birds.

Nameless to me, that is. I imagine Gemma Tganbe and Francella Bunduck had a word for them in Murrinh-Patha. Gemma and Francella were teachers at Our Lady of the Sacred Heart School in Wadeye, and today was not a holiday from learning: today was a Traditional Culture Day, a chance for students and teachers alike to leave the classroom and walk the land. This particular land, though, is not for everyone to see. Only those people who belong to it are expected: people of a single clan who share a totem creature, a language, a ritual dance. In some Aboriginal cultures, Dreamtime sites are felt to be so powerful that nobody is permitted to approach them. In many other places, outsiders are forbidden. I felt honored and surprised to be allowed here.

After the second mile the mangroves became fewer, the sea louder. Finally open water replaced the trees and the mud. On the landward edge of the beach stood a long row of red rocks, with the forest above. Gemma kept walking. So did the children, without complaint. They remained quiet when we stopped at a small bay where the sand and pebbles met a cluster of rocks, stained a rainbow of colors in long mineral swirls. Rock pools dotted the beach, the water in them warm from the sun.

Gemma began to talk. She had a story to tell, and she told it in her everyday language, Murrinh-Patha. It was the Magpie Goose Dreaming, a story that belonged to these rocks, this bay. When she stopped, the children moved forward to peer into a crevice of a long, honey-colored rock a few yards from the water's edge — a rock as tall as a grown person. In English Gemma repeated the gist of the story: how, in the Dreamtime, *ku kirrik* flew across the water and laid her eggs here; how she stepped across a couple of beaches, leaving visible tracks; how she flew inland over the red rocks and laid more eggs in the bush; how she made one final flight, depositing her last eggs at a reef in another bay. The crevice near the shoreline was her first nesting place. A big grin on her face, Gemma pressed my arm and said, "Then she stopped. I think she was exhausted from all that laying."

Dreamtime stories are for adults as well as children. The existence of special places like this one entails a responsibility: those who are linked to the magpie goose must look after the sites she left behind. The routes she took in the past are also paths — songlines — that Aboriginal people can take in the present. If they know the stories, that is. Without the stories, the land turns into real estate.

Children were climbing on other rocks, but not the Dreaming one. "The first laying was here," Gemma said. "You see the eggs?" I peered into the petrified shadows. "Used to be a big cave here," she added. "Now it's smaller. Rocks have fallen and it's changed." I didn't know if her "used to be" referred to five years or five thousand years. On an adjacent beach, children were examining X-shaped markings on a pair of flat, purple-red rocks. These were the scratched footprints of the Dreamtime goose. A boy jumped, fully clothed, into the deepest rock pool. Nobody told him to be careful.

Gemma pointed northeast across the sun-dappled bay. "See those two hills on the horizon?" she asked. "That's where my mob's from." When Aboriginal people say "mob," they don't mean a rioting horde; they mean "people." In the past Gemma's mob spoke a language called Marri-Djabin, but now most of them live in town and use Murrinh-Patha. Marri-Djabin is not yet on the *Ethnologue* list of nearly extinct languages. Give it another decade or two.

It was a long, sweltering walk back to the spot in the bush where the bus had let us off. The boy's T-shirt and black pants gradually dried, but moisture still glistened on the back of his neck. When at last we reached the shade, the group split into two circles, sitting on the ground, talking in low voices. Later in the afternoon, when the bus reappeared, some people caught a ride and went crabbing, others fishing. Nobody arrived home until well after dark.

Traditional culture. Yet there's something profoundly untraditional about this scene — apart from the presence of an outsider like me. And I don't mean the bus, for indigenous peoples all over the world are quick to adapt to useful technology. What's untraditional is that when Gemma told the children the Magpie Goose Dreaming, she spoke to them in Murrinh-Patha (literally, "language-good"). But the rainbow-rock bay beyond the mangroves isn't Murrinh-Patha country. It's the country where Marri-Djabin meets Patrick's language, Mati Ke; and the Magpie Goose Dreaming ought to be told in those tongues. The words that evoke the land ought to be the very words the ancestor spirit uttered when bringing the land to life. Yet in Mati Ke or Marri-Djabin the children would not have understood the story — and Gemma herself, being a partial speaker, might have found Marri-Djabin words slow and painful to come.

The location of a language, from an Aboriginal perspective, was decided in the Dreamtime. But the location of Wadeye — now the largest Aboriginal community in the Northern Territory — was selected by Father Richard Docherty, a missionary who founded the place in the 1930s and christened it Port Keats. He chose a spot above the all too aptly named Sandfly Creek. The missionaries ran Port Keats for forty years. Offering food, tobacco, medicine, iron tools, and Jesus, they pulled in people from separate areas and clans, expecting them to live in harmony while using the language of just one group: the Murrinh-Patha, whose creek and whose sandflies these are. As well as Mati Ke and Marri-Djabin, as many as five other traditional languages rang out through the settlement — I'm hedging my bets on the numbers, because in Australia even more than most other countries, the distinction between a "language" and a "dialect" is seldom clear. Murrinh-Patha became a lingua franca.

By the early 1970s the missionaries had grown old and unfashionable. After they packed their bags, Port Keats turned into Wadeye. In the dry season, an unpaved road connects the town with the rest of the Northern Territory; but in the wet, when the road is clogged by mud, soggy sand, and overflowing creeks, its two thousand people have no way out except by air. The recurrent isolation has helped keep Murrinh-Patha strong. For this is one of the very few traditional languages in Australia whose speakers have increased in number over the past generation. Lately it has spread beyond Wadeye to neighboring areas.

Simplicity is not a reason for the language's success. Some of its complexities seem mind-numbing — unless you're willing to take the plunge and call them mind-expanding. In its pronoun system, where English slices the world into singular and plural, Murrinh-Patha has four categories: singular, dual (with forms that vary for two males, two females, and two siblings), paucal (meaning three to about fifteen people, and again using different terms for males, females, and siblings), and plural (more than fifteen people). Each of these categories, moreover, has separate words for the first person ("we two males," for example), the second person ("you two males"), and the third person ("those two males"). "How are you?" we say in English, no matter how many people we're addressing and who they happen to be. Murrinh-Patha is a lot more precise. For "you," it compels a choice among *nhinhi, nankunitha, nankungitha, nanku, nankuneme, nankungime,* and *nanki.*

To say those words properly, you'd need to move your lips and tongue into some unaccustomed positions. Along with most other Australian languages, Murrinh-Patha has a vowel system that is simpler than ours, and it lacks sibilants like *s* and *z,* as well as fricatives like *f* and *v.* But it uses several consonants that to an English speaker seem intuitively wrong: *nh, dh,* and *rt,* for example. *Rt* is one of four "retroflex consonants" that require you to turn the tip of the tongue back in the top of the mouth. One of the commonest sounds in Murrinh-Patha and many other Australian languages is *ng* — pronounced the way we do in "singer," but often beginning a word. Strung together into sentences and conversations, what do these words sound like? In his landmark book *The Languages of Australia,* R.M.W. Dixon stated, "Australian languages generally have a euphonious sound, with a regular syllabic rhythm, something like Italian."

Back to the grammar. Some of Murrinh-Patha's pronouns are free-form, meaning that they stand on their own just like "him" and "her." But other pronouns are spoken only when you insert them into the middle of a verb. The verbs in their thirty-five classes not only swallow up pronouns, they incorporate body parts too. For anyone trying to learn the language, this means acquiring a double vocabulary: body parts, like pronouns, take on a new identity inside a verb. A nose is *thimu,* but a nose inside a verb is *yi.* (My *thimu* is in the middle of my face; you scratch your *yi.*) Eyes are *kamarl;* but once those eyes are the object of a verb, call them *ngka.* The incorporated term for a hand is *ma;* so, in Murrinh-Patha, "He will cut his hand" becomes a single verb, *puymartalnu,* or "He-hand-cut-will." The girls and boys of Wadeye master all this with ease, just as young English-speaking children nonchalantly come to terms with "pick on," "pick off," "pick at," "pick up," "pick out," "pick through," and so on.

At school, under the watchful eyes of Gemma and other Aboriginal teachers, a child becomes familiar not just with the words but with the structures and concepts implicit in Murrinh-Patha sentences like *Mangka pigunu-ka kardu makardu.* Yet the child is learning English, too. And soon, very soon, the child realizes that the structures of English are not the same as what Gemma works to instill. "Their grandmother is not here": this is an English translation of that Murrinh-Patha sentence. But the translation does violence to its true meaning: "The mother of the father of the three or more siblings is not here." A grandmother is either *mangka* or *kawu;* the two words don't mean the same thing. Partly because the school values the work of Gemma and her colleagues, Wadeye's children grow up with a solid grasp of differences like this — differences that inform the culture of their families. Many indigenous peoples are not so fortunate.

When I began my research, I hoped that if a traditional language remained strong in a community, its people would be better equipped to resist the onslaughts of modernity. Or, more exactly, they would be better equipped to turn modernity to their own use, gaining the benefits of development instead of becoming its victims. Given my preconceptions, Wadeye was to prove a challenge. Paul Black, who teaches linguistics at Northern Territory University in Darwin, had shaken his head when I mentioned Wadeye. "It's a community of lovely, warm, dedicated people," he said, "and Murrinh-Patha is solidly living. And yet I've been told there's not a car in town that hasn't been stolen at least once, and the boys regard being sent to prison in Darwin as a coming-of-age ritual."

The town used to possess a bakery, a sewing center, a brickworks, a construction yard, and a big vegetable garden. Now, for a host of reasons, these ventures have folded. From an outsider's perspective, unemployment is endemic. From a Murrinh-Patha standpoint, hunting and gathering carry on — at the local store. The town is desperately short of houses: it has bungalows where twenty people sleep. Yet when I was there one house remained locked up and vacant: the doctor's. Wadeye had no doctor. *NT News,* a tabloid newspaper in Darwin, has called the place a "hellhole" and a "war zone." The people of Wadeye have held a traditional smoking ceremony and burned *NT News.*

Some newcomers fall into culture shock. I spoke to a middle-aged teacher who had flown in a few months earlier on a short-term contract — one of forty or fifty white people in town. For reasons of privacy, I'll call her Pauline. "How on earth could you ever put this place on paper?" she said bitterly. "I still can't handle the litter. I can't handle all the locks and bolts and wire cages you need to keep anything safe. They're so inventive and creative at smashing things and breaking in." By "they," she meant the people she was here to teach. Pauline had a litany of complaints, some of them serious ("The men are violent and vicious to the women"), others perhaps not ("They don't have big attention spans"). She never spoke of an Aboriginal person by name. "Most of them don't know there's a world outside, and they don't want to know." Teaching a class of fourteen- and fifteen-year-old girls, Pauline was shocked by the students' poor command of English. "I keep telling them, if they want to be in charge of their future, they need to speak the white man's language. There's no way they can control their own destiny unless they can communicate with the person who's pulling the strings." Persuading the students to write in English was "worse than getting blood out of a stone." As for Murrinh-Patha, she often heard the girls "yabbering away in it." That's hardly surprising, for she teaches in a bilingual school.

"Yabbering" and "jabbering" are interesting words. They show up all over the English-speaking world whenever a speaker feels like sneering at animals or a minority people. Look up "jabber" in the *Oxford English Dictionary,* and you'll find quotations in which the term applies to monkeys, Flemish servants, seabirds, and Jews. It often betrays contempt, the dictionary observes, for "the speaking of a language which is unintelligible to the hearer."

Most of the other white teachers do not share Pauline's views. Although children here begin their schooling in Murrinh-Patha, learning from Gemma, Francella, and other women, by adolescence they spend most of their classroom time in English. This is a common model in bilingual schools everywhere. It seems a fair compromise between tradition and innovation — though it risks reducing the intellectual wealth

of a minority language by concentrating most of its classroom use on
the very young. I was told that teenagers in Wadeye often have a shaky
sense of Murrinh-Patha's grammatical intricacies. But many of them
rarely show up at school to learn in either language. Mark Lucas, a wid-
ower young enough to want a new professional challenge, moved here
from Sydney, where he taught English to immigrants and refugees;
needing the language at once, they picked it up fast. In Wadeye, he has
found, the need for fluent English is less obvious.

Some voices do extol the usefulness of English skills. I saw a homemade poster one day on a door of the local museum:

IF YOU DO NOT WANT YOUR CHILD TO SPEAK GOOD ENGLISH
FOR THEMSELVES TO NURSES, DOCTORS, POLICE,
GOVERNMENT PEOPLE, TAXI DRIVERS AND MANY OTHERS,
THEN DO NOT SEND THEM TO SCHOOL.
HELP OUR CHILDREN FOR THEIR FUTURE!
SCHOOL IS WHERE CHILDREN LEARN TO READ, WRITE,
DO MATHS AND HELP THEMSELVES BECOME GOOD PEOPLE.

But note the emphasis. In Wadeye, it seems unthinkable that a child
could grow up to *be* a nurse or a police officer — or even a Darwin taxi
driver. More than half the population is under eighteen. In their back-
ward-pointing baseball caps, local teenagers seem trapped between two
ways of life: the traditional culture of the elders and the remote excite-
ments of English. Neither one is fully available to them. English is now
used in circumstances both formal (the medical system, welfare, banking) and informal (bingo, discos, graffiti). But it is not seen as the local
people's property; it remains a foreign language, something that adheres to power. Or the power adheres to it. Boys in Wadeye can't dream
of becoming warriors as of old. Perhaps nobody has yet figured out
what they *can* become.

"Look, these kids are never going to be white Australians," I was told
by a veteran civil servant in Darwin. "And at the same time, they're not
going to be black American rap singers. Or Shaquille O'Neal. One of
the things that will keep them going is to keep them strong in their own
culture." But that kind of strength is now sporadic, as when the school
arranges Traditional Culture Days. Aloysius Kungul said that when he
was young — the 1970s, that is — boys would swim and fish with their
own clan group. Not any longer; and if the decline of a group identity
heightened a spirit of individual freedom, many outsiders would be

pleased. The trouble is, Aloysius added, the way freedom is expressed: "Sleep in, get up late, watch videos, play computers — then at six or seven o'clock, they start walking around in gangs. Old people tell them that's no good." But so what?

Even young people in Wadeye have begun to suffer from high blood pressure, kidney disease, and diabetes. A week after I left town, the school was due to close for "Scabies Day" — an attempt to overcome an epidemic. You could argue that the lack of fluent English in the over-crowded homes has made these sicknesses more prevalent. I met a visiting nurse who was appalled at how little the people knew about kidney failure; explaining what a kidney does, she needed to address them at the most basic of levels. But of course, she talked at them in English only. She had no grasp of the Murrinh-Patha worldview, no sense of why kidney disease was all but unknown here in the past, no idea of what it means to move within a single life span from a culture of hunters, gatherers, and warriors to a passive, sit-down society. She couldn't imagine the concept of health in the minds of the people who dismayed her. "What use," she said, "is Murrinh-Patha?"

Mark Lucas had no doubts as to the value of Murrinh-Patha: "Everything that defines who a person is, is defined by the language: their spirituality, their identity, their relationship with the environment." But he brooded about the school's emphasis on reading and writing: "We might be flogging a bit of a dead horse. I don't think it's necessary for the majority of people here to be literate in either English or Murrinh-Patha. If young people choose to live a traditional life, which sadly not many of them do, they need a visual literacy and an environmental literacy more than they need literacy in English." Ironically, Mark was running the Literature Production Centre, which over the past quarter-century has turned out hundreds of basic readers, workbooks, stories, and vocabulary lists in Murrinh-Patha. I glanced through a picture book whose hero is a mosquito-munching gecko. The story is set in Wadeye; the children in the background of the illustrations look like the readers of the book. The hope behind it all is to transform a thriving unwritten language into a thriving written one — within the context of a white-run school.

Powerless on many fronts, the residents of Wadeye have chosen to maintain Murrinh-Patha. Consider it a subtle act of defiance, and one of the rare options they have. Yet while all the Aboriginal people here speak Murrinh-Patha, some refuse to accept it as their own. Languages often coexist in a single setting, like roommates respectful of each other's private space; most bilingual or multilingual societies are not locked in strife. But the harmony can dissolve in the face of grievance, physical or metaphysical. At that point, languages become a reason (or merely an excuse) for discord. In Wadeye, some people who by ancestry belong to Mati Ke, Marri-Djabin, or another fading language still hope that the old ways of speech can be revived. They are intimate strangers to their mother tongue.

Revival is not an issue for Tiwi, an Aboriginal language spoken on a pair of islands off the north coast of the continent. At least, it's not an issue yet. Flat and thickly forested, the islands lie a half-hour's plane ride from Darwin. One day I flew to Nguiu, the main town — the *only* town — on Bathurst Island. Unlike Wadeye, Nguiu has a tourist trade: for economic reasons, the eighteen hundred or so Tiwi have been willing to market their distinctive culture. Visitors stomp the islands in regulated groups. The Tiwi have grown inured to the snap of shutters in their faces.

What the tourists glimpse is a web of language, ritual, myth, and social practice that developed here in isolation over thousands of years. To the Tiwi, Australia's mainland was a smudge on the southern horizon; until the early twentieth century they believed it was *Tibambinum,* the home of the dead. Today, carved and painted funerary poles from the islands are a mainstay of Darwin craft shops and can be bought in Nguiu as well. Yet in the town's Catholic cemetery the poles retain their original purpose: to mark the gravesite of a wealthy or important person. Plain white crosses stand side by side with flamboyant ironwood poles. It's a sign of how the Tiwi mingle new and old traditions.

Their language, however, is at the heart of a controversy. An old man called Simon Tipungwiti, wearing a World Wrestling Federation cap and sipping tea from a tin mug, alluded to it: "The young ones here, we try to protect them and show them good raising. We show them the really good way to speak the language." But I didn't grasp what he meant, so he moved on to the subject of fishing: "Many creeks in this area, they have mud crabs. And two kinds of barramundi, fresh and salt." Simon may well have been thinking that while you can't expect a foreigner to understand a topic as rich and demanding as the Tiwi language, any idiot can appreciate fishing.

Only after he'd shuffled away did I learn what he'd been trying to explain. Tiwi is still the everyday language of Nguiu, but it's spoken in two different forms. Traditional Tiwi, as used by elders like Simon, has an enormously complex verb structure. Its verbs describe not just a basic action but also the time of the action, its agent, and its object; they are, in linguistic terms, "polysynthetic." A single line of a Tiwi hymn, conveying the rough English sense "For that is what I dream about," has a tongue-twisting verb: *Pili ngiya awarra ngimatimingilimpangipulampi.* In her *Tiwi-English Dictionary,* Jennifer Lee writes: "Middle-aged and younger people can understand some traditional Tiwi. However, not many can speak it, particularly the hard verb forms . . . In speaking, young people often do not use a traditional verb form at all but a loan word from English or an imperative form of the traditional verb which they use as a free-form verb." The result is "modern Tiwi" or "new Tiwi."

It's not just a question of borrowed vocabulary. Nguiu's Mothers Club has an annual "Eisteddfod," but Welsh shows no sign of invading the island. A host of English nouns have been happily adopted into Tiwi and are now used even by elders: *anjikuwu,* meaning "loincloth" or "material," comes straight from "handkerchief"; *pajikitipuli* is, believe it or not, a Tiwi adaptation of "basketball"; *tinayijuwi* are "teenagers." So far, so good. The tensions arise when the entire syntax of a Tiwi sentence — the flow of thought, the structure of meaning — is disrupted by an alien verb. In traditional Tiwi, the phrase "she is walking" could be conveyed as *ampijirrangurlimayi.* But young people find it hard to generate such a word, even if they can guess its meaning on the lips of elders. They're more likely to use the borrowed term *wokaput* — "walkabout," that is.

To speak Tiwi, then, is to take a continual stand. Leo Weardon, who has been the Catholic priest on Bathurst Island for the past seven years, set out to learn the language — not all his predecessors had bothered to try — and has succeeded well enough to say the liturgy and read the scriptures in Tiwi. A burly, thoughtful man in middle age, he has a gaze of singular intensity. To his chagrin, he finds the language so hard that he can't deliver sermons in it. Few young people come to mass, although the liturgical wording was eased for their benefit. "I don't use English verbs when I say the mass," Father Leo told me, "but I'm aware that I'm not using traditional Tiwi. It's a simplified form. When I read the Gospel, it's in modern Tiwi." His blue eyes looked uneasy. "Of course there's an argument that when you use a modern form, you're facilitating a language's destruction."

His church is a new, unwalled structure, open to the four winds. It's a far cry from the original chapel put up by one of the best-known missionaries in all of Australia: a formidable Alsatian priest named François-Xavier Gsell. When he arrived in 1911, Nguiu did not exist. The islanders, still nomadic, still gunless, lived in fear of the white hunters who would come ashore in search of feral buffalo. The hunters killed men and animals alike, and having done so they raped the women. Gsell insisted that the murder and rape had to stop, and they did. Buoyed by success, he set out to transform the Tiwi way of life, starting with its system of arranged early marriage. Girls could be married off at birth; men were often older than their mothers-in-law. The priest used an impressive array of trade goods — everything from a hatchet, a knife, and a pipe to treacle, flour, and canned meat — to buy a frightened ten-year-old girl from her elderly bridegroom (who was already married to a dozen other girls and women). Gsell repeated the rescue purchase many times over, becoming "the priest with 150 wives." Soon his chapel echoed with Kyries and Credos emerging from the mouths of Tiwi girls and boys with new names like Hyacinth, Assumpta, and John Baptist. "The old people still sing hymns in Latin," Father Leo said with a look of bemusement. "They love it."

If the church now holds out a hesitant embrace to elements of modern Tiwi, Murrupurtiyanuwu Catholic School aims to act as a conservative force, a brake on language change. For decades its long, low buildings were called St. Therese's. Then, in 1992, the school took the name of its first Tiwi instructor. The staff at Murrupurtiyanuwu pride themselves on teaching Tiwi literacy, especially in the early grades, and they try to keep the loan verbs at bay. An experimental curriculum calls for greater depth and sophistication in the teaching of Aboriginal languages. So, when children of twelve or thirteen are not studying in English, they will be asked to "explain indigenous land management practices" and "describe reasons why the kinship system is important" — in their mother tongue. I saw a crowded back room where shelf upon shelf was packed with tapes of old people telling stories. Some of the tapes have been transcribed and published. The stories are a priceless archive. Yet on their own they won't meet the fresh, analytical demands.

Tiwi was the language of an entire small world; now that world is an offshore fragment of an English-speaking nation. It's a fragment that has lately seen an alarming number of suicides. Walking back toward the office, I passed a small building, its outer walls painted with bright murals. One of them showed a family group at a dry-season camp in the bush. Over it, someone had written:

NO MORE CULTURE FOR US.
GANGSTA GAMES WE RIDE.

Gangsta games: "For that is what he dreams about." Another wall depicted a man spearfishing from a dugout canoe. Above the water, at the point of his spear:

WE ARE THE JAIL BIRD WESTSIDE GANGSTERS
OKAY MOTHER FUCKERS.

I wonder if the boy who wrote this — somehow I assume it was a boy — understood what the words mean.

A sign on the office door announced: PURINJITI. In the past, the word meant "message stick" — a bearer of news, traveling beyond his own land, would brandish a *purinjiti* to gain safe passage through other people's territory. But here the word divulges the presence of telephones and a fax machine. The school's principal, Kilipayuwu Puruntatameri, went by the Christian name "Teresita" until she took back a Tiwi identity. She does much of her work outside the office, in an open-air sitting area with two long tables and a corrugated iron roof to protect against rain. At recess and lunchtime the staff gather here, making tea and conversation.

I sat there one morning with Kilipayuwu, an elder named Leonie Tipiloura, and one of the school's four vice principals, Leah Kerinaiua. Leah, an ebullient woman sipping Coke rather than tea, had visited the Navajo reservation in the United States and a Shuswap-language immersion school in Canada. Unlike many black Australians, she wasn't intimidated by outsiders. She accepted the need for English — "but," she added, "the community says we need our children to learn the Tiwi language first." Hence the presence of elders like Simon. Education can be tradition's enemy. Here, in principle, the two are partners.

Leah showed me a reading book intended for eight- or nine-year-olds. On each page she had circled two or three words in pencil — words that teachers say the children just don't understand. *Tirriwunga*, meaning "long grass," was one of them. It would have been familiar to small children in the past. But in Nguiu, grass is kept short. Over the isolated centuries, the Tiwi language developed a wide range of descriptive terms. Its speakers distinguished *arawunga* ("early morning before dawn") from *tokwampari* ("early morning when birds sing"), and *yarti-jumurra* ("darkness before daylight") from *wujakari* ("first light before sunrise"). Such nuances are hard for children to grasp, and adults to remember, if they always sleep indoors.

"But when it's end of school," Leonie said, "us mob go bush. We camp out one month on our land. We get a lot of bush food — copper snake, possum, wallaby, bandicoot, also sugarbag and yam." Sugarbag is a hive of wild honey, she explained, her eyes crinkled in laughter at my ignorance. "While we're there, we tell stories. How we get bush food, how we live with people. Stories at night, when we go to sleep. We make campfires and tell stories about way back, Mission days." The "we" is not just Leonie's family but much of the population of Nguiu. That shared month in the dry season helps account for the survival of Tiwi; the decline of bedtime or campfire storytelling may be a factor in the erosion of many languages.

"It's our language," said Leonie. "It's ours. We're not stopping other people from using their language. In this world today we have our own."

"They don't realize we're here all the time," Kilipayuwu remarked. She gave a long, slow laugh.

Knowing the islands now and throughout time, the Tiwi experience life on them differently from newcomers and outsiders. English-speaking Australians in the region divide the year into two or three seasons: the dry, the wet, and (sometimes) the insufferably humid buildup before the wet. Tiwi recognizes not only those three but also thirteen lesser seasons, flexible and overlapping in length, for which English has no words. Father Leo is thinking of inserting in the mass some mention of the Tiwi spirit beings. There are the spirits who turn into children, the spirits who kidnap little girls, the spirit man who lives in tall anthills and likes to play — not to mention the bloodsucking, sky-roaming spirits and the terrifying spirits of the dead. All of these have names and patterns of behavior: a spiritual ecology, if you like.

The language encourages its people to hold on to certain traditions as well as beliefs. It contains a word for "man bereaved of sibling." Or take the key term *yiminga*. According to Jennifer Lee's dictionary, it has five separate meanings. The first of them — spirit, life, breath, pulse —

suggests the word's importance. It can also signify the gallbladder, a craving for something, or the sun's position in the sky. Finally, *yiminga* means a person's maternal totem group or "skin group." To forsake the skin group, the Tiwi language suggests, would be to forsake life itself.

All the men and women I met in Nguiu believed that to be fully Tiwi you had to speak Tiwi. Identity, they agreed, is bound up in language. But for many Aborigines, such an idea is best ignored. The Larrikiya, for example, owned the country where the city of Darwin now stands. Its famous Thursday evening beach market — at which thousands of people gather to munch fast Asian food, browse for New Age crafts, listen to live music, and watch the sun slide into the Timor Sea — takes place on top of a Larrikiya burial ground. The language has been without a fluent speaker ever since, as one man breezily told me, "Old Topsy died ten or fifteen years ago." Even without Topsy and his forgotten words, the Larrikiya people, and some form of a cohesive identity, endure. Indeed, like many of North America's indigenous groups, they have begun to call themselves a "nation." It was on Larrikiya territory that I saw an Aboriginal woman standing alone outside a bar, listening to a band on the dark side of the hedge perform a cover version of Pink Floyd: *We don't need no education . . .*

At the lush campus of Northern Territory University in suburban Darwin, I met a linguist called Michael Christie who teaches in the Yolngu Studies program. The name "Yolngu" refers to a set of languages still spoken in northeast Arnhem Land, a wild, spectacular, and mineral-filled region east of Darwin. Its Aboriginal people were among the last in Australia to be suppressed; massacres by settlers lasted well into the twentieth century. Michael had a refreshing outlook on a range of topics — the Dreamtime, for example. The usual explanations of the stories make them sound utterly foreign to non-Aboriginal culture. "But it was *our* ancestors," he said with a glint in his eye, "moving across the land, singing and dreaming and talking, that made it possible for us to live in a world that we can find human." If the world seems comprehensible, it's because of the signs, tales, and knowledge that ancestors in every culture have succeeded in passing down. We too are such stuff as dreams are made on.

Michael described the extraordinary facility that Yolngu children show for language. By the age of four, they develop a kind of mental filter by which they avoid saying the name of any person who recently

died — as well as all words similar to that name. Such words remain taboo, sometimes, for years. Yolngu languages have a rich vocabulary, en-
abling speakers to express a notion in several ways; still, as an adult
learner Michael finds it hard to bypass a forbidden name, risking grief
and offense in the process. Small children navigate the shoals with ease.
The intricacies of the traditional clan and kinship system meant that
children always grew up hearing distinct languages (outsiders might say
"dialects") spoken by their mother, their father, and their mother's
mother. As a result, they learned to understand languages related to
their own, ones whose grammar was similar but whose vocabulary was
not. Multilingualism was only natural. Today, all this is in flux.

The past couple of decades have witnessed a sea change in outsiders'
awareness of Yolngu and other traditional languages. An 848-page *Concise Encyclopedia of Australia,* published as recently as 1984, contained
entries on lice, tongue worms, lawn bowls, and Rupert Murdoch — but
it had no entry on the languages spoken by the country's first inhabitants. A terse, three-sentence subsection used the past tense: "There
were hundreds of Aboriginal languages . . . Very little has survived of
many." Flash forward a decade and a half to the appearance of Lonely
Planet's *Australian Phrasebook.* Along with its explanation of grommies,
chippies, and Darwin stubbies, it devotes nearly ninety pages to Aboriginal languages — more than a third of the book.

But the change in consciousness through the 1980s and 1990s failed
to stem the erosion of the languages themselves. Goodwill is pleasant; it
is also useless. In most regions of Australia, Aboriginal languages are in
need of revival — or resurrection. Even the healthiest ancestral tongues
have only a few thousand speakers. That's nothing new: these languages
always belonged to small clusters of people. Trouble is, the old signs,
tales, knowledge, and social networks are now so outnumbered, so
hemmed in.

Even among the Tiwi and the Yolngu, Aboriginal social networks are
inevitably far different from what they were in the past. But as I found
when I drove south one day from Darwin to an isolated community
called Barunga, it's too simple to claim that ancestral languages are always losing out to English. Barunga is the site of the most famous Aboriginal sports and cultural festival in the country — the place where
Bob Hawke, prime minister in the late 1980s, promised that Australia's
government would at last negotiate a treaty with the country's indigenous peoples. (The promise has not been kept.) To reach Barunga you

turn off the main highway between Darwin and Alice Springs, following a single lane of asphalt flanked by rust-colored sand. Go far enough east, and you'd enter the Yolngu territories in Arnhem Land.

"No worries, mate," said the young Aboriginal woman on duty at the festival gate. "You'll have a great time." I went inside and found a white announcer working overtime to drum up enthusiasm: "Only four times around the oval for the Barunga mile!" "We still need a few more entries for the didge comp!" He meant a didgeridoo-playing competition. The Australian-rules football matches drew the largest crowd. Young and old — but mostly young — a few hundred people thronged around the fenced edges of the oval, reacting to the players' efforts with feeling. Often the spectators would call out in a rapid-fire idiom that was strange to me — a language in which I didn't recognize a word. Was it one of the ancestral tongues of the region, miraculously resilient in the face of English?

It was not. Australia, I learned, is home to a pair of Aboriginal languages that have enjoyed rapid growth. In numbers, they far surpass Murrinh-Patha, Tiwi, and every other ancestral language. Both are creoles, based on English but unintelligible to English speakers at a normal rate of speech. What surrounded me at Barunga was Kriol, used by more than twenty thousand people across northwestern and far northern Australia. Its cousin, spoken by Torres Strait Islanders off the tropical tip of Queensland, has the revealing name of Broken. Kriol and Broken are hidden languages. The concealment may be a source of their power.

Kriol was born on the Roper River Mission, east of Barunga, where in 1908 Anglican missionaries gathered together a few hundred Aborigines who belonged to at least eight languages. (If the missionaries hadn't done this, the murder gangs employed by a London-based multinational, the Eastern and African Cold Storage Company, might have wiped out the indigenous people.) Being multilingual, the traumatized adults at Roper River could manage to talk among themselves. But to deal with the missionaries, they needed to learn English, a language new to them. Some of them already spoke what would come to be called Northern Territory Pidgin English: its rules were basic, its vocabulary scanty. Devoid of complexity or poetry, it made no assertions of identity. But it served a purpose: communication. It was convenient.

Children created Kriol — children who, if any of them survive, must now be wizened elders. Language is the most critical facet of human experience in which a child's capacities exceed an adult's. For if small children grow up hearing a pidgin all around them, they naturally, spontaneously, take the enormous extra step of turning the pidgin into a creole. They transform a limited collection of words into a true language with its own grammar and syntax. Adults cannot do this: our minds are too set in their ways. The Aboriginal children of Roper River had no common language except pidgin English. Talking to one another in the mission's dormitories, they used pidgin as the raw material to forge something new. Children all over the colonized world have done the same, giving birth to creole languages grounded in Dutch, French, Spanish, and Portuguese as well as English. The newest of creoles is said to be developing around Juba, a city in war-weary southern Sudan, where children are creating a language out of pidgin Arabic and local tongues.

From its birthplace on the Roper River, Kriol spread to many other places in the north of Australia; or else — the history is not entirely clear — it was born afresh in two or three other places where Northern Territory Pidgin was widely used. The vocabulary of Kriol leans heavily on English, though it also includes some words from Aboriginal languages. *Mailawik,* for example, combines "week" with an Aboriginal term, *maila,* meaning "poor." If your bosses pay you every other week, *mailawik* refers to the time when you don't get paid. *Baindim* comes from "find" but adds an extra meaning: "conceive."

The traditional languages around Barunga, Roper River, and other settlements are dissimilar, and so the exact properties of Kriol vary from town to town. Its sound system and a few elements of its syntax hark back to Aboriginal models: like them, it does not use the letter *f,* and its pronouns distinguish dual forms from plural ones. *Ola gel* are "the girls"; *dubala gel,* "the two girls." For everything that English lumps together as "we," Kriol requires more precision: "we" can mean *yunmi* (you and I), *mindubala* (I and someone else), *melabat* (you and I and at least one other), or *mibala* (I and at least one other, but not you). The origins of these words lie in English, but the understanding they express is Aboriginal. Languages differ not just in what its speakers *can* say, but in what they *must* say.

As Kriol grew, it smothered the pidgin from which it was born; it also helped silence the ancestral languages that fed it; and as yet, it has showed no signs of succumbing to the English of mainstream Australia. (Further south, where pidgin was never so widespread, most of the country's black people speak "Aboriginal English," a dialect of the mainstream language.) Kriol may possibly have a short life span. But anyone who expected it to be just a temporary, in-between language is still waiting to be proved right.

How different is Kriol from English? Try saying this aloud: *Orait, sambala stakmen deya langa dat Kantri deibin maindimbat ola nenigout langa pedik naitaim.* A literal rendering might run as follows: "All right, some stockmen there belonging to that country, they were minding all the sheep belonging to the paddock at night." Sound familiar? In a Kriol selection from the scriptures, *Holi Baibul,* this is a verse from Luke's telling of the Christmas story: "And in that region there were shepherds out in the field, keeping watch over their flock by night." Abstract verses demanded extra wording, but the translators could invariably get the idea across. A line from Paul, "He has made known to us . . . the mystery of his will," became this in Kriol: *Imbin shown wi det plen blanga im . . . Nobodi bin sabi det plen basdam, bat wi sabi na.* "He showed us that plan of his . . . Nobody understood that plan before, but we understand now."

Holi Baibul came out in 1985. When it appeared, some people from Kriol-speaking towns sported T-shirts displaying a Bible and a map of "Kriol Kantri." The slogan on the T-shirt read *Dubala brom God* (Both from God). But the pride expressed by the T-shirt and the Bible are un-usual. For several years Barunga children learned Kriol in school under a bilingual program. Then a white principal abolished the program, so that classes now function in English only. The principal was following a long line of outside critics who have called Kriol "ridiculous gibberish," "broken jargon," and "lingual bastardization."

A lot of Kriol speakers also view the language with regret — it has never had many champions. A few days after the Barunga festival, I met a soft-spoken man called Musso Taylor. He is registered as a transla-tor and interpreter between Kriol and English: policemen and doctors use him as an intermediary when official duties require them to ad-dress somebody whose English skills are poor. Eloquent on other top-ics, Musso skirted around Kriol with great unease: "It's not an English sort of thing — it's sad in a way, maybe all our people have lost their own language. I mean to say, people speak a mixture." Although Kriol provides him with an income, he seemed embarrassed that I'd men-tioned it.

Adults often say they speak Kriol to their children because they want the children to learn English and have a head start in school. Unfortunately, that decision can backfire. When Kriol-speaking kids go to school, they naturally blend the classroom's formal wording with the related, casual language they already know — and the blending can make it hard for them to achieve a good command of standard English. Aboriginal parents know how different Kriol is from any ancestral language. But they tend to underestimate the distance between English and Kriol, seeing Kriol as just "blackfella English."

That afternoon at Barunga, I heard Kriol all around me. But everything I saw written down was in my own language. All the written information at the booths of the Labour Party, the Northern Land Council, and Kakadu National Park was in English; so were the price lists at the meat-pie stand and the ice cream stall. Leaving the oval and the announcer's relentless good cheer ("Everyone sign up for the spear-throwing comp!"), I walked around the red roads of the little town. The dreaded cane toads have reached Barunga — every few hundred yards I passed a squashed, obese, poisonous, dried-up corpse. At sunset, as I drove past sand devils on the single-lane track, Cher was singing on Radio Barunga. "You're listening to the voice of the bush," the disc jockey said. Cher gave way to Madonna and the power of goodbye.

Even here in the Top End, far closer to the rain forests of New Guinea and Borneo than to the skyscrapers of Sydney, the voices of the bush are likely to speak English — or, in private, Kriol. To find out more about why the region's traditional languages are falling silent, I flew from Darwin to Kununurra, a young town at the northeastern corner of Western Australia. Kununurra's airport has a big sign welcoming passengers to "The Last Frontier." I had to wait for a Greyhound bus that would carry me deeper into the state, and I passed a couple of hours in a bar — on a Sunday afternoon, there's not a lot to do in Kununurra. The available cocktails included Squashed Frog, Tetanus Shot, and Shit on the Grass (Bailey's over crème de menthe). I stuck to beer. A lone ibis prowled outside the locked tourist office. The bus was four hours late.

Eventually it took me to the old mining town of Halls Creek, the only settlement of any size in an immense area of scrubland and desert. Helicopters, light planes, and four-wheel-drive vehicles offer trips to the extraordinary striped rock formations known as the Bungle Bungles — possibly a corruption of the Aboriginal name *Purnululu*. Western Australia is divided into "shires," an incongruous term for anyone who imagines counties on a British scale: the shire of Halls Creek covers an area larger than Greece and has a population of about thirty-two hundred. It's one of several shires that make up the Kimberley, a vast region at the top of Western Australia. The region is often described as "rugged." This is like describing Mozart as "musical."

Along with adjacent parts of the Northern Territory, the Kimberley enjoys the greatest linguistic diversity in all of Australia. The languages of most of the continent belong to a single family, Pama-Nyungan. But the Kimberley contains five such families, divided into at least thirty tongues — not counting English and Kriol. "Australian languages," notes the linguist Paul Black, "seem to conspire to frustrate genetic classification." Some of the Kimberley languages may well be cultural artifacts of unimaginable antiquity. Their voices already echoed among these riverbeds, boab trees, and desiccated hills when the Sphinx was under construction in a far-off desert; and, like the Sphinx, they have outlived the ages. Their origins, relationships, and history remain an enigma.

Of these thirty languages, only three are spoken by children. It's as though twenty-seven Sphinxes are crumbling away before our eyes.

Halls Creek has been a meeting point of languages for nearly a century, ever since black children from all over the Kimberley were deported to a nearby cattle station and "Native Welfare Settlement" called Moola Bulla. By chance, the mining town had sprung up near the border between two unrelated tongues, Kija and Jaru. Now young speakers of other languages found themselves in the same area, under the sway of English. The inevitable happened: a creole emerged. Today Kriol is the daily medium for the vast majority of Aboriginal people around Halls Creek. Still, some elders use the ancient languages among themselves, and a few families living in desert outstations are bringing up children who speak fluent Jaru. A pilot who occasionally airdrops supplies to these outstations shook his head and said to me, "The middle of nowhere."

Which leaves the town of Halls Creek perched, from a white person's standpoint, on the far edge of nowhere. The gold mine and most of the cattle stations having closed down, nine in ten residents are black. Rates of rheumatic fever, anemia, and childhood malnutrition are so high that in 2000 the town's medical officer called the health of local Aborigines "so bad as to constitute a human rights issue." Reading the doctor's words, I could feel him struggling with his own language to express the pain he saw.

Like Wadeye, Halls Creek is a community of lovely, warm, dedicated people. But the clash of uncomprehending cultures can also make it a hurtful, hurting place. One morning I chatted with a gregarious Englishman who trains and counsels Aboriginal adults. "They don't waste words," he remarked. "Instead of saying 'Look, there's a green car coming along the road,' they'll say 'Green car.' Or if they see that Tony's driving the green car, they'll say 'Tony.'" The people are a lot more voluble, of course, in Kriol. That evening I walked to the "grog shop" to buy a bottle of wine. A sign was posted outside: THIS STORE IS NOT AL-LOWED TO SELL GROG FOR DRINKING IN A PUBLIC PLACE NEARBY. When the Aboriginal man in line ahead of me arrived at the cash desk, he uttered a single word: "Wine." The white clerk reached below the counter and pulled out a bottle in a brown paper bag. Looking hard into the customer's eyes — a rude act among Aborigines — he said, "Politeness! I won't be treated like a dog." The man began to reply but the clerk cut him off: "And don't start to argue, or I won't serve you next time." Contempt hung from his shoulders like a rifle. The customer stepped into the night.

One of the organizations that battle for the rights of men like him is the Kimberley Land Council. Lawrence Emery, the local project manager, was working on seven Aboriginal land claims in the Halls Creek shire alone. The process is long, immensely complicated, and linguistically fatiguing. Lawrence picked up a legal document issued by the Western Australia district of the Federal Court of Appeal and brandished it next to his bushy beard. "Our lawyer said to me, 'Can you go to the language center and get them to work on making this understandable?' Understandable for language-speaking, illiterate desert-dwellers, that is."

For people keen on maintaining the traditional ways of speech, a familiar Australian mantra is "Keeping Language Strong." But "language" has a singular meaning here. Among Aborigines and those who work alongside them, the word is commonly said without an article, "a" or "the," in front. When Lawrence spoke of "language-speaking" desert-dwellers, he meant a traditional way of speech, one that derives from the Dreaming. He meant not English and not Kriol.

There's a protocol for land-council staff to follow. "You go out there and explain in the best broken-down English what the state's proposals mean. English is often their third language, or even fourth. They'll go off and talk in language — which we don't understand — and then a senior man will come back and summarize, in Kriol or broken-down English, what was decided." Translations go back and forth. If you say, "The traditional owners will have responsibility for this site," the desert people might be baffled. But if you say, "You're the boss for this land," they understand. Lawrence was racking his brain one day over how to explain the official term "Indigenous Protected Area." Then an Aboriginal man said, "You mean a blackfella national park?" That phrase is now widespread.

Traditional culture insists that certain knowledge must remain secret — unheard not only by other groups but also by the uninitiated within a group. This need to sustain privacy can pose difficulties in a courtroom if a judge demands open access to all pieces of evidence. Aborigines have learned that it can be safer to say nothing — to pass on knowledge through their own law and initiation. Yet law and initiation spring from language. In the land-claim process, Lawrence said, "You have to prove people's connection to country prior to white occupation. So you end up hiring anthropologists to do genealogies." The proof is stronger if the people still speak an ancestral language, for then the names of a grandfather, a water hole, or a Dreaming site continue to pulse with meaning.

A cool wind was blowing off the desert on the day I strolled over to the Yarliyil Arts Centre. A nonprofit co-op, it sells the work of Kimberley artists to big-city galleries and stray visitors. Yarliyil's public area is a long room filled with paintings, many of them unframed, some piled on tables. Painted stones, spears, and boomerangs lay to one side, awaiting the absent tourists. "Most of our artists are Jaru," said Sean Lee, the center's young manager. "If the older ones are in here talking together, they'll speak in language. Speaking to me, they'll use Kriol, and I do my best to understand it. When the older ones are talking to the younger, more often than not they'll use Kriol, 'cause the younger ones won't have the Jaru knowledge. As for the young ones, they'll alter the way they speak. To me the kids will speak English the best they can. To each other, they'll use Kriol. And speaking to adults, they may use a bit of language in their Kriol. They're code-switching all the time."

Much of the art appears abstract, but, Sean said, it's representational to those in the know. He pointed out a few works by Tiny McCale, an elderly artist who is fluent in Jaru. One of her paintings depicts the Rainbow Serpent, an enormously powerful being from the Dreamtime, looking after a water hole in the dry season. The horseshoe shapes in the corners mean that fathers and grandfathers are out collecting bush tucker. I wouldn't have known any of this without Sean's explanation. For unless you grasp an artist's visual language, you see only lines and dots, ovals and rectangles. I wonder how deeply Tiny's meanings rely on the Jaru words in her mind. Younger artists — initiated into no Dreamtime knowledge and speaking no ancestral language — have begun to mix portraits of kangaroos, emus, and human beings into the seemingly abstract patterns of their work. Sean deplores this trend. Call it a visual Kriol.

I spent much of my time in Halls Creek visiting the Kimberley Language Resource Centre: an unremarkable house from the outside, a treasure-trove within. The coordinator, Cath Rouse, was an effervescent young woman from Melbourne who trained to be an accountant before moving north. "I'm from a country with the oldest continuous cultural heritage in the world," she said. "It's so amazing! I cannot fathom how it's not considered of national importance." Founded in 1984, working on a shoestring, the language center boasts an archive that includes hundreds of CDs and reel-to-reel tapes. As well as interpreting legal tracts to desert-dwellers, it has released more than fifteen hundred cassettes and dozens of videos, not to mention a shelf or two of books. "We've been tearing our hair out producing resources," Cath said. "And the producing doesn't make any difference."

After my double take, she went on to explain. Cath follows guidelines laid down by her executive committee: it's a policy that forces Aboriginal people to decide for themselves where the priorities lie. Often they have wanted linguists to record aged speakers of the fading languages — these recordings can then become the basis for written texts. "If it was me making the decisions," Cath admitted, "I'd be putting all my energy into creating the circumstances for languages to be passed down to children. People keep thinking that we, the center, are going to make sure that language survives. They don't like hearing, 'You've got to do it yourself!'"

I looked through *Ngaapa Wangka Wangkajunga,* a new book that puts into writing, often for the first time, Wangkajunga words from the Great Sandy Desert. The foreword, written by a member of the language center's executive committee, says this: "We realize that verbal practices were not enough to keep our languages alive. We needed the much appreciated skills of others who were able to put our languages into writing and so preserve them for the future." Alas, writing is not a magic preservative. Outside experts can record and publish a language, but only the speakers of Wangkajunga can sustain it as a living entity. If they appreciated their own skills as they honor the talents of outsiders, their "verbal practices" would indeed keep the language alive. How else has Wangkajunga outlasted the millennia?

One morning I spoke to Joyce Hudson, a linguist and sometime Bible translator who has worked in the Kimberley for more than thirty years. "It's the old people," she remarked, "who are wringing their hands and saying, 'We want our language back!'" Younger men and women, even if they don't wring their hands, still identify with a particular ancestry: Jaru, for example. They see their own culture as tied to a Jaru heritage. "But," Joyce added, "Kriol is now the vehicle for passing on the cultural things, and people will never admit that. 'Our identity is not Kriol,' they say. Yet Kriol is an identity language too! It's a way of saying 'I'm Aboriginal,' separate from whitefellas and high English." Australia's brand of whitefella language sounds relaxed and informal to most English speakers elsewhere. But to many Aborigines it reeks of snobbishness. Using Kriol, they can assert a black identity; they can say, *Orait, wilat wi orl wan mob.*

For the moment, Kriol is limited to the deep north. If it were to spread south, becoming a vehicle for Aboriginal identity across wide stretches of Australia, it would mark a rare event: a language gaining at the expense of English. A more immediate prospect, though, is that the sprawl of Kriol may extinguish traditional languages that survive in the central desert near Alice Springs. National movements of black Australians are based in the populous south — the Aboriginal and Torres Strait Islanders Commission, for instance, has its headquarters in Canberra. Money from the commission goes toward sustaining some Aboriginal languages. Some ancestral ones, that is; not Kriol or Broken.

Ancestral tongues are also the mandate of the language resource center, where Joyce works as project coordinator. "Many people think they can learn a language easily," she said from rueful experience. "People come in — Aboriginal and white — and expect a sort of injection. They think they can get it if we sell them a book and a tape." A few hours with the book and the tape produce a rude awakening. The center has made it easy to learn *about* the endangered languages of the Kimberley. But to learn to *speak* one of those languages is another matter. "The center's main function is not communication," Joyce has come to believe. "It's there for the maintenance of traditional identity. For the documenting of languages still spoken by older people. And for reconciliation — trying to redeem some of the wrongs." But the truth can be hard to accept. If you say it aloud, you say it softly. In the center's vision for the future, Aboriginal children raised on Kriol and English will relearn the ancient languages. "For the great majority," Joyce delicately put it, "this is very unlikely." Nostalgia can blur any dream.

The chairperson of the language center, Bonnie Deegan, is a large woman in late middle age, the mother of eleven children and the grandmother of dozens. Her hair and skin are brown rather than black, a sign that Bonnie's ancestry is not entirely Aboriginal. She's one of the "stolen generations" — victims of a national policy to remove mixed-race children from Aboriginal homes and to raise them as though they were white. The policy affected many thousands of children between about 1910 and 1970. "I was taken away from my mother when I was five," Bonnie said. "Before that I could speak language, Jaru and Gooniyandi, with her." Jaru speakers, helpless against authority, had already coined a term for policeman, *yawadaro wainowaji;* the literal sense is "chaining horseman." "But being taken away, I was in an orphanage with Catholic nuns. There were forty other girls and none of them ever spoke language. So we lost it." The orphanage stood in the coastal pearl-fishing town of Broome, hundreds of miles west of the Margaret River cattle station where Bonnie had lived as a small child and where her own languages belonged.

She was never allowed home. "We stayed in the orphanage till we were seventeen or eighteen and the nuns said it's time to go out and make our own way." Released, Bonnie made her way to Halls Creek, the nearest town to Margaret River. She never left. Decades ago, "people here would talk to me in language all the time. I didn't know what they were saying — I would just nod." In the 1980s, after the language center was established, Bonnie decided to relearn Jaru. Her success has been only partial: Jaru had been cut out of her too deeply.

Educated, ruled, and overruled in English, many Jaru people came to scorn the "blackfella language" of their ancestors. Shame drove the language toward silence. It hangs on in the desert, where isolation lessens the chance of shame. Yet it's not just the songlines and Dreamtime stories that are being quelled under the combined pressure of English and

Kriol; it's also a language's subtle meanings, the metaphors that generations of usage have made innate. In Jaru, the act of listening is treated
with huge respect. Its expressions locate intelligence and memory in the
ears. Writing in English, I naturally say "Jaru speakers." But I should
probably say "Jaru listeners." Being wise, in Jaru, is "having ears":
mangir-djaru. Being unwise or silly is "having no ears": *mangirgir-
mulungu.* What in colloquial English we mean when we say somebody
is dumb, the Jaru language conveys by saying a person is deaf.

In the Western Desert of Australia, elders would occasionally instruct a
kaditja to mete out punishment for a wrongful act. The *kaditja* was an
executioner. He might have to travel long distances to accomplish his
task. It was felt to be a sacred task; the man was not just an actor but an
emissary, suffused with spirit power. What transgressions were severe
enough to justify a *kaditja*'s fatal journey? Violation of the sacred marriage law was a capital offense. But so was the utterance of forbidden
words. An act of speech could provoke a death sentence. In the absence
of a *kaditja,* elders might sing a man or woman to death.

That's one measure of the power of language. Another is this: frustrated by their own inability to master the concepts taken for granted by
white Australians, many speakers of Yolngu and other Aboriginal languages have become convinced of the existence of a "secret English" —
a version of English that has special, even sacred force. They know how
powerful language is in their own traditions. It stands to reason, then,
that English must contain a hidden magic greater than they find in the
everyday speech of the policemen, teachers, and civil servants who control so much of their lives. Some Aboriginal people blame the government for denying them knowledge of "secret English." If only they were
initiated into this language, they too could share its power. Poor health,
poverty, and suicide would belong to a forgotten conversation.

This is a fantasy, of course. Or is it? Words do have power. Across
Australia, many of the worst massacres of Aborigines took place after
books and magazines had appeared calling them "a species . . . of tailless monkey," "the lowest race of savages in the known world," and "little less ugly than gorillas, which to my mind they much more closely
resemble than white men or the higher types of blacks." "Scarcely human," declared the *Quarterly Review.* "As a race truly irreclaimable," said
the *Illustrated London News.* In 1826 the *Colonial Times* in Hobart, the
capital of what would become Tasmania, declared: "Self defence is the

first law of nature . . . The Government must remove the natives — if not, they will be hunted down like wild beasts and destroyed!" Both halves of that sentence were prophetic. Aboriginal people in Tasmania were removed, hunted down, and destroyed. Half a century later, none were left.

The murdering pioneers could justify their deeds by means of published words. They dreamed about an empty continent, and the vision was one of freedom. But if the Dreamtime stories tell of language creating life, language can also take lives away. In the beginning was the word, and at the end.

Constructing the World

JORGE LUIS BORGES, that connoisseur of language, never had the chance to sample Tiwi or Murrinh-Patha. But he once wrote a sonnet about his attempt to master Old English — "the language of the blunt-tongued Anglo-Saxons" — while he was losing his sight. He persevered, obstinate in his desire, and able at last to recognize that beyond his own anxiety, beyond the extinct Saxon words that kept eluding him and the living Spanish words that gave voice to his struggle, "the universe waits, inexhaustible, inviting." It's a profoundly encouraging poem. Borges was never one to underestimate the intricate powers of the mind, its capacity to shape experience. That capacity exists in all human languages. Some have larger vocabularies than others, some deploy a greater variety of sounds than others, but no language is *better* than another. Languages are devoid of hierarchy. Infants emerge from the womb with an absolute equality of linguistic opportunity — whatever sounds they grow up hearing, whatever syllables they start out babbling, any fully developed language can express their needs and desires. The world is inexhaustible to everyone who perceives it.

In the past, people commonly believed that other languages deserved to vanish for reasons of basic inadequacy. In 1702 the Boston preacher Cotton Mather called New England's Indians "these doleful creatures" and "the veriest ruins of mankind." Sad and ruined as they were, "No arts are understood among them, except just so far as to maintain their brutish conversation, which is little more than is to be found among the very beavers upon our streams." A century and a half later, with the In-

dians in retreat, Henry David Thoreau encountered a small group of
Abenakis in the woods of Maine. When he heard them speak, Thoreau
— often among the most enlightened of men — resorted to an animal
metaphor: "It was a purely wild and primitive American sound, as
much as the barking of a chickaree, and I could not understand a syllable of it." Chickaree is an old name for the red squirrel. The conversation of indigenous people, then, was as brutish as beaver noise or as
primitive as squirrel chatter. Civilization required greater intelligence.

Mather and Thoreau were badly mistaken. For while technology has
become infinitely more sophisticated over the past few hundred years,
languages have not. Indeed, linguistic complexity is seldom greater than
on the lips of hunter-gatherers whose material needs are few and whose
grasp of the distant world is minimal. Languages evolve, of course. But
they tend to evolve toward simplicity. Kriol is far simpler and more flexible than the Aboriginal languages that nourished it. Italian is a slip-
shod, free-for-all language compared with the Latin from which it
sprang. English and French are now what most Abenaki people speak —
but they are not some kind of higher goal toward which the Abenaki
language has been unknowingly striving for centuries. Abenaki is a
rich and complete language, one that Thoreau might have enjoyed exploring. (He would have appreciated its six words for "moose.") Even
though Abenaki lacks a term for "scroll bar," its speakers could doubtless invent one, if they had need. Generations ago they invented a term
for white settler: *pastoni*, a person from Boston.

No language, then, merits extinction by reason of incompetence. But
there's a subtler way of kissing languages goodbye. Paradoxically, it
arises from an acceptance of the intrinsic equality among the world's
languages. We might call it complacency.

It goes like this. Modern linguistics is founded on the principles of
generative grammar laid down by Noam Chomsky in the 1950s and
1960s. Reacting against the behaviorist ideas that governed much of
American philosophy and psychology at the time, Chomsky argued
with great subtlety and force that children all over the world learn to
speak and understand by means of an innate, structured capacity for
language. ("The language instinct," this capacity has been called, notably in a book of that name by Chomsky's MIT colleague Steven Pinker.)
Human beings are hard-wired, so to speak, for language acquisition. It
doesn't matter if the language in question is Xhosa or Mandarin, Eng-

lish or Abenaki; small children will unlock its complexities at roughly the same age. Even if they can't hear a word, they can make themselves fluently understood by mastering a sign language — one that draws on the same regions of the growing brain that other children exercise by using the ears and mouth. To Chomsky, our inborn talent for expression and understanding provides strong evidence that the glittering surfaces of verbal consciousness rely on a hidden framework of "abstract universals." The universals, limited in number, are what generate the unlimited number of possible transformations in any human language. We may never be able to probe far enough beyond, or beneath, our own language to lay bare these abstract universals. But so what?

The model of consciousness adopted by Chomsky in recent years is explicitly computational. It assumes the existence of predetermining patterns that guide every sentence we speak: a Windows of the mind, perhaps. If you liken the brain to a computer, it stands to reason that the rules governing its operations are vastly more significant than the variations in its six thousand or so word-processing programs. "Thinking is largely independent of what language one happens to think in," the linguist Ray Jackendorf has stated. Or in Chomsky's own words, "We can think of the initial state of the faculty of language as a fixed network connected to a switch box; the network is constituted of the principles of language, while the switches are the options to be determined by experience . . . Each possible human language is identified as a particular setting of the switches." By such an argument, the differences between languages may have little more import than a stylistic divergence among six thousand authors with the same message to convey. A rose is a rose is a rose; a noun phrase is a noun phrase is a noun phrase; moreover, a thought about a rose or a noun phrase is a thought about a rose or a noun phrase is a . . .

Chomsky and his followers assert that all human languages depend on a generative grammar (or GG) that underlies the bewildering twists and wriggles words make on the surface of speech. They have shown how complex the mind, anybody's mind, really is. And in so doing, they have scoffed not only at behaviorism, but at other schools of linguistics. Emphasizing the shared properties intrinsic to every language, they refuse to see any merit in the "Sapir-Whorf hypothesis," which influenced many scholars from the 1930s through the 1950s. As set out by Benjamin Lee Whorf (a brilliant amateur linguist, whose lack of a doctorate has often been held against him) and his great mentor Edward Sapir, the hypothesis suggests that the language a person speaks determines the way that person thinks.

Early in the twentieth century, awestruck by the diversity of indigenous languages in North America, Sapir proclaimed that "the 'real world' is to a large extent built up on the language habits of the group." Looking for an image to evoke the power that any language exerts over its speakers, he turned to a mathematical analogy: "To pass from one language to another is psychologically parallel to passing from one geometrical system to another." The result, in either case, is disorientation.

Whorf went even further. His studies of the Hopi language of New Mexico led him to wonder if the relativist discoveries of modern physics could be expressed more easily in Hopi than in English. Perhaps English was not well suited to shape and voice the paradoxes of the quantum world. "We are constantly reading into nature fictional acting entities," Whorf noted in his late essay "Languages and Logic," "simply because our verbs must have substantives in front of them." In English, it seems unnatural to say "Flashed!" We have to say "It flashed!" or "A light flashed!" And yet, as Whorf observed, "The flashing and the light are one and the same. The Hopi language reports the flash with a simple verb, *rehpi:* 'flash' (occurred)." Does it matter that Hopi has verbs without subjects? Whorf thought so. He called it "a fact which may give that tongue potentialities, probably never to be developed, as a logical system for understanding some aspects of the universe." Decades later, researchers would claim that a neighboring though unrelated language, Navajo, has spatial concepts so different from those in English that while Navajo children may be slow to grasp abstractions like the triangle and the square, they are faster than other young Americans at mastering fuzzy sets and dynamic typology.

The model of consciousness found in the writings of Sapir and Whorf is a representational one. Even today, not all linguists are willing to follow Chomsky in granting such sweeping power to the fixed principles underlying speech: Sapir and Whorf have intellectual descendants who prefer to stress the elaborate varieties in pattern by which languages represent the world. Some are poets and romantics; others are scientists. There is new evidence, for example, that when a young child begins to learn a language and thereby to fit experience into categories, some of the brain's neural connections grow stronger, while others weaken or disappear. Our responses to stimuli in adult life depend partly on the patterns, the categories of our previous learning. So, as the French linguist Emil Benveniste has argued, "The sayable defines and organizes the thinkable." Words are not merely a garment that thoughts happen to wear; for Benveniste, words are intrinsic to thought itself. We can feel pain or joy without words. But it's hard to think of the French Revolution — or a deep-structure tree — without words.

Nearly half a century after Chomsky's initial publications, it's clear that he and his disciples have swept Sapir and Whorf aside. The vast majority of neurologists, psychologists, linguists, and philosophers now agree that the mind of a Chinese speaker and the mind of a Swedish speaker develop and operate in much the same way. In its extreme, determinist form, the Sapir-Whorf hypothesis is incorrect. Yet does that warrant a rude dismissal of all their insights? (It would seem perverse to say that every text by the philosopher John Locke should be discarded merely because, as Chomsky has shown, Locke was wrong to see a newborn mind as an empty slate.) Whorf's key point is that conceptual content can't always be easily and exactly interchanged among languages: what is said and how it is said interact in complex ways. In Sapir's judicious yet fighting words, "No two languages are ever sufficiently similar to be considered as representing the same social reality. The worlds in which different cultures live are distinct worlds, not merely the same world with different labels attached."

That notion sticks in the craw of philosophers who abide by the computational model of language. In *Language and Reality,* a widely read textbook published in 1999 by MIT Press, Michael Devitt and Kim Sterelny insist that "there are unlikely to be metaphysically significant syntactic differences between languages; the influence of syntax on thought is trivial." If this means that a good deal of Sapir and most of Whorf should be consigned to oblivion, so be it: "There is no interpretation of Whorf that is both plausible and exciting." Whorf and Sapir, they admit, may be right to say that language organizes our experience of the world. Perhaps it's true that "our minds, concepts and languages construct theories out of experience." But it is "wildly implausible," they reiterate, "to claim that our minds, concepts and languages construct the world out of experience." The world remains the same, regardless of how we talk about it.

This is, you might say, the plainspoken approach to language: the Show Me posture. What looks real is all that is real, and the labels we affix to things don't change them. "How," Devitt and Sterelny ask, "could anything a person does to his experience — how could any of his modes of representation — affect stones, trees, cats and stars?"

This quartet of words from the "real world" appears to score a pragmatic point with devastating clarity. The terms Devitt and Sterelny select are all concrete nouns. But things would quickly get more complicated if the nouns were replaced by verbs. "How could anything a person does to his experience affect sailing, smiling, soiling, and spilling?" It's not hard to think of an answer.

The same goes for adjectives and adverbs: "How could any of his modes of representation affect blind, bloated, bloody, and blue?" It won't do to respond that adjectives are only theories of experience, unless you want to suggest that nothing can be bloody or blue outside the human mind. Colors, incidentally, are notoriously resistant to fixed meanings. You can't translate a word like "blue" into another language and expect its speakers to see your particular range of hues. In 1999 a team of British researchers reported in *Nature* that the Berinmo, a remote hunting-and-gathering people of Papua New Guinea, could make no distinction between blue and green. But they distinguished between *wor* and *nol,* shades that the English-speaking researchers lumped together as "yellow." These findings give renewed proof of "a considerable degree of linguistic influence on color categorization" — and, though the researchers did not rush to say so, they offer a partial vindication of Sapir and Whorf.

Likewise, feelings and ideas are also enmeshed in our experience. They can't be translated with any greater confidence than perceptions. How could a person's modes of representation *not* affect labor, or loyalty, or love? In any language, such terms have constantly changing meanings. We don't mean by "loyalty" exactly what the word's early speakers meant in the fifteenth century. I can still remember how puzzled I was to find that the French word *aimer* spans a range of feeling that English speakers designate by both "love" and "like." To me, loving and liking are separate emotions. Not so, it appears, in Paris. By the same token, a native speaker of French might be puzzled by the English verb "know," which fails to distinguish between two mental properties: *savoir* and *connaître.* My language allows me, somewhat clumsily, to get the distinction across: on the one hand, factual knowledge; on the other, acquaintanceship and understanding. But to a French speaker, that distinction is central to how the mind interacts with the world.

The Inuktitut language goes further, much further. Inuit distinguish *utsimavaa* (he or she knows from experience), *sanatuuq* (he or she knows how to do something), *qaujimavaa* (he or she knows about something), *nalujunnaipaa* (he or she is not ignorant of something), *nalunaiqpaa* (he or she is no longer unaware of something), and two or three other verbs that mean, roughly speaking, "know." Inuktitut also has a verb, *puijilittatuq,* with both a specific and a general meaning. In general terms, "he or she is nervous." More specifically, and speaking of a hunter, "he does not know which way to turn because of the numerous seals he has seen come to the surface." My own grasp of seeing, knowing, liking, and loving is not some abstract theory my brain has constructed over the decades; it's the way I experience life in the world.

But let's put aside all verbs, adjectives, adverbs, feelings, ideas, perceptions, and surfacing seals. Let's return to the extraordinarily limited range of nouns by which Devitt and Sterelny symbolize "the world." They single out stones, trees, cats, and stars as emblematic of items that no mode of human representation can possibly affect. Is this as accurate as it is obvious? When you look at the words more closely, the self-evident truth of the proposition begins to blur.

To begin with, there's a little ambiguity in their meaning. Our collective experience has a direct impact on stars like Madonna, cats like Wynton Marsalis, and Stones like Mick Jagger. But a broader, subtler answer is this: we signal our attitude to things in the world — cats, for example — by the way we talk about them. "The cat that spent the night in the rain" may have less of a claim on our affections than "the cat who spent the night in the rain." "Who is that cat in your arms?" suggests something different from "What is that cat in your arms?" (not to mention "What is that cat doing in your arms?"). Language implies feeling. Feeling, one way or another, inspires action.

Leave the confines of English behind, and the waters muddy even further. With the aid of the *Concise Oxford Turkish Dictionary,* I decided to see how those four nouns are expressed in a language far removed from the Indo-European family to which English belongs. Turkish is the largest member of the Altaic family; thousands of years, perhaps tens of thousands, have gone by since our remote ancestors (somewhere in central Asia, presumably) spoke the same words. In Turkish, I discovered, "cat" is *kedi.* But *kedi-balığı,* far from being a "catfish" as the literally translated compound says, is what we call a "lesser spotted dogfish." A *kedi,* unlike a cat, is involved in phrases meaning "to go bankrupt," "to cause bad blood," and "to look at with intense longing." A "stone" is a *taş,* most of the time. But a stone in the kidneys or the gallbladder is *kum hastaliği* — in which case it indisputably affects your personal experience. And a *çekirdek* is also a stone, one you might unearth in a plum or an olive. Still, a Turkish stone would generally be called a *taş.* But a *taş,* I regret to say, is not always a stone. Sometimes it's what we call a chess piece. At other moments it's an allusion or an innuendo.

Are stars — the heavenly variety, I mean — any simpler? Alas, no. A Turkish star can be a *yildiz* or a *baht,* and both are tied up in human lives. *Baht* can signify "good luck" or "destiny." *Yildiz* also implies destiny, but it has the extra sense of "pole star" or "north." Finally we arrive at trees. There are several Turkish options. But the likeliest word, listed first on the page, is *ağaç.* Trouble is, *ağaç* also means "wood" or "timber." And surely the fate of trees can be profoundly affected by whether we think of them — in the mind's eye, in the same breath, always — as timber. (Consider the difference between the phrases "I like cows" and "I like beef.") English enforces a distinction between the living organism of a tree and the useful material that organism provides. Turkish does not.

Perhaps, then, the inexhaustible, inviting world does show evidence of being constructed, to a significant degree, out of our linguistic experience. Speakers of German, for example, have no difficulty creating highly precise compound words, words that appear unwieldy in many other languages. One of the key works of pre-Chomskyan linguistics was N. S. Trubetzkoy's *Grundzüge der Phonologie,* a book in which the term *Überwindungsarteigenschaften* made its grand entry. Trubetzkoy's translator needed nine English words to get the point across: "properties based on the manner of overcoming an obstruction." In a hamfisted way, such an idea is thinkable outside the bounds of German. But German, not surprisingly, was the language in which the concept sprang to mind. Similarly, poetry often fades and withers in translation because of its reliance on the highly charged, compressed, dynamic use of a particular language — the supreme expression of a single social reality.

I'm not disputing the fundamental importance of Chomsky's insights into the nature of language. Thanks to his work, we understand immeasurably more than people in past centuries about the structure of human communication. Yet as his fellow linguist Dell Hymes once observed, "The more one emphasizes universals . . . the more mysterious actual languages become." Above all, "most of language begins where abstract universals leave off." Look at the stones and stars for proof; look at the cats and trees; look at the colors of yellow. Look at the properties based on the manner of . . .

Or turn to the Mi'kmaq language. A Harvard-trained law professor named Sake'j Youngblood Henderson — by origin, a member of the Chickasaw and Cheyenne peoples of Oklahoma — spent many years as constitutional advisor to the Mi'kmaq, an indigenous group found in Atlantic Canada and Maine. He came to know their language well. Its syntax, he once stated, fits a view of reality as existing in a perpetual state of oscillation, matter becoming energy becoming matter once again: "The use of verbs rather than nouny subjects and objects is important; it means that there are very few fixed and rigid objects in the Mi'kmaq worldview." The syntax of Mi'kmaq, that is to say, allows very few objects to be easily labeled. Speakers of the language build up complex verb phrases by choosing from among hundreds of prefixes and suffixes. An intricately described action lies at the heart of a Mi'kmaq sentence — not, as in this sentence, a single brief verb buttressed by nouns. For Henderson, it's as if the rhythms and structures of the Mi'kmaq language open a door into the Mi'kmaq world. "To have to speak English," he has said, "is like having to put on a straitjacket."

It runs deep, this disparity, or disjuncture, between the Indo-European emphasis on nouns and the Amerindian reliance on verbs. It seems to be intuitively felt, and not just by writers or professors. Early in the nineteenth century a language was born amid the buffalo hunts and winter camps of the Métis on the Great Plains. The Métis were a new people. Most of the hunters in the camps spoke French; they were descended from the *voyageurs* of New France. But the women spoke Cree and Assiniboine. What they created — in the words of the language's biographer, Peter Bakker — is "an impossible language," one that "challenges all theoretical models." Its name is Michif, and it contains two sound patterns, two sets of word endings, two systems of syntax. The nouns in Michif come from French. The verbs come from Cree.

Far from being some shifting, temporary arrangement, this is the very essence of the language. To tell someone to wear her shoes, a speaker of Michif would say *Poochishkaawik tii sooyii* (the last two words echo the French *tes souliers*). Only a minority of Michif's speakers ever mastered both the parent languages. Its few remaining users, who live surrounded by the blunt-tongued sounds of English, are seldom fluent in either Cree or French. Yet during the century after its birth Michif spread as far as Oregon, Montana, Alberta, and the Northwest Territories.

By its very structure, Michif bridges the distinct worlds that Sapir posited. Today it is highly endangered. So is the Abenaki that Thoreau heard in the woods of Maine. Its neighbor Mi'kmaq, although still alive in fragments of eastern Canada, is threatened. Economic, social, and educational pressures have led many of its speakers to transfer their voices into English, and a few into French. Such is their right, their choice, their privilege. If the language falls into oblivion, a complacent response might be, "So what?" Perhaps only a fluent speaker of Mi'kmaq could give an apt reply. Perhaps Sake'j Youngblood Henderson already has.

4

Unseen and Unheard

YUCHI

MAGGIE MARSEY PARKED her white half-ton outside the unmarked circular building. Henry Washburn was here already; she could tell by the crimson half-ton nearby. The grumble of traffic along Highway 66, a quarter-mile down the hill, dwindled as she pushed open the door. Inside, a discreet plaque identified the building as the Sapulpa Creek Indian Community Center. Maggie stepped into a big office in which the computers, filing cabinets, and hard chairs had company: a table weighed down by food. The scent of barbecued spareribs had drawn a few other people to the table, where corn and peaches, salads and iced tea also awaited us. But nobody had started to eat. We wouldn't begin the noontime meal until Maggie had said grace in a language that no more than a dozen people in the world fully speak and understand.

She belongs to the Yuchi people, also spelled Euchee: an unrecognized tribe within a nation within a state within the most powerful country in the world. The rare books that mention the Yuchis often do so in the past tense. A 1979 dictionary of North American Indians called them "an extinct agricultural and hunting tribe"; a 1994 encyclopedia said that "they seem to have disappeared from the records in the nineteenth century." The authors forgot to ask Maggie's or Henry's opinion. For here, southwest of Tulsa where the streams and oak hills of the Ozarks meet the outstretching southern plains, they and other Yuchis remain, their obscurity matched only by their tenacity. Between fifteen hundred and twenty-four hundred people may identify themselves as Yuchi. Most of them live in northeastern Oklahoma, enrolled in a large and historically powerful group of Indians known as the Creek Nation.

But Yuchi is unrelated to Muscogee, the dominant language of the Creeks. Indeed Yuchi is an "isolate," a language set apart. Whereas the vocabulary of English shows a kinship to French, German, and other European languages, Yuchi contains very few words that exist in any other tongue. The Yuchis have been a distinct people for perhaps as long as ten thousand years: a people defined by language. One of Henry's license plates — "car tags," he calls them in his rasping drawl — has MUSCOGEE CREEK NATION on it. The other plate, a customized model from the state of Oklahoma, says EUCHEE.

Maggie fiddled with the microphone that Richard Grounds had handed her. It rested on her blouse, obscuring its floral pattern. She didn't act or look her eighty-two years. Yet unlike Henry, a former serviceman, Maggie has a hesitant manner and a soft voice. And for Richard — a middle-aged Yuchi who works as a research professor of anthropology at the University of Tulsa — to capture her sentences, he needs a mike. Each Monday he provides a meal for Yuchi-speaking elders and, using a camcorder, records the conversation. The words Henry and Maggie utter are what pay for their food.

Those words are mortal. Soon, perhaps now, you may be able to count the number of fluent Yuchi speakers on the fingers of both hands. Maggie and Henry grew up with Yuchi as a mother tongue. They were among the last to do so — almost everybody under seventy ignores or struggles with the language. In a few years there may be nothing left for Richard to record.

"I'm from down the line," Henry said. "I was born and raised thirty miles from here, in Bristow. And it's strange. Around Bristow, just like here, people have been around Yuchis all their lives and never even knew they existed. I said to one old fellow the other day, 'Maybe you've heard of the Yuchis?' He said, 'No, I thought you were all Creeks.'"

The old-timer could be forgiven. As a community, Yuchis have little they can call their own. Their dwellings lie scattered among the unassuming houses and farms of other Oklahomans in what, a hundred years ago, was still "Indian Territory." Pickett Methodist Chapel was once a Yuchi church; now it welcomes outsiders. For half a century the Euchee Mission School stood with its fruit trees, stables, and chicken coops on the edge of Sapulpa; but the school closed down in 1948 and its buildings were demolished. One of the town's arteries is still called "Mission Street." A lot of Sapulpans have no idea why.

"Pass the salad," Henry said in Yuchi. Richard understood the verb but not the noun; he handed a bowl of potatoes across the table. "No, no," Henry added in English. "I mean some of that rabbit food." He began to reminisce about a knife-throwing game he played at school in the 1930s — the aim was to toss the knife up and land the blade in the earth. "Wouldn't be allowed to take a knife to school these days," he said. Richard pressed him for Yuchi game-words. After a little thought Henry recalled the terms for marbles and jacks, but neither he nor Maggie could come up with the word for playing cards. Then Maggie remembered: "My mother was strict. She used to say, 'The devil's in the cards.'"

She took a sip of tea, holding the cup in a thin hand with prominent brown veins. "I still dream mostly in Yuchi," she remarked. When I asked what would be lost if Yuchi disappeared forever, her answer was oblique: "The older people used to tell us stories. They were funny. We used to laugh a lot. Now, all that's dying out. Some people still know the stories, but the younger ones don't want to hear it. They're stories about animals and — different things. But we can't tell it."

"What happens if you tell it in English?"

"In English it's not funny." And Maggie laughed. "When the older people finished the story, they used to make us spit. I don't know what was behind it."

"How would you say that in Yuchi?" asked Richard, freshly alert. She told him. "Aha," he said, "spit *out*." For him every sentence is an opportunity.

Maggie went off to the kitchen to help clear up. Henry stepped outside for a smoke. A few years short of eighty, he's a junior speaker. Some of his father's relatives were white, others black. But his mother was full-blooded Yuchi, "and she talked to us in Yuchi all the way. My father used to get on us for speaking Yuchi — he called it 'jabbering.' But I remember my mother saying, 'You need to know this language. Speak it correctly. And don't you forget it!'"

Jabbering: I recalled the stressed-out teacher in Wadeye. When Henry was a young man, he moved to California and served with the U.S. Navy in New Guinea and the Philippines. Yet Oklahoma drew him back. "I've been around here with these Yuchis for a long time," he said, looking

across the parking lot with his single eye. He comes from a big family —
"there was about ten of us at one time" — of whom four are left. His
surviving brother and sisters "can still speak Yuchi, but they're in an
area where no one else does. So they're kind of rusty." Henry has no
children and lives alone.

He butted out the cigarette after a few puffs and walked back into the
office. Henry is happy to cooperate with any and all inquirers; he enjoys
the outside interest that the language, nearing its death throes, has begun to attract. "That's really nice," he said. "Because when I was growing up, I didn't think there was anything worse than Yuchi."

Later that day I drove west from Sapulpa to Bristow, at first on the old
Route 66, a sinuous, improbably narrow road now renamed Ozark
Trail. It proved to be unsigned, unlined, unmarked, and in crying need
of repaving. The only place you could possibly get your kicks was a
clubhouse belonging to the Veterans of Foreign Wars. The Jeep Cherokee ahead of me had a sign on the rear window: YOU SAY I'M A
BITCH / LIKE IT'S A BAD THING. Junk was alight in a bonfire by Polecat Creek. Dead vehicles were common in the brush. What gives this
land its wealth is not what lies on the surface — small ranches, woods,
the occasional farm — but what's invisible below. Fields were in perpetual motion from the back-and-forth sway of pump jacks. Beyond Kelly-
ville, a tiny town with an oilfields supply store, a sign warned of a Pipe-
line Crossing.

Bristow's downtown is nearly a century old, and I imagine the brick
buildings on its main street used to display a dusty elegance. Now the
dollar store and the discount auto-parts shop have emptiness for a
neighbor, and hours pass without significant traffic. The main reason is
a Wal-Mart with a Tire & Lube Express on the outskirts. More cars and
trucks were parked in the paved meadows around it than in all the rest
of the town. And it struck me that modern English is the Wal-Mart of
languages: convenient, huge, hard to avoid, superficially friendly, and
devouring all rivals in its eagerness to expand. Yuchi, by contrast, is in-
convenient, small, easy to avoid, and nearing the final stage of a long,
slow contraction.

Bristow is one of the three main areas where substantial numbers of
Yuchis live. But even at the Polecat Creek ceremonial grounds, most of
those who follow the ancient spiritual traditions pray, chant, and make
speeches in English. Maybe the meaning is altered; certainly the *sound* is

different. When I asked Mary Linn — the leading outside expert on the intricacies of the language — what Yuchi sounds like, she replied, "It is a very soft and ethereal language when spoken by native speakers. There are tones in the language, and vowels can be lengthened when giving emphasis, so the rhythm of Yuchi is very songlike. My first impression was to answer your question, 'It is the most beautiful language in the world.'"

Back in Sapulpa, I checked the yellow pages for restaurants. Beside the listings was a multiple-choice question:

What happens to the people that do not get the victory over the beast of Revelation 13:11–18?
A. nothing
B. they are killed by the ones that do
C. there is a great earthquake and they are killed
D. they shall drink of the wine of the wrath of God.

Only "A" seemed unlikely. The answer lurked among "Appliances — Major Dealers": the wine of wrath. I turned to the page for takeout pizzas, only to find a fill-in-the-blanks question from Proverbs. This time the four choices were vengeance, anger, judgments, and wrath. Plain cheese, please.

Next morning I learned more about the wrath the Yuchis have endured over the centuries — and about their astonishing resilience, their survival under chronic pressure.

Originally they lived in what was to become the southeastern United States. Scholarly debate has raged about their place of origin: Tennessee, Georgia, Florida, Alabama, and South Carolina are all candidates. Their name for themselves, *tsoya'ha,* is said to mean "children of the sun," and in the sign language that developed on the Great Plains the gesture for Yuchi is a raised right hand, the index finger pointing up toward the sun. A mound-building, town-dwelling people, they were rich enough for Spanish adventurers to seek them out, visions of gold in the explorers' overheated heads. But the Yuchis had no gold, and the invaders burned their towns. The Spanish may also have bequeathed a legacy of viruses. Weakened by disease, the surviving Yuchis saw their power drain away. Reduced in number, they were vulnerable to attack. Early in the eighteenth century — this is the Yuchi version, anyway — they joined the Creek Confederacy, a multilingual, multiethnic group of Indians who were resisting the incursion of white settlers. Even so, Yuchi

history is one of flagrant loss. In 1714 they were massacred by Englishmen and Cherokees; in 1795 they were massacred by Americans.

Worse was to come a couple of short generations later. Wanting settlement to expand without threat of further Indian wars, Andrew Jackson ordered the expulsion of all Indians in the southeastern states. It
didn't matter whether a people had been friendly or hostile to the
whites: they had to leave. Their destination, far beyond the Mississippi,
was Indian Territory, where they would supposedly be free to live un-
hindered. Martin Van Buren replaced Jackson in the White House, but
his Indian policy was unchanged: vengeance and anger, judgments and
wrath. "No state can achieve proper culture, civilization and progress,"
Van Buren declared, "as long as Indians are permitted to remain."
Through the 1830s the U.S. Army forced tens of thousands of Indians to
abandon their homes at gunpoint and walk westward, crossing the
great river as best they could. The common phrase for this deportation
is the "Cherokee Trail of Tears." But the Cherokees were not the only
victims: Creeks, Choctaws, Chickasaws, and Seminoles also walked into
exile. Untold thousands died along the way. And among the Creeks
were the Yuchis. Richard, who is not shy of strong words, calls these
events "genocide."

In the valleys, in the highlands, on the death march, in their new
land, the Yuchis went on speaking their unique language. Some experts
consider it a single-member family within the large "Macro-Siouan
Phylum," one with remote but identifiable relatives like Dakota and
Mohawk; others insist that Yuchi fits into no recognized group. After its
speakers arrived on the plains, their numbers were so low, their communities so inconspicuous, that the Yuchis more or less dropped out of
history. Their language remained unwritten: a tongue without an alphabet, let alone a dictionary. Just about the only outsiders who knew
about the Yuchis were linguists, and the isolation they described would
fertilize some wild theories. If a few similarities exist between the
Yuchis' harvest ceremonies and the Jewish festival of Succoth, then
perhaps Sapulpa is home to a lost tribe of Israel. Or maybe the Yuchis
are descended from Minoans who escaped a sinking Atlantis. Or perhaps . . .

One of the first outsiders to study Yuchi in depth was a youthful German linguist called Günter Wagner, who spent five months in Oklahoma in 1928–1929. Wagner used an elaborate array of phonetic devices
to make sense of the sounds he heard: showing, for example, the three

kinds of consonant stops; indicating whether vowels were open, closed, lengthened, or nasalized; and distinguishing, in his words, between "a dorsal-palatal *x* (as in German 'ich') and a velar *x* (as in German 'ach')." The fruits of his research were published in English. Yet as far as the Yuchis were concerned, his writings might as well have appeared in Mandarin Chinese.

Wagner recorded a traditional story about the creation of the world. As he transcribed it, one of the sentences looks like this:

s'a'x̣dji k'a''adodɛ'hɛ na'tʠ tago'tnə ̱ κɛdjidjɩ'n ̱ κ'ʠləwɛ'ha tsoonʠ' k'ala wɛ'xtʠ tʠ κɛwɛhadji' hʠgwadjɩ'n tʠ`tawɛɫawɛ'nʠ wɛyu`wagɛ' κɛwɛ`hadjɩ'n.

A literal, word-for-word translation is scarcely less baffling. In the following quotation, each phrase or unit represents a single Yuchi word: "The earth / after it was made / there was no light / it was here / they gathered / the sun / something / she dictated / they were here / they said / those who were to make light / they hunted for / they were here." Wagner's free translation runs as follows: "At first there was no light on the earth, and so they all met under the leadership of the sun to look for someone who would light the earth." The word-for-word version suggests how foreign Yuchi is to an English speaker's way of thinking. And vice versa.

The intended audience for Wagner's work was urban and scholarly, not rural and Yuchi. Linguists in more recent years have often struggled to describe a rare language in ways that are both scientifically accurate and useful to the language's remaining speakers. But fitting the phonetic nuances of a non-Western language into a Roman alphabet can be a tricky business. Among the Lokele of the eastern Congo, for instance, the lips and tongue make exactly the same movements whether you're talking about a garbage dump *(liala)* or a fiancée *(liAla)*. The only difference is in tone: the rising pitch in the middle of the second word. Written down, the result may look unnatural. But if you want to say "I'm watching the riverbank" — *aSOolaMBA boili* — correct tone is the only thing that will stop you from saying *aSOoLAMBA boIli* by mistake: "I'm boiling my mother-in-law."

In terms of the cultural traditions contained in it, the death of any language is an event to mourn. But whereas many aspects of a floundering written language will endure in books and on line, the death of an oral language is absolute. Like some of the languages I had encountered in Australia, Yuchi flourished for more than a millennium after Anglo-Saxon and ancient Greek were no more. Yet as long as people are willing to tackle *Beowulf* and *Oedipus Rex* in the original, Anglo-Saxon and ancient Greek will remain part of human experience — aside from their dramatic afterlife in modern English and modern Greek. Oral languages have no such recourse. Their knowledge always lives dangerously. They are always one generation away from extinction.

Yuchi is in a doubly poignant state because of its lack of close relatives — the language has no cousin or brother, so to speak, with a similar heritage of meaning. Their lonely development through time has turned Yuchi and the few dozen other linguistic isolates into cultural treasures. Embedded in them may be valuable evidence about the nature of human languages — and about prehistory. It now seems possible, for instance, that Apache and Navajo bear an archaic link to the isolated Burushaski language of Asia's Karakoram Range, in what is now northern Pakistan. Language isolates "merit the protection we give to works of ancient architecture," the British journalist Simon Jenkins once suggested. "They are the archaeology of civilization, full of wisdom, legend and beauty, messages from the Earth's own time-travellers."

Those messages are important not just because of a primordial vocabulary. The words of Burushaski, Basque, Haida, Yuchi, and other isolated languages rely on a grammar that can appear wise and beautiful — or fiendishly convoluted. The complex ways in which they organize human experience remind us that language was the first great achievement of our species. Anthropologists now suspect that the outburst of language, about fifty thousand years ago, was what changed us into the creatures we are today — what made us human. Only when we had mastered grammar was our species fit for guns and roses. With its profligate wealth of noun classes, case endings, pronominal prefixes, and shape-shifting verbs, Burushaski is a linguist's dream and a learner's nightmare. While some of its verb forms have no counterparts in English, it lacks any term meaning "to have."

Early written accounts of cultures like Burushaski and Yuchi expressed surprise at the disjuncture, the apparent mismatch between technological simplicity and linguistic sophistication. That surprise (which helps account for the absurd equation of the Yuchis with Minoans or long-lost Jews) says more about the writers and their audience than about the objects of their curiosity. Until well into the twentieth century, the speakers of Burushaski had almost no wheeled vehicles, no precision instruments, and no indoor lighting except from the oil squeezed out of apricot stones. But their language is about as primitive as Proust or Bach. Yuchi, too, defies the fantasies of primitivism. In its grammar Yuchi does not distinguish, as Indo-European languages do, between humans and all other living beings. Its pronouns distinguish between *Yuchis* and all other living beings. I would stand in the same category as bears, hawks, the moon, the sun — "It's not a bad class to be in," Richard said dryly.

"How you doin'? Good to see you!" Addie George bustled into the language office, an eight-year-old great-grandson in tow. Her time was limited — she would have to drive back into town to pick up a son at work and make his lunch — but her energy seemed boundless. Black hair fell across her forehead in bangs, and behind a big pair of glasses her eyes were bright. She wore a bright red sweater above pants and running shoes. Only the creases in her face and the severe curve of her spine betrayed her eighty-nine years. In Oklahoma, as in other places, some tribal elders are reluctant to speak to outsiders. Addie was not among them.

"Now when I was little," she began, "I could say anything I wanted to in Yuchi. I did not know how to talk English. When I was six years old, my mother sent me to school and I struggled with it! I had a hard time." She stretched the vowel in "hard" so it sounded more like "haaaard." Recalling Wagner's word-by-word translation, I tried to imagine the linguistic challenges a Yuchi-speaking child must have faced at Lone Star School. "The other children talked English to me and I spoke Yuchi to them, and they thought it sounded funny. The teacher tried her best to get me to speak English. She talked to my parents — my father talked English like a white person — and so my father, every night he made me sit down and listen to him. And I finally learned."

Aaron, her great-grandson, was listening with interest. The boy seemed a little in awe of her. I don't blame him. Addie paused to drill him in Yuchi numerals; then she carried on.

In the 1920s, after years in one-room country schools, she was sent to a boarding school for Indian girls in a town called Eufaula. Addie earned good grades. But no matter how high the girls' marks, "They punished us if they caught us talking our own language. Even the

Creeks got punished. They'd make us scrub floors, and wash curtains and iron them, and clean the laundry up. And just work — work in the kitchen, clean the dining hall up, polish the tables and chairs, and make everything shine. That was our punishment." Some of the children rebelled: "We'd go way out behind the commissary building and talk Indian. To stay in practice!"

Still, Addie was lucky. Residential schools were abundant in the United States during the early twentieth century, and the punishments could be far worse. The sexual and physical abuse inflicted on Indian boys and girls has become notorious. Linguistic abuse was even more widespread. At many schools, children caught voicing their own language were beaten, mocked, humiliated. For their own good, they were commanded to forget their language. What's hard to fathom, decades later, is the absolute faith that such behavior was righteous. "We should let the old tongues with their superstition and sin die," wrote S. Hall Young, an influential missionary in Alaska late in the nineteenth century, "and replace these languages with that of Christian civilization, and compel the natives in all our schools to talk English and English only. Thus we would soon have an intelligent people who would be qualified to be Christian citizens." Christian civilization, by such reckoning, belonged to a single language. If the only good Indian was an English-speaking Indian, a child who held fast to Yuchi could be neither Christian nor intelligent.

Young was widely known as "the mushing parson." When the Presbyterian mission board asked him to translate the Bible into the Tlingit language, he refused. Better, he said, to force the Tlingit to seek God in English. His attitude was in line with government policy. "Teaching an Indian youth in his own barbarous dialect is a positive detriment to him," wrote J.D.C. Atkins, the federal commissioner for Indian affairs, in 1887. "The first step to be taken toward civilization, toward teaching the Indians the mischief and folly of continuing in their barbarous practices, is to teach them the English language." Atkins knew that some Americans, even then, considered this policy cruel. Is it also cruelty, he retorted, to force the Indian to abandon "the vicious and barbarous sun dance, where he lacerates his flesh?" He meant it as a rhetorical question. "Barbarous" appears to have been his favorite word.

Today the federal government gives modest encouragement and modest funds toward maintaining Indian languages. But neither the moral support nor the money seems likely to reverse a trend that started long before the days of S. Hall Young. In the United States as in Australia, dozens of languages have disappeared. A recent report from the National Clearinghouse for Bilingual Education listed 154 that are still in use. Of those, 118, or 77 percent, are spoken by fewer than a thousand people. Yuchi is not an exception to the American pattern; Yuchi illuminates the rule.

Addie married a shoe salesman after high school: "He was full-blood Yuchi and I could speak my language again." She also spoke it to Günter Wagner, becoming one of his youngest informants. During the Depression, she cleared the weeds out of cornfields and cotton fields for seventy-five cents a day. She raised twelve children and buried three of them; by now she has dozens of grandchildren, great-grandchildren, and great-great-grandchildren. Some live in faraway states. Few know the rudiments of Yuchi. "My oldest granddaughter, she tries her best to say things. She can say 'meat' and 'bread,' 'I'm hungry' and 'I'm thirsty,' but she can't carry on a conversation." I asked why, and Addie replied: "She needs to be around somebody that can talk, and her mother's a quiet lady. If they were around me, I'd make them talk in Yuchi! And cook like a Yuchi woman." Meaning dishes like wild grape dumplings, frybread, and boiled squirrels.

"How'd you say 'I'd like some candy' in Yuchi?" she asked Aaron. The boy had no idea, and was embarrassed to admit it. Yuchi, for him, is a jumble of elderly sounds, a few of which make unexpected sense. He put his hand over his face as he quietly said, "I forget." Addie handed him a piece of candy anyway. Then she got serious again. While Yuchi-speaking elders are still alive, "That's when people ought to get busy and learn. Even those that don't care, I still tell them how important it is. Like I heard one old woman tell me — she was a hundred years old, she used to call me 'Daughter' — 'When you pray to God, talk in your own language, Daughter. He'll bless you and listen to you because he knows you're that tribe. You talk to the Great Spirit, you use your own language.' When I heard her say that, I said, 'Well, I'll always use my language when I pray.' My thoughts come out in my prayers."

I asked her to speak Yuchi into my tape recorder, and she obliged at once. Having uttered a few sentences in a ringing, musical voice, she reverted to English to deliver a kind of oral history of her people. She told of the Yuchis' arrival in North America "from a different island," of how they lived on deer meat, wild grains, blackberries, and pecans, and of how women were washing clothes by the seashore when they noticed "big old bubbles" far out to sea. The bubbles proved to be white men's ships. Most of all, Addie talked about the Yuchis' forced march over the Appalachians. "My grandmother's grandmother was a little girl," she said. "She was tied on her uncle's shoulders with a heavy shawl. He swam across that Mississippi River, got on the other bank, took that child off, and went back to get another one." There was a matter-of-fact quality to her telling of the story: no easy rhetoric, no adverbs. "That's how they run the Indians out of Georgia and Alabama," Addie summed up. "Those that didn't make it, they drowned or froze to death. It's a hard old road."

This is not precisely what history books say, if they bother to mention the barefoot deportation of the Yuchis. But it suggests the length of a people's memory, the depth of a people's grief.

Because of the age of its speakers, the language spoken by the children of the sun is now a mostly indoor affair. Next day at the language office, I found Richard Grounds painstakingly going over a cassette that Maggie Marsey had recorded. Whatever doubts the elders may have about one another's fluency, nobody disputes Maggie's talent in the language. So when some community members asked Richard to arrange a translation of the Lord's Prayer, he turned to her.

Having been evangelized more than a century ago (and not by the likes of S. Hall Young), the Yuchis used to know plenty of Christian prayers. But the prayers, like the ancient chants in their non-Christian ceremonies, embodied an oral tradition. Literacy reached the people in English; Christianity arrived in Yuchi. "While the language was vibrant," Mary Linn was to tell me, "no one needed to write it down to save it or to teach it. Saving and passing down were all done orally, from generation to generation. But this link was broken when the younger generations didn't learn it. So they switched to English in the church" — regular preaching hasn't been conducted in Yuchi since the 1970s — "and now they want the Yuchi back." Back for religious use, that is. Back as an emblem of the sacred. To help retrieve it, Maggie performed the kind of sacred task that would once have been the duty of a male preacher — or, in earlier times, a medicine man.

Thanks to a sound-processing program on the office Macintosh, her voice was being digitized. Richard opened up the program. His computer screen resembled a lithograph showing distant conifers across a pale, windless lake, their reflections visible below the waterline. But each of the reflected conifers was a Yuchi syllable, and the spaces between the trees were the pauses in Maggie's voice.

Simple though it may appear, the translation — or reclamation — had taken weeks to accomplish. There is a delicacy in word choice; a delicacy in protocol as well. In many oral languages, the idea of God requires a verb, not a noun. And a speaker must get things right. "In the oral tradition words are sacred," the Kiowa author N. Scott Momaday has written; "they are intrinsically powerful and beautiful . . . Nothing exists beyond the influence of words. Words are the names of Creation . . . Every word spoken, every word heard, is the utterance of prayer. Thus, in the oral tradition, language bears the burden of the sacred, the burden of belief. In a written tradition, the place of language is not so certain."

Maggie's main difficulty lay in finding the exact nuances for concepts that were alien in her mother tongue. For a start, the Yuchis did not have kingdoms. She changed "thine is the kingdom" to "you hold the land." "Hallowed" became "precious, dear, expensive." A word for "heaven" was still in common memory, the literal sense being "the place where they live again," but Maggie puzzled over "Deliver us from evil" — in the Yuchi language, evil is a foreign idea. She settled on "something that's no good." The hardest term was "temptation," another notion the Yuchis had done without for thousands of years. "This one took about two weeks," Richard said. "No one could even remember preachers talking about it." Maggie consulted Henry and a couple of other elders. What she came up with was long-winded but perhaps brilliant: "Don't lead us into something we want to do, but we *don't* want to do."

The Yuchi version of the Lord's Prayer will be heard, as spoken by Maggie, on a CD-ROM that Richard and two assistants are now preparing, aided by a grant from a federal agency called the Administration for Native Americans. He showed me an early prototype. It dates from the mid-1990s, when he and an elder named Mose Cahwee took part in a multimedia workshop at the University of Iowa. Mose, a medicine man and traditional leader, died in the winter of 2001. In the prototype you can hear his voice by clicking on any of four icons: they lead to sections on numbers, animals, food, and religion. But to reach those icons you must first click on an image by the Yuchi artist Richard Ray Whitman. Having sat through an academic lecture called "Who Were the Euchee?" Whitman produced an answer of his own. He made a big collage, using oil, acrylic, and sacred earth, and copied out the lecture's title. Then he splashed a large *X* over "Were." Beside it, he wrote "Are."

"Turning the raw tapes into a functional CD-ROM is time-consuming work," Richard said. "But it's powerful, because it enables you to minimize the use of English. In most language tapes, everything is mediated through English." Within a few years he means to have a Yuchi CD-ROM with sixteen thematic areas, each one including pictures, dialogues, embedded videos, and word lists. The section on religion — even without the Lord's Prayer — was the best developed so far. It blends old photographs, video footage shot in Pickett Methodist Chapel, and the voice of Mose Cahwee leading a simple hymn in Yuchi. A black-and-white image shows a banner, now consigned to storage:

EUCHEES OF PICKETT CHAPEL

ALWAYS FORWARD

NEVER GO BACK

But how much can any CD-ROM of a vanishing language accomplish? Is it not an act of embalming? Richard's mood had turned somber. His boyish grin was absent. In graduate school, where he specialized in the history of religion, he studied German, French, Hebrew, and ancient Greek. Yet as a boy he had picked up little from his Yuchi-speaking grandmother, "and now I have the typical problems of a second-language learner, with a special twist. There are actually things I say, that when somebody else says them to me, I can't quite catch on. Or if I do, it's with a delay — because I never hear the language. I hear words, I hear sentences, but it's not a full immersion." Richard can say a limited number of things very well. He can give outsiders the impression of being competent in the language. Yuchi-speaking elders know better.

Richard went back, as his people so often do, to the Trail of Tears. Because of it, the language lost some words: generations have passed since its speakers named a starfish. Luckily, most of the medicine plants needed for their ceremonies grow in the Ozarks as well as in the Appalachians. The dances and rituals of the Green Corn Ceremonial take place each spring and summer. They remain visceral to Yuchi identity, even without Yuchi words. On the long march, Richard said, a sacred fire "was kept alive from the old home place. It was down to whatever they carried. And in some ways, our language has gone like that. We're down to just a handful — down to a few coals. But if somehow we could have a cluster of young people who can become fluent in the language, those fires could be rebuilt. That's the highest hope on my part."

The hope seemed a touch forlorn. In an effort to think positively, I pointed out that mainstream society sees Indians in a much rosier light than it did when Addie, Maggie, and Henry were growing up. Oklahoma's license plates now say NATIVE AMERICA and sport a headdress in the middle. Richard agreed that a change has occurred. "But," he went on, "I don't see that as a good thing. Before, when popular culture was antagonistic, it was clear where the boundaries were. If someone came out to the ceremonial grounds to take pictures, this was not a good thing. There was something inherently abusive about that process: these were not friends. Now it's the local anthropologist or academic who comes as a friend and says, 'Let me take the time of your elders. Let me take the investment of your community in terms of cultural knowledge.' I don't think people are very clear about the consequences." In the 1970s a white anthropologist arrived in Sapulpa and studied the Yuchis, publishing articles on the language and a book on the Green Corn Ceremonial. He stated that the Yuchis had asked him not to reveal certain aspects of the ceremonies — and he revealed them anyway. When the outside world kept its distance, Richard concluded, the issue of cultural survival was easier to confront.

That issue, which goes beyond language, elicits Richard's deepest emotions. His passion, he said, "is about carrying forward the things we have been gifted with." The ceremonial knowledge is one example. "But the most critical carrier of the ancient ways of understanding and of dreaming the world is the language itself. In Yuchi you cannot construct a single sentence without understanding a lot of things about how you see the world. It's all built into the language, it's all coded there. This is a different way of understanding." Ironically, the language's near-death experience has done wonders for Richard's career. In the 1990s he began his work fueled only by personal conviction. Lately his multimedia project has garnered money, publicity, and prestige at his university. But has it helped save Yuchi?

"I'm absolutely not willing to document the language simply for linguistic purposes," he told me with a flash of anger. His thick dark ponytail shook.

This is not about creating an academic record. I am very concerned to keep the language as part of the living community. Right now there's this small group of very talented and gifted people. And at the same time, there's this sterility. Because they're not passing the language on.

I wouldn't say this is my life's work — I would say it's my work in the lifetime of our speakers. Some other communities were slumbering when their last speakers died, and if they want to rekindle a language now, that's fine. But we're not like that. We're clear about how precious our language is. And we're still struggling to get adequate community involvement. We've tried everything, believe me. Meals. Games. Prizes. Candy. We bribe them! The really sad thing is that the kids would prefer to go to scout meetings and play at being Indian, instead of sitting with the elders and really *being* Indian.

The section on arithmetic in Richard's CD-ROM prototype goes no higher than ten. You can listen to a dead man say a numeral. You can watch some fingers moving up or down: eight . . . seven . . . six . . .

It was a fine March morning on the northern flank of Sapulpa. The waving wheat did not smell sweet, though the wind came whistling o'er the motel. Just beyond the town's main cemetery was an imposing billboard. Coming into Sapulpa, I'd see it announcing the Tulsa Arms Show ("World's Largest"). Leaving town, I'd face a giant Jesus staring down at a pint-sized sinner. "The judgment was set and the books were opened," said an Old Testament verse across the top of the billboard. Above the sinner's shoulder was a list of sins, adultery prominent among them. The sinner appeared to be in the grip of a nervous breakdown. Sapulpa has about twenty-five thousand people. The town contains one secondhand bookstore, four gun shops, and twenty Baptist churches.

And a museum, too. The Sapulpa Historical Museum occupies most of a downtown block, in premises that once boasted a hotel, a printing shop, an appliance dealer, a beauty salon, and the YWCA. I found the museum empty of visitors, though full of volunteers. A seventy-nine-year-old named Fred showed me around. He was wonderfully friendly, like so many people in Oklahoma. I saw the sewer pipe out of which the Catfish String Band once fashioned a sewer-pipe bass. I saw a screaming mannequin surrounded by pioneer dental equipment. I saw a model of the plane Fred flew in while serving as a wing sergeant major during the Second World War. His was the conflict, as it happened, that broke apart the structures of Yuchi life, creating economic opportunities for men and women alike but hastening the decline of the language. I would learn this later from Mary Linn; Fred didn't know a thing about the Yuchis.

He passed me on to Doris Yocham, the museum's director. She knew much more about Indians in the region — indeed, she had helped organize two reunions of men who once boarded at the Euchee Mission School. I had read that its students were whipped for speaking Yuchi, but Doris denied it: "The boys were not mistreated here. They have very good memories because it prepared them for life. One of them was on the Bataan Death March, and he said that the school had prepared him to face it."

Photographs along a single wall showed the town's minority peoples. The display was equally divided between blacks and Indians — most of whom, including "Chief Sapulpa," the local founder, were Creeks. "Originally," a caption said, "the Euchees/Yuchis were sun worshippers and were among the most superstitious of the Indian tribes." "Superstitious" is a loaded word. Yet in other respects the labeling seemed progressive: "In 1867, the Creek Nation was organized under a written constitution, and 44 towns were established." Indian nationhood is not always endorsed so readily in the heartlands of conservatism. "We accepted the Mission students," Doris told me. "Of course there were always a lot of Indians around here. I grew up watching the Indians come to town on their wagons. My own father was part Cherokee." I hope my eyebrows didn't rise too high. You couldn't have found a paler-looking lady. "The Indians were so conservative," she added. "They only took what they needed to have. It's a shame the white man ruined it all."

Might museums outside Sapulpa have more to say about the Yuchis? One morning Henry Washburn guided me through a labyrinth of turnpikes and expressways to the Gilcrease Museum in northwestern Tulsa. The Gilcrease claims to house "an unparalleled collection of Native American art and artifacts" as well as "the world's largest, most comprehensive collection of art of the American West." It stands on a hill above 460 acres of gardens and woods. That day the oaks were still bare, the magnolias just coming into bloom. Curving plate-glass windows in the Vista Room delivered a spectacular view over forests that could, by a small stretch of the imagination, be remote from any major city. "Must have been three years since I was here," Henry remarked. But the atmosphere of high art, or the school groups roaming the museum, made him taciturn. He said nothing in front of Thomas Cole's painting *Last of the Mohicans:* a few noble savages, dwarfed by even nobler mountains. In the permanent galleries of art from the American West, one triumphant painting had the title *The Hayfield Fight — August 1, 1867. 2,500 Sioux Defeated by 19 White Men.*

A small room was devoted to Indian art of Oklahoma. I hoped to find some work by the likes of Richard Ray Whitman, who plays with contemporary styles as he explores the meanings of tradition. But the artists displayed were all dead. "Any Yuchis here?" I wondered aloud. "I doubt it," Henry said. "I kind of doubt it." And he was right. If Yuchi work formed any part of the collection, the Gilcrease was keeping it well out of sight.

I was ready to leave, but Henry lingered in front of a Creek painter's depiction of village women pounding corn. For some reason the image brought to mind the fate of his mother's tongue. "When the language goes," he said, "the government will be able to say there's no such tribe as the Yuchi. We'd be just like the Vietnamese scattered around here — we'd be nobody. We're nobody anyway, as far as that goes."

Henry and I shared a quick meal of Kentucky Fried Chicken in a Tulsa mall before I dropped him at home. Pulling up in his driveway, I heard a rooster crowing.

"Your neighbors keep chickens, eh?"

"No, I do."

"Oh. For the eggs or the meat?"

"Well, neither one. They're fightin' chickens."

I couldn't think of anything to say, but Henry went right on. "I raise 'em. They're tryin' to make it illegal now. My neighbor doesn't like 'em — that's why he put up that big wooden fence."

On my own again, I drove south to the town of Okmulgee. When the asphalt had finally succumbed to ranchland, calves tottered beside their mothers on the young grass. "Redneck Corner" comprised a gas station, a convenience store, and a trailer called Indian Smokeshop. The afternoon was wearing on, and I wanted to visit the Creek Council House Museum: the headquarters of what, late in the nineteenth century, had been a quasi-independent nation.

Dumped in Indian Territory at the end of the Trail of Tears, the surviving Creeks had done well for themselves. By the terms of a treaty with the United States in 1856, they ran their own education system as one of the "five civilized tribes." Washington made them a solemn promise of autonomy. The Council House, an imposing two-story building, dates from 1878. It contained a courtroom and legislative chambers, Okmulgee being a capital of sorts. But a generation later, preparing for the birth of a state, U.S. authorities abolished the governments of the Creeks and their fellow "civilized tribes." Washington wanted to hand out land to settlers, and it needed the "surplus" acres that the Indians held in common. In the 1920s demolitionists almost tore the Council House down.

The building was saved and is now an impressive museum, focusing on the achievements of the Muscogee Creeks. I would have been unimpressed, though, if I'd been Yuchi. In the guidebook they warrant a single mention: "1620 — The Yuchi are conquered and enslaved by Muscogee; their language resembles no other indigenous language in North America." "Conquered and enslaved": the Yuchis beg to differ. Otherwise, throughout the Council House, they are ignored. They are made invisible. The guidebook mentions William Bartram, a Quaker naturalist who traveled through the South just before the American Revolution; but it omits his praise of a Yuchi community as "the largest, most compact town I ever saw." An old map of Indian Territory hung on the museum wall, and peering at the Sapulpa area I found a stream called Euchee Creek. The name has disappeared. In the 1990s some Yuchis applied to the U.S. government for permission to leave the Creek Nation and gain the status of a separate tribe. The application failed.

I stepped out into a downtown that had a vaguely disconsolate air, as though the heart as well as half the buildings had been ripped out of Okmulgee. Across the street from the Council House, Xanadu Apparel rubbed shoulders with Yours Truly Salon (Full Service) and Boy Howdy Variety Store. Notebook in hand, I made an odd spectacle. A boy on a bicycle stopped to ask if he could help with whatever I was doing.

What I was doing, for much of my time in Oklahoma, was trying to puzzle out the patterns of Yuchi. Richard lent me a rare copy of Günter Wagner's grammar to make sense of, if I could. The complexities begin with the Yuchi fondness for creating intricate compound nouns; the word for "lemon" means "peach big yellow sour ones," and "railroad" becomes "wagon inside burns its road." But many languages do this sort of thing. (The state bird of Oklahoma, for example, has the English name "scissor-tailed flycatcher.") What's more problematic is the way that Yuchi verbs can be altered by an object. Depending on whether you want to put a pencil, a ball, or a cup inside a bag, you must choose one of three words for "put." Things that lie on the ground, things that sit, and things that stand are in need of separate verbs.

Like Hopi, though unlike English, Yuchi has a cluster of stand-alone verbs that take no pronouns. When flakes are tumbling out of the sky, we say "It's snowing" even though the "it" means nothing. Yuchi has a verb that gives the news single-handed: *cra' 'ę*. "It burns," "it melts," and "it thunders" are further examples. So is the word that completes a story: *djilɛ'* (roughly, "it is said"). The grammar suggests that a Yuchi story, like a fire or storm, is a natural phenomenon — or was.

Yuchi kinship terms are more problematic. Take the word *dots'onɛs'ię*. According to Wagner, it can mean "my father's sister's daughter" or "my father's sister's son." We'd say "cousin" and have done with it. But *dots'onɛs'ię* can't refer to cousins on the mother's side of the family; Yuchi has a different word for them. And yet *dots'onɛs'ię* also applies to "my sister's son," "my brother's daughter," "my sister's daughter," and "my brother's son" — everything we mean by "nephew" or "niece." The language is saying, it might appear, that relationships are not defined by gender.

But hold on. Whatever you're using *dots'onɛs'ię* to mean, you say the word only if you're a girl or woman. A boy or man uses other terms: *tsɛsonɛ'*, *dis'anɛs'ię'*, or *di'yanɛs'i'ę*, depending on the precise relation. In Yuchi, some words vary according to the sex of the speaker. "My mother," "my father," "my father's sister's husband": these terms stay the same. But "my brother," "my sister," and "my daughter" are said differently by men and women. This system does not resemble Mati Ke, where gender taboos have the power to thwart all conversation; but neither can it be likened to English, where words are perceived to exist independent of any speaking voice. In his book *Phonology as Human Behavior*, Yishai Tobin defined language "as a constant struggle for maximum communication with minimal effort." Maximum communication, agreed. But I'm not sure how accurate it is to say that Yuchi (or any other ancient, isolated language) demands minimal effort of its speakers.

"Features that make Yuchi difficult to analyze," scribbled another linguist, James Crawford, on a rough sheet of paper in the early 1970s. He listed five: contractions, homonyms, vowel harmony, "what appears to be arbitrary nasalization of vowels," and "no formal distinctions between noun and verb, or any word class." Crawford died with his analysis of Yuchi incomplete. It was left to Mary Linn, a generation later, to write the language's first complete grammar. Fortunately the quality of spoken Yuchi had stayed high, even though the quantity of speakers had fallen very low. This is one of the world's few languages, Linn wrote, that can be classified as stative/active: "Instead of encoding the notion of 'subject' and 'object' on nouns, like we do, Yuchi cares about the ability of that subject or object to initiate action, i.e. the animacy of the noun." Does it sound straightforward? Wait. "In Yuchi, this notion is completely controlled by the nature of the verb itself, not the nature of the noun participants."

I headed downtown for a coffee, thinking again that for anyone except a small child, second-language fluency can pose a daunting challenge. In Oklahoma, more than any other state east of the Rocky Mountains, the challenge needs to be faced head on. For the condition of Yuchi is echoed and re-echoed throughout the state. Most of its twenty-seven Indian languages are disappearing. Only three — Cherokee, Creek, and Kickapoo — "have a lot of speakers, including kids. Choctaw and Comanche may also have some kids that speak it. But after that, no other tribe in Oklahoma has children speaking fluently. And that's the easiest way to know whether a language is on the way out."

I was sitting across a table in the Mission Street Café from Greg Bigler, a Harvard-trained lawyer with a mustache, a long black ponytail, and bags below his middle-aged eyes. It was a working afternoon and he'd come straight from the office, sporting the yellow sweatshirt of the Groundhog Day Run in Ponca City. An attorney for many tribes, Greg also serves as president of the Oklahoma Native Language Association. The title is misleadingly grand: only a few people are active in the group, which organizes workshops for teachers and distributes some models and tools for language learning. Those models, he stressed, don't depend on money. "A lot of the time, tribes or communities will gear their language programs based on what they can get funding for. Funding is great, there should be more of it, but there's so much you can do without it. The first thing is, if you've got an aunt or an uncle or a grandma, spend time with her! Tailoring a program to funding is a mistake, especially if you're down to a few dozen speakers."

The best way to learn a threatened language, Greg kept saying, is by intensive talk with an elder. Among native peoples in California and Arizona, master-apprentice programs have been shown to work; but they demand an investment of twenty or thirty hours a week. "And most people can't commit to that. So you go down the sliding scale as to how much time you have: classroom learning, language camps, and so on. And then it depends on the skill of the teacher." Good teachers create opportunities for pride. Native people who don't speak their ancestral language are often hesitant to look bad in public; they may be embarrassed or ashamed at their lack of fluency; they're nervous about saying things wrong. They fear failure. Fluency seldom develops in front of a blackboard.

"But the only *wrong* thing," Greg went on, "is not to do anything. So if you're twenty-five or thirty-five now, stop blaming your parents for not speaking the language. Stop blaming the government or the schools. Go ask your grandmother to speak to you. Do something. Do whatever you can."

Greg is a Yuchi. His law practice is based in Sapulpa. His mother, Josephine Bigler, speaks the language well; his aunt understands it but sometimes stumbles over words. Greg has been wrestling with Yuchi for nearly twenty years. In the 1980s, by his own account, "I got tired of this community wanting to have meetings about how its language was disappearing, and I decided that instead of having meetings, we should have *classes*." Years later he abandoned the classes. "Yes, we can get the kids to count from one to ten, and to speak a moderate level of introductory phrases. But my personal goal was fluency. And the only way to do that is a lot of intense, one-on-one work."

How fluent he is in any given month depends on how much time he's spent around his mother. If he has been with her a lot, Greg understands her Yuchi fairly well. Sometimes he can reply with confidence. But then the rest of his life takes over again, and his Yuchi skills begin to evaporate. The lack of materials only sharpens the frustration.

It's not that the lexicon of Yuchi is mired in the preindustrial past. Inventing words has never been a problem, especially with Maggie Marsey, Mose Cahwee, and other fluent elders willing to devote so many hours to the rescue effort. Other indigenous peoples have occasionally been less fortunate: their elders have preferred to take a language with them to the grave. Better, they felt, to keep it private than to see it mangled, compromised, eroded, or transformed in the mouths of the struggling young. Yuchi contains dozens of recently minted words. Months before his death, Mose Cahwee put his seal of approval on terms like "videotape" and "cassette tape": *k'ala bE thlE gOdEnA hOhû* (literally, "something turns words catches").

The problem lies in the acceptance, diffusion, and rapid recall of such words — and, before that, in their spelling. The above term for cassette tape uses Richard's orthography. In the language classes he has adopted a kind of teaching-aid spelling, full of accents, underlinings, and capital letters in unlikely places. It avoids some of the symbols Wagner scattered around; it gives no indication of pitch, for example. But without the musicality, Richard warned, "This is as simple as it can get." Indeed, fluent speakers might be hard-pressed to recognize the meaning of a sentence spoken with the wrong music. Yuchi has three sounds that English conveys with the letter *a*. Richard gives each of them a different sign: *A, a,* and *@*. He adds extra symbols to show when a vowel is nasalized — a key distinction, for it affects a word's meaning. Trouble is, Mary Linn's grammar uses a much simpler system, one that she says was developed in cooperation with Yuchi elders. Greg follows her approach. Very little has been written in Yuchi — but it has been written in several ways.

The point is not that one particular system has truth, beauty, or accuracy on its side. Whatever alphabet you adopt, you still have to master the spoken language. The point is that a tiny community of speakers and learners finds itself uncertain and divided over spelling. As I would discover among the more numerous speakers of languages like Provençal and Mohawk, this kind of split is all too common.

Greg has graduated from a great university; he has traveled widely; he has an absorbing job. His passion for Oklahoma's languages intrigued me. Why should the fate of Yuchi or any other endangered language matter to him so much? Greg sipped his coffee — or, in the syntax of a Yuchi sentence, "man the / coffee the / it he sipped" — and stayed silent for an unusual length of time. Above the air conditioners, the Dixie Chicks blared through the café's speakers: "Goodbye, Earl . . ." Finally Greg spoke: "It's a gift that we were given, and I'd hate to see us lose it. I don't think you can quantify it in terms of dollars or knowledge — it's just like saying 'Why do we care about art and music? Why do we care about our children?' It's part of us.

"If we lost all of the literature that was written before 1900, it wouldn't stop us eating or breathing. But there'd be some intangible loss that could never be recovered."

Just how hard is it to come to grips with a dying, unwritten language? A couple of days later, I saw for myself.

The weekly Yuchi class was supposed to begin at 6 P.M., but a few minutes ahead of time the community center was dark. Richard looked happy as he stepped out of his little car, for he had his children with him: Renee, a girl of fourteen, and Alan, a redheaded boy of twelve. They spend much of the year with their mother, a white woman in another state, and Richard had driven several hundred miles to pick them up for their spring break. His black hair hung loose. As soon as the building's doors were unlocked, Henry Washburn limped over from his half-ton, his eye patch taped to his face. He was visibly in pain.

It was 6:25 when Richard called the class to order. About a dozen adults were chatting in the room, along with seven or eight children. One girl wore plastic bunny ears above her black braid. Maggie Marsey, having arrived in the nick of time, said a brief prayer to begin. For some years she had avoided the language classes because her husband, a Muscogee Creek, didn't want her there. Candace, a blond teenager with a Yuchi grandparent, padded off to the kitchen in search of aspirins and coffee for the elders.

Richard looked at Maggie and said, "How would you greet somebody if you meet them in a store?"

"*sÂngÂ'lA sOnOlA?*" she replied.

Richard wrote the phrase on a long sheet of paper and taped the sheet to a wall. Looking at his transcription, I felt all sense of familiarity dissolving. To anyone embarking on Yuchi, the sounds, the rhythm, and the pitch are already strange; so is the word order; now, at the evening classes, capital letters, accents, and apostrophes took on a novel meaning.

We practiced speaking the phrase. I felt a brief, idiotic surge of pride at having memorized a Yuchi sentence.

"How would you translate that?" Richard asked.

"Doin' all right?" said Maggie. Miked, she was just about audible. Richard turned to Henry for a reply. My ears heard a curious muddle of syllables, which Richard decoded with a purple marker: *n@dAsE s@ zOnû.*

Underneath, in green, he added Henry's own translation: "I don't feel very well." When Henry repeated the sentence, Richard found he'd missed out an *lA* in the middle.

Maggie was feeling all right, or wouldn't admit otherwise, so Richard asked her for a second reply to the question. Listening closely, struggling to decipher the sounds, I heard *"na gathli eh zona."* Richard wrote it up: *n@gk@thle'ê zOnû*. "And how would you translate that?" he said.

"Nothin' wrong with me."

"Who's ready to try?" Richard asked. Alan's arm shot up, and his father punched him cheerily on the shoulder. The boy repeated the old woman's words.

"Hey," Henry said, "that's all right!"

Richard underlined the *ê*. "That seems to be the stress," he said. "The air is cut off a little bit before that." He drilled us all. "I think everybody does better," he added, "if we say it without looking at the sheet of paper. It doesn't really help."

A tall, sturdy-looking man called Danny Cahwee shook his head. He was a son of Mose Cahwee, but his mother was a Pawnee and he could speak neither of the ancestral languages. "It helps me," he muttered.

"What we're trying to do," Richard explained, "is get you to listen to the sounds and then *say* it, not *read* it."

After that, things began to get hard.

"nedzAt'ê wahA'ês'ε Onû?" said Maggie. "How's your father?" This is womantalk. It doesn't matter whom Maggie is addressing; only a girl or woman can pose the question in this way. She repeated the words a few times, making the rhythm clear.

Henry tested Renee on the phrase. "That's good," he remarked. In his voice, the word "good" lasts about four times longer than when I say it. "They been away for months," he muttered, "and they can say it better than these folk."

"How would you say this in mantalk, Henry?" Richard asked.

"nedzAt'ê wahA'ê'hOnû?" The wording was similar to Maggie's, but a female sibilant near the end had been replaced by a push of male air.

A broad-shouldered, gray-haired man spoke up for the first time. Carlin is a Chickasaw — another of Oklahoma's "five civilized tribes" — married to a woman who's part Choctaw, part Yuchi. Now he told us how to inquire after a father's health in Chickasaw. "Our language is not as complicated as Yuchi," he added. "The men and women say the same thing."

Richard decided it was time to order dinner: not frybread or boiled squirrel, but pizza. A collection bowl appeared. While we fished for quarters and dollar bills, Henry patiently explained how a man would ask after somebody else's mother. The best learner seemed to be Candace, the blond girl. Her brain was young enough to absorb what my brain kept wanting to spit out. But I wasn't alone. All around me, adult brows were furrowed in the struggle to master these perplexing cadences and symbols. Concentrating on "your mother," I missed "my mother."

"*sÂnga'ê s'ε Onû*," Henry said. "She's all right."

But wait: who exactly is the mother being spoken about? The terms for Yuchi relatives don't apply to other people's parents. Richard asked, "If your mother or father was a non-Yuchi — they could be Creek or anything else — how would you say that, Maggie?"

She began to quiz the men on how our father, or our mother, was doing. The answer depended on the pronoun embedded in the question, and the differences kept eluding me. "My father, she's doing fine," I must have mumbled. "My mother, nothing wrong with him."

With stomachs now starting to growl all over the room, Richard asked Maggie to drill the class in verbs. "To eat" is irregular in Yuchi, so he settled on "I want." But Maggie, never having learned a European language except English, seemed unsure why Richard was so keen for her to repeat, devoid of context, the Yuchi expressions for "I want," "I wanted," and "I will want."

Carlin had his hand up again. If a non-Yuchi man learned to speak fluent Yuchi, would he count as a Yuchi, grammatically speaking?

Nobody seemed sure. The question has seldom arisen; the question does not arise; the question may never arise. In this classroom setting, Yuchi did not sound soft, ethereal, or songlike. Maybe it was inevitable that the language would appear awkward in its new role as an object of study, its mysteries exposed and analyzed on the basis of outside principles and teaching styles. But were these the right principles, the best styles? Mercifully, the pizzas appeared.

In the kitchen a couple of Yuchi women were trading stories with Carlin. "I was brought up traditional," he said. "Now I'm one of only ten or twelve people who can speak Chickasaw rightly. Of course there's another thirty or forty who can speak it . . ."

He paused, uncertain. "Wrongly?" I suggested. Carlin laughed. But he didn't disagree.

He told of an early date with Juanita, the part-Yuchi woman he later married. He was speaking Chickasaw; she was speaking Choctaw, a closely related tongue. After a few minutes she announced, "I want a cigarette." Carlin didn't respond; he was paralyzed by surprise.

"I want a cigarette!"

The Choctaw word for "cigarette" has a different sense in Chickasaw: it means "kiss."

"I felt kind of flattered," Carlin said. "I was thinking, 'Either this girl is awful brave, or else . . .'" He granted her request.

When the class resumed, the main activity seemed to be distributing prizes to the children. Candace and Renee took charge of drilling the younger kids in Yuchi phrases. Anyone who blurted out a correct "How's your father?" could reach into a plastic bag and grab a yo-yo, a ruler, a puzzle, or some candy. I wondered if a yo-yo stands, sits, or lies on the earth.

"We're in the payoff round," said Richard, his lament about bribery forgotten. He was watching his son and daughter; he was enjoying himself. But Henry, sipping another coffee, said nothing.

Richard didn't accept my comparison of English to Wal-Mart. I discovered this one sundrenched morning while driving along a side road south of Sapulpa. Henry was in the other front seat, Richard in the back. "You get the point?" I said, pleased with my own ingenuity. "Just like Wal-Mart is swallowing up the neighborhood hardware stores, English is swallowing up the neighborhood languages." Richard got the point; he also saw its weakness. "At Wal-Mart," he said, "you can still buy the stuff that smaller stores used to sell. Languages aren't like that. Languages are unique. English doesn't sell the other merchandise — it eliminates the other merchandise."

We were looking for Josephine Keith, possibly the youngest fluent speaker of Yuchi, and neither man was confident of the way to her home. Josephine seldom appears at the noontime meals or evening classes. But since she was barely seventy years old, Richard had assumed he would have plenty of time to work with her — until, soon after Mose Cahwee's death, she underwent surgery for cancer.

Sapulpa now sprawls as far as Lone Star School, where Maggie Marsey and Addie George once wrestled with English. A sturdy brick building, it languishes among weeds and wildflowers, the windows smashed or boarded up. Richard urged me farther south, then west down what proved to be the wrong side road. Through the car's open windows, beyond someone's ragged home, came the agile, buoyant song of a finch. The area is dotted with creeks (and also Creeks). Yuchis, as ever, are harder to find. At last we crossed a bridge over Polecat Creek and turned hard right onto a gravel road that swung past farmland and juvenile woodland. Richard leaned forward and said, "We're arriving at the last household in the world where Yuchi is spoken every day."

I noticed Josephine's old farmhouse — a green roof, a clutter of debris by the door — before I saw its replacement, just across the yard. After two husbands and five children, Josephine was living with none of them. Instead she was taking care of her uncle, Maxey Barnett, a man of ninety-three. We found him rocking on the new porch in a sliver of sun, an Oklahoma Farmers Union cap over his blue check shirt, bedroom slippers on his rhythmic feet. Henry's greeting was heartfelt, for Maxey is one of the very few elders still capable of fluent mantalk. Interpreting his mantalk, however, is an art, especially when Maxey leaves his dentures out. That morning, while the rest of us trooped into the living room, he stayed with the sunlight on the porch. The first people were born, according to traditional Yuchi belief, from earth and the blood of the sun.

"*sÂngÂ'lA sOnOlA*, Josephine?" said Richard, giving her a hug. She said she was doing fine. Her hair was still black, her movement steady, but her voice had a quaver to it. Above her easy chair, a painted eagle clasped the Stars and Stripes in its talons. I remembered that another Oklahoma language, Comanche, served as "code talk" among U.S. forces in Europe during the Second World War, just as Navajo was deployed in the Pacific theater. Military planners were confident that no Nazi could decipher Comanche.

Josephine too had gone to Lone Star School. "I was about six years old," she said, "and English was *hard*. But the other kids tried to help me and the teacher was real nice." The same story. The same pain.

Maggie Marsey pulled up in her white half-ton. She lives just a short drive away. As she walked in, Josephine said, "Maggie and I, that's all we talk — our language." I sat back and did some addition in my head. Not counting Richard, who is neither old nor fluent, the four elders gathered here made up at least a third of the fluent speakers the Yuchi language can muster. Their combined age was over 320. "Not that we're getting old," Josephine said with a sort of smile, "but we're forgetting things." They talked about the warm weather. Their language was rich in words for how weather feels on a body; but if it had a term for "degrees," no one could remember it. Slice open a wild persimmon, and a Yuchi can predict the weather in the pattern of its seeds. "Could predict," I mean. "Predicted." "Used to predict."

The knowledge that the language is disappearing can make its last speakers perpetually anxious to say it right. Yet languages depend on noisy use, not silent perfection. "I knew a couple of people," Henry remarked, "who spoke only English to their grandkids. I said 'Why?' They could hardly speak English themselves. And the man said, 'We might get something wrong.'" Josephine was defensive on the topic of grandchildren: "I try telling mine some words, like what animals are called." She didn't like to admit that none of her children can hold a conversation in Yuchi. "Gary, he's learning — I try to teach him traditions, for them to carry on." A few minutes later the truth came out: "I never did teach Yuchi to my kids. They can speak a few words, that's all. I thought it would be hard for them."

Josephine did what she believed was right. She didn't understand that her kids could have mastered Yuchi as well as English; she didn't know that the mind of a preschool child can absorb languages as effortlessly as a mop soaks up spilled water. She raised her family in the 1960s, long before anyone in Oklahoma heard about the research in Montreal indicating that bilingual children have greater mental flexibility and form concepts more easily than children who speak a single language. Her kids were grown and gone by the time Hawaiian researchers showed that young children in a bilingual program end up learning English better than their counterparts who get no Hawaiian at school. In the twenty-first century, MRI scans and other brain-imaging tools would prove that bilingualism helps the brain development of small children. But in rural Oklahoma, decades ago, Josephine didn't realize that language never had to provoke an either-or decision. She only wanted her kids to do well. She loved them. She did her best.

And now she was tiring. We got up to leave. Henry limped to the porch to converse with Maxey Barnett. Tape recorder in hand, Richard charged after him. But Maggie Marsey stopped me at the door. Something urgent was on her mind, and she would have no other chance to enlighten me. "My great-grandma was on the Trail of Tears," she said, looking straight into my eyes. "They didn't have nothing to eat. One of the babies was crying. She saw one of the mothers leave it and go on. She told me." Then Maggie said goodbye.

Richard didn't grasp many of the old man's slurred expressions — later Henry would interpret them, phrase by phrase, in the language office. Maxey talked about the watermelons and potatoes he grew on this land; he complained about the scrub forest that was springing up, burying the fields. So much effort, vanishing year by year into the shade . . . The farmer's cap perched at a rakish angle on his head. He was almost the age of Oklahoma, and his grip on my hand was firm. "Y'all come back!" he called in English, lifting his right arm to the sky. He stood there, a child of the sun waving in the springtime light, until we were invisible.

Dont Vori, Bi Khepi

A FEW YEARS before I saw the Jesus of Sapulpa and the Wal-Mart of Bristow, I paid a brief visit to São Luis, a port on the northeastern coast of South America. It was founded by the French — a tropical sister to St. Louis, Missouri — and constructed by the Portuguese. Eventually it became the capital of one of Brazil's poorest states. Isolated from tourists, surrounded by the Portuguese language, I thought I'd slipped the surly bonds of English. But then I noticed a sign for Windy Hamburgers, and another for Swing Motel, and another for Futurekids Computer Learning Centre. Such is the way of our world. If you want your burgers to have wind, announce the fact in English.

The number of people who speak English as a mother tongue is approaching four hundred million. More than one and a half billion may speak it as a foreign language, fluently or otherwise. The combined total far surpasses the number of speakers for any other language in history. Previous lingua francas were far narrower in their geographical reach. They too had an impact on local and regional cultures — Latin, for instance, overrode and extinguished Gaulish, the ancient Celtic language that once thrived in France — but no lingua franca has ever enjoyed the political, economic, cultural, and military power that now accompanies English. It is the working language of untold numbers of international companies and organizations; a huge majority of scientific and technical journals appear in no other language; it's what the White House and the Pentagon talk. Shridath Ramphal, co-chairman of the Commission on Global Governance in the 1990s, has said that "there is no retreat from English as the world language, no retreat from an English-speaking world."

At the end of his book *English as a Global Language*, David Crystal nervously peered five centuries ahead. "Will it be the case," he asked, "that everyone will automatically be introduced to English as soon as they are born (or by then, very likely, as soon as they are conceived)? If this is part of a rich multilingual experience for our future newborns, this can only be a good thing. If it is by then the only language left to be learned, it will have been the greatest intellectual disaster that our planet has ever known." No language appears capable of challenging the supremacy of English. In the distant future, it is more likely to shatter into mutually incomprehensible fragments than to be displaced and supplanted by Chinese, Spanish, Portuguese, or any other language we can name. The question is whether English, by then, will have silenced most of the languages in the world — whether Mati Ke and Yuchi will have been joined by languages now as well known and widely spoken as Russian.

When Vladimir Putin took over as president of Russia in the year 2000, one of the first things he did was to create a language committee. He was worried about the state of his language, and he wanted it to maintain as much purity as possible. Like all such committees, this one has found success hard to achieve. Many of the dangerous, impure words are terms from the brave new Moscow: *biznismeni, defolt, keeleri.* Contract killers, that last word means. Good old-fashioned murderers are just not the same as *keeleri.* Sometimes the English source-words are shortened. In Moscow slang, *fresh* means freshly squeezed orange juice, and *breik* is breakdancing. If a hip young businessman wants to reassure his girlfriend, he may tell her, *"Alscool, bebi."* Perhaps she still needs cheering up? *"Dont vori, bi khepi."*

Of course Russian has a long way to go before it falls into genuine danger. But these are the first steps on the road: the infiltration of foreign phrases as well as isolated words; the use of English terms *(bebi, khepi)* for which home-grown equivalents exist. Power does not lie just in bank accounts and gun barrels. Power lies in the words that govern behavior.

The people of Africa have known this for centuries. English started out there as the language of the British Empire. It was one empire among others, one colonial language among others. The Kenyan author Ngũgĩ wa Thiong'o, who grew up in the 1950s, mastered English at a school where to speak his mother tongue, Gikuyu, was to risk punishment and ridicule. Under the name James Ngugi, he spent nearly twenty years composing novels and plays in English. "In schools and universities," he wrote, "our Kenyan languages . . . were associated with negative qualities of backwardness, underdevelopment, humiliation and punishment." Finally he dropped the "James" and began writing in the language of his family. Ngũgĩ felt that to continue his work in English would be to accept a legacy of subjugation. His decision aroused a baffled anger, both inside and outside Kenya. "It was almost as if, in choosing to write in Gikuyu, I was doing something abnormal. But Gikuyu is my mother tongue!"

Kenya was independent, yet in Ngũgĩ's eyes English still reeked of imperialism. Elsewhere in Africa, though, it was no longer just a colonial idiom. It was a language of liberation. The Soweto riots that shook South Africa's apartheid regime in 1976 began as a dispute over language. During their first six years in school, black children were allowed to speak their mother tongue; but once they hit high school, the government obliged them to divide the day between English and Afrikaans. Nobody objected to English. It was Afrikaans, the language beloved by their oppressors, that black students hated to learn. The first martyr of the riots — Hector Peterson, a thirteen-year-old boy — was among a crowd whose placards read AWAY WITH AFRIKAANS!

A generation later, when apartheid had been scrapped, Coca-Cola stopped placing Afrikaans words on its South African labels. In Zaire, meanwhile, the residents of Kinshasa — whose rapid population growth had forced Montreal to stop calling itself "the second-largest French-speaking city in the world" — hurled insults as the country's longtime despot, Mobutu Sese Seko, fled the country. Watching the motorcade of the sick tyrant speed through ravaged streets to the airport, people shouted, "We don't have to speak French anymore!" Mobutu's replacement made English an official language.

These days, speakers of French in various countries feel insecure. The main broadsheet newspaper of French-speaking Montreal, *La Presse*, calls itself "le plus grand quotidien français d'Amérique." Understandably, it attracts many of Quebec's best journalists. But their prose is often riddled with anglicisms — not just sprinkled here and there, but studded through entire articles. Nathalie Petrowski, a columnist who likes to cast a withering eye on English-speaking Canada, once wrote an article that carried the headline "Les boys, les girls, le cash." Montreal's French speakers are in a majority. Yet it's inconceivable that an article in *The Gazette*, the English-speaking counterpart of *La Presse*, could have the casual headline "The Garçons, the Filles, the Argent." A short day's drive down the St. Lawrence River, the city of Rimouski — which has only a few hundred native English speakers amid a population of fifty thousand — contains a student hangout called Coyote Bar. "Mercredi: Classic Rock," it promises; "Jeudi: Ladies Night." In the summer of 2002 it advertised for new employees by saying, "Nous engageons Boss Boy, Barmaid, Serveurs/Serveuses, Shooter Girls, DJ."

Quebec's provincial government is often a bitter rival of Canada's federal regime. Still, both Quebec and Canada are members of the international Francophonie — a loose grouping of nations and territories where French, once the international language of diplomacy, continues to be widely spoken. That's the theory, at least. Today a third of all members of the Francophonie use English when they deal with the United Nations, even though French is an official language of the U.N. One of the latest defectors is Vietnam: for decades a French colony, never a British or American one. Quebec's international affairs minister, Louise Beaudoin — a woman known as a hard-line advocate of political separation — explained the decline in French by saying, "I believe that English is so attractive it's used without thinking." *Air bags,* among young people in Paris, has come to mean breasts, and *fax* is shorthand for flat-chested women. (I guess this usage qualifies as "attractive.") In a recent book called *La Mort du français,* the French writer Claude Duneton predicted that his language would disappear within sixty years.

Other European languages too are struggling to resist the tidal wave. As the twenty-first century began, names like Siegfried and Hildegard were rare among German babies. In their place crawled a swarm of little Justins, Jessicas, Kevins, and Steves. Job ads in one of Germany's leading newspapers, the *Frankfurter Allgemeine Zeitung,* have appealed for German professionals to fill vacancies like "Junior Product Manager," "Customer-Support-Representative," "Pharma-Marketing-Trainee" and "Marketing Manager in Non-Food." In the country's business circles, a familiarity with English is now essential. Indeed, the nation's largest bank has begun to dispense with bilingualism. Board meetings of the Deutsche Bank are held in English only. In June 2000 Rolf Breuer, the chief executive of the bank, was challenged about the absence of German at these meetings. He replied, "So what?"

Dozens of new English words have become German words too: *das Web-Design, die Bypass-Operation, der Cursor, der Startup-Phase.* Verbs that have appeared in German include the likes of *downgesized* and *outgesourced.* It's as though German is beginning to give up the creative struggle to invent its own terms — as though its speakers are consuming language, rather than producing it. English expressions have proliferated, not just expressing up-to-the-minute concepts but replacing time-honored words: sudden coinages like *der Team, die City, das Display,* and *die Party.* "We've reached a point where the borrowing has got too much," the London *Observer* quoted Ole Wackermann as saying. Wackermann speaks for Verein zur Wahrung der deutschen Sprache, a German-language defense group. "A language that fails to keep up, that loses its ability to create new words and relinquishes the old, is in danger."

In Europe, Germans and Russians are not alone in deploring *dieser Trend.* By way of resistance, Poland has passed a law to banish such terms as *supermarket, venture capital, sex shop*, and *music club* from the national language. They arrived in Warsaw, as in Moscow, soon after the death of Communism. A few of western Europe's small nations have been flirting with English for longer. As far back as 1976 Denmark's minister of education declared that the aim of schools' compulsory English courses was "to make Denmark bilingual, with English as the best medium after the mother tongue." In the early 1990s the Netherlands came close to substituting English for Dutch in virtually all of higher education. Merita-Nordbanken, a Helsinki-based bank that is among the largest in Scandinavia, now insists that all its official communication — even by e-mail — be conducted in English. SAS Airlines is controlled by the governments of Norway, Sweden, and Denmark; in 2002 the main part of the airline's Web site functioned in English alone.

David Graddol, a language researcher at Britain's Open University, has said that in Sweden, the Netherlands, and Denmark "you can't live a full life as a citizen without speaking English. Some domains — business, science, even intellectual discussions — are in English now." A couple of generations in the future, citizens of those countries who insist on speaking their national language may be seen as hopelessly out of date. Dutch too is on its way, some think, to becoming an affectation, a mouthful of nostalgia — the verbal equivalent of wooden clogs.

After Atlanta was awarded the 1996 Olympic Games, and Sydney the games for 2000, neither Americans nor Australians embarked on a crash course of foreign-language learning. They were confident the world would come to them, trying to speak the language of the hosts. But when Beijing won the right to hold the 2008 games, about six hundred thousand residents of the Chinese capital were told they would have to learn English if they wanted to keep their jobs. Taxi drivers, sales clerks, and many government officials had no choice: unless they could demonstrate a basic grasp of English, they would be fired. The city's radio waves overflowed with English lessons.

China has some way to go before it catches up with its neighbors. In the 1990s the *Far Eastern Economic Review* called English "Asia's premier language," "part of the identity of a new Asian middle class," "the single common link among the region's wildly diverse peoples," and "Asia's unifying tongue and its language of opportunity." Across the world's biggest and most populous continent, English is often seen as a key to economic growth. It can open other doors, too. In countries like Burma and Tibet, where growth has arrived without democracy, English performs the job it used to perform in South Africa: acting as a language of resistance, a way for oppressed people to make their plight known to the wider world. Aung San Suu Kyi — like Nelson Mandela, Martin Luther King Jr., and Mahatma Gandhi before her — speaks English. The despots in dark glasses do not.

Once they had a chance to vote on the matter, the subjugated people of East Timor were clear on what they didn't want: Indonesian soldiers occupying their country. In 1999 they broke free after nearly twenty-five years of Indonesian rule. The occupiers destroyed much of East Timor as they left. Shocked surviving Timorese, as they wandered through the wreckage of their capital city, Dili, found themselves facing hard questions about what they *did* want.

One of the main issues involved the choice of a national language. The older generation of freedom fighters preferred the colonial tongue, Portuguese, seeing it as central to East Timorese civilization. Most of the young rejected that; schooled in Indonesian, they had no desire to embark on basic Portuguese. Despite the unsavory political baggage that Indonesian carried, some people wanted to continue using it. Still others plumped for Tetum, the most widespread of the nation's fifteen indigenous languages. But having been suppressed by the Indonesians, it too was foreign to many Timorese.

So a fourth option arose: English, the language of the global marketplace, the Dili moneychangers, and many of the U.N. soldiers who were safeguarding the country's freedom. Independence is no time for nostalgia, the proponents of English said. Even though it's the mother tongue of nobody in East Timor, is it not essential to prosperity? Fretilin, the party that won the first legislative election, called English "a vital tool for the dissemination of our ideas" and proposed to make it, "to a certain extent," a working language of the new administration.

The leading specialist on East Timor's languages, an Australian linguist named Geoffrey Hull, has advised the country's leadership to promote Tetum and Portuguese. But positive reinforcement alone may not do the trick. Hull also says that foreign companies should be forbidden to label products in English only, that all English-language TV programs should be subtitled in Tetum, and that advertising in English should be banned. If Tetum and Portuguese are to thrive, he warns, the use of English must be limited. For "English is a killer language."

That's not how it's viewed in Malaysia. The country has a magazine, *Junior,* that could hardly be more different in tone from magazines aimed at teenagers in Europe and North America. Instead of features on fashion, movies, and the music industry, one recent issue contained articles on giant pumpkins, Christmas carols, and Stonehenge. There was a long book review of *Rich Dad, Poor Dad:* "It exercises the mind to think of possibilities and options which will eventually make the person stronger in terms of achieving financial targets." There was an article about a Web site called thinkgeek.com. And, taking up more space than nearly everything else in *Junior* combined, there were English lessons.

They came in various forms. A vocabulary test on the letter *u* asked for definitions of words like "unequivocal," "ubiquitous," and "umbrage." Sixteen closely printed pages entitled "Language Wisdom" consisted entirely of English exercises. An article on strategies for passing the Malaysian university entrance test concentrated on English fluency: "You don't study a language, you live it . . . Speak and read in English whenever you can." *Junior* cautioned its readers against dating; instead, a columnist gave advice on English skills. "You must read consistently and write a lot," she told an anxious student who had asked "What can I do before it is too late?" "You have to read almost all your free time to make up for all that you have lost."

English is the mother tongue of almost no Malaysians. In number of speakers, the national language, Malay, is followed by Chinese, Hindi, and Tamil. *Junior* draws readers from each of those groups, because English is one thing they can agree on: it's desirable to them all. The magazine's publicity doesn't bother to claim that *Junior* is fun; it urges teenagers to "read *Junior* for self-improvement." Mastery of English, it appears, is the quintessence of self-improvement.

Flipping past the pages on antonyms, prefixes, suffixes, and punctuation, I came across a general-knowledge quiz for young Malaysians. It had questions on Babe Ruth and the Statue of Liberty. It inquired how tall the towers of the World Trade Center had been. And it asked the location of Coca-Cola's headquarters. The obvious theme is the United States. But the subtler theme, I think, is power.

Power is language. In a courtroom, when a trial ends, only the judge has the power to "pronounce a sentence." Worries about pronunciation have led, in South Korea, to a fast-growing syndrome: English envy. As the *Los Angeles Times* reported in April 2002, rich parents in Seoul and other cities have begun hauling their toddlers to plastic surgeons for a frenectomy — a membrane-slicing operation designed to lengthen the tongue. The procedure does nothing for a child's ability to speak Korean, but it supposedly helps in the pronunciation of English. With their longer tongues (so the theory goes), Korean children will be able to say "right" and "wrong" without fear of "light" and "long."

Devotion to English, like any faith, demands proof of commitment from its adherents. In this case, the little children pay the price of their parents' zeal. Futile for linguists to point out that the sons and daughters of Korean immigrants in Australia and North America learn to distinguish *r* from *l* just like other kids; futile to explain that Korean and Japanese people often confuse the letters for the simple reason that their own languages don't enforce that phonetic distinction. A frenectomy, like a circumcision, is a covenant of sorts. It requires a child to be subjected to serious pain in return for the promise of intangible rewards. Snipped membranes are becoming the foreskins of Seoul.

Frenectomies aside, many Korean infants were already spending several hours a day in front of TV sets watching English-instruction videos, and some Korean children were suffering anxiety attacks from the pressure to achieve fluency. "English makes children's lives hell!" declared a cover story in a national magazine. By 2002 the language had become a business worth three billion dollars a year in South Korea alone. "Learning English," said the host of an English-language talk show, "is almost the national religion."

No religion could want a more effective evangelist than China's Li Yang. Even before the spur of the 2008 Olympics, the former disc jockey claimed to have taught English to more than twenty million Chinese people in a decade. His workplace, as often as not, is a football stadium, where he induces packed crowds to yell out phrases like "No pain, no gain!" "I have heard so much about you!" and "Don't mention it, anytime!" Li's meetings have a political edge — the man's Web site says that his personal motto is "stimulating patriotism, advocating national spirits, conquering English and revitalizing China." But few of his students show up for the politics. They're looking for a chance to progress in English outside the constraints of a classroom, where if you make a public mistake you lose face. The coolest way to learn is to participate in the high-decibel rallies of what Li calls "Crazy English." Above a rock 'n' roll beat, he tells people to overcome their inhibitions and speak English as fast as possible, as clearly as possible, as loud as possible. Crazy English precludes embarrassment.

Li has led People's Liberation Army soldiers in shouts of Crazy English atop the Great Wall. He has done the same with Shanghai brokers on the floor of China's leading stock exchange. His slogans include "Learning English is a piece of cake!" "Make the voice of China be widely heard all over the world!" and "Make 300 million Chinese speak fluent English!" This exclamatory pastime is now a multimillion-dollar enterprise. "The best way to love your country," the *Times* of London quoted Li as saying, "is to learn English, get an MBA and run a great business." As well as being a nationalist and a gifted performer, the man is a realist. "Chinese people don't learn English because they love it," he explained, "but because Coca-Cola and Microsoft rule the world."

It was a task once assumed by the British Empire, and no love was lost between Beijing and London as long as the British ruled Hong Kong. While the Union Jack fluttered above their heads, people in the territory were careful to maintain their Chinese identity. But as the deadline drew near for London to relinquish control, English names in Hong Kong became trendy. Civic Wong. Neon Chan. Jackal Chang. The territory was suddenly alive with people calling themselves Apple, Sherlock, Civil, Cinderella. As long as a name sounded fresh and English, its meaning didn't matter — any term would do. Shining Sun. Beauty Bee. Businesses followed suit; one company took the name So So Shoes.

In the Hong Kong of the mid-1990s, English was starting to assume the decorative role it had already played for a generation in Japan. There, English has many uses. One of them is to be a fashion accessory — a language whose function is glamour. It doesn't matter if the glamour carries little or no semantic meaning; the mere atmosphere of English is message enough. The language acts like a brand name. It soothes. It titillates. For its internal market, Japan has produced a soap dish that says "Beautiful time partner," a pencil case that reads "Your soul, spirit, pride, passion and yourself. Oh, skull and crossbones!" and a T-shirt that asks, "Would you like to make some love? Nope. You have to lost weight, right?"

Writing in the *Atlantic Monthly* in November 2000, Barbara Wallraff cast doubt on the idea that English is becoming the language of the world. She observed that the number of mother-tongue speakers of English is still dwarfed by the number of mother-tongue Chinese speakers, and that a few other big languages, such as Spanish and Hindi, are also growing fast. While English is widely spoken in foreign classrooms, the exact total of second-language learners is impossible to pin down. Many people find it in their interest to overestimate their command of English. The language still has a long way to go before it is truly global.

All this is true — and beside the point. When it comes to science and business, technology and entertainment, politics and engineering, the dominance of English is incontestable. It is the common idiom of the world's elite, the repository of global ambition. It has become, if you like, the *defolt* language of the planet. *Alscool, bebi.* A century from now, perhaps only the poor, the old, the isolated, and the stubborn will be unable to function in English.

Wallraff's article elicited dozens of replies and commentaries on the *Atlantic*'s Web site. A Scotsman living in the long-contested region of Alsace noted that parents on the French side of the border with Germany want their kids to learn English ("What's the point of learning German?"). Their neighbors across the Rhine share the same desire ("What's the point of learning French?"). The European future, to this correspondent, appears monolingual: "This is sad. Language is at the heart of a country's culture. There is something rich and satisfying about French. Subtle and appealing. But it will become a handicap. The Internet will see to that. I only hope I am wrong. Europe and the world will be a sadder place."

Another respondent was blunter: U.S. English, he said, is destined to dominate the world. "Commerce demands it and the growing need for universal law supports it. It's not even much of an issue . . . It's pretty much unstoppable short of nuclear winter." For this man, a language is a tool, a verbal machine. Other correspondents raised questions of diversity and cultural nuance, provoking a terse rejoinder: "Nuance is highly overrated. In business and law the LAST thing I want is nuance. In nuance is a legal case. I want stark, bleak, naked, cold and heartless clarity in my business documents. And that is what I shall have."

If clarity is winning out over diversity, the dream of Ludwik Lejzer Zamenhof is coming true at last. Part of the dream, anyway. Zamenhof was a Jewish eye doctor in Bialystok, a city that now lies in eastern Poland near the border of Belarus. In the 1870s, when he began his life's work on languages, the city stood in the heartland of Yiddish. It was a crossroads for Russians and Poles, Jews and Gypsies, Germans and Ukrainians and Lithuanians. Zamenhof's father taught languages in Bialystok, but the young man rebelled against such work. "In that town," he was to write, "an impressionable soul might . . . become convinced at every step that the diversity of languages was the single, or at least the primary, force which divided the human family into unfriendly parts."

So he set out to invent a new language — a language whose rules are simple, straightforward, and free of annoying exceptions. Zamenhof built its vocabulary from a mixture of Romance, Germanic, and Slavic roots. All its nouns end in *-o*, all its adjectives in *-a*, all its adverbs in *-e*. No letters are silent. Thanks to the systematic use of suffixes and infixes, the language has the virtue (if it is a virtue) of predictability. A tree is *arbo;* a small tree is *arbeto;* a big tree is *arbego;* a forest is *arbaro.* Near is *proksima;* far is *mal'proksima.* True is *vera;* false is *mal'vera.* Hot is *varma;* you can guess the word for cold. But try as he might, Zamenhof couldn't get away from ideology. Man is *viro;* woman is *vir'ino.* A husband is *edzo;* a wife is *edzino.* At the base of the language is maleness; anything female is an afterthought.

If everyone were to speak his rational idiom, Zamenhof thought, conflicts between nations would dissolve. In 1887 he published *An Inter-*

national Language: Preface and Complete Grammar, a book whose goals were as grand as its title suggests. The author used the pseudonym of "Dr. Esperanto" — Dr. Hopeful, that is. Esperanto became the name of the language and of an entire movement, complete with flag and anthem. Enthusiasts took it up around the world. Thousands of books would be published in Esperanto. Millions of people would learn it. Bertrand Russell and Leo Tolstoy were among its early advocates, Umberto Eco and Václav Havel among its later admirers. You can now find Web sites devoted to the language. It may still have a couple of million speakers. Yet the enthusiasm is gone: Esperanto is fading away.

The main reason is the sprawl of English. Amid the polyglot confusion of eastern Europe — a confusion that was, of course, immensely creative — Zamenhof never imagined that any existing language would become so dominant. He conceived of Esperanto as neutral territory, a realm of the mind where all peoples could gather as equals. A noble ideal, while it lasted. But his language came without factories or stock markets. No government would issue decrees in it; no studio would make movies in it; no army would fight on its behalf. Lacking any sort of power, Esperanto didn't have a hope.

Leaving the Grave

MANX

H E WAS A FISHERMAN. Born in 1877, he grew up within sight
of salt water. He lived in Cregneash, a village near the southwestern coast of the Isle of Man, and on clear evenings, if he
stood at a back window of the family home, he could see the
coast of Ireland catching the sun to the west. Ned Maddrell was a boy
when he began work on the sea. His native island lies at the geographical center of the British Isles, and he soon grew familiar with many of
Britain's ports. Manx boats, laden with mackerel, cod, and herring,
would ply the waves south to Wales, east to England, and north and
west to countries where Gaelic was spoken. Maddrell's first language
was the Manx form of Gaelic: a Celtic tongue, branching away from
early Irish, that had been in use for a thousand years. Yet by the late
nineteenth century it had collapsed as a language of common use. Only
in a few villages like Cregneash did it hang on.

Maddrell never forgot his Manx, though when he was living and
working off the island he used English as a matter of course. He spent
years away from Man. Then, in his retirement, he returned. After the
Second World War, not many islanders were left who shared his mother
tongue. Blessed with rugged health, Ned Maddrell would outlive them
all. He watched as his island was transformed from a struggling tourist
resort to an offshore banking haven. He saw an influx of new residents
who had no clue about Man's Celtic heritage. As the years slipped by, he

acquired a modest fame as the last speaker of Manx — the man with whom a language would be buried. Tape recordings were made of him. Pictures were taken: a geezer with a broad smile, a cloth cap, and wary eyes. Plainspoken, anonymous for most of his life, Maddrell had never expected to be famous, least of all because of the language he happened to speak as a boy and remembered, more or less, in his old age. He was three years shy of a century when he entered the reference books.

"Manx began to decline in the eighteenth century," writes R. L. Thomson in *Language in the British Isles,* "and formally ended on 27 December 1974 with the death of the last native speaker." Daniel Nettle and Suzanne Romaine, in *Vanishing Voices: The Extinction of the World's Languages,* say that "with [Ned Maddrell's] death, the ancient Manx language left the community of the world's living tongues." Sometimes the date of extinction is pushed back. The first edition of the *Cambridge Encyclopedia of Language,* for example, claims that "the last mother-tongue speakers died in the late 1940s."

But you can still hear Ned Maddrell speak.

If you go, as I did one autumn afternoon, to the Manx Museum in Douglas, the capital city of the island, you'll find a small display on the Manx language and its last native speakers. By picking up a black, old-fashioned telephone receiver, you can listen to their elderly voices: John Kneen and Harry Boyle, chatting about work on a farm; John Tom Keighen, deploring the low wages paid to rural laborers; Eleanor Karren and Ned Maddrell, discussing the keeping of a cow. Maddrell's voice is firm and strong, although even in a brief conversation he struggles to find a word or two. In extreme old age, he retained many proverbs from his youth. *T'eh cabbyl mie ta breimeragh tra t'eh jannoo yn ushtey,* he announced one day: "It's a good horse that farts when it pisses."

His wife did not speak Manx, a fact that Maddrell occasionally turned to his advantage when a tape recorder lay at hand. He was reminiscing about the Irish ports when out came this — in Manx, of course: "I'd been fishing out of Crookhaven for a long while, and I met a girl there and I was courting for almost three years, two years, and her photograph is in my home now. Isn't it a good job that my wife doesn't understand that? It would not do to mention her name at all, it wouldn't. She was a nice girl." A transcription and translation appear in the three-volume *Handbook of Late Spoken Manx,* edited by the scholar George Broderick. A close look at Maddrell's actual words shows that his Manx was speckled with English expressions: "priest," "one day," "fond," "bloody liar" . . . It's typical among the final speakers of any language: when you have nobody who can answer back, your vocabulary crumbles away.

Maddrell was aware of his linguistic failings: "I remember when I was able to speak Manx as well as English, better than English too, but . . . after I left Cregneash and went out into the world, I wasn't hearing any Manx and it almost left me." In one story he told of his cousin, the skipper of a Manx fishing boat that sailed into port in Sutherland, in the far north of Scotland. Maddrell's cousin approached two women who had eggs to sell. "How much do you want for them?" he asked in English. The younger woman turned to her mother and said in the Scots form of Gaelic, "How much will we take from them?" "They're only Englishmen," the old woman answered, also in Gaelic. "Take a lot from them, take plenty!" "We're not English!" the skipper said. "We understand everything." The women were baffled but the eggs came cheap.

Near the telephone that plays the voices of Maddrell and the other dead speakers, the Manx Museum has a display entitled "Reasons Not to Speak." I counted six — the distillation of comments by long-dead islanders who had given up on the language. Manx isn't spoken in school, they said. It's too much effort to learn. It's useless off the island. Even on the island, English is more useful. English has status and prestige. And finally, Manx can be a secret code, a weapon for excluding other people. A resident of the northern village of Sulby spoke eloquently on this: "The Manx language is dead and it deserved to die because the last use it was put to in our house was to enable our parents and grandmother to carry on a conversation between themselves which my sister and I did not understand." Across the long decades, the man's irritation is palpable. His grievance outlived the language — he thought.

Scholars spent decades waiting for Manx to die. As long ago as 1909, visiting linguists began to record its aging speakers on phonograph cylinders and portable tape machines. Many of the results can be found in Broderick's bilingual handbook. Conversation often had an elegiac tone: "There used to be four looms in Cregneash." "There was no cinema in those days." "Light the candle, it is twilight." One speaker used *jouyl*, the Manx word for "devil," to mean an automobile. The handbook also contains a few practical utterances, such as "Pick the dead flesh out and you'll be all right": *Teiy yn coghal ass as bee oo kiart dy liooar.* The meaning of *coghal* is precise: "core of a sore, big lump of dead flesh after an opened wound, tears in a weal." A language redolent of farms and fishing gear, Manx had expertise in wounds and weals.

Brimful of sturdy consonants like *j, k,* and *v,* bursting with vowel hordes like *eea* and *iie,* it looks like no other Celtic language. The reason — ignominious to some — is that its spelling was invented after the Reformation by a pair of bishops who wanted Protestant texts to be available to their flock. In the sixteenth century, next to nobody spoke English on the island. The system the bishops devised has its share of difficulties but, for better or worse, it makes Manx letters fit English pronunciation more closely than the notoriously difficult match of sounds and letters in Irish. Take *vie,* the Manx word for "good." It's pronounced the same as the English verb "vie." The Irish word for "good" can also be pronounced that way — but it's spelled *mhaith.* Speakers of Manx don't face all the silent letters of Irish, nor the imposing clusters that figure in so many Irish words: *dhch, chn, thfh,* and the like.

As the number of its fluent speakers diminished, Manx began to lose the intricacies of its ancient syntax and grammar. Unlike Yuchi, it unraveled as it shrank. Manx has, along with all the other Celtic languages, a complex system of consonant mutation (also known as "lenition") — a tailless *kayt,* or cat, is always liable to turn into a *chayt* or a *gayt.* The mutations affect only the initial consonants of words, and they don't change the meaning; their purpose is euphony. By the time Ned Maddrell was young, the mutation system of Manx was in flux and other patterns had begun to dissolve. "The position regarding noun genders in Late Spoken Manx is that they hardly exist at all," Broderick remarks. "The genitive singular case with a separate form has largely disappeared in Late Spoken Manx." You can almost hear the man sigh. "Very little has survived of eclipsis." Same goes for the possessive adjective, not to mention the synthetic verb. Amid all these losses and reductions, the personal pronoun gained strength. This too can be ascribed to English influence.

Purists might wonder what was left in Late Spoken Manx. But then purists have never been very keen on the island tongue. "From the beginning of its career as a written language," the Irish scholar T. F. Ó Rahilly said of Manx, "English influence played havoc with its syntax and it could be said, without much exaggeration, that some of the Manx that has been printed is merely English disguised in a Manx vocabulary. Manx hardly deserved to live. When a language surrenders itself to foreign idiom and when all its speakers become bilingual, the penalty is death."

The purists, the visiting linguists, the reference books: all of them are wrong. On a global level the triumph of English may seem unstoppable, but on a local level you can find innumerable tales of a bullheaded refusal to submit. Call it tribalism or call it an attachment to heritage: whatever term you use, it's a phenomenon that will not go away. Manx is a splendid example, and a surprising one. For it is alive and — if not exactly *well* — fighting hard for breath. The fighters are bilingual and determined. Many of them are also young. At least 150 people have serious ability in the language, and a few dozen speak it on a daily basis. Manx is a test case for rebirth.

It took me a while to be sure of this. Indeed my first journey left me wondering if Manx was still a linguistic corpse. Renting a *jouyl,* I drove southwest from Douglas to the little town of Colby. The trip didn't take long. All distances are short on the Isle of Man; from tip to toe, it's barely thirty miles in length and eleven miles wide. I had an introduction to Winifred Crellin, an elderly spinster who has lived on the island all her life. Might she recall the Manx language with nostalgia or pleasure? The Esso station on Colby's slender highway was selling local cabbages as well as fuel, and the cloth-capped attendant wanted to quiz me about the Toronto islands — "I used to live there, you know." He finally gave me directions to Miss Crellin, who shared a modest bungalow with her younger sister Margaret. They moved to Colby when the old house and garden at Greeba, a village eight miles away, began to seem too large for comfort.

"To you," Margaret said, welcoming me with tea and slices of bran loaf, "the island is small. But for us it was a big change, this part of the island."

As a country child in the 1920s, Winifred might well have come into contact with aged speakers of Manx. She insisted otherwise. Even when they were girls, the four sisters in her family knew nobody who spoke the language well. The only words Winifred said she had ever learned in Manx were *Kanys ta shiu?* — "How are you?"

"You could count in Manx at one stage," Margaret reminded her.

Winifred looked angry at the memory. "That was when I was nearly finishing school," she retorted. "They took some notion to teach it, I don't know why. The form below me was taught the Lord's Prayer in

Manx. But our mother used to say there was no point in learning Manx, because other folk weren't talking it. We grew up with the idea that there wasn't much point in keeping it up." When the Crellin sisters were children, the old command "Don't be speaking the roughness!" was still remembered on Man. English felt smooth. English felt suave. The psychological impact of that linguistic shift, its emotional gravity, has perhaps never been measured.

I finished my bran loaf. As I put on my coat in the sisters' little hall, I happened to praise a painting by a Manx artist: bright meadows, gray-green hills.

"Lovely, isn't it?" said Margaret. "The fields of heaven."

Back on a rain-spattered side street in Douglas, I asked the manager of my guesthouse for advice on Manx culture. A mustachioed Geordie with silver earrings and a gold neck chain, he is, in the local parlance, a "comeover." Out of season, his trade depends on English and Irish workers newly hired by local companies and in need of something re-sembling a home. "They look after their Manx people first," he said without bitterness, as though in their shoes he would do exactly the same. The island's mix contained other elements, too. "King William's College, out past the airport — it's a boarding school, like. They come from Arabia, China; they've got all breeds and nationalities."

Perhaps the Isle of Man is still getting used to all these comeovers. A lack of job prospects meant it used to specialize in emigrants, not im-migrants. For many decades the English treated it as a vacation refuge, complete with miniature railways and horse-drawn trams, but by the 1960s package tours to the Aegean and the Costa del Sol had lessened the mass appeal of an exposed island in a northern sea. Mindful, perhaps, of its long history of smuggling, Man reinvented itself as an offshore banking center — a tax evader's delight. Its success was spec-tacular: new money poured in. Leafing through the yellow pages, I dis-covered seventy-six choices under "company registration agents" and forty under "banks and financial institutions," including Habib Euro-pean Bank, Meghraj Bank, the Bank of Bermuda, and the Royal Bank of Canada. What draws them all to the hilly streets of Douglas are the money-making opportunities that come from the Isle of Man's semi-independent status as a "Crown protectorate." It is not, and never has been, part of the United Kingdom, nor is it bound by the banking rules of the European Union. Today the island's population has risen above seventy-five thousand, about half of them born elsewhere. Unemployment scarcely exists.

The Isle of Man issues its own banknotes, stamps, and coins, although with typical pragmatism it accepts United Kingdom currency as well. The local pound coin has nothing but the English language on it; the 10p coin mixes English and Latin; but for just 2p you get a pair of words in Manx — the Gaelic name for the place, *Ellan Vannin*. Appearances to the contrary, "Man," or *Vannin*, has nothing to do with maleness (it may derive from Manannan, the Celtic sea god; it may be a pre-Celtic survival). Likewise *Ellan*, the Manx word for island, only happens to resemble a girl's name. But these two linguistic accidents have a striking effect: what sounds, in English, the most masculine of islands becomes, through the softer consonants and rhythms of Gaelic, a place with a feminine ring to it.

The guesthouse manager could offer no advice. But he handed me something better: a scribbled note of invitation, signed by Brian Stowell.

Manx is "a doomed language," declared a metaphor-prone Anglican priest as long ago as 1859, "an iceberg floating into southern latitudes." Its meltwater ride to extinction has been predicted for generations. In this regard, the only surprising thing about Ned Maddrell was his longevity. The Manx, however, are not always predictable. Outsiders looked at Maddrell and saw the last of his kind; easy to imagine him beside a deserted shore in a black-and-white photograph by Edward Curtis. Insiders looked at Maddrell and saw a colorful old chap ready to pass along his knowledge and his memories. Young, idealistic islanders have rarely taken a shine to radical politics — but some of them have long displayed a fierce interest in Manx.

Half a century ago an article appeared in a local newspaper, *Mona's Herald*. On New Year's Day in 1953, a teenage boy in Douglas happened to read that article. Its subject was the dwindling Celtic language and culture of the Isle of Man, and it inspired the boy to seek out one of the language's most resolute speakers, a wholesale fruit importer named Doug Fargher. Ned Maddrell had taught Fargher some of his Manx; Fargher had picked up the rest from books. In those days the island was bleeding population and lacking confidence. The boy already hated the widespread assumption on Man that everything Celtic was inferior. He began to hang out with Fargher and one of his friends and employees, Leslie Quirk. Soon the boy became proficient at the language they and a few other people spoke in private. Good jobs were few on the island in the 1950s, and the young man — Brian Stowell — decided to leave. He was to spend most of his working life teaching physics in Liverpool, a four-hour ferry ride away.

The shock and delight of learning Manx — of discovering a new past that was also his own — never left him. Even while he lived in England, Brian was among the most ardent advocates of the island language. Having mastered Irish Gaelic, he translated an Irish learners' course into Manx. He recorded Manx-language songs, edited a Manx-language newsletter, and wrote essays in and about the language, notably for a book called *Towards a Celtic Future*. Perhaps all this had started off as a youthful pastime. But it didn't stay a pastime for long; it became a passion.

In 1991 the passion drew him home. The island's government — spurred by a poll showing that more than a third of all residents wanted Manx to be taught in schools — created the job of Manx Language Officer: a civil servant paid to encourage a linguistic rebirth. Brian applied and was hired. He helped design and run a program that now sees about eight hundred children a year take a weekly class in Manx. While the lesson doesn't begin to make them fluent, it exposes them to the language's sound and feel. It gives the children a sense of pride, even ownership: their home is the merest speck on the map, but something unique and valuable arose there. In his retirement Brian began to promote Manx on the Internet. Sunday mornings he hosts a language show on Manx Radio; Monday evenings he teaches a class for adult learners.

I met him in his house on a dripping Douglas street. We sat at his dining room table while an enormously fat Manx cat sprawled over a nearby armchair, its eyes the only bodily part that moved. Manx cats are rare, the gene that causes taillessness being linked to spina bifida, and a Japanese TV crew once arrived on Brian's doorstep hoping to film the animal in motion. The cat declined to cooperate. Lifted up and dropped onto the carpet, it yawned and went back to sleep.

That's the story, anyway. Brian told it with a slight gleam in his blue eyes. Islanders, he later said, don't like anything to be analyzed. "In Liverpool I was used to people being totally abrasive and upfront. But in Man, people will smile politely at you if you say anything they don't agree with, then go and stab you in the back." I think I believed him, just as I think he was telling the truth when he said that a mole in the police force had discovered that a file was being kept on the bishop's daughter simply because she was learning Manx. It sounded like the lead-up to a joke, but the punch line was serious: "In the eyes of the United Kingdom government, anyone who's fostering a Celtic language is political by definition." Advocates of Manx have been known to call the language an anchor for their Celtic souls. Yet Brian has had to battle for recognition from his supposed allies, too. In a typical skirmish, he took on the Celtic Film and Television Association after they snubbed the Manx as nothing more than a subset of the Scots.

Most islanders, he conceded, "relate naturally to England. It's a survival tactic. They know there's a cultural connection to Scotland and Ireland, but in terms of what side their bread is buttered on, it's always been England. That's why it was so important for the Isle of Man to stay loyal to the British crown." Some think the teaching of Manx opens a Pandora's box: "disloyalty to the crown. But the abiding characteristic of the Manx establishment is ambiguity. Loads of maps don't even show the Isle of Man — just Great Britain and Ireland — and the Manx government likes it that way. It's an attitude of 'We're not here, don't bother us.'"

Perhaps Brian's pungent sense of irony had sharpened during his long campaign to haul a language back from the grave. "Doug Fargher instituted Manx-language evenings in pubs in the sixties and seventies. Up until then, learning Manx was associated with trying to read the Bible." He paused for effect. "There's still a strong whiff of death about it." When I mentioned an upcoming "community eisteddfod" (shades of the Tiwi Islands), the Welsh term annoyed him: "'Eisteddfod' took over from the perfectly good word *cruinnaght,* or gathering." Pause. "We're ashamed of existing."

Fluent speakers of Irish or Scottish Gaelic can understand Manx. Does that make it a mere dialect? Brian insisted not. Along with the discrepancies of spelling between Irish, Scots, and Manx go smaller differences in vocabulary, grammar, idiom, and pronunciation. "Very often in Manx," he told me, "there is an English way of expressing something and a Gaelic way of expressing it. Since written Manx first appeared in the 1500s, it's been okay to say *T'eh dooiney mooar* (He is a big man) as well as the true Gaelic expressions *T'eh my ghooiney mooar* (He is in-his big man) and *She dooiney mooar eh* (It's a big man he). But to say the equivalents of *T'eh dooiney mooar* in Irish or Scottish Gaelic is just wrong." One explanation for this is Ó Rahilly's: that Manx is irredeemably corrupt. But recently another Irish scholar proposed that the flexibility of Manx grammar is derived not just from the corpulence of English but from the lingering influence of the Vikings who ruled the Isle of Man a thousand years ago.

In the Manx Museum's library I looked through a few issues of *Carn*, a magazine that tries to link Celtic readers everywhere. Its articles appear in English and all six of the Celtic languages (even Cornish, which died a couple of hundred years ago; efforts to rekindle it have been damaged by infighting among the kindlers). A writer bemoaned "the now substantially minoritised Manx people, our rapidly vanishing culture, our shattered national psyche." The Manx are familiar with disparagement, some of it self-inflicted. In 2000 the Celtic League held its annual meeting on the island. Delegates fumed at the BBC, whose programming "makes no provision for the distinct cultural identity of the Manx people," and they complained about property speculation, "remembering that Mann is an island nation where the frustrated home-seekers' only option is emigration."

An island nation. I had arrived on the Isle of Man, I confess, thinking of it as an offshore fragment of England: a place distinguished by tailless cats, motorcycle races, financial sleight of hand, and, oh yes, a private language. What surprised me was how widely it seemed to be accepted, and not only among the disciples of the Celtic League, that the island is indeed a nation. Inside the Manx Museum lies the "Manx National Gallery." An islet off the southeastern coast — it contains both a twelfth-century chapel and a sixteenth-century fort — was, according to a plaque above the heron-busy shore, "acquired for the Manx nation in 1984." The buyer was Eiraght Ashoonagh Vannin, or Manx National Heritage. I recalled something Brian Stowell had said: "We still remain a largely secret country."

To grasp a little more of the secret, I decided to venture away from the heavily populated south. One afternoon, defying the rain squalls and the early darkness, I headed north over a slaty mountain in search of the home of Yn Cheshaght Ghailckagh — the Manx language society. "It's a big journey," a Manxwoman had warned me. "A remote place," a Manxman had said. Indeed, as the crow flies I was about to drive a full twenty-five miles.

Yet I don't mean to sneer. The island's hills, twisting roads, and shape-shifting weather seem to magnify space and distance. I was looking for a disused school down a side road outside St. Jude's, a hamlet whose name does not appear on standard tourist maps, and I wasn't altogether sure of success.

But John Crellin had switched on the lights in the building and left his car in the road. I found him at a table in the smaller of the school's two rooms, poring over a handwritten account book. Since he sold his cattle, the language society has taken up much of Johnny's time — he struggles to perform an unpaid job that he calls "librarian" and might as well call "general manager." Better still, think of him as the heart and soul of Yn Cheshaght Ghailckagh. He packs up its aging merchandise for sale, one or two items at a time; he takes care of the archives and correspondence; he looks after the building, making sure that the visiting members of the Women's Institute and the Ramsey Beekeepers' Association behave themselves, and resisting efforts by younger members to waste money on such frivolities as an indoor toilet. He even stores some of the society's innumerable books in his farmhouse loft.

"We sell books all over the world," he told me, bustling to prepare two mugs of steaming tea. "Utah, the Netherlands, Japan, you name it. We've sold as far south as Tasmania and as far north as Alaska. A lot of linguists buy our stuff for the curiosity value. I had a request from a fellow the other day for a Manx book that was 'yellow with age.' He was a collector, you see. It's a strange old world."

I was wondering if Johnny might use one of the dialect expressions that survive in the island's English — terms like "ayr" (father), "graney" (unwell), "baraghtan" (bread and butter), and "aley" (a rough spot in the sea, likely to hold fish). All these terms, and many others, were lifted from Manx Gaelic. In the absence of their feeder language, such words are now scarce. Instead, Johnny's words had an obsolete formality that reminded me, as his looks did not, that the man must be well into his seventies. His step was unfaltering, his pale eyes needed no reading glasses, and his hair had as much brown in it as gray. But his English recalled the past: "We had no proper telephone number or anything appertaining to the society"; there are "various electronic aids to promote intercourse among the people." By intercourse aids, he meant nothing more risqué than cassettes, videos, Web sites, CD-ROMs, and the like, all of which enable Celts to grasp the languages of their cousins across the sea. "It's wonderful," Johnny said. "I can remember when you had to wait and hope for a secondhand dictionary. But one of the problems now is that people haven't got the time. They're bothered by television, filling their heads full of absolute rubbish. Or they're off out in the car. In the old days, people would sit down after their tea and read a book."

Which is one of the ways he picked up the language: by reading grammars as a sailor in the Royal Navy while war raged about his vessel in Malta and the Far East. After the war he came home to farm, meeting other enthusiasts, taking the odd language class, and speaking Manx as and when he could. Remembering the ex-sailor I'd met among the Yuchis, I was ready to call him "the Henry Washburn of the island" until I realized: Manx was not a childhood memory for Johnny Crellin, it was a grown-up choice. For a decade he spoke the language every day with Leslie Quirk, a widowed friend who came to live at St. Jude's. But a year before my visit his friend moved into an old people's home. Johnny's wife is Scottish. She does not speak Manx.

Johnny is, above all, a Manx patriot — a Manx nationalist, I mean — with an acute displeasure at his culture's fate. Brian Stowell had mined a rich vein of irony by saying that when tourism was declining in the 1950s and 1960s the island tried a New Residents Policy "that attracted half the remains of the bloody British Empire. They rapidly became known as 'When-I's' because they kept saying 'When I was in Poona' or 'When I was in Nairobi . . .'" The New Residents Policy proved less successful than the slightly later turn to offshore banking. But Johnny Crellin had little taste for irony. He preferred to denounce. "There's no longer a country in the control of Manx people," he said. "All the major industries are foreign owned. The biggest and wealthiest farms are foreign owned. And the whole financial sector has helped destroy our nation."

Yet the island's government dances attendance on the banks, and in recent years the government has given strong support to the language. Why? His answer was cynical: because the money industry "depends on this being a separate entity. If Man were deemed to be nothing more than an appendage of Lancashire County Council, the financial sector would be ruined. So the government is now turning its attention to Manx culture." Laws that are passed by the island's parliament must be promulgated in Manx as well as English. The gesture is not purely symbolic; it also ensures a constant updating of legal and technical vocabulary in Manx. But in Johnny's opinion, the parliament can't be trusted. "The majority of people here are not Manx. This means, in the political scene, Manxmen being outvoted on Manx projects."

I wondered how long it might take for him to see a newcomer as a

Manxman. Other people had told me about comeovers who adopt the island's culture with delight, even becoming "more Manx than the Manx themselves." Yet in the Manx National Gallery a caption describing the sculptor Bryan Kneale had said: "A true Manxman — his grandparents were steeped in the traditions of the countryside — Kneale has achieved international recognition . . ." Was that, then, the definition of a Manxman? Or could you be truly Manx even if your grandparents came from Timbuktu? I remembered the ingrown Celtic vanity so mercilessly satirized by the Irish writer Flann O'Brien in his novel *The Poor Mouth:* "May I state that I'm a Gael. I'm Gaelic from the crown of my head to the soles of my feet — Gaelic front and back, above and below . . . and every sentence I've ever uttered has been on the subject of Gaelic. There is nothing in this life so nice and so Gaelic as truly true Gaelic Gaels who speak in true Gaelic Gaelic about the truly Gaelic language." Either your identity is sealed by your ancestors, or else your culture has to be willing to open up to the intrusive, threatening world. It's an issue whose implications are being tested and played out among dozens of minority peoples around the world.

As I left the old school Johnny Crellin was already turning off its lights, shedding darkness on the curling plaster, the dartless dartboard, the tea bags and powdered milk, the beekeepers' modest library, the grammar texts yellow with age, the furred volumes in Irish and Welsh, the records of Yn Cheshaght Ghailckagh dating back to Ned Maddrell's youth, the cupboards full of books unopened since their ailing owners bequeathed them to the society . . . What will become of all this once Johnny Crellin can no longer take care of it?

But elegy would be misplaced. Yn Cheshaght Ghailckagh has persevered. By dint of bloody-mindedness it has pushed from the nineteenth century into the twenty-first: a resource, a reproach, a reminder.

Compared with members of minority groups whose languages fell silent long ago, Manx speakers are lucky. Heroic efforts have been made in recent years to revive the Wampanoag language, unspoken in its Massachusetts homeland for centuries. Under such a weight of silence, revival is extremely hard. Big terms survive in a seventeenth-century Wampanoag Bible: crucifixion, ascension, salvation. Little terms — the uncounted words and phrases needful for lullabies and lovemaking, cooking and fishing, adult banter and childhood play — rarely show up in scripture. When the outside world looked at photographs of Ned

Maddrell and his tombstone, it assumed that Manx had expired as surely as Wampanoag. "Save the whale, yes," said an article in the London newspaper the *Independent* in March 2002. "But save, say, Manx (the last native speaker on the Isle of Man died in 1974) — forget it."

Many old words and verbal locutions have indeed disappeared from Manx. In private, though, the heart of the language did not stop beating. Its pulse was frail and irregular, but it never ceased. The little words were never lost. Ned Maddrell came to be a symbol of the language. He was never its only voice.

To hear one of Manx's most eloquent voices, I made my way to the tiny cathedral city of Peel on the island's west coast. The fields of heaven stretched to the brink of the Irish Sea. Offshore, an ancient sandstone castle dominates St. Patrick's Isle. Ten centuries ago, when Norsemen controlled the North Atlantic, Peel was familiar to the Viking kings of Mann. A few Manx words, such as *giau* (creek) and *baatey* (boat), are rooted in Norse. But Peel's later reputation, courtesy of the fishing trade, was "kipper city." Parking outside a supermarket, I walked across the street into an old people's home. The heat was high in the building; even before I climbed the stairs to room 25, I was feeling uncomfortably warm.

The room was small. You'd have been hard-pressed to swing a cat in it, tailless or otherwise, and I wasn't sure where to put my coat. A medicine bottle shared space with pens and a radio on the bedside table; a crucifix hung near a washbasin. A paperback French-English dictionary lay open on the narrow bed, while *La Langue brétonne en 40 leçons* stood propped up on the desk. The radio blared from some other room whose inhabitant must have been almost deaf. But Leslie Quirk was not deaf in the slightest, nor was his mind reduced. No one else has ever compiled lengthy observations on Breton grammar from the perspective of Manx.

"He's practically a native speaker," Brian Stowell had said. And Brian should know, because he learned some of his Manx, half a century ago, from the mouth of Leslie Quirk. "I got my first Manx from my grandmother," Leslie told me. And she was a native speaker, so a chain of speech remains intact. "She saw that all my schooling would be in English, and she got mad and said, 'I'll see that you get some Manx.' I knew the Lord's Prayer off in Manx at least five years before I did in English. I was a little fellow and she'd be kneeling at the bed with me. 'Don't let anybody tell you it's a rubbishy language,' she said, 'because it isn't. I know it's a good language.' And technically, linguistically, she was right."

Leslie can say this with authority because he understands nine or ten languages, not including German, "which I didn't get on with at all. I'm very fond of Old English but I don't like the Modern English — I don't take to it. Old English is more difficult: more adventurous, so to speak." The pinkish red complexion of his face and bald head clashed with his bright yellow shirt and green trousers, but Leslie didn't care. He had ideas on his mind, not color schemes. He also made Modern English fresh in my ears again, saying that at King William's College in the 1920s, "I took six years of porridge, I reckon — we were ruled with a rod of iron and half-starved into the bargain," or describing his years on the family farm as being "fastened to the cows' tails on the land." The effect of all this ruling and fastening was that Leslie's Manx had gone into grievous decline by the time he learned that Caesar Cashen, a fisherman turned shopkeeper on Market Street in Peel, was teaching Manx classes at night.

"The Bible was our textbook," Leslie said with a beam. "Our Manx was the 'Behold!' type rather than the 'Look!' There was one old fellow of eighty-three with a big bushy beard who would sit there in the middle of the room. One day he started telling Manx stories and we thought, 'He's making awfully good progress!' But as it turned out, he could already *speak* the language. He wanted to learn to *read*."

Some years later Leslie found himself in Caesar Cashen's shoes. His own teaching was unorthodox, because his students "would learn through fun. It was a novelty — I taught them to remember by verses and songs." Manx has a difficult range of words for what, in English, we'd have to call "already up," "already down," "coming up from down," and "coming down from up." Leslie got the point across by translating an English nursery rhyme, "The Grand Old Duke of York." "I've got a grasshopper mind," he said. "I want to learn! If you take Breton now, I can't speak it at all, but I've got a good knowledge of the irregular verb endings, some of which are *very* irregular. You see, I get some pig by the tail and it'll try to pull me homeward."

Even if Breton is a hobby for his tenth decade, Manx is something more. The language allows Leslie, looking back over most of a century, to justify his time on earth. As a Manx rhyme has it, *Gloyr dy row hood's, my Yee, dy braa / Son ooiiley ny bannaghtyn jeh y laa* (Glory may there be to you, my God, / for all the blessings of the day). Leslie has the grace to bless. He knows he played a role in rescuing a language from the grave.

He showed me down the stairs, worrying that I'd wasted my time in driving all the way to Peel to see him. Useless for me to protest. "I'm totally optimistic about Manx," he said at the front door. "It's huge strides ahead in the schools, compared to what it was. It can go one way or the other, but it's got a chance now that it hasn't had for a long time. Old fogies like myself, it doesn't matter — we hope to be translated into the spirit before very long.

"But the language has got children now."

That evening in Peel, I went to a concert featuring the voices of Manx musicians. The sponsor was Feailley Ghaelgagh, an annual Manx-language festival held across the island. Down at the harbor a glossy new museum called the House of Manannan straddles the lucrative frontier between culture and tourism. To face the music, I had to follow sixty or seventy people through a back door of the museum and enter its small auditorium through a chamber devoted to the Vikings. Inside, dry ice wafted through the stage floor. It half-hid the replicas of intricate Manx crosses with simulated Celtic fog.

The master of ceremonies made a point of speaking Manx first. To avoid giving offense, he also translated what he said. A pair of Manx flautists performed, bowed, and said nothing. They were followed by Caarjyn Cooidjagh, a small choir of men and women who made their way gingerly past the crosses and the resurgent dry ice. With superb precision and flair, they gave voice to a somber, haunting melody that wives of fishermen used to sing by the harbor while they waited for their men's return: *Geay jeh'n aer ta my ghraih er y cheayn* . . . I reveled in the texture and rhythms of Manx: its chunkiness, its muscular flow from the singers' lips. They moved on to a fast-paced traditional ballad and a newly written love song. But for some reason the master of ceremonies had failed to introduce the conductor, a shy woman who looked embarrassed to be onstage, and when she and the other performers left they did so in ragged haste, not bothering to bow.

After the music came an awards ceremony. Yn Cheshaght Ghailckagh was giving out its annual prizes, and Brian Stowell stepped up to act as presenter. He mentioned the society's motto, *Gyn Chengey Gyn Cheer!* (No language, no country). One prize was intended for the city of

Douglas, which had agreed to make new street signs bilingual, but no-body showed up to collect the plaque, so Brian put it back on the floor. A young executive from a supermarket chain bounded onto the stage to accept an award — he was English, and had spent only a few years on the island, but his willingness to say *Gura mie eu* as well as "Thank you" won him a warm hand. The supermarkets, like the capital city, have be-gun to post bilingual signs. Two children got prizes for making progress in Manx. They seized their certificates and kept silent. On this public, semi-official level, I thought, the language has a long way to go.

At lunchtime the next day I drove down the coast to Port Erin, home of the Isle of Man Seal Sanctuary. Small though it is, the island has a profusion of animal welfare groups: a hedgehog hospital, a cat sanctu-ary, a pets' aid league, an SPCA, a horse and pony welfare agency, a Basking Shark Society ("unique among wildlife organisations the soci-ety is the only charity working solely with the basking shark"), even a Home of Rest for Old Horses. But I wasn't looking for seals or other fauna; I wanted a hotel called the Falcon's Nest. In a daylight sequel to the night before, Feailley Ghaelgagh was sponsoring a musicians' workshop. I arrived far too early, and to escape the enthusiasm of the hotel owner's wife ("We were in Vancouver and Whistler last sum-mer — wonderful, and so reasonably priced!"), I strolled around the lit-tle town. Jackdaws perched on multicolored Christmas lights, newly strung between the sky-blue lampposts. The tide advanced on dogs walking their owners along the beach.

The workshop started slowly in a back room. Musicians straggled in, many of them bleary-eyed, a few with children in tow. I noticed a tall man with short gray hair who had, the previous night, been one of the maroon-shirted singers in Caarjyn Cooidjagh. Now Bill Corlett was sit-ting alone over a ploughman's lunch. I interrupted it.

The choir's name, Bill told me, is pronounced "Cur-jin Coo-ja." Hav-ing begun with a few people getting together to sing at a festival in the late 1980s, it now has about fifteen members. They sing almost exclu-sively in Manx — for love, needless to say, not money. Fewer than half the choir's members speak the language well. Bill, a no-nonsense man who works as a highway maintenance engineer, did not include himself among the fluent. He joined the Royal Air Force in his teens and spent more than a decade off the island; back home, his interest in Manx ar-rived too late for it to trip off his tongue. "Unfortunately, I have no affinity for languages apart from my own. Phil Gawne" — he gestured toward an intense-looking man of about forty with a shock of black hair over his forehead — "started teaching myself and my wife, virtually on a one-to-one basis, and maybe if we'd carried on with that, I'd be further ahead than I am now. I've taken various classes but you get bogged down in the grammar, don't you?"

I didn't know, but I nodded. Bogging seemed all too plausible. Manx is simpler for English speakers to spell than other Celtic languages, yet the syntax remains a challenge. Its sentences generally begin with the verb, not the subject. Small children easily make the grammar work for them; adults find the task more onerous. Heads already spinning from the mutating nouns, they run up against verbal phrases whose structure goes against the grain of English. Instead of "I like," a Manx-speaker can say *s'mie lhiam* (is good with-me). In place of "He does not like waiting," *s'olk lesh fuirraghtyn* (is bad with-him waiting). It's not just a new way of talking that students learn — it's a new, or rather a very old, way of thinking.

Bill sipped his Coke and said, "I came into it when I was thirty-one. You haven't got a hope!" He laughed, but not cynically. Whatever his dejection about not mastering Manx, he was still committed enough to give up a family Saturday in favor of the workshop here.

"But you need to meet Annie Kissack," he told me. "Let me get her over."

He got up and said a few words to a dark-haired woman just sitting down at Phil Gawne's table. I recognized her from the concert: the self-effacing conductor of Caarjyn Cooidjagh. Forsaking her drink and her family, she took a chair beside Bill. He'd called her "the driving force" behind the choir, and at close quarters, listening to the rush of her words, I could see the determination he meant.

"I never thought we'd have a choir," Anne said. "It was an accident, really. But the choir's an ideal thing if you like music. The name means 'friends together' — it sounds stupid when you put it in English, I'm sorry — but we really are all friends and relatives. I've got no formal training, but I knew a lot of Manx songs, because as a child I was under the influence of Mona Douglas. I was in her youth group, Aeglagh Vannin, in the sixties. It was very small, mind you. In those days it was *really* a minority thing to do."

I'd heard of Mona Douglas before. Through the mid- and late twentieth century, most of the people who fought to save the Manx language were men (in his *Short History of the Manx Language*, Brian Stowell gives twenty-nine names; twenty-six are men). Mona Douglas was the leading exception. She collected and performed innumerable dances, stories, and songs. Where tradition had grown a little feeble, she had absolutely no compunction about fortifying it with her own inventions. Purists might quibble. But the impact of her work was to keep tradition alive. Every endangered language needs such a woman.

Anne's eight-year-old son Ewan carried her lunch over from the other table. He wolfed a few mouthfuls of chips before leaving the meal with his mother. Phil Gawne had brought out a fiddle from its case under the table and was experimenting with a tune.

"There's a couple of academics who are the authorities on Manx," Anne was saying, "but by and large, everyone else is just getting on and doing it. People don't get passionately engaged about what's proper — we're quite blatantly here to look at Manx from our own needs. Phil and I have set about raising our children in Manx as much as possible. One or two other families are doing the same. But it's not easy. There's so much vocabulary that wasn't there from the nineteenth-century sources — words for 'dummies' and 'nappies,' for example."

In my country I'd have said "pacifiers" and "diapers," but I knew what she meant.

"So what did you do?"

"Oh, we did find something. For 'nappies' it was the word for padding, I think. Sometimes two or three words are going round for about ten years, till one seems to emerge as the favorite."

Some linguists call the result "neo-Manx." Fortunately their strictures don't trouble the people who go on using the language, creating fresh traditions every day. The language contains a host of young words and English borrowings. Yet in some ways the Manx now being uttered on the island is closer to the old verbal structures than was the Manx Ned Maddrell spoke. Not even a Brian Stowell is likely to scale the heights of biblical rhetoric, just as nobody in New York or London is likely to wander down the street saying, "We desire to hear of thee what thou thinkest." By the same token, principals in London or New York schools presumably don't ask their students, "Yo, what's up?" Every language has different levels of formality. As Brian had explained to me, "The Manx spoken now is a sort of halfway house between the Bible and the Manx in George Broderick's handbook." It is not a slurred slang.

By seeking to build a Gaelic-speaking community around the nu-

cleus of their own family, Anne and Phil are following an initiative
launched in the late 1960s by Irish speakers in Belfast. The Shaw's Road
community, as it came to be known, was founded by idealistic couples
who had learned Irish Gaelic as young adults. They built eleven houses
on the edge of a working-class estate in west Belfast, determined that in
those houses Irish would be dominant. Elsewhere in the city, even in its
Catholic and republican areas, the language was not often heard. The
nationalist or republican movement comes draped with symbols, but
these couples preferred to act. (In so doing, of course, they became a
symbol.) An Irish-language primary school, Bunscoil Phobal Feirste,
stands at the center of the enclave. It started off in 1971 with nine children in a mobile hut and now has a permanent building used by several
hundred. That's one measure of the success of the Shaw's Road community. Another is the lack of surprise that spoken Irish attracts on the
streets of west Belfast. A language long associated with rural retreat has
acquired an edgy urban base.

Ewan came and stole another handful of chips. With a look of tri-
umph, he climbed onto his mother's lap. The triumph was short-lived,
because his five-year-old sister, Kitty, promptly clambered onto *his* lap.
Anne sent the children back to their father and reverted to Caarjyn
Cooidjagh: "Nobody has ever said to our faces that we should sing in
English — but you've got to be assertive. You've got to say, 'We're a
Gaelic choir!' Otherwise you'd be swept away." If new tunes or lyrics are
needed, she writes them. The singers are all under fifty, so the choir has
no debilitating need to cling to the past. "Older people associate Manx
with poverty," she added. " 'You'll never get on with that,' they say, or
'What use has it ever been?' But the younger people don't feel that. And
this is a wealthy island now for the most part."

I didn't ask about what I'd felt the previous night: a diffidence, a
hesitancy. But looking at a Scottish musician across the room, Anne
brought up the subject herself. "The Irish and Scots don't really know
what to make of us," she said. "We've never had the tradition of courtly
poetry — any literature we've had has been introverted religious poetry — and often Irish and Scottish people are looking for something
grander. There was a tendency, ten years ago, for musicians to do a bit
of Manx and then move on to Irish. Everything you heard was aiming
to be an Irish reel or a jig."

The regret in her voice disappeared: "But people are more confident
now. We're grounded here. We need to have pride in ourselves."

A man with an acoustic guitar and a soft tenor voice had begun to sing in Manx, and after a few verses a flautist took up the melody. Three fiddlers launched into a mournful tune that imperceptibly stirred, quickened, spiraled, and overflowed into a song to set the blood afire. The room was now alive with music. And I realized, sipping a fresh beer, how critical a role music can play in the survival of a small language. Music can haul Manx out of the classroom and its dutiful lessons; music offers the hesitant lips a shortcut to joy. Learning Manx or any other endangered language can feel like a burdensome duty. Thanks to music, it can also be a pleasure.

Each of the six Celtic languages has been pushed westward, driven back against the tides of the Atlantic. The stronghold of Scottish Gaelic lies in the remote Western Isles; the heartlands of Irish are the western fastnesses of Kerry, Connemara, and Donegal. French keeps nudging the Breton language farther and farther west in Brittany, just as English long ago forced its way into eastern and central Wales. Cornish survived longest within a few miles of Land's End; and as for Manx, although its present-day speakers are sprinkled throughout the island, the village that acted as its bastion was Cregneash, at the far southwest, facing out as though for rescue across the Irish Sea.

Its setting is remarkable. From the nearby town of Port St. Mary, you climb a long hill past a Stone Age burial ground until, if you look back from the summit, a large chunk of the Isle of Man falls away into the distance: the airport, King William's College, the old capital of Castletown, farms and coastal villages, golf courses and sheep-speckled moorland. Keep going, and all this disappears behind the hill's brow. In front of you, to the west, lie a few houses and a land that drops into water. Ned Maddrell lived here, as did Harry Kelly, Eleanor Karren, Ned Faragher, and other men and women who kept a tenuous grip on Manx when everyone on the other side of the hill had let the language go. After they died, years passed in which the village heard only English phrases on the wind.

On a blustery Sunday afternoon I entered the tall house of *Yr Greinneyder,* the one who stirs things up. Phil Gawne was waiting for me — his story emblematic of a profound change in attitude to Manx, desperation giving way to hope. We sat in armchairs near the old fireplace while in a pasture that begins outside his window a pair of dark horses grazed and ran. Phil is a farmer's son; he still enters plowing competitions. They provide a break from his part-time employment and full-time commitment: to stir the embers of Manx into a flame.

"I started out down on my grandmother's farm," he said. "Things really hadn't changed that much for the best part of a century, the way people dealt with each other. Mealtimes, we'd be gathering in — all sitting round the table, eating traditional Manx fare, spuds and herring and meat pie. The older I was getting, the more I can remember conversations starting out with 'He's the brother of such-and-such' or 'That fellow's a cousin . . .' Everybody knew everybody else's parentage and all their family trees. And then, more and more, there'd be talk of the newcomers. But nobody had anything to say."

To a lot of bright children, that kind of intimacy would be suffocating. It would fuel a desire to spurn the hearth, its chains of belonging. The word "insular," after all, means "of an island." Rebels, doubters, or outcasts might well take insularity as a reason to flee. But Phil was neither a doubter nor an outcast, nor was he at that stage a rebel. Even as a boy he thirsted to learn about his own community. He was annoyed to find, in high school, that the Isle of Man scarcely appeared on the curriculum. At the time he did not speak Manx.

"The farmers used to gather on a Sunday," he went on. "There'd be yarns and patter, and things would be coming out. But then the newcomers would bring in totally new subjects of their own, like what they'd read in the Sunday papers. So the brash conversation was taking over and the old stories were dying out. And gradually it seemed to me that the Manx people were bending over backwards to make other people feel at home."

Yet he sailed to England, enrolling in a science program at Liverpool University. During his first weeks in Liverpool he noticed an advertisement for an Irish-language class. The teacher proved to be Brian Stowell, who was ready and willing to teach Manx instead of Irish. Phil's three years on the mainland were also his first years of Manx.

After his studies Phil returned to the island. He took further language lessons; he also became a regular at a Castletown pub "where the influence of a few pints of beer and three or four really good speakers meant that within a few months I was speaking Manx fluently, though perhaps not competently." He had no desire to continue in biochemistry; and anyway the island had no jobs in that field. So he trained as an accountant. It was the early 1980s, and Phil played a small part in clearing up the mess after a bank's spectacular collapse. The work radicalized him.

Many of the smiling comeovers, he believed, were "not only diluting my culture and spoiling my environment, but they were also extremely corrupt and, in some cases, criminals. I found it really stressful, and after sixteen months I left. I just couldn't stand it. Everything I was doing — having to play golf, go off on yachts, swill gin and tonics — seemed totally wrong."

Phil turned to self-employment. He built stone walls; he made jewelry. He also turned to arson.

Loads of these £200,000–£300,000 homes were being built, while a lot of Manx families were looking for first-time homes in the £40,000–£60,000 bracket. And there was nothing for them. It wasn't just two or three nationalist nutcases — a lot of people were very disgruntled that the finance sector seemed to rule the roost. The government wasn't listening to the people, only to the financiers. That's the way it seemed.

So we started to campaign. Initially it was just daubing slogans around. Then it was burning luxury homes down — ones that were almost completed, but not occupied yet. A lot of people still tell me that if we hadn't done that, we wouldn't have the respect we're treated with now. It's a terribly sad thing to hear. But most people tell me that the democratic means would have got us nowhere.

He was arrested, convicted, and sentenced to sixteen months in prison. Two other men received slightly longer sentences. Upon his release Phil gave himself over to the language. He joined Yn Cheshaght Ghailckagh; he sang in Caarjyn Cooidjagh; he helped found Feailley Ghaelgagh, the Manx-language festival. After Ewan's birth, he and Anne Kissack took what may well prove the most radical step of all: they and another family started a Manx-speaking play group.

Flash forward a few years, and Phil Gawne has become a quasi–civil servant. Paid by the publicly funded Manx National Heritage and the Manx Heritage Foundation, his job is to stir up the language. In practice, a lot of the stirring takes place in the four Mooinjer Veggey play groups (the name means "little people," or fairies). About sixty children now attend these play groups; many of the parents and even teachers come from England, Ireland, and Scotland. Since none of the adults grew up speaking Manx, they're all starting from the same position — an equality of ignorance, you might say. If the language is being reborn through the immersions of Mooinjer Veggey, it's not on an ethnic basis.

Farewell to the old, constricting definition of what it means to be truly Manx.

"There's a danger," Phil admitted, "of forever talking things up, of believing your own rhetoric. But from what I can see, Mooinjer Veggey has actually worked." He sounded almost surprised. "The children are going home and using Manx in the home, singing Manx folk songs, teaching words to their parents. It's such a good feeling."

The phone rang: his father was calling to chat about plowing and horses. I watched the sky and the cold sea beyond the sloping pasture. When Phil sat down again, I asked the question that had been growing in my mind over the past couple of hours: whether he ever despaired of the perpetual struggle and wanted to give up the fight.

"I often think it would make sense to give it up," he confessed. "But I never think that I *should*. Everybody has their bad days, of course — if I have a bad day at the plowing match, I think I'll never go plowing again. And I realize there's only so much you can do. I can't stop the Isle of Man I know and love from being changed. But I can influence the way it's being changed. That's why I've latched onto the language in a big way."

It's not for its own sake, then, nor out of a passion for linguistic diversity or Celtic philology that Phil Gawne has made the survival of Manx so central to his life. For him, the fate of the language is intertwined with the island's whole identity. Writing in a local newspaper, he once called the language a "firmly anchored lifeline" without which "Manxness is in danger of being sucked into the void of 'dumbed-down' Euro-American trash." The rhetoric risked becoming a rant, but there was no ranting in his careful words to me: "The music, the Gaelic way of storytelling, the folklore — all these things come out of the Manx language. It's the one thing you can put your finger on and say, 'This is unique to the Isle of Man.' I know there's absolutely no economic reason to learn Manx. But the language is almost like a peg to hang the culture on."

He looked, as ever, resolute. Only once did I read hesitation in his face: when he suggested that "perhaps the best thing that ever happened to the Isle of Man was the new residents drive and the finance sector. It's a difficult thing for me to admit that. But if we hadn't gone ahead with it, we'd have continued to despise our own culture, and we probably wouldn't have had the interest in the language." Along with the wealth came security in the present and confidence in the future, soon followed by curiosity about the past. The language revival draws on all three qualities.

Phil had a new project in mind and, some weeks after I left the island, word came through that it would go ahead. The island's government has promised to fund a primary school where Manx, not English, will be the language of instruction. The school will give the diminutive graduates of Mooinjer Veggey a place to carry on speaking Manx throughout their childhood. Much work lies ahead in creating a full curriculum — the language has no atlases or encyclopedias, for example. But a thriving Manx-language school, more than any other initiative, would prove that this remains one of the world's living tongues.

Anne Kissack arrived home with Ewan, who had been rehearsing a pantomime in English, and gently chided her husband for failing to offer me a cup of tea. She chided him again for not showing me the sights of Cregneash; and when I'd finished a mug, she lied bravely ("I need a bit of fresh air") and walked me around the village. Manx National Heritage owns many of the buildings, intending to keep the place as a living folk museum — if that's not a contradiction in terms. We passed the thatched and whitewashed cottage where a cantankerous, gray-bearded Manx speaker named Harry Kelly used to live; we passed a smithy and a grim-looking church. Eamon de Valera, the prime minister of Ireland, visited Cregneash in the 1940s to meet its Gaelic speakers; today the village doubles for rural Ireland in TV shows, ads, and movies like *Waking Ned Devine*. Chickens were running free over a footpath. Night had begun to fall, but there was nothing fuzzy about this particular Celtic twilight: in the brisk wind, the houses stood etched in dramatic clarity.

As I said goodbye, Phil handed me a recent survey of Manx speakers and learners. At first glance the results were encouraging for a man of his convictions: on the subject of national identity, a large majority of respondents said they were "Manx, not British" or "more Manx than British." But one question, I thought, had elicited a troubling response. Asked whether "learning Manx is a hobby for me," sixty-two people agreed, thirty-two were neutral, and only twenty-nine disagreed, six of them "strongly."

Can this or any language survive if most of its speakers see it as a hobby? After all, a language is not a stamp collection or a piece of folk art; you can't just pull it out of a cupboard when you choose. A language needs continual use. But I remembered Phil's stern and forthright words: "No matter how few speakers you have, it's always worth continuing the fight to save a language. Looking at Manx from the outside in the early seventies, anyone would have said it was a complete and utter waste of time to try and save it. There was just no chance whatsoever."

I kept thinking of Phil's dark-haired children. Ewan and Kitty represent the oral tradition at its most elemental: the passing on of words and expressions from an old Manx-speaking woman to her grandson, Leslie Quirk; from him to Brian Stowell; from him to Phil Gawne; and now to the lips of a further generation. Ewan and Kitty eat breakfast in the very kitchen, they sleep in the very bedrooms where, a century and a quarter ago, a family named Maddrell lived. By accident or by fate, their house was once the home of a Manx-speaking boy called Ned.

The Verbs of Boro

anzray: to keep apart from an enemy or wicked company
mokhrob: to express anger by a sidelong glance
zum: to wear or put on clothing for the upper part of the body

I WAS FEELING LOW. I had spent the day wading through academic books about language and my head hurt. It appeared more and more unlikely that I would ever grasp the phonetic meaning of a "lengthened, front unrounded, half-open, lax voiced vocoid" or a "voiceless, laminal post-alveolar stop with slight aspiration and a high off-glide." Linguistics has a scholarly code that excludes the uninitiated, and it had begun to seem to me that the more you love languages, the harder this code is to learn.

Returning to the crowded stacks of the university library, I began, almost at random, to pull books off the shelves. I didn't know exactly what I wanted — instinctively, perhaps, I was searching for some proof of humanity among those dust-dry grammars and theoretical speculations. I was looking, I suppose, for a book that would lift a language off the page. The first candidate I found was *A Practical Introduction to Tonga,* published in London in 1953. Forget the South Pacific: Tonga, in this case, refers to a language spoken in what is now Zambia and was then called Northern Rhodesia. The author, C. R. Hopgood, aimed his book not at scholars or students, and still less at the Tonga-speaking people themselves, but at junior officers of the British Empire. He was determined to school them in grief.

Hopgood's first lesson begins with the words *Ba-ntu ba-fwa* — "The people have died" — and proceeds to the Tonga phrases for "The thing is dead," "The small object is dead," and "The ferocious animals are dead." Lesson two starts off with "Get up, you little beast" and lurches ahead to "The animals bite." By lesson four, the syntax has become more complex ("The baboon is eating up all of the people's food") and the mood is growing ever darker: *Bu-ntu bwa-ngu bwa-mana*, "My humanity is finished." Lesson seven bears a modest resemblance to the Book of Job. "My goat has aborted"; "His sheep were attacked by wild dogs"; "My sheep's hut has fallen into disrepair": all these mishaps lead up to the dignified distress of "Wild boars have sadly depleted our crops." Were upper lips ever quite as stiff as that? The empire finds it hard to restore order. In the end, Hopgood can offer nothing more sanguine than a Tonga version of "It is bad not to hoe. Such neglect of agriculture brings troubles. It results in poor stamina."

I abandoned the stresses of farming life in the Zambezi Valley and returned to the stacks. Eventually I found myself glancing through a volume published at Gauhati University, in the Indian state of Assam, in 1977: *A Descriptive Analysis of the Boro Language*. Which language was that again? I didn't know and at first I hardly cared. What caught my attention was that Pramod Chandra Bhattacharya had dedicated the book to the memory of his son Amiya Kumar, dead at the age of twelve, a boy "who is no more in this world." Dr. Bhattacharya had researched and written the volume, he said, "against a number of personal and national calamities which occurred during 1952–64," some years before the calamity of his son's death. Humble to a fault, he offered his apologies "for my poor expressions not only in Boro, but in English."

I took the book back to my table and sat down with it.

egthu: to create a pinching sensation in the armpit
khale: to feel partly bitter
khonsay: to pick an object up with care as it is rare or scarce

Boro, I learned, is a language of northeastern India that spills over into neighboring countries: Nepal, Bhutan, Bangladesh. Most of its speakers live on the north bank of the Brahmaputra River. The language goes by other names too: Mech, Kachari, and (now the most common) Bodo. Whatever name you choose, it's one of well over two hundred languages in the fertile subfamily of Tibeto-Burman. Nearly all these languages, being indigenous to a small area, have never had great numbers on their side — Boro is one of the very few that may be spoken by as many as a million people. Its speakers are usually fluent in Bengali or in Dr. Bhattacharya's mother tongue, Assamese. Bilingualism is doubtless an asset on an individual level, but for a language with as little clout as Boro it can also be a prelude to permanent silence. No nation, state, or province uses Boro as an official language; bigger languages are muscling into its territory; many of its speakers suffer wretched poverty; most of its linguistic relatives are even smaller and more obscure.

Yet Boro has its partisans. The desire to sustain it stands at the root of a political movement that strives to create a new Indian state of Bodoland — or, in the movement's most extreme form, a sovereign, fully independent nation. "Despite being the sons of the soil," one Boro leader protested in the Indian parliament, "we people have been neglected, discriminated, oppressed, suppressed and misruled ever since Independence." A few days after my chance discovery in the library, I surfed the Internet and came across an interview with U. G. Brahma, president of the All Bodo Students Union, who complained that "under the pressure of aggressive Sanskritization, several Bodo subgroups have forsaken the Bodo language and culture. This poses serious threat to the survival of our Bodo culture as a separate entity."

As I knew from living in Quebec — and as I had witnessed on a tiny scale on the Isle of Man — nationalist movements often draw their most potent energy from fears of language loss and cultural erasure. To make a quasi-mathematical formula out of the idea, you could say that any advance of the global is likely to produce a defense of the local. Advocates of Boro who found the students and politicians too mild-mannered have formed a guerrilla army, the Bodo Liberation Tigers. In the past few years the most violent or desperate among the separatists have begun to massacre Hindi- and Bengali-speaking migrants settling in their homeland.

Unlike many endangered languages, Boro does exist in written form. Indeed it exists in two written forms: the Roman alphabet of the West and the Devanagari script of India. Feuds between their partisans seem to have consumed more time and anger than the common struggle against outside enemies. This too is a tale with precedents.

gobram: to shout in one's sleep
gulun: to bend after overthrowing or uprooting
ur: to dig soil (as the swine do), to move curry (while cooking)

Looking at these verbs, rolling them around in my mouth, I was re-minded of the first time it ever dawned on me that languages could not be translated on an exact, word-for-word basis. As a boy I took pri-vate French lessons from a chain-smoking spinster cousin of Albert Schweitzer who had somehow fetched up in a basement apartment in Lethbridge, Alberta. One day I tried to say, "I'm hungry." French, how-ever, demands not an adjective but an abstract noun: *J'ai faim,* I have hunger. Likewise I have thirst, I have fear, I have nine years. You can't just reproduce the English parts of speech; you have to re-create the idea. You have to search, often gropingly, for the best possible equiva-lent. For a unilingual child like me, this was a radical, scary notion. When you venture outside the confines of a mother tongue, you must embrace uncertainty. And yet English and French are related languages with a long overlapping history and a mountain of shared vocabulary. How much harder is the search — how much rarer is a precise equiva-lent — when two languages have little in common? The verbs of Boro challenge me, not with *déjà vu* but with *jamais vu.*

It's not only a language of verbs, of course. Under the discreet fluo-rescent lights of the library ceiling, a few nouns also stood out on Dr. Bhattacharya's crinkled, yellowing pages: *bokhali,* a woman who carries a child on her back; *gansuthi,* the first-grown feather of a bird's wing; *zogno,* the sound produced by a mixing of mud and water if you thrust your hand into a crab's hole. How could anyone resist a language whose expression for "slightly humpbacked" is *gobdobdob*? Boro has a whole range of terms for calling out to animals: ducks, pigeons, poultry, cows, buffalo, pigs, cats, puppies, and grown-up dogs all demand words of their own. In contrast to English, which asks its speakers to say "Ah!" "Oh!" and "Hey!" in a variety of moods, Boro is blessed with twenty "interjectional exclamative particles" to express everything from insult to affection, repentance to irritation, terror to sympathy. It also has a folk song in which the singer comforts a young bride with the reassur-ing information "Ants prepare their food store with the help of their saliva."

Unless I have severely misread Dr. Bhattacharya, though, the glory of the language lies elsewhere.

> *onguboy:* to love from the heart
> *onsay:* to pretend to love
> *onsra:* to love for the last time

Verbs like these go beyond all borders: the ideas or sentiments they express transcend the culture that articulates them. I can't imagine I will ever need to express the noise that mud and water would make if I refused to let a sleeping crab lie; as far as I'm concerned, *zogno* is a word that can happily stay in Boro. While I love the surprising verb *dasa* — it means "not to place a fishing instrument" — I accept, with some reluctance, that my own language might have little use for it. But *onsay* and *onsra* are a different story. Having met those words in Dr. Bhattacharya's book, how can I do without them? I covet them, just as I covet the verbs for expressing anger by a sidelong glance or for feeling partly bitter. They are more than just fresh sounds on the tongue; they are fresh thoughts in the mind.

Poring for the second time over Dr. Bhattacharya's painstaking text, I recalled a passage by the lawyer Rupert Ross, whose book *Returning to the Teachings* explores some of the vexed encounters between Cree and Ojibwa people in northwestern Ontario and the forces of the Canadian legal system. Ross says those encounters are made trickier, and justice harder to achieve, by the distinct worldviews that underlie the speakers' languages: "My Aboriginal friends talk a great deal about what it's like to have to use English all day, and they generally describe it as a strain. If we truly recognized that we occupy a universe of constantly transforming things, people and relationships, then we would have no choice but to discard our heavy reliance on nouns to capture and describe it." Yet that reliance is woven deep into the fabric of English. Nothing could be more difficult to discard.

Is Boro a language, like Cree and Ojibwa, in which the world appears to be constantly transforming? Dr. Bhattacharya reports that if *onsra* is said in a different tone, it has a different meaning: "to arouse the female oracle for the last time."

gagrom: to search for a thing below water by trampling
goblo: to be fat (as a child or infant)
gobray: to fall in a well unknowingly

It's possible, I admit, that some of these words have simple English equivalents that Dr. Bhattacharya failed to find. I'm somewhat dubious about his explanation of *kholab:* "to feel tedious for an odd smell." And while I accept his faith that a Boro proverb effectively means "an honest person is troubled," I'm still puzzling over his literal translation of it: "The cat clears its bowels on mild soil." Amid the movable curries of the

Brahmaputra, bowels seem to be a preoccupation. Where English offers a tedious-feeling sentence like "A great man behaves honorably," Boro conjures up a smell: "A big man farts straight behind."

Still, you might retort — especially if you happen to be an admirer of Noam Chomsky — the two phrases mean the same thing. In *Aspects of the Theory of Syntax,* Chomsky wrote: "It is possible to convey any conceptual content in any language." An extraterrestrial, he once suggested, would see all human beings as speaking a single language. We earthlings may be forgiven for choosing a variant perspective. As the critic George Steiner once noted, Chomsky's ideas "could account, with beautiful economy and depth, for a world in which men would all be speaking one language, diversified at most by a moderate range of dialects." In fact, however, the luxuriant profusion of tongues on the planet challenges any simple notion of evolutionary benefit to our species. The incredible diversity of human languages is surely just as remarkable as the hidden similarities of their grammar.

Besides, there's more to any language than just its ability to express conceptual content. "Languages," said Ken Hale, a colleague of Chomsky at the Massachusetts Institute of Technology, "embody the intellectual wealth of the people that speak them. Losing any one of them is like dropping a bomb on the Louvre."

> *asusu:* to feel unknown and uneasy in a new place
> *gabkhron:* to be afraid of witnessing an adventure
> *serrom:* to examine by slight pressing

A quarter-century after Dr. Bhattacharya's descriptive analysis was published, linguists are again at work on Boro. Unlike the imperial Hopgood among the Tonga, they are carrying out their labors on behalf of the local people. But their motives are zealous. They think they have God on their side.

On an American Web site I found news of the language's speakers under one of their other names: "As in most animistic cultures, the Mech live in fear of the spirits of nature. Only through appeasement can they have peace or success in life, but no one is sure when or if the spirits are appeased. The Mech need liberation from such oppressive beliefs." They are, as a result, now featured in a series of "Unreached Peoples Prayer Profiles." After a quick sketch of traditional Boro culture, the Web site requests a few prayers: "Ask God to grant wisdom and favor to the mission agencies that are targeting the Mech." (The verb "targeting" merits some thought.) "Ask God to anoint the Gospel as it goes forth via radio in their area . . . Ask God to speed the completion of the *Jesus* film and other Christian materials into the Bodo language."

My first instinct is to urge the Boro to use the missionaries' *asusu* and to *anzray* them, keeping *onsay* in reserve for emergencies; otherwise the Boro may soon pass beyond *mokhrob* to a destructive *khale.* (Pardon my nouns.) Yet it's not that simple. The missionaries change the culture, but the culture is changing anyway. Even rural Assam is subject to the forces of globalization, and the tribal peoples of northeastern India face a host of pressures — environmental and economic ones among them. As well as calling for prayer to save the oppressed souls, the missionary Web site warns that "a large percentage of Mech have encumbered unmanageable debt."

By continuing to speak their language, the Boro won't get rid of their debts, save their forests, or halt the influx of outside settlers. But they may be a good deal more likely to withstand the corrosive despair that accompanies these pressures, avoiding the self-hatred that comes when a culture implodes and disintegrates. J.R.R. Tolkien, a linguist long before he was a novelist, once noted "the part played by the cultivated Icelandic language, in spite of poverty, lack of power and insignificant numbers, in keeping the Icelanders in being in desperate times." Pride in their own tongue could give the Boro, too, a better chance of sheer survival. Who knows — the anointed Gospel might even play a role in a drama of language preservation.

Otherwise, chaos beckons. "A hare dies due to its shit" — Boro sayings are not for the squeamish — "a deer dies due to its footstep; a man dies due to his mouth."

> *bunhan bunahan:* to be about to speak, and about not to speak
> *khar:* to smell like urine or raw fish
> *khen:* to hit one's heart

The Lion's Tongue

PROVENÇAL

ONCE THERE WAS A WRITER who revived a language. His name was Frédéric Mistral and he grew up in Maillane, a country town in the deep south of France. He was born in a whitewashed farmhouse just outside the town in 1830, two short generations after the convulsions that had killed a king. Those convulsions had also intensified the long, slow process by which the language of Paris was coming to dominate the farthest corners of France. Frédéric was a bright young man. But unlike many other bright young men, he felt a profound attachment to his home. He loved its traditions: how on All Souls' Day, for instance, children would place sweet food at the foot of their beds to appease the spirits of the dead. In his high school days he was mocked for the local expressions he liked to use — most of his teachers and classmates thought it only right and proper to emulate the language of the capital, the city of light. Frédéric was schooled in its elegant cadences. But the language of Molière and Voltaire was not his own. It is said that even as an adolescent Frédéric vowed to restore "the sacred mother tongue." His own mother tongue: Provençal.

It was a language that combined local roots with a long and distinguished literary history. Provençal literature had sprung to life seven centuries before Mistral, on the lips of troubadours. Writing and singing in Provençal, poets like Peire Rogier and Arnaut Daniel invented the rules and dreamed the grand romance of courtly love. In the process, they taught Europe how to shed the confining skin of Latin — still the language of church and government — and use the vernacular idiom, making art out of common speech. As Lawrence Durrell once observed, "The slumbering language woke to the touch of new music, new words, new passions. Indeed, until this poetry asserted itself, the whole love-transaction was hardly on a higher plane than baronial pig-sticking." Provençal was also the language of the freethinking Cathars, whose anticlerical speculations would be brutally stamped out by armies from the north of France. The crusade against heresy had the side effect of stifling the troubadours.

Perhaps the tolerant, unorthodox atmosphere in the region encouraged the troubadours and allowed the Cathars to emerge. In the twelfth century feudal control was already fading; wealth was becoming palpable. Or perhaps the young Provençal language — with its ease of rhyme, its lightness of touch — helped give rise to the troubadour movement. It was a time, unlike ours, when every self-respecting poet was multilingual. A late twelfth-century poet called Raimbaut of Vaqueiras wrote a love poem in six stanzas using five languages in turn: Provençal, Genoese, French, Gascon, and Portuguese. In the last stanza, showing off like a jazz musician, he deployed them all. It's futile to attempt a translation of such a poem, for its central meaning lies not in Raimbaut's profession or pretense of love but in his sheer linguistic extravagance.

For a good millennium, Provençal was the mother tongue spoken, sung, and heard every day by most of the people living in southeastern France. A broad statement, and one that needs qualification: Provence remained independent until the end of the Middle Ages. Even then, the act of union with France gave the region much autonomy. Until the French Revolution Provence made many of its own rules, and it went on speaking its own language. Not long before Mistral's birth, a bishop of Marseille insisted on preaching his sermons only in Provençal.

In the intellectual landscape of Europe, Provençal is not some puny tributary but a major river system. After the decline of the troubadours, admittedly, its literature shrank into mere convention. But in the mid-nineteenth century it again became a force to be reckoned with. The reason was Mistral. Having read the troubadours, he knew what his language was capable of. In 1854 he and six friends launched a poetic brotherhood with an invented name: the Félibrige. Its aim, Mistral an-

nounced, was "that our children, instead of being brought up in contempt of our Provençal customs, and instead of envying the baubles of
Paris or Madrid, should continue to speak the language of their cradle,
the tender language of their mothers, and should remain on the farms
where they were born . . . and that our people, instead of wallowing in
ignorance of their history, their great past, their true character, should
understand their claims to nobility." If they valued their own identity
and kept apart from wicked company, the people of Provence need look
up to no one. The Félibrige manifesto aimed to hit the heart.

Mistral's first major poem, *Mirèio*, was an epic of thwarted love.
Never one to shrink from a challenge, he declared at the outset of the
poem that he meant to do for Provence what Homer had done for ancient Greece. Though he fell a little short on that score, he was already a
cultural icon by the time he entered middle age. Poetry was Mistral's
lifeblood. Yet he was also a lexicographer, a verbal curator, even an anthropologist of sorts. After *Mirèio* he began work on the monumental
Tresor dóu Felibrige: a labor of love and immense energy that would end
up as a two-volume dictionary of the Provençal language and an encyclopedia of Provence.

Along the way Mistral created a spelling, too. Reasoning that the cus-
tomary medieval spelling bore little resemblance to how people actually
spoke, he modernized the way his language was written. It was a controversial project. Some of his contemporaries attacked him, partly bitter at his attempt to unify the many dialects of southern France. Mistral
brushed such criticisms aside. Though he based his written vocabulary
on the speech of his own area, he freely adapted terms from elsewhere.
It was a composite language, but Mistral went on calling it "Provençal."
Under his guidance, the language again became respectable.

His fame kept growing. The man was revered. More than that: he was
loved. In 1894, when he attended a bullfight in the Roman arena at
Nîmes, twenty thousand people are said to have stood up as he walked
in, shouting "Mistral! Mistral!" His last major poem, *Lou Pouèmo dóu
Rose,* was the tale of a doomed affair between a young man and woman
of different social classes as their boat traveled the Rhône, destined for a
fatal accident. It sounds like James Cameron's *Titanic* in miniature,
published fifteen years before the *Titanic* sank.

In 1904 Mistral won the Nobel Prize for literature. He was the first —
and, apart from Isaac Bashevis Singer, still the only — writer to receive

the Nobel for work in a minority language, a language neither used nor promoted by any government. With his prize money Mistral founded a museum in the city of Arles to honor the traditions of Provence. Homage continued to pour in. He became known as "the lion of Arles." When he died in 1914, just before the Great War, Mistral had every reason to believe that his poetry would endure and that his language would survive.

To walk into her house was to walk into the dark. Even when Nini Albertini switched on two or three lamps, speaking all the while in rapid-fire French, the house absorbed and swallowed up the light. I sat down in a small room whose only window was shadowed by the leaves and jutting branches of a great fig tree, a tree conceivably as old as the seventeenth-century *mas* itself. The *mas* — a Provençal word for farmhouse, widely used in the south of France even by people who know nothing of the ancient language — was sheltering Nini's family long before the Revolution. Around its heavy walls and red-tiled roof grow the lime and cherry trees, the olives and almonds that have fed unbroken generations. Yet the *mas* and its half-wild garden are no longer rooted in the countryside, but stand surrounded by the growing town of Saint-Rémy. And Nini, long settled into widowhood, has no children of her own.

She bustled and talked, bustled and talked. Only when I agreed to taste one of her homemade liqueurs, an infusion of nuts in local wine, did she pause and sit down. The liqueur was dark brown, almost black. She told stories then of her great-grandfather, who saw his first airplane in 1914 and thought the world had come to an end; of her father, a soldier in the Great War who found among the remnants of a church the egg-sized grenade and the chunk of stained glass that Nini keeps on a mantelpiece; and of her mother, whose photograph hangs on a whitewashed wall of the dining room. The dark-eyed young woman inside the frame wears *la capello*, a lace scarf and wimple that formed part of the traditional costume of Provence. Nini looked up at her and sighed.

"True Provençal came to a stop in the time of our parents," she said, meaning (I think) the early twentieth century. "My mother told me how they ridiculed her language. It was a terrible thing. The teacher would strike a child across the knuckles with a ruler if the child was caught speaking Provençal." Unselfconsciously, she lifted her hands and hit her own chest, rattling a necklace that hung down over her sweater. "It's an awful thing to come home from school feeling that your mother tongue is ridiculous. The hurt went very deep."

After the second great war Nini moved to the city of Avignon, training as a nurse and doing social work in a prison near the Popes' Palace. Eventually she married a Corsican. Adult life slipped by, its chores and its pleasures in French. A decade ago she returned to the *mas,* having nursed her husband, her mother, and her sister through long and painful deaths. Living alone there, Nini began to write poems. She bought a heavy book whose pages were blank. Before long her poems had filled it. Remarkably, these poems came to mind in Provençal, a language Nini rarely hears in daily life. She bought another book and filled it, too.

I listened to her read a few of these poems. A stillness came over her then, and her voice grew softer, higher, younger. It became, indeed, the voice of a girl, evoking the cypresses that sway above the fields and roads of Provence, or praising the beauty of her youthful mother, or defying what some would call inevitable: that Provençal itself will die. Although tens of thousands of people still know how to speak it, the vast majority of them are old, and only a handful still use Provençal as much as French.

The poem that struck me most, "Lengo Nostro," tackles the language's disappearance head on. In it Nini compares Provençal to a seed lost in gravel soil. Lost, but not dead; the seed is merely waiting for spring. Nini doesn't just speak *about* the vanishing language; she talks *to* it: *Où milan de toun pople / Car sarrian ourfèlin / Sè parties per de bon* (In the midst of your people, we'd be orphaned if you left for good).

I blinked as I stepped out of the cool *mas* into a sunlit afternoon. The trees that overhung a small statue of the Virgin Mary had shed a drift of russet leaves onto the car's windshield. Nini was still waving as I drove down the lane and out into Saint-Rémy. Heading northeast, I crossed from the *département* of Bouches-du-Rhône into the *département* of Vaucluse — official subtleties that hark back, like so much else, to the revolutionaries of 1789. They could do nothing about the past of Provençal. But, puffed up with idealistic fervor, they were determined to revoke its future. The revolutionaries put an end to regional autonomy, decreeing that all across France the language of instruction must be French. Zealous for a rational future, they saw minority languages like Breton and Provençal as rife with stupidity and superstition. It took several turbulent decades before their centralizing orders were fulfilled. The surprise, even so, may be not that Provençal is in such failing health but that it continues to exist at all.

It exists; yet it's virtually invisible. Looking for proof of its survival, or even its noble history, can seem akin to chasing the wind. The morning after visiting Nini, I walked around La Roque Alric, the hilltop village where I was staying with friends. The village's name comes from Provençal: its houses cling to the southern face of a tall dramatic rock, *la roca* in the old tongue. La Roque Alric has a town hall, public toilets, and a church, but no school; its few dozen permanent residents do not include a child. Some homes lie empty except in late July and August.

The village cemetery stands on a ridge. I climbed the long stone steps, pushed open a gate, and entered a small world apart. The ruined wall of an eleventh-century Romanesque chapel borders the cemetery, and a handwritten note beside a wire barrier asks people to go no farther; the risk of damage is too great. The note is in French. So are the inscriptions on all the tombstones, even the oldest, lying flat on the pebbly earth since 1861. The widow of an old man named Joseph Allègre had put up a fine monument in the 1920s, but now it was leaning precariously against an ivy-covered wall, shoved there with four or five other slabs rendered irrelevant by the expanding dead. Newer graves displayed chrysanthemums and color photographs.

If Provençal is anything here, it is a ghost. Outside the cemetery walls, rowanberries and rose hips weighed down the yellowing bushes. A hawk revolved above the valley, watching the cloud shadows pass.

La Roque Alric had two or three times as many people when Joseph Allègre was a boy. He almost certainly spoke Provençal at home. But if he went to school, he learned to read and write in French. In 1863 the school inspector of the Apt and Carpentras district, not far from La Roque Alric, had written: "I know of absolutely no school where the teaching is performed in patois, and if it were otherwise, the instructor would be severely called to order." Provençal has long suffered from the prejudice that it's nothing more than "patois" — an uncouth dialect, a corrupt degeneration of French, unworthy to be heard in a classroom or spoken in a court of law.

Now that Provençal no longer poses a threat, France has begun to wake up to its richness. A fifteen-hundred-page bilingual dictionary, *Français-Provençal* and *Francés-Prouvençau*, was published in the 1990s.

(Notice that even in the Provençal version French comes first.) Leafing through it, I gained the impression that the longer a Provençal word happens to be, the more likely it is to resemble French. Of course, a sentence that looks recognizable in print can be impossible to understand when spoken fast with a heavy accent. But on the page, it's the short words that carry the weight of linguistic difference. "Elle grogne toujours" (she's always grumbling) is unrecognizable in Provençal: *Delongo reno.* The idioms vary, too. If you're staring in French defiance, you "look at someone under his nose." In Provençal, the phrase is similar but not identical: *Branda li moustacho en quaucun.* You wag his mustache.

The standard Provençal grammar dates from 1952. It observes that a few sounds must be pronounced in un-French ways. *Ch* needs to lose its northern softness and acquire a "ts" sound — so while *chin* is close to a French dog on the page, it becomes "tsin" in the mouth. *Machoto,* a Provençal barn owl, looks Spanish but sounds Japanese. The language is full of triphthongs, as in *pièi* (then) and *biòu* (beef). Unlike French and English, it regularly omits personal pronouns in front of verbs, so that phrases like "I am," "we are," and "you are" are each expressed by a single word: *siéu, sian,* and *soun.* The author of the grammar, Xavier de Fourvières, is usually as rigorous and unsmiling as you might expect, but even a grammarian can't help having fun with interjections. The language, you can thus be assured, is rife with expressions of aversion and disgust, from *Bouai!* to *Puai!* and from *Isso!* to *Pòu!*

To venture far beyond what academic linguists would consider permissible, it might even be said that the sound of Provençal bears something of the same aesthetic relationship to the sound of French that the landscapes of Paul Cézanne do to the landscapes of Claude Monet. French is full of silent consonants and soft endings. Its liquid notes quiver on the tongue, just as Monet's water-filled visions of Normandy shimmer on canvas. Provençal has a harder, rougher texture, reminiscent of Cézanne's dry light. The French version of an insulting Provençal rhyme, about the supposedly flea-ridden cushions made in the village of Cabrières, goes like this: *À Cabrières / ils font des coussins / pleins de puces.* Provençal looks similar: *A Cabriera / fan de coissinieras / plenas de nieras.* But it gives the jaw more work to do.

Today the region enjoys a reputation for picturesque splendor: outsiders see Provence as fashionable, even glamorous. It wasn't always so. Nini told me that until the 1840s, when Italian laborers dug an irrigation canal that brought water to the fields around Saint-Rémy, even tomatoes were absent from the local diet. Provençal speakers in the past dined on onions and beans, rarely accompanied by meat. Country life was often a matter of sheer grinding poverty. And so, leaving their stony fields to be battered and dried by the sun, farming families moved to the cities: Marseille, Nice, Avignon . . . Contrary to its popular image, Provence now ranks among the most urbanized regions of France. The old language still has a foothold in remote villages, but no village is remote enough to escape the stresses, fractures, and opportunities of a modern economy. Peasants who have lingered stubbornly in their ancestral *mas* can turn into millionaires overnight if they choose to sell.

It was, then, Avignon where I looked next for news of Provençal: Avignon, the domain of medieval popes; the city where Petrarch met Laura, a vision of beauty who inspired so much of his poetry. Nini, who takes a fierce pride in local tradition, had shown me a petition about the Provençal language from an Avignon group called Parlaren. The group's president, Jean-Claude Roux, invited me to his home to discuss the future of Provençal. I was about to enter a linguistic war zone.

Roux lives in a less than fashionable district outside the medieval walls. An Islamic butcher's shop is a couple of minutes' walk away, not far from a side street named Impasse Pétrarque (perhaps some well-educated bureaucrat had wanted to make a literary point). Orange paper pumpkins hung in an upstairs window of the school beside Roux's house, and a lizard no bigger than a child's finger scuttled through a fence into the playground. Roux, a big man in a flowery shirt, met me at his gate. He ushered me through the garden, where a ladder stood propped against a tall persimmon tree. Fat, reddish orange fruits were visible among the higher branches. "They come from the Orient," Roux remarked, "but they grow very well here. This tree has been fruiting for a month already." He gave a barking laugh. "Maybe persimmons will become traditional to Provence!"

And why not, anyway? A culture can't hope to survive if its users resist change on all fronts. When a language ceases to invent or borrow words, it's surely in its death throes. Even Nini, a staunch believer that "Provençal can gain ground only by virtue of its traditions," had gone on to say, "But they have to be real traditions, ones that the young can take part in. Not just the sort that tourists applaud. Not just what people call 'folklore,' but a culture that is truly alive."

Roux showed me into a big front room where papers and magazines were piled in shambling heaps, among them copies of the magazine he publishes nearly every month: *Li Nouvello di Prouvènço*. The magazine gives his name a little differently: Jan-Glaude Roux. In French his surname is pronounced "Roo"; in Provençal it turns into "Rooss." From his name onward, the man has a double identity. He also has demands.

"What we want," he said, "is for Provençal to be officially recognized as a regional language of France, in exactly the same way that Breton and Basque are indisputable regional languages. We'd also like Provençal to be taught to young people in the region, no matter where their families come from. It's absolutely untrue to say that learning Provençal is a useless exercise. From the moment you begin to live here, you're faced by the Provençal identity and the Provençal character. That simply has to be recognized."

It sounded plausible to me at the time. Provençal is a proper language, Roux kept insisting, with at least seven dialects: one for Marseille, one for the Rhône Valley, one for the Alps, and so on. What's spoken in south central and southwestern France, he assured me, is a separate though related language. Occasionally I felt a certain unease about the politics behind his polemic: "Half of all the people in Provence do not have a Provençal origin. A lot of them arrived here from north Africa. And so we find ourselves in a very delicate situation. Provençal people are obliged to share their resources with others who don't come from Europe." No hint that immigrants might mean anything more than a dilution and a threat.

In conversation, Roux emphasized the health of his language. He claimed that it has as many as two hundred fifty thousand speakers. He told of a Web site. He said that books continue to appear in Provençal. He mentioned a weekly TV show featuring *Tintin* in Provençal translation. But copies of his magazine had a somewhat different tone. Though many of the words eluded me, my French and basic Spanish allowed me to work out the gist. And it was clear that an article on the TV programming now available to Bretons and Berbers in France also deplored the lack of broadcasts in Provençal.

An ornate wooden dresser stood on one side of the room. The photos on top showed a blond boy and girl, all smiles, who live in the Dordogne, a few hours northwest of Provence.

"Do you talk to your grandchildren in Provençal?" I asked.

Roux's answer was uncharacteristically brief: "That's difficult."

He invited me to a Provençal class he would be giving the following night in an old district of Avignon. Searching for the classroom, I lost my way among the sinuous narrow roads of the walled city. Voices I heard in the twilit streets were speaking Arabic — Muslims in France now outnumber practicing Catholics — but the small businesses had names like Liberty's Bar, Indian Ranch Market, Hot Attitude, O'Neill's Irish Pub, Dock Games Center, even Bloomsbury's English Tea Shop. In twenty-first-century Avignon, Provençal is at best a fourth language. Signs in English wished me a HAPPY HALLOWEEN — a festival that has taken France by storm. Only a funeral home was trying to promote the indigenous tradition that Halloween has supplanted. FOR ALL SAINTS, its placard urged (in French), THINK ABOUT THE CLEANING OF YOUR TOMB.

Roux's class met in an upstairs room beside a medieval church. Nine students, four or five of them beyond retirement age, were sitting at a long table under harsh fluorescent lights. One man sported the first beret I'd seen in France. Beside him sat a woman with bright red lipstick, dyed chestnut hair, and (sadly for her pronunciation) no teeth. A black-and-white Michelin map of coastal Algeria decorated one of the walls — a map that must have been printed at least forty years earlier, when Algeria was French property.

Like the Yuchi class I had witnessed in Sapulpa, this one was pitched to beginners. Roux gave the verb *estre* a nationalist spin — "When you learn English or German, you start with the verb 'to have.' But for us, 'to be' is the universal verb, and so we start with that." A portable blackboard stood at the front of the room, and Roux repeatedly filled it with grammar in capital letters, his belly protruding from his check shirt as he bent to write and erase, write and erase. "Remember," he warned, "*estre* is its very own auxiliary." His students had little chance to speak Provençal, and when they did Roux was quick to correct them. He was particularly keen to make sure their spelling was correct. For no apparent reason, he launched into a lecture about the warring twelfth-century dynasties of Barcelona and Toulouse. I began to lose track of time, listening to occasional footsteps on the stairs, a car's horn in the gathering night, the bells that pealed from the stone tower next door . . . The class was looking expectantly at me.

"Were there questions you wanted to ask, monsieur?" Roux repeated.

What I really wanted to know was why, given these students' hunger to master a fading language, Roux was keeping them so quiet. But instead I posed a standard question: "Why are you interested in learning Provençal?"

"Our grandparents spoke the language," one elderly lady replied, "and we still carry the memory. It remains in the ear."

"It's a sort of intermediary," a younger woman suggested, "through which we can learn an entire history."

"And are you learning it for cultural reasons only," I added, "or do any of you have a political motive?"

The reasons were purely cultural, they said. Roux gave me a sour look: "Maybe you were expecting them to show up with Kalashnikovs, *quoi?*"

I asked no further questions. But as I made my way through the dim square outside, a black-goateed man named Guillaume — the youngest member of the class — caught up with me and asked if I'd like to talk some more. We walked to the small apartment that he shares with his girlfriend, Céline, a student of medieval art. Guillaume was training to become an archaeologist. Sitting on a kitchen chair, I drank a glass of sweet pale muscat and listened to a familiar refrain.

"I know Provençal is a rich language," Céline said. "My grandparents spoke it a lot. But my parents used it much less, and I hardly understand it at all. We know something is being lost. We're just not quite sure what it is."

Neither is anyone else. Roux's contention that Provençal is a true language remains a matter of strenuous debate. Next afternoon, in search of a second opinion, I strolled past bookstores, bakeries, and cybercafés to the University of Avignon.

Patric Choffrut's office lies in a complex of buildings that center on a medieval convent. Before the university moved in, the main building served as a hospital — Nini Albertini worked here as a nurse. Choffrut, who was sporting a natty tie, dark shirt, and jeans, proved to be a middle-aged bundle of intellectual activity. He kept looking for books and papers on his overflowing shelves, then either brandishing them in triumph or swearing in fury if he failed to unearth them. One of those papers was an election brochure from 1998, when he ran as a candidate for the regional parliament, representing a party called Région-Provence. I might have voted for him if I'd been living here; the platform seemed clear and forward-looking ("A European region open to the future . . . A cultural identity that must not disappear . . . A land of integration"). But Choffrut won only two percent of the vote.

He turned some of his energy to the European Federation of Maisons de Pays, an association of thirty-two minority groups trying to sustain local cultures under siege. Like Phil Gawne on the Isle of Man, he engages in political activism; but, like Richard Grounds in Oklahoma, he performs his work inside a university. Choffrut is now the federation's president. He showed me its new directory, which is dedicated to "those whose language and existence are threatened . . . to all the gagged peoples." The English version of the directory has the inelegant title *Those Europeans Who Want to Speak and Live Their Language.*

It describes the idiom of his own region in even less elegant terms: "Provençal Occitan-Oc language." When I asked Choffrut to explain the wording, he was forthright: "Provençal is not a language. It's a dialect of Occitan."

"But when I was talking to Jean-Claude Roux —"

Choffrut exploded. "Roux and his friends say that Provençal is a separate language, but this is linguistically stupid. It's also political suicide. These people are right-wing, rural, narrow-minded — they've frozen Provence in the nineteenth century. They're *passéistes.* What they're doing, those assholes, is weakening us just at the time when we're fighting for recognition from France."

"Assholes" is not a free translation, by the way; we were speaking English. Following the breakup of Choffrut's marriage, he moved from Paris to Avignon — leaving his academic colleagues in the capital speechless with amazement — and began to live with a woman from Minneapolis. Unlike the painstaking English of most French people, Choffrut's is fast and profane.

For him, the language still hanging on in nooks and crannies of Provence is but one variety of a larger entity called Occitan. After the collapse of the Roman Empire, he explained, Latin evolved into a pair of related idioms across the territory that is now France. The names that distinguished these idioms were the names for "yes": *langue d'oil* and *langue d'oc.* In Paris and the north, *oil* evolved into *oui* and *langue d'oil* into standard French. Across the south of France, things were more complicated. The *langue d'oc* gave birth to several dialects, one of them being Provençal.

If a Provençal man met a woman from Gascony in southwestern France, they might be hard-pressed to understand each other's accent.

But pronunciation is not everything; whatever their accent, people from Dublin, Houston, and Sydney all speak something they call English. Likewise, the Provençal man and the Gascon woman would be using a common language. Choffrut calls it Occitan; others prefer the old name *langue d'oc*. (Roux, however, would say the man and woman were speaking two different languages.) In linguistic terms, Choffrut believes, it's impossible to separate the Occitan dialects of southern France from Catalan (spoken in northeastern Spain), Balearic (on the island of Majorca), and Piedmontese (in northwestern Italy). We divide these idioms out of habit and convenience, Choffrut suggested; but the divisions don't reflect the facts. To him, "There is only one language of Latin. The difference in language is a difference in our heads."

That's a provocative, subversive statement — and an overstatement, no doubt. But it reflects a central truth about the way language is actually used, as opposed to the way languages are generally written about. Most people in Barcelona and Paris would scoff at the notion that they speak the same language. Yet Catalan imperceptibly shades into Occitan, Occitan blurs into the jumble of Alpine idioms known as Franco-Provençal, and Franco-Provençal slides into a regional version of mainstream French. Where does a language end? Where does a dialect begin? No hard and fast answers exist, especially when a language (or dialect) has never been adopted by a modern government. "A language is a dialect with an army," one old joke goes. It's often close to the truth. But not since the Middle Ages has Occitan (or Provençal) had soldiers. Free from the demands of generals, politicians, and civil servants — nobody has ever had to pay income tax in the language, either — Occitan has kept a high degree of flexibility in both its syntax and its vocabulary. Even a well-known word like *mas* has rivals: elsewhere in Occitan territory, a farmhouse can be a *granja* or a *bòria*. Not surprisingly, that Gascon woman and that Provençal man might end up communicating in French.

Years ago Choffrut made a deliberate and radical choice. One of his grandfathers lived in the Auvergne region of south central France; his other grandfather came from Provence. His heritage also includes Alsace, Paris, and Algeria. Out of this hodgepodge of possibilities, Choffrut decided, in effect, to create his own roots. Identifying with his grandfathers, eventually moving to Avignon, he became an Occitaniste. It was an act of will and imagination. At the university, he teaches Occitan Studies.

Intellectually speaking, the Occitan movement makes a good deal of sense. The trouble is that most people (even in France) don't base their lives on intellectual decisions, nor do they choose their roots. Inadvertently, *Those Europeans Who Want to Speak and Live Their Language* hints at the difficulties facing the Occitan cause. Many minority cultures are easy to define: Basque, Breton, Welsh, and so on. But the directory includes entries for four regions of southern France, one of them being Provence. It also has a separate entry for Occitan as a whole. I take this to be a tacit recognition that the movement's expansive ideals must be grounded in local communities. Even Choffrut talks not only about Occitan but also about Provençal.

"I used to speak it more frequently," he confided. "Ten years ago I spoke it almost every day. Now it depends on who I meet. I used to joke around with the secretaries in Provençal. They understand it, but they won't answer back. Once you've started off speaking French to someone, you have to force yourself to speak Provençal." Choffrut calls himself "left-leaning"; as an adult, he converted to Judaism. A politically engaged lover of ideas, a gourmet cook who knows his wine, a rumpled-looking professor who spent much of his youth in Paris — you'd have a hard time finding anyone who conforms more closely to the stereotype of a French intellectual. Yet he rejects the adjective. "We're so weak," he said; "the French have split us up into so many different units. At the Revolution, the French imposed their laws on us. We're not respected. That's why I'm so mad." The slander against Occitanistes is that "we're dangerous, we're terrorists, we want to separate from France." But a minute later: "We are not French!"

He's not ready to concede defeat. If and when France ratifies the Council of Europe's charter of minority languages, either the Occitanistes or the Provençalistes stand to gain official recognition, heightened status, and serious money. But for the moment, nobody can agree on what the language is, where its borders lie, or how many people speak it. (Estimates for Occitan vary wildly, from well under one million to well over three million; for Provençal, the guesses are far lower.) Choffrut pointed to a group of bilingual Occitan schools — the Calandreta network — as proof of growth. Yet you only have to scratch the surface of his optimism to find bitterness rising like a welt. "We're very touchy about the correctness of our language," he admitted. "You want so much to preserve it, you are killing it."

Was the language growing, or was it dying? Choffrut has a friend,

Bernard Vaton, who lives in the nearby town of Orange. As a parent, Vaton serves on the board of the local Calandreta school — the name in Occitan means both "lark" and "young apprentice." He also teaches the language to adult beginners. Thinking his evening class might make a good contrast to the methods of Jean-Claude Roux, I caught the train to Orange. A short, bald man was waiting outside the station in a two-seat BMW.

Neither his teaching nor his Occitan leanings paid for the car: Vaton works as an architect and urban planner. As he swerved through the ancient town — I forced myself to listen to his polemic, though I'd have preferred to concentrate on the magnificent Roman buildings we were zooming past — he told me that throughout the south of France there are more than thirty Calandreta schools and roughly seventeen hundred students. (It sounds like a lot — until you remember that the region's population is about thirteen million.) The movement's heartland lies in the southwest, toward the Spanish border. His own area, Vaton conceded, is a weak link in the chain; the Orange school is one of just three in Provence.

The school has taken over a former agricultural college on the edge of town. As we approached it, I mentioned the humiliations that Nini's mother and other Provençal speakers had endured long ago. Vaton gave an eloquent shrug: "I spoke Occitan to my parents, but if I used it in school, I'd get my knuckles rapped too. I used an Occitan word in an essay once, and the teacher wrote 'barbarous regionalism' in the margin. He also lowered my grade." He pulled into the school's parking lot just as I noticed black graffiti on a wall across the road: ORDURE and LA FRANCE AUX FRANÇAIS. The nation's constitution is unbending: "French is the language of the Republic." To be an Occitaniste in Provence, even now, is to run a certain risk.

Vaton showed me around. Lights had come on in the asphalt playground where some pupils were kicking a soccer ball around, waiting for their parents to pick them up. The Calandreta facilities looked somewhat makeshift, its few computers clearly secondhand — to attract pupils, it tries to avoid charging fees, even though the government classifies it as a private school. "We'd like to be in the public system," Vaton said, "but a lot of people still have the idea that if you teach in a minority language, you must be against the republic." The fund-raising campaigns rarely stop. Lately the school received a large donation from a woman who lives on the Caribbean island of Martinique.

The evening class consisted of four women, two of whom had children at the school. "I'd hoped for more of you," Vaton admitted. Mattresses and teddy bears lay piled up at the back of the classroom. Even in an Occitan school, rules of French grammar were inscribed on the walls: "Règles de clause," "Les signes de ponctuation," and so on. Vaton rolled up his sleeves, took a deep breath, and started to lecture in French. An hour later, he was still lecturing. By comparison, Roux had been a model of enlightened pedagogy. One of the few times Vaton stopped for breath came when his mobile phone rang, emitting a shrill parody of Beethoven's "Ode to Joy."

He talked about the need for a common Latin parlance: "It's not normal that people who speak in Romanian, Spanish, Italian, and French should have to communicate with each other in English." He talked about how the troubadours had codified the language, "and that's why we all write the same. If everyone wrote the language the way it's pronounced in their neighborhood, it would be chaos." Like Roux, he veered into dynastic history, talking about François I and Eleanor of Aquitaine before jumping ahead eight centuries to the Institute of Occitan Studies: "It took off during the last war, when people in the Resistance spoke Occitan so the Germans couldn't understand what they were saying." Swinging his arms with enthusiasm, he told the class they mustn't be afraid to speak Occitan — and gave them little chance to do so. "The story of the tonic accent is very important," he declared. "I insist on it."

The women dispersed into the night. "I've been teaching like this for twenty-five years," Vaton said. "I really enjoy it."

Driving me back to the railway station, he stopped beside the great Roman stadium. "I grew up just over there," he said with a casual wave. "This is what inspired me to become an architect." In such a town the very air reeks of history — eight and a half centuries ago a count of Orange was among the proudest and wittiest of troubadours. Opposite the stadium stands a bilingual plaque in honor of Frédéric Mistral. *Aurenjo la pompouso,* he called the city. The French version changes *pompouso* to "opulent." Vaton drove on toward the tracks.

The train back to Avignon was even faster than his BMW. In short order the Popes' Palace appeared in the distance. Walking out of the bright station, I recalled Patric Choffrut's bitter answer when I asked him why Occitan's survival touched him so deeply: "The question is moot. Twenty years ago it was extremely important for me. Now I really

believe it's fucked. We're dead. The language is dead. I think it's disgust-
ing. To me, it's a massacre. If they finally kill us, we will have lost a trea-
sure."

I respect Choffrut's passion as well as his intellect. But I don't believe
that Occitan is dead, nor do I think that "they," the French, are the only
villains of the piece. Infighting can wound a language just as grievously
as frontal assaults. While the causes that endanger languages cut across
all continents, each language also has unique tales of loss and resistance.
Provençal stands out not only because of the fading glory of its literature but also because of the mutual hatred among its would-be saviors.

When Mistral created a Provençal spelling, speakers in Avignon and
Arles were delighted. But others in the south of France were far less
happy — a division that persists to this day. Jean-Claude Roux, laying so
much emphasis on proper spelling in his beginners' class, was insisting that the students write in Mistralian style, as opposed to Occitan.
Before reading her poems Nini Albertini had told me, "I refuse to accept that Provençal, the language for which Mistral battled so fiercely,
should be made to disappear into Occitan." By contrast, Patric Choffrut
had charged that "Mistral cut us off from the other Latin languages.
The way he writes makes it very weird. I admit, his version is written
more like the way the language is sounded, but it has less relation with
all the other Latin languages."

The result is a dimming language (or dialect, if you prefer) whose remaining speakers feud about spelling. When Orange was run by social-
ists, the council put up bilingual signs beside the roads leading into
town: ORANGE/AURENJA. That's how you spell the place in Occitan.
But a conservative party won the next election and within a few weeks,
egged on by Roux, it changed the signs to Mistralian spelling: ORANGE/
AURENJO.

I needed to learn more about Mistral. The poet's *mas* is now a museum, and one weekend afternoon I drove to Maillane — the quintessence of a sleepy country town — hoping to find fire there in the embers
of his language. The chic restaurant across the road had a Provençal
name: L'Oustalet Maienen (the Maillane house). But its menu was in
French alone. So was the long list of regulations in the entrance hall of
the Musée Mistral. And so was the expensive guidebook. "It's thanks to
Frédéric Mistral," the guide informed us — I was one of six people on
the obligatory tour — "that Provençal is still spoken a little today." A

woman from Saint-Rémy, she knew where the land mines lay. "Frédéric Mistral was not against France," she declared, keeping a wary eye on a couple of Parisian visitors. "He simply hoped that France would become a federation."

The guide did not explain that Mistral was a late offshoot of the Romantic movement, which swept across western Europe in the decades before his birth. As such, he inherited that movement's exaltation of language. Provençal, in Romantic eyes, was capable of collective grandeur, and Mistral was determined to ensure it lived up to its potential. But if the Romantic movement gave language the power to forge national identities, it also turned language into a weapon. Language could break nations as well as make them. In an age when great writers exerted a political influence undiluted by the pollsters, public relations experts, lobbyists, and media consultants of later decades, France had reason to be wary of the man.

We drifted through the rooms on the ground floor. Paintings of Mistral jostled photographs of Mistral below busts of Mistral beside statues of Mistral. Usually he sported a wide-brimmed hat above a wispy beard. Looking at a faded photo of a portly, hatless gentleman who was evidently not Mistral, I discovered it was Theodore Roosevelt, who took a moment from his presidential duties in 1907 to send the poet a signed picture of himself with "high regard and esteem." In the next room, Pope Pius X proved to have done the same. The kitchen had a gun hanging high on a wall, its barrel aimed at a painting of a *nature morte*. In the heavy afternoon, I felt as inert as the canvas fruit.

And then we climbed the wide staircase, and my mind woke up. An engraved proclamation outside a bedroom was dated 8 September 1940. It conveyed the homage of Marshal Pétain — "head of the French state" — to Frédéric Mistral.

September 1940. The Luftwaffe and the Royal Air Force are dogfighting in the skies over Britain; the German army has overrun Belgium and the Netherlands, and its soldiers are ensconced in Paris; but in Vichy, the leader of a puppet regime can spare the time to celebrate a writer who has been dead for twenty-six years. Mistral deserves homage, Pétain says, because he was inspired by the Latin race. Following the poet's superb example, the marshal declares his "invincible resistance to all those who would *nous déclasser, nous niveler, nous déraciner*." It's a hard yet crucial phrase to translate: Pétain will resist all those who would bring us down in the world, who would flatten us out, who would tear us away from our roots. In quasi-fascist circles, *déraciné* was often a code word for "Jew." No wonder the Resistance fighters who spoke the southern language wanted no part of Mistral.

I had just reached the section where Pétain promises that a glorious new France will soon emerge, grounded in the country's traditional virtues — virtues which Mistral had supposedly incarnated — when the guide realized I was paying the text too much attention. "It was actually written by Charles Maurras," she hastily said. "He admired Mistral very much. Now, come and see the poet's bedroom . . ."

But I had no interest in his blankets and bedpans. It wasn't just the lingering taint of fascism: Mistral was a poet fighting to save a beleaguered culture; he died long before the Nazis came to power. You can't hold him responsible for the sins of future disciples who would swoon in the embrace of fascist apologists like Maurras. (In Brittany, too, the Nazis tried to bolster a minority language with the aim of weakening the French state; today some Breton nationalists refuse to condemn their collaborating forebears.) What bored me was Mistral's aura of sanctity. He accepted, even exulted, in the role of grand old man. After his death Provençal would become a language of the old, the poor, the out-of-the-way — and a few scruffy activists.

I forced myself to remember the initial radicalism of his cause. The year before Mistral's birth saw the appearance of an instruction manual called *Les Provençalismes corrigés*. It was popular enough to go through many editions between 1829 and 1880. The manual's author, J. B. Reynier, was determined that "correct" French should vanquish all local expressions. He saw Provençal terms as a menace. No word was too trivial to arouse his ire. In place of *Qué!* (What!), Reynier told his readers, "Say, according to the circumstances, *Hé! Hé bien! Quoi! Que dis-tu? Qué* is a Provençal word which must absolutely be avoided when speaking French." Such was the intellectual climate in which Mistral grew up. The irony is that although he always called his language Provençal, what he created or re-created was a composite, somewhat along the lines of Occitan.

He lived in Maillane, but when people called him a lion they situated the lion in his favorite city, Arles. I went there on a warm morning near the end of October. According to a time-honored Provençal saying, *Pèr Sant-Jude e Sant-Simoun, / Li champ cargon lou mantèu blanc* — "On St. Simon and St. Jude's Day, the fields put on their white coat." (It sounds a lot better in Provençal.) But the day's golden sunlight carried no sign of frost, let alone snow, even on the high, boar-filled hills. One of the minor side effects of global climate change is to render the old sayings untrue.

Arles was the capital of the Roman province of Gaul, and its ancient grandeur is still evident. I liked its slightly dilapidated air, the whiff of drains among the Roman columns: the city doesn't bother to tidy itself up for visitors. Yet it's not averse to hype, as I discovered by reading a fragment of Mistral's verse on a plaque in the town hall:

> Arle!
> O, tu que siés estado
> Tout ço que l'on pòu èstre,
> La metroupòu d'un empèri,
> La capitalo d'un reiaume
> E la matrouno de la liberta . . .

Not just a capital and an imperial metropolis, but the matron of freedom as well? No wonder Mistral was so popular here. Of course he may have sung the praises of every town in Provence. The Museo Arlaten, the fruit of his Nobel, would give anyone pause for thought.

As I walked in, a middle-aged woman in traditional costume welcomed me and took my money. When I asked if she or any other staff members spoke Provençal, she looked a little nervous and said, "Nobody here, monsieur." I pressed the point and was referred to a Madame Pinet at the city's tourist office. "And where is that?" "Near McDonald's."

I decided to see the museum first. A glass case in the entryway holds the Swedish Academy's certificate to Mistral, signed by Alfred Nobel. But once you climb the stairs you have to fight your way past a speechless army of bric-a-brac: shoes, wigs, dolls, shawls, brooches, costumed mannequins, religious paraphernalia, all of it belonging to a world that seems as distant from our own as that of the troubadours. A framed magazine from 1904 shows a huge crowd crammed into a Roman theater. "The feast of the Virgins of Arles": entertainment for the masses. A photographer had captured Mistral in the midst of the decorative virgins, listening to a poem being declaimed in Provençal. It was picturesque. It was all too picturesque.

The old, handwritten labels have Provençal names. The newer, clearer labels are all in French. I learned that in Provençal an ungainly zinc bath from the nineteenth century is a *bagnadouiro;* a copper warming pan (its twin had been hanging on the wall of Roux's office) is an *escaufeto*. How many people need such words now?

Beyond the traditional flutes, the traditional jugs, the traditional bowls — beyond all this lies a shrine. The shrine is meant to be the climax of a visit. A small room, it contains the usual bust of the poet on a shelf. But in the middle of the room is a cradle. VISITOR, declares a sign in French, BOW PIOUSLY BEFORE THIS CRADLE. IT IS THE CRADLE OF FRÉDÉRIC MISTRAL, THAT IS TO SAY OF THE RENAISSANCE OF ONE OF THE MOST BEAUTIFUL LANGUAGES SUNG ON THE LIPS OF MEN. The cradle stands behind tall sheets of glass, resting on an ornate wooden base where carved cherubs frolic. Inside the cradle lie a baby's dress (black with blue stripes), a lace cap, a leather pillow — and, where the head should be, some long strands of hair. Something, you might think, is missing.

Enough already! I left the Museo Arlaten without either bowing piously or finding the oil painting featured in its brochure, a painting in which this cult of grandeur attains its ridiculous height: Mistral surrounded by the main characters from his poems, all of whom gaze adoringly while a shaft of golden light bathes the poet from above — a bookish messiah, transfigured among a choir of literary saints. When the messiah died, did he take his language up to heaven?

The metaphor is only partly mine. Never shy of a rousing image, Mistral once compared the Félibrige to Jesus' apostles, who received the gift of tongues at Pentecost: "When our Redeemer descended from heaven to earth, the official, universal, and obligatory language was that of the Caesars. The language was no less official than the slavery of the time. But Jesus, the Son of God, wanting his disciples to have in their hands a means of freeing the people, performed a miracle for them, which . . . approximates to our Félibrean cause." The apostles were given "languages of fire." Thus equipped, they went out to remake the world. The story can be read as a biblical defense of language diversity, exactly what the story of Babel appears to explain as a curse. With Jesus as well as Mistral on their side, no wonder Provençal speakers in the nineteenth century felt inspired by the challenge.

Unfortunately, perhaps, the Félibrige did not confront the political and educational systems of France, which legitimize one language alone. Whether or not he confused himself with the Redeemer, Mistral made the mistake of thinking that his aesthetic, nonpolitical victories were enough. These victories could only be temporary, for he accepted the power structures that had already marginalized Provençal. He also sowed the seeds of future trouble by consistently favoring the dialect of Avignon and Arles over those of other cities in southern France. His best poetry, to be sure, stands up to time. But the meaning of his other triumphs has emptied away. Denied all status by a centralizing regime, his language faded during his illustrious career: even before his death, Mistral had turned into statues. Today, if Provençal is to have a hope of revival, it needs new metaphors, new modes of rebellion. What it doesn't need is the veneration of an unread poet — a veneration that tames, declaws, and all but castrates the man.

On the pavement outside the museum, a vendor had spread out cheap posters. Mistral was absent yet Píkachu was there, along with Bart Simpson, the Little Prince, the French World Cup–winning soccer team, and Che Guevara, miraculously transformed into a global consumer icon. A roundabout walk to the tourist office took me past the cultural center that Arles has established in its old Hôtel-Dieu, the hospital where Van Gogh recovered after slicing off his ear. At the library — now called not a *bibliothèque* but a *médiathèque* — I was told that nobody on the staff could speak Provençal, but perhaps if I drove to Saint-Rémy . . . In a bookstore owned by the publishing firm Actes Sud, I asked if they published anything in Provençal, and watched the young clerk's face break into a scowl before he answered *"Non, monsieur."* Why should this of all languages be a cause of shame? A women's clothing store had the name L'Arlésienne — but instead of wearing *la capello* or the ancient costumes of Arles, the mannequin in the window was dressed as a ghost in a witch's hat.

Madame Pinet was absent from the tourist office near the golden arches. Indeed, she might not return until tomorrow. In a very un-French style, the staff members were sporting badges that gave their first names alone. Martine passed me on to Francette, who consulted with Jacqueline — none of whom spoke a word of Provençal. So much for the lion's tongue in the lion's chosen city.

Once there was a writer who failed to revive a language.

Enough of cities. I decided to spend a morning wandering the wine-dark hills around La Roque Alric. The mayor's son-in-law was rumored to speak Provençal, and perhaps I could speak to him . . . But no, he would be hunting wild boar. As soon as light seeped through my bedroom window, I heard a crackle of gunshots in the distance. Not the wisest morning for a stroll.

Then Nini Albertini phoned up with an invitation. She knew an elderly gentleman in Saint-Rémy who still belonged to the Félibrige. Nearly a century after Mistral's death, it survives as a cultural body whose members, spread across the south of France, agree to promote what they call the "langue d'oc." Would I care to meet the man?

So I drove to Saint-Rémy again, found Nini waiting in her garden, and took her to the home of a retired civic functionary named Marcel Bonnet. Or, in Provençal spelling, *Marcèu* Bonnet. He lives in a stone house on a slope above the main square. Back in the years before his stroke, he would have had a pleasant walk to his job in the town hall. Now one side of his round, bespectacled face is twisted, and his speech and movements alike are heavy and slow.

It took some time for me to realize what a distinguished amateur scholar he is. At first, sipping his wife's homemade lemon wine and nibbling from a plate of olives, I didn't pay him enough mind. Sitting in the big dining room, its lights blazing against the shadows, I was content to listen to him and Nini rambling on about their childhood before the Second World War. "You went to the nuns' school," he said to her, "and I went to the lay school. Our grandparents didn't talk to each other. They would have been shocked to see us sitting in the same room like this." Imagining those decades of mutual silence in a small Provençal town, I thought: Some traditions deserve to die.

To be fair, the silence was a product of political and religious disputes; it had nothing to do with language. When Monsieur Bonnet first went to school, in 1928, more than half the boys in his class spoke Provençal. But now? His wife is not a speaker (she nodded with enthusiasm, her expression hard to interpret). When Monsieur Bonnet uses Provençal with friends, one of the main topics of conversation is how few of them are left to speak it. Nini gave a regretful nod. "We don't sing in the fields any longer," she said. "I think it was the tractor that did it."

I finished the lemon wine and wondered how much longer I had to stay. But then, spurred by a remark Monsieur Bonnet made about the Jews of Provence, I asked what he knew about Judeo-Provençal, also called Shuadit — a dialect (or language) that emerged in this area during the Middle Ages. Mass deportations under Marshal Pétain brought

Judeo-Provençal down in the world, flattened it out, tore it away from its roots. Its last speaker is said to have died in the 1970s.

Monsieur Bonnet livened up as much as his body would permit. Disregarding a protest from his wife, he moved ponderously to a book-filled study, its shelves protected from daylight by floor-length curtains at the window. He knew where to look. Within seconds he was trudging back, clutching a copy of *L'Astrado,* a bilingual journal published in the nearby city of Nîmes. The issue contained his lengthy essay — in Provençal only — about Judeo-Provençal. "But I'm not an educated man!" he protested again, and I was wishing I'd had the sense to disbelieve him sooner.

Only later, hours after I had left, did I wonder why he'd described and analyzed an extinct idiom in one that may soon join it. For Monsieur Bonnet is a pessimist. "The Provençal language is finished," he told me, oblivious to Nini's discomfort. Are members of the Félibrige supposed to say such things? For once, I wasn't asking questions. I was too busy looking at a small, leather-bound book he had retrieved from elsewhere in the study. *Poésies Hebraico-Provençales du Rituel Israélite Comtadin* had been published in Avignon in 1891: a trilingual edition in which a page of Hebrew verses was followed by a page alternating French and the purest form of Judeo-Provençal.

> J'ouvre mes lèvres en jubilation
> Ca co è lou gran mestre.
> La crainte de l'Éternel en partage
> Desur tambourin e viouloun . . .

I noticed the name of the translator: "His Majesty Dom Pedro II of Alcantara, emperor of Brazil." Was that Borges's ghost hovering at my shoulder?

Dom Pedro was an emperor in exile and poor health. He had ruled Brazil for more than fifty years. As well as carrying out his political duties, he translated Isaiah from Hebrew into Latin, and *Prometheus Bound* from ancient Greek into Portuguese. He knew a smattering of Sanskrit and Babylonian — and he wrote an essay in French for the *Grande Encyclopédie* about an Amerindian people called the Tupí. But in 1889, after he defied Brazil's big landowners by abolishing slavery, the old man was deposed by a coup. Dom Pedro fled to the south of France and set to work on the poetry of Judeo-Provençal. The book appeared just before his death.

The doorbell was ringing: Monsieur Bonnet had other guests. I handed back the *Poésies* with immense reluctance.

Nini was uncharacteristically quiet on the walk to the car. She was still troubled by her friend's conviction that Provençal — "the mistress of languages," she called it — was doomed. Had Mistral, after all, led to a dead end? I pointed out four children who were wearing Halloween masks as they roamed from door to door, plastic bags in their hands. But Nini wasn't in the mood for chitchat. She needed to sort out the language question. She needed to set her mind at rest.

Finally she settled on an image. She'd already used it in her poem "Lengo Nostro," but it would work in conversation too. The image might well be an illusion. No matter: remembering it, speaking it aloud, Nini would again be free to turn her thoughts to the world.

"To understand the fate of Provençal," she said, "think of an olive tree. I can remember a terrible frost we had in the 1950s, when some people said all the trees were dead. They said we'd have to turn to other crops. It's true the farmers had to cut away many, many dead branches, even some of the trunks. But the roots weren't dead at all. The roots were full of energy. And when the time was right, the olive trees came back to life."

Indeed, Provençal poetry did not come to an end with Mistral and his disciples. On my last day in Provence, in a little town called Apt, I met one of Mistral's heirs — a description that Sèrgi Bec might well reject. But surely there's a Mistralian defiance and cockiness in the title of one of Bec's many poetry collections, *Siéu un païs* (I Am a Country). I had found it on the shelves of a dingy bookstore in Arles. Published in 1980, *Siéu un païs* is a bilingual volume written in French and Provençal, prefaced by what the author calls "an open letter to the Occitanistes." In the letter he discusses both the necessity and the failure of Occitan.

Bec agreed to meet me at a local café and lead me back to his house. It was market day, and the streets of the old town were closed to traffic. Somehow I squeezed the car into a coffin-shaped space beside a plane tree, near a sign, supposedly in English, that warned: ATTENTION: SUBMERSIBLE PARKING. (If the Calavon River flooded, the parking lot would be submerged.) Perhaps the same translator was responsible for the English version of the town's tourist brochure. It reported that religion had once been "the main worry of life in Provence."

At lunchtime the market stalls began to close. But the odors of sausages and cheese, of fish and olives lingered until city workers hosed down the streets. I had to dodge a jet of water as I looked through the window of Apt's main bookstore. One of Bec's recent works was on display: an illustrated notebook of natural history. Yet like all the books in evidence, it was in French, and the author's first name was given not as "Sèrgi" but as "Serge." The bookstore had a yellow poster on the door, inviting parents of young children to attend an information session about a proposed bilingual school in French and Provençal. IT'S POSSIBLE! the poster said. I strolled to the café.

I'd never have found Bec's house if he hadn't shown me the way. Retrieving my car from the submersible parking, I followed his silver Renault up a hill overlooking the Calavon Valley and along the narrowest of lanes. The house was full of modern paintings, dried flowers, an oriental doll; its large rooms basked in untraditional light. I'd been scrutinizing the cover of *Siéu un païs,* which shows a worried-looking poet with thick dark hair and sideburns, wearing a corduroy jacket, hands in his pockets. Two decades later, the tall man smoking a cigarette across the dining room table had pale gray hair. But Bec didn't seem as old as sixty-seven. He had a sort of military uprightness — and as a young man, indeed, he'd served as a soldier with the French army in Algeria. Perhaps that experience had left him tired of useless wars. He was certainly tired of the linguistic battles still raging over Provençal.

"I've had enough of it," he told me. "I can't tolerate it — it's intellectual idiocy to be fighting over how a language should be written. And it extends as far as outright hatred. Fireballs have been thrown — it's unbelievable. But I'm not a traditionalist, I'm a man of today. All this nonsense about the traditional costume, I don't agree with it in the slightest. It irritates me. I even ask myself if I should go on writing in that language. And yet I love it."

In his open letter to the Occitanistes, Bec spoke as a veteran campaigner for the Occitan cause. By 1980 he had published eight books in Occitan, becoming recognized as one of its leading literary voices. But he'd grown disillusioned, feeling that while the movement had reason on its side, "it takes no account of subjective reality." The Occitan movement finds itself trapped in a ghetto of universities, he charged; it has failed to attract people who still live off the land, not to mention those who work in factories, shops, offices, and studios. Pure reason matters less than spoken words — the words that flow from the mouths of the living. If speakers of the language choose to think of it as Provençal, so be it.

Bec has maintained that principle ever since, balancing between the two hostile factions. Sometimes his later poems use Occitan spelling, sometimes Mistralian. He wants to keep his readers alert, hoping they'll see past a word's appearance. Yet many of his readers never realize he has dealings with the old language — in his novels, plays, and works of nonfiction, he writes in French. An author has to make a living, after all. Nobody could earn a week's breakfast writing in Provençal.

I asked him why he continues to use Provençal for his poetry, and although the question was hardly a new one, he struggled with it. "It's a language marvelously suited to poetry . . . But that's not the real reason. It's because, because, I'm a man of duty. I owe this much to my parents and my heritage. Provençal is not my mother tongue; my parents spoke French when I was around. But between themselves, they spoke Provençal. That's what I was bathed in, if you like." Strange and compelling, I thought, that an old man should feel he owes it to his parents to write poems in a language they chose to shun in his presence. Among poets, Provençal still has a certain charisma.

Bec shared my reservations about Frédéric Mistral. In fact, he went a lot further. "Mistral bores me stiff. All right, I'm exaggerating, but I can't stand the people who say, 'Mistral is all that matters' — the ones who can't get through a single speech without referring to Mistral. When I speak in public, I make a point of never quoting him. There are people, even now, who keep saying, 'Mistral has written . . .' Well, fine. But even if Mistral said otherwise, today you have to thresh the grain with a machine."

He paused to light another cigarette. "What he wrote was valuable for the period. But now it makes me sick. When they crown a queen of Arles in traditional costume and have a public reading of Mistral's poems, it's unbearable. In the end, it works against Provençal. Of course I want to preserve a sense of tradition, of rootedness. But I also want an openness to the world."

I had the disturbing impression of having stirred something up in Bec, something he preferred to leave untouched. Whatever subjects I raised — French fiction, the state of Provençal (or Occitan) publishing, even the bilingual school project in Apt — he dismissed with sardonic lucidity. The school project is a fine idea; but to move beyond the realm of ideas, it needs money and commitment. Don't hold your breath, he implied.

There was one more topic I had to broach. I was almost dreading it.

"And do you use Provençal in your daily life?"

"Of course," he said to my surprise. "But less and less. And partly it's because I find the words are missing. I speak Provençal to a certain extent when I go into a village. Sometimes there are meetings where I use it. But mostly, I speak it at funerals. The women gather together in one group, the men in another, and we speak in Provençal. The men talk about the harvest and they talk about hunting. It's curious — at that moment you feel the weight of tradition, and the tradition rises up again. At funerals, something leads us to speak spontaneously in Provençal."

Bec and his black setter walked out into the warm afternoon to see me off. He urged me to take care on the winding lane back to the main road. I waved goodbye, but I hardly saw the man any longer. There was a vision in my mind that refused to go away: a little crowd of people, most of them even older than the priest, who stand on the high steps outside a medieval church and gaze down toward the vineyards and olive groves of a gray-green valley. Their ears still ring with the music of departure — peace, eternal rest, perpetual light — and their minds are restless with the past. There, in that field, the dead one used to go courting; that was the grove struck by lightning in the great storm . . . But a horn sounds in the distance, and the people in the crowd become aware that they're not as strong as they would like: after a time, the complaining muscles and veins and bladders require them to move. As they shuffle down the church steps, taking precautions not to fall, they bid farewell to each other one more time in the language of their youth; they bid farewell to the language of their youth.

Melting at the Edges

L ANGUAGES CAN VANISH from all sorts of causes. Disease, warfare, genocide, political repression, sheer bone-grinding hardship: all these have killed their share. Natural disasters have destroyed a few; unnatural disasters, vastly more.

Eastern Canada, where I live, has not been left unscathed. The St. Lawrence Iroquoians — the people who discovered Jacques Cartier sailing down the great river in 1535 and who welcomed the explorer into their midst — disappeared within decades of Cartier's visit, probably because of their abrupt exposure to European illnesses. Like so many peoples in the Western Hemisphere, they had no immunity to invasion. A hundred years later, the Neutral people in what's now southern Ontario were overrun by warriors of the Iroquois Confederacy armed with new weapons and old hatreds. Some of the survivors joined up with the conquerors, but the Neutral language dissolved. The Beothuk — the original "Red Indians," fond of gracing their bodies and homes with ocher paint — fled from Irish and English settlers along the coasts of Newfoundland, only to starve in the desolate interior. Their language may well have evolved in isolation for several thousand years; all that remains of it are a few word lists, their reliability dismal.

Such are the casualties of history. Yet throughout history, even as languages died, new ones arose to take their place. Maori, Afrikaans, some Romany tongues, many of the sign languages, a host of creoles and pidgins: these are young languages, ones that diverged from their parent within historical time. And even now, on occasion, a language is born. Nicaraguan Sign Language dates only from the 1980s, when deaf children — brought together for the first time by a Sandinista government that aspired to educate them but had no idea how to go about it — created a linguistic system of their own and then began to transmit it to their elders.

Exciting though they are, such events are far outweighed by the massive loss of languages now occurring among indigenous peoples on every continent. To the ambitious, the rebellious, the curious, the disaffected — to the young, in a word — dominant cultures hold a magnetic power. And as we've seen in Oklahoma and Provence, mother tongues fade without the young. In Canada attrition, not repression, accounts for the disappearance of Scottish Gaelic from the Ottawa Valley, the Eastern Townships of Quebec, and most of the areas in the Maritime provinces where settlers used to speak it every day. Little by little, child by child, Gaelic froze on their lips. Warfare reduced the Hurons from a powerful nation to a mere remnant — a few thousand people living on the outskirts of Quebec City — but attrition led them to forsake the Huron language. The last elders to speak it died early in the twentieth century. To converse with Huron people today, you need to use French. In French Max Gros-Louis, a former chief of the Hurons, once told me: "We are a nation that doesn't have a language. This is almost shameful. It would be a matter of pride to take our language back."

Gros-Louis was aware of the force and beauty of what had been lost. In Huron, the verb we might translate as "to calm down" meant "to make the mind like a field prepared for planting." To say "They greeted him with respect" required but a single word: *tehonannonronkwanniontak*. Literally, "They greased his scalp many times." We know this — in fact, we still know a great deal about the language — because of the many grammars, gospels, and hymnbooks compiled by Jesuit and Recollet missionaries before the fall of New France. Huron, like Latin, has ended up as an idiom of ceremonial chants and leather-bound books. Unlike Latin, though, Huron has had little influence on surviving languages. Worn away to oblivion, it is a grandparent of nothing.

The process of language attrition can be both visible and audible. I had glimpsed it in the graffiti at Nguiu, where Tiwi is up against the allure of "gangsta games," and heard it in the streets of Avignon. Like so much else, the phenomenon is global. Attrition may be happening every day on the south shore of Baffin Island in the Canadian Arctic, in a small town named Kimmirut. This is an isolated spot — for much of the year the only access is by a small plane, which flies in two or three times a week when the weather allows — but isolation isn't what it used to be. The town's main language is Inuktitut, spoken by the Inuit (or as some outsiders persist in calling them, the Eskimos). The Inuit make up at least ninety percent of residents. They were never vanquished in battle; they never saw their land snatched away by outsiders; and unlike most of the other indigenous peoples in North America, they speak a traditional language that the reference books list as secure.

Stay a little while in Kimmirut, keeping your eyes open, listening to local people, and you're liable to find security melting at the edges.

The hunter veers off the frozen bay and drives his snowmobile up a narrow road into town. DRIVE SLOW, says a sign on a warehouse facing the sea. An April wind whines against the brightly painted houses, but in his skin boots, parka, and black tuque the hunter doesn't feel the cold. He is attentive — every time he arrives in the community, turning away from the big, heel-shaped rock formation that gives Kimmirut its name, he sees something new. For this outpost, nestling below its tiny airfield, is not his own place. He comes from a town on the mainland barrens, hundreds of miles away. All winter long, he has been staying with a few other young offenders at a treatment center — a cabin, really — an hour's ride from town. Living close to the land, eating country food like raw walrus, char, and caribou, speaking his ancestral language, the hunter has had a chance to heal.

He slows down as he passes the school and the scattered houses, some of them with tethered dogs in front, one with a pair of polar bear skins stretched out to dry on racks against the wall. Ravens are playing in the sunlit air. A road heads up to the police station, where a white officer lives; the young hunter has no reason to go that way. Instead he drives to the Co-Op — one of the town's two stores, and the only one that will make a purchase from an unknown carver like him. For the hunter is also an artist. Climbing off his snowmobile, he reaches inside his parka to be sure the sculpture is still intact. The sign on a wall of the building is in the southern language, the southern alphabet, and he ignores it.

He walks inside, waiting a few seconds for his eyes to adjust to the dim light. Then he pushes open a second door into a second world.

The store that enfolds him is selling cigarettes, detergent, blue jeans, tea bags, Canadian flags, fishing tackle, garbage cans, ammunition, brownish bananas, washing machines, baby formula, CDs of country music, socks, knives . . . English nouns are everywhere. A pound of Raisin Bran costs more than seven dollars. The hunter bypasses all this. He goes to the office of the Co-Op manager. The man is busy with paperwork, and the hunter has to stand outside his door for several minutes. He transfers his weight from one foot to another. In his parka he is beginning to feel hot.

"Now, Mr. Samuel," the manager calls in what the hunter does not recognize as a strong Newfoundland accent, "what have you got for me today?"

The hunter is not fluent in English. But the manager speaks no Inuktitut. The young man walks into the office and sits on the edge of a chair. He stares for a second at the manager's humming computer. With a nervous smile, he grabs at an inside pocket and pulls out a plastic bag containing a small, heavy, stylized bear. He carved it out of Baffin stone. Thousands of miles to the south, he has been told, shoppers are hungry for such carvings. The manager peers at the bear with his pale eyes. He turns it over, scrutinizing the rough paws.

"How much?" the manager says.

"Sixty dollars," says the hunter in a small voice. For the size of the stone, and the time he spent transforming it into a bear, he thinks it would be only right. He would have liked to ask for seventy.

"I don't see sixty. I see forty-five."

The hunter is disappointed, but other carvers have warned him that the manager will refuse to bargain. Authority belongs to him. Anyway the hunter's English is not yet good enough for him to defend the price he wants. He must improve it. Then he will be able to argue for what he deserves.

"Okay," he mutters.

The manager scribbles down the number on a slip of paper for the hunter to take to the store's cashier. She is an Inuk — a person — and she speaks the people's language. But she doesn't speak it loudly, or the manager would object. She intends to keep her job; she doesn't want a confrontation. The hunter pockets his money and quickly leaves. He could spend it all within two minutes if he stayed.

The cashier works another hour in the store. Then she goes upstairs for an afternoon shift as waitress in the pink-walled coffee shop. Her friend is still cleaning up from lunch. The only customer, staring out at the *Misty Michelle,* a fishing boat in the iced-up harbor, is a gray-haired southerner wearing a denim jacket. He is staying here for a month while he fixes trucks, snowmobiles, and other equipment at the airfield. Yesterday she heard him complain to the manager about "the natives." "A lot of 'em use their culture as an excuse not to do any work," the manager agreed. "I like hunting too, but I work here seven days a week." Another day she overheard the manager saying that one of her cousins, a hunter and carver with five young children, is "lazy as a cut dog." She had to bite her tongue to keep from asking exactly what "cut dog" means.

It's partly out of deference to the mechanic that she says hello to her friend in English. But also, in truth, she likes the money and the feeling of worth that a job gives her; and the job belongs to English. Occasionally, if the coffee shop is empty, she takes one of its old southern newspapers over to an arborite table, reads the photographs, and slowly puzzles out a story or two. At home, talking to her husband and her children, she prefers Inuktitut — except when they watch TV, of course. Sometimes she teases her husband because he doesn't catch the laugh-track jokes.

An Inuk comes in and sits down, his back to the window. The waitress recognizes him: he's a member of the family who suffered a snowmobile accident on the trail from Iqaluit to Kimmirut a few days ago. The family spent two nights on the tundra before setting off toward town and being rescued. The man is wearing a light jacket and army camouflage pants; sunglasses balance on top of his head. He orders a cup of tea and a cookie. When the waitress brings them over, she can't refrain from asking him questions.

"You guys make an igloo or what?"

"Tent," he says. His English is jerky. "We had everything. Right under the rock."

"How come you guys start walking?"

"Like, if you're not feeling too good, get out and do something. That's what my grandpa used to tell me." And then, thinking of his grandfather, he says a couple of sentences in his own language. The waitress retreats.

A few minutes later, having finished his tea, he gets up to leave. "*Tawauvusi*," he calls to the two women.

"Yeah, goodbye," the waitress says.

The man puts on his sunglasses and steps out into the sun. The angle and warmth of it tell him that soon the geese will be flying north over Baffin: it's almost time for the spring hunt. Tall grasses and a broken-off willow already stick up above the snow. The man is thinking in Inuktitut again when he hears a voice saying, "Afternoon, young fellow!" He needs a few moments to realize who is speaking: a former police officer from somewhere in Ontario who moved up to Kimmirut the previous year to work as the town administrator. The right words of response are slow to arrive on his lips.

With barely fifty houses and four hundred residents, Kimmirut ranks as one of the smaller communities in the young territory of Nunavut, a word that means "our land." Inuktitut is an official language of the territory. But the town's administrator, its wildlife officer, its policeman, the managers of the hotel and both the stores, the school's principal, most of its teachers, the coordinator of the visitor center, and the airport manager are all *qallunaat*— southerners. Only a few of them can easily function in Inuktitut.

The administrator is not among that few. As he stands outside the Co-Op, clutching a rented Hollywood video, he wonders why it took the rescued hunter so long to answer a friendly greeting. The reticence of the locals sometimes annoys him. There is so much he wants to do for this place — so many changes he could make! He'd like to introduce a bank branch, but although he has tried to explain the concept of interest to several Inuit, he's not sure that they entirely grasp it.

"Hello! Hello!" a small child calls out to him in English.

"Hello there! How ya doin' today?" he responds.

"Hello good!" says another child, giggling. She's dressed in a T-shirt, pants, and shoes.

"And a very good afternoon to you. You must be feeling a little chilly, I guess."

"What?"

With a wide smile, the administrator gets back on his snowmobile and chugs off to the school. He wants to see the principal to check on the details of a bingo game to be held that evening in the gym. Profits will go toward paying off a debt that was incurred last fall, when twenty Kimmirut teenagers flew south as part of a student exchange. In return, twenty southern kids stayed here for nearly a week, stretching hospitality to its limits in a town chronically short of living space. The students have promised to keep in touch by e-mail. A laptop will be among the prizes tonight. But the jackpot prize is a return flight to Ottawa: a chance to escape to a world full of surprising objects like trees and squirrels, fences and traffic lights. A world of power.

Somewhere a dog is howling. Nearing the school, the administrator waves at an old man perched on a low crate in a crawlspace underneath a house. The man's face is thin and bespectacled, but his hair is still thick and black. Houses in the town rest on metal stilts without foundations, and this crawlspace happens to be the studio of one of Kimmirut's most celebrated artists. Many years ago one of his carvings was an official wedding gift to Prince Charles and Princess Diana. The old man wonders, occasionally, what became of it. He began, decades ago, by carving oil lamps and slivers of ivory; but the money proved best for stone bears, and now he does little else. Using a small ax, he chips away at a block of serpentine. His fingers are familiar with the cold. At the moment, coated by dust, the stone looks gray. But when he's finished, it will be a dark and glossy green.

While he works, he listens to the Arctic service of CBC Radio. "Honey, I'm Home" by Shania Twain leads into an interview between the show's host and the head of the Kitikmeot Corporation, in the faraway town of Taloyoak. The old man tries to follow the talk, but the gist of it keeps eluding him. Even in an exchange between two Inuit, strange terms keep pushing in: *Red Dog Mine, cooperation, mining symposium, Aboriginal Achievement Awards* . . . The artist was born in a hunting camp and lived on the land, remote from any community, until the 1970s. He couldn't go back there now, and not only because of his age. His son, who instructs youngsters at the local school, has married a teacher from the south. Sometimes the grandchildren speak in English, and he has to ask his son what's on their minds. Their Inuktitut conversations, he has begun to notice, are sprinkled with the hammer sounds of their mother's tongue. What is this *see-dee-rom* he keeps hearing about? He knows the meaning of *apple,* but why does an apple need a *mouse?* Even his wife can fumble along in English. If the two of them are alone in the house and a dealer or curator phones up, he hands the machine to her.

The wind has risen again. A sheet of particle board half shields the old man from the dancing snow. "What will the next change be?" he wonders. *Aaksurulauqsimajjaajunniirasugittailigitsi.* Looking up for a second past his neighbor's satellite dish, he sees a young hunter in a parka and a black tuque heading out by snowmobile toward the frozen bay.

10

The Words That Come
Before All Else

MOHAWK

THE FIRST TIME I ever sensed the power of the Mohawk language, I was hunched over a student desk at McGill University in downtown Montreal. It was a damp February afternoon in 1997, mild enough for smokers to huddle in small groups outside the tobacco-free arts building. A short walk down the hill, a plaque proclaims this to be the site of Hochelaga — the Indian town whose inhabitants fed and puzzled over Jacques Cartier four and a half centuries ago. The Breton explorer decided that the great river that had brought him here would be called the "Saint-Laurent," and he christened this hill "Mont Royal." Both names have lasted.

Inside the building, several hundred people had given up part of their weekend to cram into a windowless amphitheater. It was the climax of a conference looking into the doubtful fate, the 440 recommendations, and the 3,537-page report of the Royal Commission on Aboriginal Peoples. The federal government had set up the commission after the 1990 Oka crisis, with memories still fresh of masked Mohawk warriors eyeball to eyeball with heavily armed Canadian soldiers. The confrontation, a few miles west of Montreal Island, had lasted eleven weeks. By the time of the conference the memories had faded in society at large, although they remained crystalline among the Mohawks. Swiveling my desk, I noticed a good number of native men and women in the crowd: Mohawks had been joined by Crees, Hurons, and people from other groups that many Canadians still call "tribes" rather than "First Nations." Up on the stage, the grand chief of the Assembly of First Nations — a handsome, brooding Cree man called Ovide Mercredi — sat down near a neoconservative newspaper columnist named Andrew Coyne. The two did not shake hands.

A man with a dark blue shirt, a ponytail, and suspenders bounded to the podium. He stood there for a minute, waiting for the hubbub to subside. I didn't realize, at the time, that Ernie Benedict was the founder of the Native North American Travelling College, the holder of an honorary doctor of laws degree from Trent University, and the man who had once presented an eagle feather to Pope John Paul II at a huge outdoor mass. No wonder a McGill lecture hall held no terrors for him. Benedict was seventy-eight years old. He didn't look it. Nor, when he opened his mouth, keeping his eyes half closed, did he sound it:

Ohenton karihwatehkwen ne'e ayontati' niya'tewenhniserake tsi teyonte-nonhweratons. Akwekon enhskat tsi entitewahwe'nonni' ne onkwa'nikònra, tanon tenyethinonhweraton' ne onkwehson'a ne'akwekon skennen akenhake'. Etho niyohtonhak ne onkwa'nikònra . . .

In these words, or ones very like them, Ernie Benedict was giving succinct thanks for harmony and peace. But he didn't stop there. Still speaking in the Kanien'kehá language — otherwise known as Mohawk — he went on to do what he and other traditional Mohawks do before any ceremonial occasion, any religious gathering, any political meeting, any formal celebration. He confirmed his gratitude to the food plants and medicine plants, to the waters and wild animals, to the trees and birds and rain-bringing thunders . . . Lengthy, convoluted, dense with meaning, his words flowed out into the audience like the unexpected music of a dream.

I was struck by the tension in the crowd, the way surprise soon turned to anxiety. It wasn't just the French- and English-speaking Canadians sitting in the big room who could not begin to understand Ernie Benedict, a small man who seemed to grow in stature as he spoke, swaying slightly, declining to make eye contact with anyone; it was also the members of other Indian nations. How long would he go on? *Tete-watenonhweratons tsi shekon tewatkahthos ne karahkwa tehohswathèton' ro'tarihàton' ne kèntho onhwentsyàke . . .* Coyne leaned forward, pushing his head into his hands. In the unlikely event that he chose to recite the

Ohenton karihwatehkwen in its full splendor, Benedict might be standing at the microphone for two hours.

Not so. A few minutes after he began, he pronounced a refrain for the last time, *Etho niyohtonhak ne onkwa'nikònra,* and switched to English. "We have had the help of all creatures from our Mother, the Earth," he said. "We will now return that love in thanks and greetings." Such greetings have been uttered for centuries, not only in Mohawk and English but also in the languages of the five other nations that make up the Iroquois Confederacy. They were — and still are — a people for whom oratory counts. Occasionally delivered in a long form, more often abbreviated, the greetings are both a prayer and a pledge of allegiance: a defining statement of belief. Under the artificial lights, Benedict greeted and thanked all the creatures of the world, moving on from terrestrial beings to the sun and "our grandmother the moon, who, we believe, is faithfully performing her task." A purpose of the great prayer — the Iroquois thanksgiving address, it's generally called, although a literal translation would be "the words that come before all else" — is that by the time a speaker falls silent, "now our minds are one." Glancing at the panel waiting to speak, I thought it an unlikely prospect.

Sure enough, after Benedict sat down, Andrew Coyne stood up to denounce. The Royal Commission on Aboriginal Peoples had recommended, along with much else, a concerted effort to keep traditional languages and cultures alive. But to the newspaper columnist its report marked "a fundamental departure from liberal-democratic values." By highlighting the value of cultural difference, Coyne said, the commission displayed "the folly of identity politics" — a folly that led to "the elevation of identity above other concerns like fairness or freedom." The report appeared to accept that "real nations are ethnic or cultural ones." Coyne disagreed. There was, he argued, "something narcissistic" about the claims of aboriginal peoples and Quebecers alike. Above all, the report placed an unacceptable stress on collective rights and called for "a retreat into a traditional culture that is ill-suited to the demands of an industrial economy."

He left the podium to meager applause and scattered cries of "Shame!" Yet nobody, I suspect, was shocked by Coyne's polemic. He had said, clearly and forcefully, what a host of non-natives have always thought: Our law is the law. Our language is the language. Rights are individual. Differences will fade away.

"My voice has been angry for quite a while," the following speaker,

Ovide Mercredi, began in a tone of bitter quiet. He never looked at Coyne, but most of what he said over the next twenty minutes was a cold response. Coyne had attacked the royal commission's appeal for a third order of government, an indigenous order, as threatening Canada with something alien: a racially based system of authority. "I don't have any difficulty with the idea of racial government," Mercredi retorted. "I see it every day of my life." The longer he spoke, the angrier he seemed. His questions became rhetorical: "Have you seen us win anything lately? Are we getting our land back? Our resources? Are our languages guaranteed in your laws? Is the money spent on English and French being spent on the Cree language, the Ojibwa language, the Inuktitut language, and other indigenous languages of Canada?"

He mentioned those three, I imagine, because out of the fifty-three or so aboriginal languages still used in Canada, they appear the most likely to be spoken a couple of generations from now. Next to Navajo, Cree is the most widely heard native language in North America. It may have more than eighty thousand speakers, concentrated in small reserves across much of northern Canada and in the poor neighborhoods of cities. But even Cree speakers, like Mercredi, worry about eroding dialects and abandoned words. The Canadian constitution grants official status to English and French, giving indigenous languages no legal recognition. Most of these languages are now in a parlous condition. Of the six languages belonging to the Iroquois Confederacy, Ernie Benedict's is the healthiest. Statistics are unreliable, as traditionalists refuse to recognize the jurisdiction or comply with the census demands of either the United States or Canada, but it's clear that Mohawk still has hundreds of fluent speakers, as well as thousands of people who speak a limited version.

That day in Montreal, Ovide Mercredi kept going back to what he had just heard, or to what he thought he had heard: "'You'll never survive on this land unless you assimilate to our society. Speak like us, dress like us, think like us.' This is what's called individual universality. There's other names for it, like cultural genocide and racism." At times, Mercredi said, it doesn't pay to be mild mannered: "Those who sound the angriest, win. Let us not be ashamed to express our anger." Finally he changed language. Using the tongue he had learned as a small boy amid the lakes, swamps, and evergreen forests of northern Manitoba, he spoke a few sentences in Cree, paused to look at the crowd, and then gave a rough translation: "I live different from you. Not that I hate you.

But because I like the way we live ourselves, as people. The future must be different."

With Cree words behind him, his anger appeared to dissolve. "I apologize for my tone of voice," he said at last. A man in the crowd shouted, "No!" When Mercredi sat down, most of his listeners stood up. A few steps away from Coyne's right ear, a woman beat a huge drum.

I never forgot its sound. Years later, waiting in the lobby of radio station CKRZ in the little town of Ohsweken, I could still recall the force of that moment, the sudden strength of that drum. The station, whose logo shows an eagle feather dangling from a musical note, broadcasts from a strip mall called the Iroquois Village Centre. Several thousand people in Ohsweken and the surrounding Six Nations reserve, an hour's drive southwest of Toronto, identify themselves as Mohawk. Only twenty or thirty of them are fluent in their ancestral tongue. Maintaining it is a bruising struggle; reviving it, a rare ambition.

Mohawks made this fertile corner of the continent their home when their leader Thayandanegea — known in history textbooks as Joseph Brant — led almost two thousand Loyalist Indians and a few dozen black slaves westward from New York in 1784. Most of Thayandanegea's followers belonged to the Iroquois Confederacy. They were refugees. After the Revolutionary War, in which the majority of Iroquois supported King George III, Americans torched their towns and farms in revenge. The Six Nations reserve has always been multiethnic; only a quarter of its first settlers were, like Thayandanegea, Mohawks. As the settlers' population grew, the racism they faced was overt and unashamed. The author of a book entitled *The Six Nations Indians in Canada* (1896) had this to say about "the Indian" in general: "There is slight ground for thinking him capable, under the most favorable auspices, of perilling the eminence of the white, in respect of intellectual attainment." So ended a chapter called "His Intellectual Equipment." It was followed by "His Discomposing Levity."

I looked up to find Brian Maracle striding into the lobby with easy familiarity. A onetime host of *Our Native Land,* broadcast across the country on CBC Radio, he's the author of two well-received books and a former reporter for the Toronto *Globe and Mail,* English Canada's leading newspaper. Spiffily dressed in a leather jacket and black cap, he was clutching a handful of CDs from his own collection. His partner, Audrey Bomberry, followed him into the cramped studio, holding a few more CDs. She sat across the table, her lips close to a microphone. Brian would be handling the controls. After a sound check, he cued up a Buddy Holly song. *Tewatonhwehsen* was about to begin.

Tewatonhwehsen (Let's have a good time!) is the name of the only show that CKRZ broadcasts in Mohawk. Since 1993, when Brian Maracle left Ottawa and moved to the reserve — the most populous in Canada, and (in spite of white land grabs) one of the largest — he has become more and more passionate about the fate of his ancestral language, a language he barely spoke as a boy. Eventually he abandoned his writing career, devoting himself instead to keeping Mohawk alive. The weekly radio show is fun. It's also a means to an end.

Brian motioned for silence, turned on his microphone, and began to speak. Over Audrey's shoulder, he could survey the parking lot of a Chinese restaurant, a denture clinic, and a branch of the Royal Bank of Canada. A snapshot of suburbia: not what outsiders expect an Indian reserve to look like. But Six Nations is a complex and divided place, just as the Mohawks are a complex and divided people, resistant to generalization. There are small-scale farms on the reserve, and longhouses that host traditional Iroquois ceremonies; there's also a studio, owned by a Maori immigrant, that specializes in video production, CD duplication, digital recording, and graphic design.

Robbie Robertson, the lead singer of The Band, often came to Six Nations as a boy; it was the home of his mother, a Mohawk. But this evening Brian wasn't in the mood for The Band. When the red light above CKRZ's studio door went off, he snapped his fingers to a livelier beat. "I always like to start with Buddy Holly," he explained, "because he's the best." A staff member shouted from the lobby: "A kid phoned in, wanting Britney Spears." "This program is a Britney Spears–free zone," Brian called back.

Audrey introduced a haunting tune by a singer who goes by the name of Cherokee Rose. Cherokee is a distant relative of Mohawk: it's one of fifteen known languages in what scholars call the Iroquoian family. In Mohawk, I noticed, Audrey's voice is quieter and more hesitant than Brian's. She too has lived away from Six Nations and has battled for fluency in middle age. As the song was playing, the couple debated how to translate Hootie and the Blowfish into Mohawk. They settled on "Hootie and the fish that has a potential to get bigger." "The show is only an hour," Audrey told me later, "and the response we get is mostly positive, even from people who aren't speakers. They say, 'It gives me a good feeling to hear it on the radio.' A lot of people don't understand a word, but it's their one tenuous link to the language."

Silence is threatening to overtake Mohawk and all the other Indian languages the Iroquois refugees brought with them. Around Ohsweken, Seneca and Tuscarora have fallen by the wayside; likewise Oneida, a language so close to Mohawk it's sometimes described as a little brother; even Onondaga, the central fire of the great confederacy, has just a few speakers left in Canada and a few more in New York. At Six Nations, Mohawk is now in tacit competition with Cayuga, a language that flourishes nowhere else. A good deal of the reserve's cultural energy has gone into saving Cayuga. Bloodlines and language don't always match: Audrey's father was a Mohawk, but the indigenous language he spoke was Cayuga. CKRZ broadcasts Cayuga classes five mornings a week; the University of Toronto Press has just published a fat Cayuga-English dictionary; the Woodland Cultural Centre has poured time and money into the language. Cayuga is also the main language here of traditional religion.

Despite all this effort, Cayuga may have fewer than a hundred fluent speakers. Mohawk, though rare at Six Nations, is more widespread: a short day's drive to the northeast, in three communities near Montreal, the language endures on the lips of elders, activists, a very few children at home, and many more pupils at school. At Six Nations schoolchildren can take intensive classes in Mohawk or Cayuga. An important gesture of affiliation or identification, these classes have not yet led to a language revival beyond the school.

This week, Brian was happy to find, the only commercial he had to read was for a Sunday bingo game sponsored by the radio station. "Sometimes," he said, "I'm supposed to read these ads saying 'Chicken nuggets for $1.59 on Tuesdays at McDonald's.' I read 'em in Mohawk. Hasn't come back to me yet!" When I put in a request for Bob Dylan, Brian improvised a Mohawk introduction for "Mr. Tambourine Man." Then he moved on to the soundtrack from a German film. Nobody could accuse him — or most other Mohawks, for that matter — of being parochial.

But *Tewatonhwehsen* is only a sideline — a chance for Audrey and Brian to use the Mohawk language in play. The rest of the week is a harder slog. Much of the year they teach an adult immersion course to a devoted handful of students who somehow arrange to spend five days a week, seven hours a day learning a language they feel is rightfully theirs

— a language, like a phantom limb, whose absence hurts. One of the students was a young mother who wanted to raise her children bilingually; a second was a traditionalist who saw Mohawk as a foundation of his identity; a third was a high school guidance counselor on sabbatical. "The Mohawk teaching situation here is very bad," the guidance counselor told me. "We've got a mishmash of abilities. Some are fluent but can't write it. Some can read but can't speak it. Some know it but can't teach. The immersion program to me is the key. I never dreamed I'd be able to do the *Ohenton karihwatehkwen* like I did this morning."

The classes take place in a pale bungalow on an Ohsweken street that looks like any other in small-town Ontario. The nearest business boasts the name Red Indian Mini-Mart. Inside the bungalow, every day begins and ends with the words that come before all else. The students can measure their progress by the ease with which they give greetings and thanks. Brian understands their difficulties better than many other teachers of indigenous languages because he too has had to grope toward fluency. "Just because you're a speaker," he said, "doesn't mean you're going to be good with this group. Some of the elders use shortcuts and slang, or they speak really fast." A metaphor sprang to his lips, reminding me of his past life as a writer of English: "You got a little child who's just learned to walk — you don't put him in a race, or he would be left behind. I'm no marathoner. I'm no Olympic hurdler. To a fluent speaker, I'm like a kid. And these students are like little kids."

Some things in English don't translate well into Mohawk, Brian told me: "'I didn't know what I was getting into' is hard to say in Mohawk. Because in Mohawk you either are or you aren't. English is so vague and sloppy, you don't really know what somebody means." From an opposing standpoint, of course, the supple ambiguities of English are a large part of its genius. "But," Brian went on, "there are other things in Mohawk that you can't say simply or easily in English. You'd need time to explain everything, and the interpretation can vary so much from speaker to speaker. In Mohawk we have to describe not only *where* things are but *how* things are — how they exist. We're much more specific than English."

From an English (or Indo-European) perspective, Mohawk has its ambiguities too. For one thing, it does not reflect our understanding of linear time. "We have this concept in Mohawk," Brian said, "that can refer to either time or place. If I want to say 'I washed all over the wall,' I might use the same phrase as 'I washed the wall all day long.' By adding a particular suffix to a word, we extend the meaning of that word over either time or space."

"A thing that keeps us going," Audrey explained above George Harrison's "Here Comes the Sun," "is that we have to do this. For some people it's a choice. For Brian and me, it's not — it's what we need to do." Only an experience of immersion, they believe, can create a grasp of a language so unlike the students' mother tongue; and only a grasp of the language can bring full understanding of what it means to be *Onkwehon:we* (an Indian, or one of the "real people"). Brian interlaces his English conversation with *Onkwehon:we* and *Kanyen'kehá:ka* (people of the flint), though he avoids saying "Mohawk." That name goes back to a term meaning "man-eater," conferred on the nation by one of its enemies.

Whatever you call it, the language is built on root words. They demand an intricate series of prefixes and suffixes. "But if I use the wrong prefix," Brian admitted just before he turned the mike back on, "there's just a couple dozen people here who would know. If they're listening." Light glinted off his glasses.

That morning he and one of his students had been discussing an episode of *The Simpsons*. The student had asked how to say, in Mohawk, "Homer got smarter." Brian had been stumped. He figured out an answer halfway through a rhythm and blues number by Clarence "Frogman" Henry. In Mohawk, he explained with a look of relief, you'd say, "'Homer has a bigger *o'nikonhra* than he had before.' Some things can't be adequately translated, one of them being the root word for intelligence. *O'nikonhra* is the root of hundreds of words, all of them involving something that goes on inside you. Not just inside your head! One part of it is your thinking, but another part involves feelings and attitudes. *O'nikonhra* is the root of 'I am sad' and 'I understand something' and 'He is good-natured.'" Then the Frogman finished.

It was 6:30 P.M., almost time for CKRZ's *Music Mixx* (the return of Britney Spears, no doubt), and Brian cued up a final song: "Smoke Gets in Your Eyes" by the Platters. In Mohawk they became "the big plates." Brian dedicated the song to his sister. He and Audrey gathered up their CDs and strolled out of the studio, back into a world of English. In the jingle-jangle evening, I went following them.

The Mohawk nation emerged in the foggy ruins of time in what is now central New York. It served as the "eastern door" of the Iroquois Confederacy — the allied nations lived farther west, around what would come to be called the Finger Lakes. Mohawks had a vivid reputation for cruelty: they were feared by the white invaders of their country and by other Indian peoples alike. (As late as 1950, posters for a Hollywood movie called *The Iroquois Trail* used phrases like "The Terror of the Tomahawk!" and "400 Miles of Frontier Fury!") This reputation obscured the fact that the Mohawks, like all the Iroquois, were an agricultural people who raised corn, beans, squash, tobacco, and sunflowers. A matrilineal society, guided by clan mothers, they adhered to laws that were imparted, they believe, centuries ago by a semi-divine being of Huron origin, Tekanawi:ta, the Peacemaker. The greeting in several Iroquois languages — their equivalent of "hello" — is "peace."

Today there is but one small Mohawk territory on the ancestral land, and not many Mohawks live there. Their society is one of remnants. Apart from their share of Six Nations and their village in the Mohawk Valley, Mohawks have two other communities in Ontario, two in Quebec, one in the Adirondacks of northern New York — and one reserve, Akwesasne, that straddles the boundaries of New York, Quebec, and Ontario, causing migraines among police officers, immigration agents, and customs officials. Each of these communities has a private history, a local identity, and a separate way of speaking the language (at Akwesasne, for instance, an *l* sound is prevalent in words where most Mohawk speakers use *r*). In addition, thousands of Mohawks work in cities far from "the rez." They have shown a particular gift for bridge building and other ironwork high in the air. Mohawks had a hand in building the World Trade Center, the Empire State Building, and many other Manhattan landmarks. In 1949, when Joseph Mitchell wrote a *New Yorker* article about them, Brooklyn's Mohawks still tended to speak their ancestral tongue at home. More than a hundred Mohawk men were employed as ironworkers in New York City on September 11, 2001. Yet by then theirs was no longer a living language of Brooklyn.

As an outsider, I knew that Mohawk society is plagued by divisions. Band councilors who cooperate with federal agencies in Canada and the United States are seen as traitors by Iroquois traditionalists; the band councilors rightly say they are elected, and the traditionalists rightly retort that voters form a small minority of the population. Both groups have had their problems with Mohawk nationalists. Sometimes Mohawks themselves refer to the three groups as shorthairs, longhairs, and warriors. But the longhairs suffer a further division: some attend longhouses that follow the teachings of the nineteenth-century Seneca prophet Skanyatariyo (also known as Handsome Lake), while many others scorn Skanyatariyo's innovations. Some Mohawks call themselves Canadian, others American, and many others recognize no sovereignty except their own. Some are willing to bring lucrative casinos into their territories and to earn revenue from sales of duty-free cigarettes; others are not. Some Mohawks think retaining and regaining their ancestral language should be a priority; others do not. I knew the outlines of all this, but I was still innocent: I imagined that at least those Mohawks who want to preserve their language would be able to agree among themselves.

"The Mohawk language is based heavily on agreement," David Maracle told me. "Nouns, genders — everything has to agree." He paused. "That is literally the first and the last time that Mohawks agree on anything."

David grew up in Tyendinaga, a reserve on the Bay of Quinte in eastern Ontario, where a second group of Mohawk refugees found a home after the American Revolution. Of its few thousand residents, only a handful are adept in Mohawk. But those few take pride in speaking the purest form of the language — a Mohawk unadulterated by other peoples' words and intonations. David (if you go back far enough, he must be related to Brian) learned to speak Mohawk by hanging around elders at Tyendinaga as a teenager in the 1960s. He ended up teaching Mohawk language and culture at the University of Western Ontario, a few hundred miles away. No one else has churned out so many Mohawk books, tapes, pamphlets, and other language-learning materials. While Brian admires this material and uses it at Ohsweken, Mohawks farther to the east are wary of it. They see it as promoting the Tyendinaga dialect, not the language fighting for breath in their own communities.

David's spellings are different from those used by Mohawks elsewhere; indeed, his very alphabet is distinct. Mohawks have argued about whether they should use an apostrophe to indicate a glottal stop (think of the charged space in the middle of the English phrase "Oh-oh!"; such a pause is a crucial element in many Mohawk words). They have argued about falling and rising tones, about *t* versus *d*, about *k* versus *c* and *g*, and about the mere existence of *h*. Published sources spell Tekanawi:ta, the name of the Peacemaker, in at least five ways, most often as "Deganawidah." In the face of such disorder, language advocates began to push for that least glamorous of get-togethers: a standardization conference. One was finally held in 1993, with the aim of establishing a single Mohawk orthography. The meeting resolved many of the outstanding controversies, yet it failed to establish whether the language has a place for the letter *y*. In most Mohawk communities, *i* is used instead. But at Six Nations — and in David Maracle's writings — *y* continues to appear. This means that no consensus exists about the people's very name. Is it *Kanyen'kehá:ka* or *Kanien'kehá:ka*?

Such are the natural difficulties that arise when people from several communities set out to turn an ancient oral language into a written one. Most Mohawks feel an intense loyalty to their own place. But the rivalries between those places stand in the way of a united language. Nobody wants to feel that his or her own speech, so jealously guarded against the encroachments of the outside world, is being shoved aside in favor of somebody else's dialect. Consider it Occitan and Provençal writ small. If time is running short, tempers can be short, too. Spelling easily becomes a political issue. An Abenaki filmmaker named Alanis O'Bomsawin once phoned David Maracle at 8 A.M. on a Saturday to ask his advice. She had made a feature-length documentary about the Oka crisis, *Kanehsatake: 270 Years of Resistance*. Only at the last minute did she realize that in titling the film after the Mohawk community at the heart of the struggle, she would have to choose a particular spelling: either "Kanesatake" or "Kanehsatake." "And if we don't spell it a certain way," David remembers her explaining, "some people say they're going to take their names off the credits."

O'Bomsawin later made a short documentary about a young Mohawk woman whom police arrested at the end of the confrontation. Of fourteen women charged with obstructing justice and participating in a riot, she alone was not granted bail, because she refused to give a name the court would recognize. Her name, she insisted, was Kahentiiosta. Asked to provide an identity in English or French, she kept silent. The crown prosecutor, Pierre Teasdale, complained: "It's as if I said my name was X and it's really Y. People could start coming to court calling themselves anything." Kahentiiosta was eventually acquitted — under her preferred name.

There's a traditional Mohawk story that suggests the power of silence and the danger of inappropriate words. The story tells of how Tewiske:ron — the evil twin in many tales of the dawning world — and his grandmother stole the sun and took it to a faraway island. Teronhiawa:kon, the good twin, went to retrieve it, helped by the beaver, the rabbit, the spider, and the hawk. But the whining, mouthy otter insisted on going too. The others paddled to the island and told the otter to keep quiet in the boat while they performed their tasks. This he did. But on the return journey, as the group escaped with the sun hidden in a bag, the otter couldn't keep silent any longer. In his excitement, he began to talk very loudly. One of the others hit him with a paddle, breaking his bottom jaw and pushing it back into his head. To this day, otters have a very short jaw. The sun remains safe in the sky where Teronhiawa:kon hurled it.

Indians' power of silence can be unnerving. A mystique grew up around it in the minds of European settlers and early American writers. For decades Hollywood promoted an image of North American Indians as stoic and monosyllabic: "How!" The irony is that indigenous languages are rich, expressive, and, in many cases, anything but monosyllabic. Much information can be clustered in a single word. An English sentence like "I am bringing sugar to somebody" is a single verb in Mohawk: *tkhetsikhe'tenhawihtennihs.* Word order is flexible in the language. But the order of elements *within* each word adheres to certain rules.

A Mohawk verb — any Mohawk verb! — is polysynthetic. Not only does it describe an action; it must also indicate the agent, recipient, and time of that action. That's not all. The verb may include up to six of what grammarians call "positional classes." First comes a pre-pronominal prefix, such as "away," "not," or "should." Then comes a pronominal prefix, such as "you all and I" or "they and I" (Mohawk has six ways of expressing relationships that English lumps together as "we"). Next in line is a reflexive and reciprocal aspect, showing whether an action is happening to the self. Only then does the incorporated noun root appear, followed by the verb root — the word's core. Last of all comes a suffix, providing a marker of time and announcing whether the action is habitual or momentary. "Not / they and I / self / mirror / look / habitually": *Yah teyakwatatkens.* Or, to put the notion into English, "We don't always look at ourselves in the mirror."

To think in Mohawk and to think in English are to highlight different qualities in the mind and in the outside world. "Car," "truck," "train," and "wagon" are all the same in Mohawk, not because the language has failed to catch up with the industrial world, but because those items perform the same task: transporting people from one place to another. In Mohawk grammar, objects matter less than actions. The language has no separate terms for "breakfast," "dinner," and other meals. In place of our question "What did you have for breakfast?" a Mohawk speaker will ask, "What did you eat this morning?" Likewise, a Mohawk "table," instead of being verbally cut off from its main function, is literally "what you eat food on." The language keeps highlighting the reasons why things exist. For the English phrase "There was a table on the rug," a Mohawk speaker would say, roughly, "What you eat food on stands on the hemp material in the past": *Kentskahràke watekhwah-ratsherotehkwe'.*

David has compiled several dictionaries of root terms. Only by mastering the roots, he believes, can adult learners of the language hope to generate their own Mohawk sentences with any fluency. Sometimes the roots are so broad in meaning that they produce a crowd of elaborations. *Ori:wa,* for instance, can have the sense of "matter," "thing," "reason," "fault," or "business." The dozens of verbs arising from it include *kerihwakanon:nis* (I handle the business), *katerihwakatenhstha'* (I swear), *kherihwanon:tonnis* (I question someone), *tetkherihwa'serakwas* (I answer someone back), and *thiya'tewakerihwara:'on* (I am fidgety; I feel guilty). Root words on their own may have no meaning. Outside a dictionary, they exist only in living kinship to all the other elements in the language. The basis of any Mohawk word involving a house is *-nonhs-*. A houseboat is *yononhsa'kerha;* a house cat is *kanonhsa'keha takohs;* "I have a nice house" is *wakenonhsiyo.* But *nonhs* by itself, David says, "would be incomprehensible to any fluent speaker who has never studied the grammatical aspects of the language."

I asked David if he ever grew seriously frustrated with his language work. Three decades of teaching and writing and publishing — and in the number of its speakers, Mohawk has continued to decline. "You mean pulling your hair out?" he replied. "You mean screaming? There are days when standing on a street corner, naked and covered in dogshit, seems a better way to go. What happens is, I just ignore it for a week. Then I end up back at it. This is what I'm supposed to do, I guess."

The Mohawk Institute, a residential school for more than a century, was an imposing, three-story, silver-domed building that stood among extensive grounds on the edge of the Ontario city of Brantford. By 1970, however, residential schools had gone out of fashion. Indeed they were an embarrassment. The Mohawk Institute was closed down and transformed into the Woodland Cultural Centre, run by Six Nations and other indigenous communities. "But some of our people won't ever come in here," admitted the director, a genial, Cayuga-speaking Mohawk named Amos Key. His office, a former dormitory, has a skylight cut into the ceiling of what had been a place of darkness. "For a lot of them, it's a struggle." He spoke frankly about the errors of the past, not all of which had been perpetrated by white people. "Talk about English and French — we had our own two solitudes. We had our own pecking order. There was religious persecution and marginalization even inside Six Nations. For healing and reconciliation to occur, we need to recognize we did this to each other."

I drove back by night to my home in Montreal. The journey, along the shores of Lake Ontario and the St. Lawrence River, followed a route that Mohawks may have known — and related Indian peoples would have occupied — centuries ago. Their grandmother, the moon, was faithfully performing her task. But the road below was a trail of feeder lanes, exit ramps, nuclear power plants, megaplexes, service stations, furniture galleries, gazebo sellers, strip malls, billboards, doughnut shops, warning signs, superstores, car dealers, home appliance depots, air compressors, fast-food outlets, heavy metal stamping plants . . . Somewhere in the midst of all the nouns lay Toronto, the largest city in Canada, lauded by foreign writers like Pico Iyer and Jan Morris as an intercultural model of the global future. I couldn't help wondering what space was left amid the glowing concrete for the people whose land this had been before it was flattened, paved, cemented, and used up.

Mohawks often wonder the same thing. At Kahnawake, a fifteen-minute drive from downtown Montreal provided the Mercier Bridge is working smoothly, the annual powwow bears the name Echoes of a Proud Nation. It takes place in a couple of fields outside town in mid-July, often the sultriest weekend of the year. Tourists and locals get together to sample corn soup and strawberry juice, to check out the booths selling dreamcatchers, beadwork, and New Age music, and to watch the costumed dancers. One year when I attended, the head male dancer was a Michigan Ojibwa, the host drum was beaten by Assiniboines from southern Manitoba, and the master of ceremonies had moved into Navajo territory from Pennsylvania. According to my souvenir program, a sponsoring business was East of Texas Westernwear in Kahnawạke (Visa accepted). The program described the Grand Entry Song as "probably an imitation of rodeos and Wild West shows."

But what, exactly, is the proud nation that the powwow claims to echo? Is it Mohawk, Iroquois, or pan-Indian? Speakers of all Iroquois languages use the term *Onkwehon:we* — "the real people." Dakota, Inuit, Innu, Haida: these names also mean "the people." Many indigenous languages, it seems, preserve a timeworn privacy — a willingness to exclude — that native people themselves may no longer see as desirable or even possible. Is assimilation the only option? One alternative is a hybrid native culture transcending the barriers of language. It would have the merit of being inclusive. Everything apart from English would be relegated to the realm of the picturesque: the odd chant, the old half-understood name in the midst of ersatz rodeo songs and East of Texas Westernwear. In the words of Christopher Jocks, a Mohawk whose family roots are in Kahnawake and who teaches religion at Dartmouth College, "I fear that without our languages it is all too easy for us to become cartoons, caricatures of ourselves."

In his 1996 book *Back on the Rez,* Brian Maracle not only described his joy at rediscovering Mohawk customs; he also explored with great sensitivity and nuance the vexed meanings of tradition. His favorite festival at Six Nations, Noyah, takes place on New Year's Day. But the custom and even the name have nothing to do with Iroquois antiquity; they emerged from the *Nieuw Jaar* celebrations of the seventeenth-century Dutch. Noyah survived, changed, and ended up as a valued part of Six Nations tradition. Cultural identity, then, can transcend a shift of language. Ask the Irish (most of them). Or read Brian Maracle on the subject: "Just because we started speaking English doesn't mean we also started playing cricket and eating kippers. No, we still play lacrosse and eat corn soup and we still have an attitude regarding the future that is hard to pin down."

But Brian was unhappy about the logical conclusion to be drawn from that remark. Perhaps, after all, the attitude regarding the future won't endure far into the future; perhaps the corn soup will arrive ready-made in a Campbell's can. Nine pages later, he was emphatic: "Without the language, our ceremonies, songs and dances will cease . . . The Confederacy will cease to function . . . The names themselves will lose their meaning. Without the language, we will lose our traditional way of thinking and our distinctive view of the world." And when all that is gone, what point will there be in hanging on to Mohawk land?

The Mercier Bridge cuts a swath through what was supposed to be Indian territory forever. So do three highways, a rail line, and the St. Lawrence Seaway. To construct the seaway, the government of Canada confiscated more than a thousand acres of Indian land, thereby cutting Kahnawake off from the rapids that give the place its Mohawk name. The community took the issue to the United Nations; a former Egyptian diplomat wrote a book expounding its case. To no avail. Standing in the bleachers above the powwow dancers, a strong-armed spectator could turn and hurl a stone that might, with a little luck and a following wind, hit a freighter on its ponderous journey to the Atlantic. Kahnawake is not a remote place: its eight thousand or so residents are immersed in the life and languages of greater Montreal. Many of them work in the city — a couple of them cut down a dying tree in my garden. Mohawk students can be found at several of the city's leading private schools and both its English-language universities.

Yet Kahnawake can seem like a quintessential working-class town. Idealistic German tourists, hoping to meet up with timeless wisdom, have been distressed to learn that this is a community fond of country music and heavy metal, one whose residents tend to be serious about bingo, passionate about wrestling and hockey, anxious about obesity and diabetes, and proud of their numerous war veterans. Don't come here looking for a Green Party vision of indigenous America.

What, then, distinguishes Kahnawake from any other blue-collar town? The Mohawk language, among other things. For more than two decades Kahnawake has had a Mohawk-immersion school for young children and a Survival School for adolescents. Church services are said in the language. Occasionally you hear it spoken on the street. The morning announcer on radio station K-103 ("The Monster") slips effortlessly between English and Mohawk. A Young Women's Singing Society performs traditional Mohawk music; at least one longhouse holds rituals in the language. Entering the community by road, you pass a sign telling drivers KAIANEREKOWA IS OUR CEREMONIES AND MUST BE PROTECTED. (In English that word is generally translated as "the great law of peace.") The town maintains an extensive Web site in Mohawk as well as English. Despite all this, few young people and families at Kahnawake use Mohawk frequently, casually, unthinkingly. But together it adds up to a continuing presence — a willed refusal to let the language vanish without a struggle.

Parents whose children attend the Mohawk immersion school are given a calendar with a set of goals on it. Second on the list — right after understanding oneself through Mohawk language and culture — is "to develop respect and appreciation for the gifts of the Creator and to acknowledge thankfulness through the *Ohenton karihwatehkwen.*" Yet it's one of Kahnawake's many paradoxes that "traditional" religion here is anything but traditional. No surviving Mohawk community is as old: it began in 1669, as a settlement founded by a French priest a few miles downriver, and moved to its present site in 1716. Mohawk was a living language around the island of Montreal long before English swaggered in. But from the start Kahnawake was known as a town of "praying Indians." Praying to Jesus, that is.

It has its own saint, Kateri Tekakwitha, a half-blind, smallpox-scarred convert who died at twenty-four after engaging in penitential practices so extreme they ruined what was left of her health. Today Rome recognizes her as a "patroness of the environment." Kateri's parents were Algonquin and Mohawk; many of her fellow believers had no Mohawk blood at all. Kahnawake became a place where French Jesuits gathered up and watched over Christian immigrants from many Indian nations. The praying Indians were excluded from the Iroquois Confederacy, and when hostilities broke out in 1776 the men of Kahnawake declined to fight. Yet the town needed a lingua franca, and by virtue of numbers Mohawk grew to dominate. Over time the town's multinational origins were partially forgotten, and it came to be a Mohawk stronghold — militantly so, at times. To a large degree, language created Kahnawake's identity.

"One thing about Mohawks," Melvin Diabo told me. "If there's a crisis, you can count on them to come through. I'm counting on that spirit of self-preservation now." A scholarly-looking man with wavy gray hair, Melvin runs the Kahnawake Language Centre. "I can make Mohawk extremely difficult, even for Mohawk speakers," he happily remarked. But his horizons stretch far beyond his own community. Melvin won a Latin prize as a student of the Jesuits in Montreal; he grew up to marry an Irish woman, and can chat knowledgeably about the revival of Hebrew in Israel. "We're always on the lookout for innovative ways to make sure our language doesn't disappear," he said. "People over sixty here speak Mohawk. More importantly, they think in Mohawk."

"We're boring," Billy Two Rivers interrupted. "Really we are." Melvin looked pained at the notion, but his friend forged ahead. "What we need to develop is more recreational clubs. Mix in with the youth. You gotta recapture communication. I'll do it on every occasion I can — I'll come in and speak to the children. They'll speak English to me, and I'll hit them with Mohawk."

Billy Two Rivers is old enough now to collect a pension, but I wouldn't want him to hit me. He still weighs close to the 220 pounds he carried as a professional wrestler. In the 1960s he spent six years in Britain, entering the ring in a feathered headdress and doffing it to reveal a Mohawk haircut. Occasionally he would do a war dance. The crowds loved the act, and the man. After returning to North America, he performed in the movie *Black Robe*, where the Mohawk language stood in for Huron, and he provided a chunk of native eloquence and timeless wisdom in an obscure live-action version of *Pocahontas*. He also spent two decades on the Kahnawake council — when he called himself "chief," it wasn't just an act. "How is the Welsh language doing these days?" he asked with interest.

Trying to explain why his language, unlike Welsh, had faded, Billy went far back in time. "The nature of our economy," he said, "required that we men work in groups. As voyageurs. As guides. They spoke among themselves in Mohawk, although they had to be multilingual to speak to the Indian nations across the country. The harvesting of oak forests — our people were involved, working in gangs, if you want to call them that. The steel trade — riveting, raising, connecting — again, it required the men to work in a group. Mohawk was the working language of our men, and that dictates the language of the home, right up to about 1948. They went to New York, Boston, Detroit, Buffalo. If a newcomer came into the group, he had to learn the language fast."

I wasn't sure that men dictate the language of the home, and Melvin didn't seem certain about it either ("Mothers are the natural teachers. Men are your diplomats and your warriors"). Over the past century Kahnawake saw a slow growth in non-Indian residents, as Mohawks again began to marry outside the community. Not so slowly, radio and TV appeared on the scene. "Our biggest fault," Melvin said, "is using that media as a babysitter." The 1950s were a key decade in the process of

language shift. Mohawk men switched to English on the job just when
Roy Rogers, Ed Sullivan, and the Three Stooges entered their homes.

Melvin was a student then. He recalls his mother's stern request:
"'Son, can I talk to you privately?' I was thinking, 'Oh-oh, what did I do
wrong?' She said, 'Have you forgotten where you come from?' 'I don't
know,' I said, 'What do you mean?' She said, 'I talk to you all the time in
Mohawk and you always answer me in English. Son, you're going to live
in two worlds. I encourage you to know English — but don't forget your
Mohawk. Because the way things are going, you're going to lose your
language. And if you lose your language, you have no business saying
you're a Mohawk.'" I'd heard similar tales in Oklahoma and the Isle of
Man. But at Kahnawake the story had a political bite. "Next thing you
know," Melvin's mother warned him, "the government will say, 'You
work like us. You think like us. You talk like us. Guess you're one of us
now.'"

I didn't go looking for politics. I didn't want to write about politics. Yet
with Mohawks the subject is difficult to avoid. It came up once when I
asked Tiorahkwáthe, the Kahnawake councilor who handles language
issues, about his devotion to Mohawk. He gave a range of reasons, rang-
ing from the aesthetic ("Our language is very picturesque, everything is
descriptive") and the religious ("In English, most people even forget to
thank the waters each and every day") to the sensual ("When you're
speaking in the language, it's like having a three-flavored ice cream: vanilla, chocolate, raspberry. But when you do the translation into English, you take out two of the flavors"). Yet his first response — "So that
we don't become part of the melting pot" — was political.

Mohawks are passionate about maintaining their identity and holding on to what little power they still have. Their language won't put
bread on the table, but, many residents of Kahnawake believe, it can
help preserve their separateness in the face of a mainstream society
still hell-bent on assimilation. And so, in January 2002, Kahnawake put
its own language law into effect. *Kaianerenhserón:ni ne Onkwawem-
ma'ón:we Aóntston ne Kahnawake* arose from a declaration made by the
community's elders in the winter of 1998. "Fearful of the loss of our
beautiful Kanien'kéha language," the elders urged the Mohawk Council
of Kahnawake to take action. What emerged was a law that sets out "to
revive and restore Kanien'kéha as the primary language of communica-

tion, education, ceremony, government and business within the Territory of Kahnawake."

That may be a quixotic ambition. In practice, English is too deeply embedded in the community to be uprooted now. But the law still matters. It requires all institutions of Mohawk government to implement a language policy for their employees within two years; it assures those employees that they will be able to work in Mohawk; it gives residents of Kahnawake the right to have local court proceedings conducted in the language; and it requires applicants for all public-sector jobs to speak Mohawk or promise to learn it. As the local government is by far the biggest employer in town, these rules are significant. Staff will have to be retrained. Tangible rewards await those who soldier ahead with their Mohawk-language studies. For private businesses, the law is softer. Although they "have a moral and ethical obligation to protect, promote, use and encourage" the language, they won't be punished if they ignore it.

Kenneth Deer, the editor of Kahnawake's newspaper, the *Eastern Door*, praised the language law as tough and valiant. "We can't afford not to pay the price," he wrote. "One hundred years from now, what kind of Mohawks are we going to be? We are less Mohawk today than one hundred years ago. How much less Mohawk are we going to be in 2100?" For him the answer will depend on whether the language endures. Deer made an explicit comparison that other people in his town have shied away from: he noted that despite the recurrent mistrust between Mohawks and French Canadians (a mistrust four centuries old), Kahnawake's language law takes Quebec's Charter of the French Language as an inspiration. In turn, other native communities are looking at Kahnawake as a potential model. Soon after the Kahnawake rules went into practice, the language commissioner of Nunavut called for a new law to protect Inuktitut.

No residents of Kahnawake will call the language law crazy. In a close-knit community whose politicians wield considerable power, it can be risky to speak out against any of the leaders' big decisions. But there's a huge difference between hoping that a language survives and making sure it does. Like many other minority peoples, Mohawks often find themselves wanting their language to endure — and not wanting to make the sacrifices that desire may entail. The Kahnawake language law begins to call their bluff.

Yet in the town that was once by the rapids, nothing is simple. Fault lines shift and blur. I spent an hour with Philip Deering, a man of great intelligence and subtlety who had acquired a reputation as a tobacco smuggler in the 1980s. Now he was working on an MBA. But he felt I needed to learn more about the *Ohenton karihwatehkwen*. "The greetings part is an expression of love," he said. "If you track the root down, it's love. It's an expression of love toward all the elements of creation. It's an expression of great lovingfulness — if you can say that in English." Philip had been hesitant to meet me, expressing a fear that I would betray the truth. I assumed he meant a journalistic betrayal over tobacco, or the Oka crisis, or the language law. But no, he meant the betrayal that words induce when languages have different meanings.

Mohawk names, for instance, don't just identify a person you meet on the street. They also have a spiritual dimension — Onkwehon:we traditionally receive them during a longhouse's midwinter rites — which is why some fluent speakers of the language oppose the Mohawk Council of Kahnawake's attempt to fix Mohawk names on street signs. If a name is sacred in the spirit world, should everybody and his uncle be using it to indicate the road to the garbage dump? Names make a political statement, too. Kahentiiosta employed hers as a political act at the end of the Oka crisis. Tiorahkwáthe, the Kahnawake councilor, used to be known as Jimmy Gilbert. Then he abandoned the name by which most of his friends and colleagues knew him.

But taking an indigenous name doesn't always mean ditching a Western one. Kanerahtenhá:wi Hilda Nicholas, to give her full name, runs the language center in the small Mohawk community of Kanehsatake. I mean no disrespect by referring to her henceforth as Hilda; most Mohawks do the same. She's a friend of Marianne Mithun, a California linguist who may well rank as the foremost academic expert on Mohawk; on her desk I noticed a book about Estonian sociolinguistics. Again it struck me how sophisticated the Kanien'kehá:ka are. How humiliating — how absurd, as well — it must have been in the summer of 1990 to hear themselves mocked in the Quebec media as *les sauvages*.

Kanehsatake's thirteen hundred or so residents live beside a French-speaking town called Oka that was, until that year, known only for a provincial park (complete with nudist beach), a Trappist monastery, and a pungent cheese, which the monks silently made and widely sold. Then the town decided to expand its nine-hole golf course. The expansion would have meant bulldozing a Mohawk cemetery and chopping down the pine trees on a sandy hill claimed by the people of Kanehsatake as their own. Some of them took up arms to stop the bulldozers. Activists from far beyond Kanehsatake arrived to help out — or, in other eyes, to stir up trouble. Amid the pines that summer, a brief gunfight left a white policeman dead and led to a long, tense standoff, punctuated by the noise of helicopters, rifles, and sirens and followed, when the exhausted Mohawks and their supporters had finally laid down their weapons, by dozens of arrests.

Hilda didn't speak directly about those events. But the news she wanted to tell me was political. Since the crisis ended, Kanehsatake has experienced a building boom, largely thanks to federal money. A police station, an elders' center, a clinic, and, newest of all, a Mohawk immersion school have been built. Along with the usual facilities of an elementary school, this one boasts an Oral Tradition Room. Yet the language center recently saw its budget cut. "This is the painful struggle we're always left with," Hilda charged. "We're always set up for failure. They don't want us to succeed." "They" meant the government of Canada, and perhaps its people too. My government; my people. She had nothing kind to say about the five-year, twenty-million-dollar Aboriginal Languages Initiative the federal government launched in 1998. "By the time each community gets anything, you're lucky if you get two to three thousand dollars a year. And they expect you to save a language on that? What do they take us for — fools? Of course we know what's going on. They're still carrying out their intentions when they sent people to the residential schools."

In Kanehsatake, Hilda admitted, Mohawk is losing ground. Yet there are people in their forties and fifties here who know the language; the gap between elders and children is narrower than at Six Nations or even Kahnawake. The immersion school is a grassroots initiative, not something imposed on Kanehsatake from on high, and parents are committed to its success. Local elders are busy with language initiatives of one kind or another; several are working on Mohawk versions of previously untranslated books of the Bible. All in all, optimism about the language should be conceivable here.

But Hilda had a message she wanted to get across, and I was a vessel she could use to attack the Canadian government's indifference. "I have a ten-year plan for how to preserve our language in this community," she said. "I've got eighty percent support from people who live here.

But everything's held back by funding. It's very frustrating. These are the struggles we go through. I've said to them, 'Take it seriously.' I've said to them, 'Stop insulting me.'"

In an essay on the significance of language diversity, Marianne Mithun discusses a Mohawk verb: *ia'teiakohahiia'konhákie'*. Karihwénhawe' Dorothy Lazore, the coordinator of the Mohawk standardization project, happened to use the term one day in a story she was telling about her mother. In context, it meant "she was crossing the street." But when split into all its components, the word looks like this: *ia'-te-iako-ha-hiia'k-onhákie'*. David Maracle (or Tawit Kanatawakhon-Maracle) spells it another way — but regardless of the spelling, every syllable, every glottal stop is there for a reason. To hold numerous units of meaning, the verb keeps growing, incorporating nouns inside itself.

Outside the pages of books like this, how much really depends on the way a woman is depicted as walking across a road? Mithun's answer: "Noun incorporation is done for a purpose. It creates single words for what are portrayed as single concepts or events." Speakers of Mohawk are free to play with the language; they aren't required to incorporate. If they choose, they can extract a noun from the verb so as to give it greater emphasis. We can achieve something like the same effect — "The street, she was crossing it" — but in an awkward, even artificial manner. "The grammatical categories of the language," Mithun says, "represent those features of situations that speakers have specified so often that they have become routinized." In short, the definitions and meanings that Mohawk grammar has made routine are not the ones embodied by English. "It is this diversity, the result of millennia of development, that makes the loss of these languages irreparable."

In *Back on the Rez,* Brian Maracle makes a similar point with a different kind of example. "John carefully paddled his canoe through the rapids yesterday," we'd say in English. A Mohawk equivalent could take several forms, but typically it would go like this: "yesterday / through the rapids / his canoe / carefully / he paddled / John." Brian compares the English version to a movie scene in which the camera focuses first on John, then on his boat, and finally on the scene around him. In the Mohawk version, time and landscape take precedence, followed by the boat and then by a man in the boat; personal identity comes last of all. "These two movies," Brian writes, "represent two drastically different ways of looking at life . . . The way that the English-speaking world

structures its sentences explains to me, in a small way, why western society is so self-centred and narcissistic, why it is so fixated on the cult of
the individual and why it is so obsessed with celebrities."

His condemnation of English was written, of course, in English. In
the years after *Back on the Rez* appeared, Brian took his condemnation
to its logical conclusion. Abandoning English: not a good career move
for a writer. But teaching Mohawk, he insists, has its own rewards.

One morning in late winter, wet drifts still clinging to the cornfields, I
drove a short stretch of the way back up the St. Lawrence toward Tyendinaga and Ohsweken. But this time I turned off the freeway at the eastern Ontario town of Cornwall, and followed the signs saying BRIDGE
TO USA. The bridge's first span carried me as far as a narrow island in
the icy river, where a three-dollar tollbooth lay in wait. A few hundred
yards ahead was the U.S. Customs office. Instead of passing through
Customs and climbing the bridge's second span, I took a sharp left onto
Kawehnohkowanen:ne, better known as Cornwall Island. I was listening
to radio station CKON, "your Seaway Valley sports authority." "The
voice of Akwesasne," CKON calls itself in other moods.

Cornwall Island is one of four disconnected parts of Akwesasne. On
the American side of the bridge, just outside the "reservation," stand a
huge General Motors foundry as well as Reynolds and Alcoa aluminum
works. Pollution from the heavy industry beside the river and the Great
Lakes has turned the wild creatures of Akwesasne ("land where the par-
tridge drums") into toxic dumps. On its shores, at the heart of a continent that traditional Iroquois think of as Great Turtle Island, a turtle
was discovered to have 3,067 parts per million of PCB in its body fat —
sixty times the amount needed to qualify as hazardous waste. A New
York State wildlife pathologist once called Akwesasne "the worst place
in the world to be a duck." Rife with smugglers and automatic weapons,
it has also been one of the worst places in all of Indian country for fac-
tional violence.

In only a few minutes I reached the eastern edge of the island, overlooking Iroquois territory in Quebec and New York. "Mohawk territory" would be the normal phrase — but according to a strong oral tradition in Akwesasne, the community, whose founders settled here amid
the turmoil of the mid-eighteenth century, is descended from Ononda-
gas as well as Mohawks. With bone-dry Indian humor, a modest restaurant where the road stops is called The End. Akwesasne, like Kahna-

wake, doesn't bother with house numbers and street names; glancing in the rearview mirror, I saw I was driving much too slowly for the locals' pleasure. Somewhere between an emu ranch and the protective palisade of the Native North American Travelling College, I found the white, two-story home of the most beloved of all Mohawk elders, a life chief under the ancient system of "condolence": Ernie Benedict.

His wife, Florence, called him in from the snow-filled back yard. He was chopping wood to feed the kitchen stove. By now he was eighty-three years old. A couple of decades had gone by since he served as resident elder to Canada's Assembly of First Nations. As he walked in to shake my hand and sit down, I noticed a black pen in the pocket of his green check shirt. His study was lined, ceiling to floor, with books. Copies of *Canadian Geographic* lay on a side table in the living room above a picture book, ready for visiting grandchildren, entitled *The Flintstones' Wacky Inventions.* Ernie's voice was softer than I recalled; but of course, the only time I'd heard him speak he'd been standing in front of a McGill University microphone. English is his second language — he and Florence speak Mohawk between themselves — and he deploys it precisely, without the floury repertoire of "like" and "you know" and "kind of" that thickens so many people's speech.

I asked him about the central concepts of Iroquois law: *skennen, ka'-shatstenhsera,* and *ka'nikonriio.* "Peace," "power," and "righteousness" are the common translations. But the word "power," with its connotations of struggle and politics, saws and drills, may convey a misleading impression of the Iroquois ideal. Or so I had been told by Philip Deering of Kahnawake, and when I mentioned this Ernie smiled and said, "That's what I think. And it's a reason, I guess, for trying to hold on to other languages. For some, it helps enlarge their thinking. Maybe for others it's a challenge they don't want to take."

What was missing in the standard translations of those terms? He closed his eyes to concentrate. Through a living room window I watched downy woodpeckers and red-winged blackbirds lining up at a feeder suspended from an old maple tree. "Well," Ernie said finally, "with *skennen,* the same word used in another context is *skennenha:* slowly, quietly. With *ka'shatstenhsera,* there's strength in there. There's also a bit of speed implied: *yo'shatste tsi rotorihatye* means 'he's driving along with great speed.' So, the first is slow, and the next has speed. With righteousness, *ka'nikonriio,* you have different words. Something that is nice. Something coming very close to — sometimes used as a word for — law. The fact of *ka'nikonriio* is also — beautiful. Or good. So, goodness and the law are the same."

I had the impression that a three-hour philosophy seminar had just been compressed into a couple of minutes.

Could Iroquois culture survive in the English language alone? Again Ernie let the silence gather before answering. Outside, snow particles danced in the sun. When he spoke, he used the term *Haudenosaunee* rather than Iroquois. "It's almost impossible. I can't think the Haudenosaunee identity could go into future society unless they did have the language. There's so many strikes against the Haudenosaunee way of thinking — people saying 'What good is it? It's a thing of the past!' Myself, I think it is that whole difference in the way of thinking that is an argument for its survival." I remembered what Ovide Mercredi had said in Cree, years earlier: "I live different from you. Not that I hate you. But because I like the way we live ourselves, as people. The future must be different."

Ernie's thoughts turned to the *Ohenton karihwatehkwen* — the Haudenosaunee thanksgiving address, the words that come before all else. In Mohawk, he ventured to say, "you're free to add on many little adjectives and particles, embellishments to the word that do not translate into English very well. It would spoil the flow of English. But in Mohawk it's just pulled right along, because each word is a complete thought or a sentence. So in English you have shortcuts." And it's not just a matter of embellishments. Ernie lowered his voice, cleared his throat, and uttered what sounded like a few words in his own language. No, it was a single word: *entitewahwe'nonni'*. "At the beginning, they say 'Now that the people have come together.' The word in Mohawk has a whole range of meanings. One is that 'We are able to fit into this space.' And it also has the meaning 'Now we have all come and we are open, we are receptive to what's going to happen.' Or, 'We will be wrapped up in it.' Then the idea of body is implied. So, 'Our bodies together are able to fit into this place.' I mean, that's only one word. But it takes all that time to explain it in English."

A broad smile broke out on his creased face. "If you try to explain it all in English, you lose the whole flow. People will probably walk away." Ernie laughed and his long hair shook and the laughter hung in the air, and I remembered what Philip Deering had told me months before: for many Haudenosaunee, even now, the *Ohenton karihwatehkwen* gives meaning and justification to life.

11

Humboldt's Parrot

AT THE BEGINNING of the nineteenth century the German scientist Alexander von Humboldt arrived in South America. Most of it still belonged to the stagnant Spanish Empire. Humboldt and his companion, a French botanist named Aimé Bonpland, would spend five years exploring a region that had dropped out of European consciousness since the forced departure of the Jesuits decades earlier. Having spent a few months in the coastal lowlands around the small city of Caracas, the two men ventured by foot, mule, and canoe into the vast interior. Before Humboldt, no European or North American had realized what an incredible diversity of animal and plant life flourished in the tropics. In what would soon become Venezuela, Humboldt found pristine forests, broken occasionally by Indian settlements. Their residents, unlike the Mohawks far to the north, had avoided the wrath of foreign armies. But even here colonization had left a bitter legacy. Many of the indigenous peoples had been weakened and diminished by epidemics. Often the survivors lived at small mission stations scattered along the rivers that drained and shaped the jungle.

Humboldt rarely had a chance to speak his native language in South America. For the most part he relied on Spanish and French. During his years away from Berlin, he is said to have discovered the electric eel, made the first accurate drawings of Inca ruins, given the Brazil nut its scientific name, crossed the Andes four times, and recognized the cold current off the coast of Peru that still bears his name. There was nothing, it seems, he didn't want to know. Curious and knowledgeable about a host of scientific disciplines, Humboldt was also a linguist. His great multivolume work *Travels to the Equinoctial Regions of the New Continent* includes much firsthand news of indigenous languages. Along the upper reaches of the Orinoco, for example, the sheer abundance of languages surprised and troubled him. Spanish was of little use. And without a lingua franca, "a traveller, however great may be his talent for languages, can never hope to learn enough to make himself understood along the navigable rivers."

We live among shadows. The dodo and the passenger pigeon have fresh company every month: since human beings began to dream and talk their way across the earth, thousands of species of animals and plants have died out, and today many thousands of others are at risk. Previous episodes of mass extinction probably followed a collision with some errant heavenly body. Now the asteroid is us. Hunting, the oldest profession, still endangers some animals — the last wild gorillas and chimpanzees are turning into "bush meat" daily. But far more creatures have fallen into danger as an indirect result of human behavior: the ravaging of forests and coral reefs, the use of chemical pesticides and industrial pollutants, the technologies of modern farming . . . These forces take their toll on minority cultures, too.

Like languages, species can vanish by accident and oversight; often their demise is casual. Most of the victims are neither large nor photogenic. One of the smallest birds to become extinct was a flightless songbird called the Stephens Island wren, which disappeared in 1894 from its single home, a green rock off the New Zealand coast. Over the millennia, free from the usual predators, the bird had lost the power to fly. Stephens Island's only human inhabitant was a lighthouse keeper, and the lighthouse keeper had nothing against wrens. But for company he kept a cat named Tibbles — and Tibbles exterminated the species.

On a visit to the Rocky Mountains a couple of years ago, I dangled my left hand off a walkway beside a natural pool in Banff National Park, eighteen inches above a bed of brown-green algae. A dragonfly skimmed the surface. The algae rippled in the wind. "Pond scum," you might say. Except that this particular scum harbored a few diminutive mollusks: *Physella johnsoni*, the Banff Springs snail, which is known to survive in just five ponds near the town of Banff. The snails occur only where lukewarm water spills out of Sulphur Mountain, smelling as rotten as the name suggests. Notable, under a magnifying glass, for their tiny black eyes and their coiled, globelike shells, the snails devour the algae that grow in the sulphurous water. Even the largest of them are no bigger than a small fingernail.

If you dip your hands into a pond while wearing insect repellent or sunscreen, you endanger an endangered species even further. Over the millennia, the snails have adapted to a delicate environment containing large amounts of dissolved gypsum, little oxygen, and no artificial chemicals. Human swimming in the ponds — tempting, despite the odor, but illegal — has destroyed some mats of algae, and with them the snails' eggs. "Are snails just as important as grizzly bears?" asks a Parks Canada leaflet. "You bet they are! . . . Healthy populations of Banff Springs snails indicate the integrity of their unique hot-spring ecosystems. It's all just a matter of scale." The snails used to exist at nine springs in the area; from four, they have disappeared.

To conserve Banff Springs snails, unlike languages, we don't have to think about psychology. Give the snails a chance, and they'll breed. The only necessary task is to safeguard their habitat. All the snails require is for their turquoise, algae-laden pools to be left untouched. In the heart of Canada's most popular national park, that's easier said than done.

Still, the idea that we have a moral duty to preserve *Physella johnsoni* — so small, so impossible to cuddle, so lacking in what you might call animal magnetism — is uncontroversial. To humans, the creature is useless. Yet time, energy, and money are being spent to grant the snail a future. Consider this a sign of the intellectual success the conservation movement has enjoyed over the past century. Many populations of animals continue to suffer a grievous decline. But the public relations battle on their behalf was won decades ago.

The more that human actions show up the fragility of the natural world, the greater lip service we pay to the fight against extinction. Words like "ecosystem" and "biodiversity" now trip off the tongues of children (the concept of linguistic diversity, by contrast, is still unfamiliar to many adults). From their earliest days in preschool and nursery school, children learn about endangered species. There are coloring books about big-eyed sea turtles whose eggs are stolen by poachers, whose nesting sites are destroyed by bulldozers, and whose digestive systems are choked by plastic. Guilt precedes literacy: it's a heavy weight to lay on a two-year-old. Extinction, once a shocking idea, holds few surprises anymore.

Only forty-seven Indians were left at the village of Atures when Humboldt and Bonpland arrived there, and in the absence of its Jesuit founders, the Catholic mission was in "the most deplorable state." San Juan Nepomuceno de los Atures, to give the place its full title, had been built in 1748, taking the last of its names from the Indian people of the region. Barely half a century later, the Atures had disappeared. Humboldt found that the families living in the wretched settlement spoke languages called Guahibo and Maco. According to a Guahibo tradition, the Atures, hunted by yet another people called the Caribs, had fled to an island in the Orinoco. There they died out. If the tale is true, it's likely that disease, not warfare, killed them. All that survived of them, Humboldt learned, were their tombs in a mountain cave high above the great river: "the place of sepulchre of a whole nation destroyed."

He climbed to the cave one evening, stopping to admire the view over savannahs stretching far to the west. Looking down on the Orinoco, he could see the cluster of forested islands where the Atures were rumored to have taken refuge. A great rock jutted out of the granite mountain. In a hollow of the rock Humboldt counted nearly six hundred skeletons, varnished with "odoriferous resins" and decorated with red paint. Each skeleton reposed in a palm basket. On the ground nearby were earthenware vases also containing bones. Humboldt chose several skulls and three complete skeletons, one of them a child's, and as darkness approached he loaded them onto his mules. He intended to ship the bones to Europe for scientific study.

Night had fallen by the time he left the cave, and the starlight above the mountain was matched by a resplendent display of fireflies on the slopes below. Humboldt noticed the wild begonias and the sweet-scented vanilla growing near the entrance to the tombs. When he arrived back in the village, the local people became aware of a different smell: a resinous odor, coming from the backs of the tired-out mules. They knew what it meant, and they made sure Humboldt saw their fury. But if they were furious, they were also powerless.

Rare species of wildlife that range over a wide territory — sea turtles, tigers, Siberian cranes, and so on — are among the hardest to conserve.

Many of these creatures are also slow growing and slow breeding. But when any population shrinks to just a few dozen individuals, the threat of extinction calls for drastic measures. You may want to eliminate human traffic, as Australia did when it turned a flat, dry, grassy woodland in central Queensland into a national park closed to the public. The woodland — once part of Epping Forest, a big cattle station — is the only remaining home of a species called the northern hairy-nosed wombat. Park wardens have fenced in three hundred hectares, keeping all livestock out and encouraging the native grasses to regenerate. The wombats are imprisoned in their own small wilderness. Human intervention led, indirectly, to their death everywhere else: clearing of forests, competition from sheep and cattle, infestations of foreign grasses. Now, human intervention — habitat management, genetic research, supplementary feeding, and so on — is the wombats' best hope. At last count their number was down to sixty-five.

Languages need a larger habitat than hairy-nosed wombats or hot-spring snails. But people who want to help languages endure face a similar challenge: to find a way of encouraging them to reproduce. Queensland and the Rocky Mountains are two of the many areas where indigenous languages might benefit from a gift of energy, money, and outside expertise. Even so, for the purposes of language reproduction, no external gift matters as much as self-belief. If mothers, fathers, and grandparents want to speak a language with their children, that language will survive. But if mothers, fathers, and grandparents are constantly told that their language is an old-fashioned relic, unfit to be uttered in a classroom or a factory and useless for their children's future, then few of them are likely to keep up the struggle.

Human environments, we now realize, are in perpetual transition. Change has always occurred; stasis is death. In an oral culture, word-for-word repetition may well be less faithful to tradition than creative adaptation. A language, unlike a wombat, can't be fenced in — its speakers can't be denied access to the world. Some kinds of change — vaccination programs, for instance — can even save a language by forestalling fatal epidemics among its only speakers. The future is not always a menace. But to ease the transition from the old ways, a minority culture needs the chance to adapt on its own terms.

The most damaging changes are often unintended. A generation ago, disaster was inadvertent when it fell upon Ladakh, a Himalayan valley at the far northwestern edge of India. The valley's people, who are Buddhist and ethnically Tibetan, speak Ladakhi, a language distantly related to Boro. Until the mid-1970s the great snowpeaks of the Himalayas isolated their communities from all but the most intrepid outsiders. Then the government of India built a highway to connect the valley to the rest of the country, and the people of Ladakh learned that they were "underdeveloped." They had no TV sets, no refrigerators, no recorded music. They lived in mud houses. Economists drove in and told the people they were poor. For the first time, they began to feel imprisoned in their own small wilderness. Within fifteen years of the highway's construction, Ladakh's self-sufficient local economy had been undermined by cash and credit, and its ancient forms of knowledge were being eroded by government schools in which Ladakhi children came to believe that their culture and language were inadequate for the modern world. The highway could not be unbuilt.

"Young children I had never seen before used to run up to me and press apricots into my hands," wrote the Swedish anthropologist Helena Norberg-Hodge in her book *Ancient Futures: Learning from Ladakh.* "Now little figures, looking shabbily Dickensian in threadbare Western clothing, greet foreigners with empty outstretched hands. The films they see and the tourists they meet make their lives seem primitive." No longer do the Ladakhi people stand at the center of their own lives; instead they are conscious of existing on a periphery, far from the "real life" taking place in New Delhi or New York. Young travelers from rich countries flock to Ladakh, hoping to find an unspoiled refuge from the materialism of their own societies. Instead they pass on the very values they are yearning to escape. They don't speak Ladakhi. They don't drink butter tea. Searching for the wisdom of the ages, they encourage the locals to speak English and sell soft drinks. Defenders of highway building and globalization can rightly say that the Ladakhis are richer than before. But it would be hard to claim they're better off.

If Humboldt had cared only about ornithology, he would still have found much in Venezuela to keep him busy. The nation contains forty-three species of birds that are known to exist nowhere else, some of them with memorable English names like the "handsome fruiteater" and the "guttulated foliage-gleaner." A secretive, insect-eating, ground-dwelling bird called the Tachira antpitta was last seen in Venezuela in 1956, and no one can be sure if it's extinct — rare birds, like rare languages, sometimes survive unexpectedly.

But the explorer had much else on his mind. Among other things, he wanted to trace the relationship of the vanished Atures to the surviving Indian peoples of the region. In the Orinoco's "labyrinth of petty nations," this proved to be a hard task. With no history texts to help, Humboldt realized that the best way to work out the labyrinthine interrelationships would be by "the analogy of tongues. These are the only monuments that have reached us from the early ages of the world; the only monuments which, not being fixed to the soil, are at once movable and lasting, and have traversed time and space." His perceptions echoed — or did they influence? — the work of his older brother Wilhelm, one of the great linguists of the early nineteenth century, a man convinced that each language contains an inner form expressing its speakers' vision of the world. "There can never be a moment of true standstill in language," Wilhelm was to write, "just as little as in the ceaselessly flaming thought of men. By nature it is a continuous process of development."

Leaving the village of Atures, Alexander von Humboldt moved along the Orinoco to a mission settlement by the name of San Jose de Maypures. There two other indigenous languages were spoken. He arrived by night, struck by the solitude of a village where he could hear nothing but the calls of nocturnal birds and the clamor of a distant waterfall. Even in the middle of the night, however, the mosquitoes were ravenous. In the morning, scratching his bites, he walked around Maypures: it didn't take long. The little church, built of palm trunks, stood on a plain below the waterfall. Seven or eight huts surrounded the church, and in some of them women were making pottery. Humboldt admired these huts for their "appearance of order and neatness, rarely met with in the houses of the missionaries." Nearby, plantains and cassavas were being cultivated. The introduced goats had been devoured by jaguars, but descendants of the Jesuits' black-and-white pigs had managed to survive.

Maypures had another domestic species, too.

The greatest concentrations of linguistic diversity are found in the tropics. Languages thrive where the web of biological diversity is also at its most intricate: in tropical rain forests, above all. More languages are indigenous to Venezuela than to all of central and eastern Canada — an area many times its size. Where food is abundant, territories don't need to be large. Where food is scarce, territories expand. The same principles hold true for both biological and linguistic evolution.

The wet, hilly, verdant island of New Guinea — now divided between the nation of Papua New Guinea and the Indonesian-controlled region of Irian Jaya — has given birth to about eleven hundred living languages. One in every six languages spoken on the planet comes from this island. (These are languages, remember, not dialects.) In New Guinea each valley, each mountain, each tributary, each bay seems to have a language of its own. Five times more languages are native to the island than to the entire continent of Europe. New Guinea is also a hotbed of biological diversity on a scale almost inconceivable in colder realms. In 1996 Conservation International sponsored a team of scientists to assess biodiversity in the Lakekamu Basin, a lowland rain forest in Papua New Guinea. Some of the sites they visited were already being logged by transnational companies. Working in an intact forest just a single square kilometer in size, the scientists counted more than two hundred fifty species of ants. A single month in the Lakekamu Basin was enough for the research team to discover twenty-three species of previously unknown insects, eleven new species of frogs, seven new species of reptiles, and three new species of fish.

Unknown to Western science, that is. Often the indigenous people of a region have been familiar with a "new" species since time immemorial. One such species, the Arnhem Land long-necked turtle, lives in the far north of Australia. I first heard of the turtle at the visitor center in Nitmiluk National Park. A few minutes' walk away, orange-red cliffs overshadowed a river whose relentless waters had pushed a deep gorge through the Arnhem Land plateau. Until the year 2000 the turtle that lives in rock holes above the river had neither an English nor a scientific name — a name, that is, in the dead language used by taxonomists. The animal's small size and flattened head, along with its habit of feeding on water lilies as well as fish, distinguish it from *Chelodina rugosa*, the northern long-necked turtle. Yet the Gagudju, one of the Aboriginal peoples of the plateau, have always known that *burrungandji*, the "new" species, is not the same as *almangiyi*, the "old" one. It's just that nobody from the outside bothered to ask them. The Gagudju language is now endangered; it belongs to a very few old-timers. In tribute to Gagudju, the Australian scientists who formally described the species have given it the Latin name *Chelodina burrungandjii*. If and when

Gagudju vanishes, what other environmental knowledge will vanish with it?

Language centers in many countries are fighting against the clock, recording the words of elderly speakers before time silences them. I think of *Ngaapa Wangka Wangkajunga,* a word book in an Australian desert language that is, like Gagudju, at risk of extinction. An old woman called Dolly Snell enriched the book with dozens of Wangkajunga terms for plants and bush tucker — essential knowledge in an arid environment. Perhaps her knowledge can be transferred across languages; perhaps not. Neither she nor the linguist who compiled the book had a precise English word for *karlijita* ("an edible grass seed"), *nartutaka* ("a small plum-like fruit from bushes that grow on hills"), *ngalyilka* ("a small edible mushroom"), or *purti-purti* ("a plant similar to bush tobacco. Eating this plant will make a hungry person feel full"). The language reflects its value in the environment: Wangkajunga may have as many words for lizard as Wall Street does for financial instruments. In the future, perhaps, zoologists will find that the language had reason to distinguish *lungkurta* ("a blue-tongue lizard") from *lungminka* ("a blue-tongue lizard") and *ngintul* ("a blue-tongue lizard"). They may well be able to clone a duneful of *lungkurtas* on demand. But by then, other kinds of meaning that went with the Wangkajunga knowledge system will no longer be available. A language can never be cloned.

In an appeal for action, not just rhetoric, biologists are warning of the consequences that lie in wait if the loss of biodiversity continues apace. They say that self-interest, not just altruism, warrants a major shift in behavior. Biologically diverse regions can better withstand drought and other natural (or unnatural) stress. Many of our most common and effective medicines derive from wild plants, but Western scientists have studied only a tiny proportion of plant species for their medicinal value. If potential cures for crippling diseases are being shredded into pulp or shipped across an ocean as plywood, we may never know about them. By "we," I mean the mainstream cultures of wealthy nations. Indigenous peoples often know a great deal about the natural world, and part of the knowledge lies embedded in their languages. In the isolated Haida language spoken in British Columbia and Alaska, the name for a common plant means "leaf remedy of the grizzly bear." If the Haida people lose their language, the plant will revert to "alum root," its old meaning forgotten. Might human lives be saved thanks to words like *th'alátel* — literally, "a device for the heart" — a term in the endangered Halkomelem language, also native to British Columbia, for wild ginger?

Biologists and environmental activists can threaten as well as plead, warn as well as cajole. Until very recently, linguists have done little except analyze and describe. You can debate a politician about the intrinsic usefulness of an old-growth forest, pointing to the long-term economic benefits of tourism and sustainable harvesting — but sustaining an ancient language may not boost anybody's gross domestic product. Most visitors to Bathurst Island want to see Tiwi funerary poles and dine on locally caught fish; but after they hear a sentence or two in Tiwi, they want to see those poles and eat that food in English. A language is not a commodity (wild ginger notwithstanding); trade rules don't apply to it. Forget the economics of language, then. But it's also tough to argue on purely moral grounds that a threatened language has the right to be protected. Individuals have rights, companies and governments insist that they have rights, animals may or may not have rights — but languages?

When forests are cut down, the rights of local peoples are usually ignored. The peoples scatter or die. So do their languages. Now, almost in desperation, some linguists have begun to adopt the tactics and metaphors of biologists. Linguists have been learning to act as partisans, campaigning on behalf of the languages they once set out to study in a cool, neutral light. At last they are speaking out about the resilience that comes with diversity; they are condemning the wanton advance of bulldozers and chain saws; they are pleading for niches of equilibrium to remain undisturbed. In short, they are warning of the dangers inherent in what the biologist Edward O. Wilson calls an "impoverished and homogenized world," one in which a few dominant life forms have overrun and erased the diversity that used to sustain us.

But by dominant life forms Wilson means creatures like rats and starlings, cane toads and zebra mussels. Linguists mean the tongue I'm using now.

In the village of Maypures Humboldt was delighted to see not only black-and-white pigs, but also "tame macaws around the huts of the Indians, and flying to the fields like our pigeons . . . These macaws, whose plumage glows with vivid tints of purple, blue and yellow, are a great ornament to the Indian farmyards." He had noticed the species near other tropical rivers, and had tasted its cooked flesh: "black and somewhat tough." Ever punctilious in his descriptions, Humboldt called it "the largest and most majestic species of parrot with naked cheeks that we found on our travels." It was, almost certainly, the blue-and-yellow macaw, a species that still survives over wide stretches of South America.

Other macaws have been less fortunate. Of the eighteen recognized species, all of them native to Latin America, two are extinct and a third, Spix's macaw, perches on the brink. The last wild member of the species lived in eastern Brazil until it disappeared in October 2000, leaving a few dozen captive specimens divided among a Qatari sheik, a Philippine industrialist, and a Swiss entrepreneur. The species is not just a commodity but a trophy, the birds' rarity a symbol of their owners' power. The International Union for the Conservation of Nature describes the status of seven other types of macaw as vulnerable, endangered, or critical. Only eight species appear safe.

Amid the shadows of the huts in Maypures, Humboldt was shown a talking parrot. It too was a trophy of sorts. He didn't specify whether it happened to be a blue-and-yellow macaw or a member of a different species. It was an old bird, a feathered survivor. But the local people insisted that "they did not understand what it said." When Humboldt asked why, he was told that the parrot "spoke the language of the Atures" — the language of the people whose resinous bones his mules had carried off the granite mountain. The Atures language had died out among humans. It was last heard coming from a bird's beak.

Ways of Escape

YIDDISH

N O FEELING on the left side," a man behind me said. "Something coming from a disc in his neck. He had to have the operation immediately or else he'd be in a wheelchair for the rest of his life." It was the last night of a four-week run of *The Great Houdini*, a play at Montreal's Saidye Bronfman Centre, and the 320 seats were packed. Admittedly, some members of the audience had trouble schlepping up the stairs to their seats. In a metropolis where more people speak French at home than any other language, the program was printed in English. But the show took place in neither of those tongues; *The Great Houdini* was the annual production of the city's Yiddish Theatre. As the lights went down I noticed a woman in a chestnut wig, heavy makeup, and a black leather jacket. How long, I wondered, since she passed her eightieth birthday? I should live so long.

The play began. If it had been in English, I would have called it a Broadway musical. But, as a Yiddish proverb goes, "If grandmother had balls, she would have been a grandfather." This is a language for realists. The opening scene, set on Coney Island, featured aging women wearing bloomers and tights that might have been a trifle risqué back in 1894. Two gentlemen in their sixties did a creditable song-and-dance number. In its leisurely fashion, the play was tracing the career of a Hungarian Jew called Erik Weisz. When he was a boy, his family emigrated to America and he became Ehrich Weiss; then he transformed himself more radically into the magician Harry Houdini. If he wanted, he could make a parrot disappear. His shtick was the art of escape. Even so, the Yiddish-speaking past kept pulling him back — or so the script argues.

I followed the story by reading the overtitles that flashed in French and English above the wide stage. Sometimes this was enough to provoke a weird cognitive dissonance. "England, England, keeper of the light," announced one overtitle. The other read, "England, England, pays grandiose." "*Toyt is toyt!*" Houdini's brother said. Or, "Death is death." Or, roll the Gallic drums, "La mort est irréversible." In deference to the pious, the Creator's name was rendered as "G-d" in English, though it remained "Dieu" in French. Even to an outsider like me, the overtitles were not always necessary, for the speeches contained a heavy smattering of English. Talking to his beloved mama (a woman whose influence he never could escape), Harry said: "*Ir meynt az ikh fil gut vegn dem?* Theo is in business, Nathan is a lawyer, Leo is in medical school, *un ikh? Shlep zikh arum fun eyn office tsum andern.*"

It's not only for convenience that I give the Yiddish text in the familiar Roman alphabet; that's also how it appears in the script the actors were using. Outside the theater not all the performers could speak fluent Yiddish, let alone read it. Yiddish is a complex offshoot of German. But normally it's written in the twenty-two letters of the Hebrew alphabet and must be read from right to left. The language looks, excuse the expression, more exotic than it sounds.

At the interval I glanced at Montreal photographs in the arts center's basement and at postmodern Toronto paintings on the main floor. I also listened to the schmoozing crowd. Most of the conversations were being held in English, a few in French, and only one in Yiddish. "I hear she's not doing so well lately," a woman said with a sigh as I clambered past her into my seat. A bright-eyed man turned to me and asked, "Are you enjoying the play?"

"Yes, I like it a lot."

"Do you understand the Yiddish?"

He took it for granted I was Jewish. I hadn't the heart to tell him otherwise.

"No, not very much."

"A pity." The man would not relent. I began to fear he was a nudzh. "Did your parents speak Yiddish in the home?"

"Not a lot, I'm afraid." While not exactly a lie, this was a profound understatement.

"I'm seventy-six," he went on, "and I'm one of the fortunate ones. My parents could speak English but we had to speak Yiddish to my grandparents. They couldn't understand any English. Could yours?"

Could mine? No matter what I told him, I would feel like a schmo. "Kind of like your situation," I mumbled.

The man nodded and began to praise his grandson. The boy attends Bialik High School in Montreal — one of the few secular schools in the world that maintains compulsory Yiddish classes. "You should hear him talk. You'd be amazed!"

The lights dimmed, saving me from further dissembling.

In the second half of the play, Harry — distressed by his mama's death in America at a time when he was performing in Europe — visits Margery, a shiksa spiritualist recommended to him by Sir Arthur Conan Doyle. Shimmering and billowing, the woman fakes a maternal apparition, at which the unnerved magician cries out, *"Mama . . . Mama . . . dos bistu? Ruf mikh on mit mayn yiddishn nomen."* After a long pause the ghostly voice has to admit she can't remember her boychik's Yiddish name. *"Du shvindlern!"* Harry shouts at Margery. *"Mayn mama hot fargesn mayn yiddishn nomen? Du shvindlern."*

This was the moment, I thought, where the Yiddish language came into its own. Instead of remaining a picturesque effect, a chance for applauding pensioners to revel in sounds from their childhood, Yiddish became essential to the action. To win success, Harry had disguised his origins, but, the scene suggests, he had not forgotten them. By using language to expose Margery as a fraud, he was showing that bilingualism can be a liquid asset. It can make you less credulous, less easy to fool. It gives you an extra line of defense. Harry died when he forgot to keep his guard up; a goyish boxer punched him in the stomach before he'd readied himself for the blow. The boxer was a medical student at a university that had, at the time, a strict quota on Jews — McGill University in Montreal. For Houdini, this was the city of no escape.

A few days later I talked to Irwin Block, a journalist who had spent his evenings over the past month playing Conan Doyle in a deerstalker cap. On him, it looked good. The cast was replete with businessmen, dentists, and teachers; the phonetic coach worked as a maxillofacial surgeon in his spare time. One of the regulars, a property manager, had been absent from *The Great Houdini;* he was recovering from a multiple bypass. Despite the ailments and afflictions of her cast, the theater's director, Bryna Wassermann, has always insisted on mounting new work. *The Great Houdini,* in its Yiddish incarnation, was a world première.

During the Vietnam war Irwin had been one of the rare Western reporters based in Laos. An agnostic, he seldom ventures into even the most progressive of synagogues. But a few years ago he felt a pull back to the secular culture of his childhood. He joined a Yiddish choir and started collecting Yiddish poetry. "Then I discovered the thrill of being onstage, and now I'm hooked. Even though the rehearsals are all in English, this has definitely improved my Yiddish — when you're singing, you have to understand every word.

"It's fun, it's entertainment, and it's rewarding. I'm part of a community, too. Trouble is, the core audience is dying."

Yiddish was created by the Ashkenazim — the Jews of Europe. Its origins are unclear, but, according to the commonest theory, it emerged a thousand years ago in the Rhine Valley between lands that were destined to become France and Germany. The first speakers were probably Jews hightailing it out of France and into the vicinity of Cologne. It's a fusion language with layers and hidden depths, one of the deepest layers being made up of terms from Romance languages such as Old French.

The Jews who had the chutzpah to haul those words into Germany also knew Hebrew and Aramaic, a related language from biblical times — or at least the men and older boys did. Hebrew is the language used in most of the Jewish Bible, whose first five books, the Torah, enjoy an ineradicable holiness in the minds of devout Jews. (Before the creation of our world, many believe, God chatted with the angels in Hebrew.) Aramaic joins Hebrew to form the idiom of the Talmud, a multivolume set of commentaries on the Torah and the prime object of study in Jewish religious academies. Jesus, in all likelihood, spoke Aramaic. At least one in every ten Yiddish words derives from Aramaic and Hebrew. Their importance may exceed their number. "Without Hebrew," Lucy Dawidowicz once wrote, "Yiddish appears dull and listless . . . The Hebrew words wore top hats. They have dignity, style, tradition, elegance. These qualities they bring into Yiddish."

From the banks of the Rhine, Jews spread out to other German-speaking parts of Europe. Having mastered the language of their neighbors, they began filling its nooks and crannies with terms from Hebrew,

Aramaic, and old French. Then they migrated east, settling in regions that would enter history as Poland, Lithuania, Belarus, Hungary, Ukraine, and Romania. Regions, that is, where most of their neighbors spoke a Slavic tongue. And so, because Yiddish was always permeable, informal, a language without the exact vocabulary and exacting grammar of Hebrew or Latin, it took on a Slavic layer too. (In *The Joys of Yiddish* Leo Rosten calls it "the Robin Hood of languages.") A single Yiddish word often blends a pair of sources. One example is the word for pickpocket, *kesheneganev,* which marries the Polish word for pocket with the Hebrew term for thief.

Nearly all the Jews who stayed behind in central and western Europe relinquished Yiddish — Karl Marx, Franz Kafka, Gustav Mahler, and Albert Einstein did their work in German. Dutch Jews also abandoned Yiddish — although some Yiddish words, such as *schofel* (shabby), took root in modern Dutch. In the cities of eastern Europe, Yiddish remained a minority language; only in the little shtetls did it shape the speech of entire communities. But at times of need, even the village Jews had to communicate with the gentiles around them. Users of Yiddish, like users of Romany, are almost never monolingual. Gentiles rarely bothered to learn Yiddish, or Romany.

The vagaries of history make it hard to talk both accurately and casually about Yiddish and its speakers. Take one of the centers of Jewish life and learning before the Holocaust: the city of Vilna, also called Vilnius, also called Wilno. Here, more than anywhere else, Yiddish became the language of an urban elite. Here, Yiddish was eminent. The speech of Vilna enjoyed the highest prestige of the language's three main dialects (Polish and Ukrainian versions being the others). But where was Vilna? Not counting all the times of war when it fell under occupation by the armies of France, Germany, and Sweden, Vilna belonged to Lithuania during the Middle Ages, Poland through most of the seventeenth and eighteenth centuries, Russia during the nineteenth, Poland again after the First World War, and the Soviet Union after the second. Go figure. Today it's back in an independent Lithuania. Its Yiddish speakers have been described as "Polish Jews," "Russian Jews" and "Lithuanian Jews." Nationalities come and go; the Jewish aspect of the city remained constant, until most of Vilna's Jews were wiped out.

Harry Houdini was one of millions of Jews from central and eastern Europe who, between 1880 and 1920, boarded ships for America. They were fleeing the recurrent pogroms that shook pre-revolutionary Russia. Soon they launched a full-throated Yiddish culture on what was, to them, a young continent. Montreal, Los Angeles, Chicago, and Philadelphia were among the cities where Yiddish theaters, newspapers, and book publishers thrived. A Yiddish vaudeville sprang up, featuring performers who could switch at the drop of a hat from dances and off-color jokes to sentimental religious songs like "Fraytik af der nakht iz yeder yid a meylekh" (On Friday night every Jew is a king). The heart of the culture lay in New York, where Second Avenue acquired the nickname "the Yiddish Broadway." Yiddish words were quick to enrich the local vernacular — words like *klutz, dreck,* and *schlock.* Few languages are so rich in expressions of complaint and dismay.

As a Jewish fusion language, Yiddish was not unique. Sephardic Jews — who were welcomed in Moorish Spain but would be expelled by its Christian conquerors — created a language variously called Ladino, Judezmo, or Judeo-Spanish. Jews in parts of north Africa and the Middle East spoke Judeo-Arabic; smaller groups developed Judeo-Persian and Judeo-Provençal. In all these cases, Hebrew and Aramaic elements mingled with a dominant overlay of words from the majority culture. Yiddish stood out, however, by virtue of the sheer number of its users. Early in the twentieth century as many as ninety percent of the world's Jews were Ashkenazim. Most of them spoke Yiddish. Then the Holocaust turned the language to ash.

So the story goes. But in fact the collapse of Yiddish is neither so simple nor so abrupt. True, millions of Yiddish speakers died at the hands of Hitler and his willing executioners. But millions of other Yiddish speakers grew safely old outside Europe (not only in the United States but also in the likes of Canada, Australia, Mexico, and Argentina), passing on less and less of the shtetl language to their children and grandchildren. From the start, Jews did well in America: Hollywood was merely the greatest of their inventions. But while many of their turns of phrase were finding a permanent home in that other fusion speech known as American English, a torrent of English words — and, more damagingly, English grammatical structures — breached the leaky walls of Yiddish. The welcoming nature of American society, from a strictly linguistic standpoint, posed a menace to immigrant tongues. *Fentster* is the Yiddish word for window — but as the story goes, one Yiddish speaker says to another, "How do you say *vinde* in English?" Immigration led to integration; integration, to assimilation.

It was a sadder, uglier story inside the Soviet Union, where Jews, Leon

Trotsky above all, had played crucial roles in the October Revolution. By way of reward the 1920s saw a rich flowering of Yiddish. Birobidzhan, an especially isolated corner of eastern Siberia, was even declared an "autonomous Jewish district." In its snowy forests, Yiddish enjoyed official status. But when Joseph Stalin turned against the Jews, Yiddish became an unacceptable language, one that Jews in cities like Moscow and Leningrad were smart to forget. Anti-Semitism, that old czarist disease, now took on a Communist twist. To succeed, even to survive, Jews had to live in Russian. Not even Birobidzhan was exempt from the terror. Many Jews were desperate to escape to the new state of Israel. About sixty Yiddish-language books were published in the Soviet Union in 1948; during the following decade there were none. In August 1952 Stalin ordered the execution of some of the language's best writers.

Assaults on Yiddish were nothing new: it had long been under fierce attack from other Jews. To the eighteenth- and nineteenth-century reformers of the Haskalah, or Jewish enlightenment, Yiddish was nothing more than "Jargon": an uncouth corruption of German, fit for nebbishes. "Down with filth, spider webs, Jargon, and every kind of refuse!" declared Daniel Nayfeld, the editor of a Polish-Jewish journal in the 1860s. "We need a broom, a broom!" Nayfeld believed that European Jews should speak and write the languages of the Gentiles around them. A linguistic cleansing, he thought, would be a moral and intellectual cleansing too.

Nayfeld launched his attack just when Yiddish books and newspapers were proliferating. He saw their success as a threat. Most Yiddish writers were men — men who aimed many of their stories at women. This was a new audience, a hungry audience. For centuries Jewish girls had been discouraged from reading and writing; reading was a male prerogative because it took place in *Loshn-koydesh*, the holy tongue, sacred in its blend of Hebrew and Aramaic. Holiness adhered to men. What remained was *mama-loshen*, the mother tongue, the wagging tongue of women: Yiddish, the language of the home. Entering the house of God, a man was expected to leave his home behind. Was Yiddish serious enough? Was it masculine enough? Such questions didn't bother the women.

In literary terms, the language came into its own at the very moment when it was being squeezed from two sides. Its authors had to contend, not only with ill-tempered assimilationists like Nayfeld, but also with the zealous partisans of modern Hebrew. The founder of Zionism,

Theodor Herzl, considered making Yiddish the common idiom of Jews in Palestine — it was, after all, the daily language spoken by the over-whelming majority of the world's Jews. But in the mid-1890s he decided instead that Hebrew should be the common tongue of Jews in the Holy Land. If his motives were partly pragmatic (Sephardic Jews did not speak or understand Yiddish, leaving only Hebrew to act as a national language of Zion), they were also psychological. Herzl wanted Jews to free themselves from the weight of self-mockery and self-hatred that seemed inextricable from *mama-loshen*. He wanted them to be "real men." Real men spoke Hebrew.

A guerrilla warfare between Yiddish and Hebrew went on for dec-ades, as though the meshugge world had only enough space in it for one Jewish language to thrive. Some champions of Hebrew sniped at Yid-dish because it ranked low in social prestige and had few social graces. In 1904, for instance, the poet Chaim Nachman Bialik sent a letter to the Yiddish writer Sholom Aleichem: "I am sorry that you don't write He-brew . . . The time has finally come for you to stop dallying so much with the 'servant girl.' At least fulfill the conjugal duties of a man toward his wife with the Lady, and go to the servant girl only to satisfy your ap-petite." Bialik's kvetching reveals not only his sexism but his view of He-brew as duty and of Yiddish as pleasure. (Admittedly, Bialik had a way with images. He also said that reading the Bible in any language except Hebrew was like kissing your bride through her veil.)

Prejudice went both ways. In the 1920s the advocates of Yiddish in the Soviet Union ruthlessly suppressed Hebrew, which they equated with backward religiosity. At the same time, Hebrew militants in Pales-tine insisted that a free Jewish society could allow no place for Yiddish theaters, newspapers, and schools. British soldiers had to guarantee the safety of Jewish audiences trying to see the movie *A Yiddishe Mame*. Even after the founding of Israel, its leaders decreed that survivors of the Holocaust should speak Hebrew in the new country. Yiddish stank of defeat, of humiliation — and too many people liked it for comfort. How could a desert bloom in the cadences of the ghetto?

Yiddish can still be heard in Israel, thanks in good measure to the in-flux of Jews from the former Soviet Union. Many older immigrants have found Hebrew difficult to master. But on Israeli TV, Hollywood movies take on a Hebrew flavor — even the Yiddish terms are translated into Hebrew. "What an irony!" a Jerusalem columnist called Sam Or-baum told me. "Yiddish is more mainstream in American English than it is in Israel!" Orbaum saw Yiddish in present-day Israel as "a quaint, obsolete remnant." It has left a few incongruities. Arabs who buy and sell secondhand goods in the street still cry out, *"Alte zachen! Alte zachen!"* Old things, old things.

Yet with the flight of time and the confident spread of Hebrew through Israeli streets and homes, an odd thing began to happen. Yiddish — whose words had been uttered by the millions of Jewish dead and were still alive among those who had escaped — took on the aura of a holy tongue. Hebrew was now a worldly success. Thanks to Auschwitz and Bergen-Belsen, Yiddish became sacred.

That's one interpretation, anyway. In Jewish culture there are always other, competing views. What's not to like? I think of Ron Finegold, a slight and scholarly Orthodox Jew who works as reference librarian at the Jewish Public Library in Montreal. "I see Yiddish libraries that were built up sixty or seventy years ago being thrown out now," he said one day, "because nobody can read them. It's all being abandoned — don't tell me it's carrying on! I keep a few things, the rarities, but all the common or garden things, from Sholom Aleichem on down through the books from the thirties and forties, I don't keep at all."

This may be sad, but it's not sacrilegious. Ron drew himself up to his full height and said, "I've never seen this kind of throwing out of holy texts."

A bitter October day in a northern suburb of Toronto. I maneuvered off the long gash of Highway 401 and found my way to a hectic street corner dominated by a fiberglass statue of a blue-eyed moose. Chava Rosenfarb lives on the tenth floor of a tall building here. High above the moose, her plate-glass windows look out over other glassy towers. A mural composed of ceramic tiles dominates the living room of her apartment: it shows two young people strumming guitars in a green, idyllic setting. The young people are her children. Chava made the mural herself. The pastoral scene on the wall and the scraped sky beyond it are a far cry from the narrow streets of Lodz where, as a young poet behind the barbed-wire enclosure of the wartime ghetto, she became one of the last major writers of Yiddish.

She was dressed all in black, although tiny embroidered flowers were visible on her blouse. I sat near the mural and picked from a big plate of green grapes and another of cookies. "Enjoy!" she said twice. Chava ate nothing herself, but she drank a cup of strong coffee while she talked.

"It was a bustling, lively culture until the Holocaust. Poetry, drama, novel writing, and all kinds of creativity in the Yiddish language. Not to speak about songs — Yiddish is famous for its songs. And then it was eradicated like with the cut of a knife." At the gates of Auschwitz she remembers seeing the elegantly dressed Dr. Mengele, wearing gloves, greeting Jews half-mad with fear, dividing the feeble from the able-bodied, the men from the women . . .

She said goodbye to her father there and never saw him again. She was in three camps. At Bergen-Belsen, in April 1945, she fell sick with typhus fever. Then the camp was liberated. Somehow, Chava had survived. So had her teenage sweetheart, a brilliant young man named Henry Morgentaler. After the Nazi surrender, they scoured Europe for each other — and, amazingly, they found each other. By 1950 Chava had published three volumes of poetry. She was also pregnant. The couple managed to emigrate to Canada, where a stranger on the winter train gave her a Golden Delicious apple: "This was for me the taste of Canada. It was a very festive feeling." When the train pulled into Windsor Station in Montreal, a small crowd of Yiddish writers were there to welcome her. One of them kissed her hand. "They made me a reception in a big public hall, and with my big belly I went up to speak and tell them about my experiences."

Even in Canada, life was not chivalry. Henry Morgentaler resumed his medical studies, interrupted by war, at l'Université de Montréal. To support his studies, he worked as a shipper of parcels. Chava took a job in a factory. She would get up at 4 A.M. to write, having no other time of day that was her own. But instead of poetry she began to write a major novel based on her wartime experiences. She felt a kind of moral duty to describe, with the utmost accuracy, what she had heard and seen. A cherry tree, brought from a shtetl, had flowered improbably in the Lodz ghetto. It became a symbol of hope. Chava named her novel *Der boim fun leib* (The Tree of Life). It was finally published in 1972: some critics call it a masterpiece.

In the meantime, there was domestic life. "Both children when they were very small spoke Yiddish," Chava told me. "And then one day my son was a young child and we went to the beach, and there was a non-Jewish boy there. He tried to speak to my son. And my son answered him in Yiddish. So this boy turned to my husband and asked, 'Does he speak *language*?' My husband and I were stunned. And suddenly we realized that for our children to communicate with others, they had to know English." Not only did the children attend school in English; the family also began to speak English at home.

Chava's daughter, Goldie Morgentaler, has retained her mother's tongue — she made a Yiddish translation of one of Quebec's most celebrated plays, *Les belles soeurs*. Abraham, the little boy on the beach, grew up to be a doctor like his father. "He knows a few words," Chava said, then reverted to the truth: "But no, he's lost his Yiddish." *Yee-dish*, she pronounces it, with a long opening vowel. The telephone interrupted our conversation: a friend calling from Paris. Chava kept the call short. Even so, I had time to hear how her voice softened and grew richer when she was speaking her own language.

Her insistence on memorializing the ghetto, using the very words of the ghetto, led to marital dissent. If her son was unable to read her work, her husband preferred to ignore it. "I didn't want to get back to the pain and the suffering," Henry Morgentaler told the writer Elaine Kalman Naves, who prepared a CBC Radio program about Rosenfarb's work. "She felt she had a duty to be a witness to the past — I wanted to live in the here and now. The past created nightmares for me. Being a doctor is like undoing the nightmares I suffered, undoing the evil of the past." Five years after *Der boim fun leib* was published, the couple divorced. By then Morgentaler was a household name in Canada: the country's most famous abortion doctor, constantly testing the limits of the law. He was revered by millions and reviled by millions. Chava — the writer for whom a Yiddish welcoming committee had braved a snowstorm at Windsor Station — was anonymous. One by one, the welcomers died off.

Her work appeared in Montreal for a time. But the secular Yiddish culture in Montreal — in all of North America, indeed — began to dissolve. For the past few decades Chava's work has been published in Israel. None of her books, she says, is printed in editions of more than a thousand copies. Her readers "are all scattered, all over the world. I don't have many readers anymore. It's not for pleasure I write!" Until the mid-1990s she was a mainstay of a Yiddish literary journal, *Di goldene keyt*, edited in Tel Aviv by the great poet Abraham Sutzkever (himself a partisan who survived the Vilna ghetto). But then *Di goldene keyt* ceased publication. A body blow for Chava, it was also a last-ditch incentive for her to translate her work into English. "I need to have a readership!" she told me. "And now I don't have it anymore. There are single individuals here and there who read my books — but nobody buys them. Finished with buying. There are no bookstores with Yiddish books. So I felt a need to break out into wider waters, the major streams."

So far two of her novels have appeared in English. But, growing old in Montreal, Chava Rosenfarb became lonely. Finally she moved to Toronto, where a sister also lives. Perhaps the solitude is less burdensome now; perhaps. "What affects me most," she wrote in an essay entitled "Confessions of a Yiddish Writer," "is the continual sense of isolation that I feel as a survivor, an isolation enhanced by my being a Yiddish writer. I feel myself to be an anachronism wandering across a page of history where I don't really belong. If writing is a lonely profession, the Yiddish writer's loneliness has an additional dimension. Her readership has perished. Her language has gone up with the smoke of the crematoria. She creates in a vacuum, almost without a readership, out of fidelity to a vanished language, as if to prove that Nazism did not succeed in extinguishing that language's last breath, that it is still alive."

The language of Goethe and Hitler is the source of at least two-thirds of all Yiddish words. But apart from its critical infusion of Hebrew, Aramaic, Slavic, and Romance vocabulary, Yiddish has a spirit and even a structure that make it something other than just a variant dialect of German. From his vantage point in Jerusalem, Sam Orbaum struggled to define "an ineffable element in Yiddish that is impossible to pin down or describe. It's more than a language: it's an attitude. Guilt, the persecution complex, distrust of the goyim, the belief in pervading anti-Semitism, are examples. They're attitudes that directly evoke emotions best expressed in and by Yiddish."

In his *Grammar of the Yiddish Language,* Chava's friend Dovid Katz spends a fair amount of time describing not just the way Yiddish speakers utter words, but the way they move their heads and bodies. As Katz explains, an adjective diminutive "is often accompanied by a gentle forward and downward thrust of the head and the opened palm of one hand, with optional horizontal vibration of the same hand and its fingers, and a slight smile." The thrusting, opening, smiling, and vibrating go along with a slow, falsetto pronunciation of the diminutive, which serves to sweeten an insult or soften a criticism. Similar expressions and gestures go with adverbial diminutives, which a fluent speaker would use to convey meanings like "quite cleverly, but not exactly brilliantly" or "sort of late, but not too late."

Yiddish is full of what Katz calls "satiric characterization": a reper-toire of stock epithets, often accompanied by a lifting of the eyebrows and a shaking of the head or shoulders. The phrase *a fayner man* seems to mean "a nice guy." But when it's used as a satiric characterization, it suggests the opposite: "What a bastard!" Likewise *a krasavitse*, instead of meaning "a beautiful woman," can be used to imply "not a good-looking woman at all." Different in form are the "psychoadverbial in-serts" — phrases that can stand alone, spoken fast in a clipped tone, making clear a listener's attitude to what a speaker has just said. To il-lustrate psychoadverbial inserts, Katz gives the Yiddish for exchanges as pointed as these: "I'm jumping off the roof." "Well, go ahead. Don't come crying to me!" Or, more subtly, "You don't like them, right?" "God forbid. When did I say that?" If Yiddish is often prone to senti-mentality, it's also a language in which intonation puts the kibosh on vocabulary — a language in which subversion is kosher.

Yiddish has a variety of words that mean "question." It has at least eight ways of saying "think." Because some of its verbs factor ideas down to individual grammatical elements, they're "inherently analytic" — this is a linguistic statement of fact, not a value judgment on my part. But speakers of the language are making value judgments all the time. If you're talking about a couple of professors, you must decide whether to call them *profesorn* or *profesoyrim*. Are they menschen who warrant your respect, or schlemiels who do not? Masculine nouns are especially prone to the use of diminutives that convey, with a single word, ideas of "lousy artist," "small-time lawyer," "incompetent teacher," and so on. Yiddish (not that it's unique in this) also has a linguistic feature with the evocative, menacing name "devoicing assimilation": voiced conso-nants like *b* and *d* are "devoiced" by other consonants that follow on, so that the vocal cords no longer vibrate. A traditional Yiddish greeting: "How is a Jew?" The traditional answer: "How should I be?"

Enough already! Dovid Katz hails from Brooklyn, the son of a Yid-dish-language poet. He lived for many years in England, running a Yid-dish Studies program at Oxford University. But in the 1990s, after com-pleting his invaluable grammar, he moved to Lithuania, taking charge of a Yiddish Institute at the university in Vilna and directing its Center for Stateless Cultures. About four thousand Jews inhabit Vilna now, only five percent of the prewar total, and very few of them are native to the city. "I have this sensation that Yiddish is a mist on a morning field," Emmanuelis Zingeris, a leader of Lithuania's Jews, has said. "It's disappearing before our eyes like a dream that never was." *Alte zachen, alte zachen.*

When he's not in his office, Katz spends some of his time driving out into the latke-flat countryside of Lithuania, Belarus, and eastern Poland, visiting small towns and villages and searching for elderly Jews who somehow managed to escape the Holocaust. Often these survivors can still converse in Yiddish, though they may not have done so for decades. Katz's typical method is to walk into a Belorussian or Lithuanian town, stand in the market square, and accost a passerby in Russian: "Hi. Please forgive me, I speak Russian very poorly. I have a question. Are there any dirty Jews like myself in this town?"

Shy, he isn't. "To find a shtetl Jew here, a shtetl Jew there, is to me exhilarating," he said on a BBC Radio documentary about his work. "The whole soul of a place is still there. The shtetl is real — it's not some romantic imaginary concept we dreamt up after the Holocaust." More difficult for many to swallow is Katz's denunciation of the much-revered March of the Living, which brings young Jews from across the world on a pilgrimage to Auschwitz. "Not to take them to one surviving Jew," he told the BBC, "it makes me sick . . . And it falsely, from a historical point of view, isolates the Holocaust from the Jewish civilization that was destroyed." That civilization had a language, a music, a literature, and a name: *yidishkayt.*

"There's a need to really sing aloud the songs of the Holocaust period," Hankus Netsky declared. He was standing at the front of a small theater in Camp B'nai Brith, whose buildings nestle by a modest lake in the Laurentian mountains an hour's drive north of Montreal. A Boston-based composer, teacher, music historian, saxophonist, pianist, and accordion player — as well as the founder and director of the Klezmer Conservatory Band — Netsky was one of the star faculty at KlezKanada, an annual five-day summer camp for people of all ages. KlezKanada bills itself, precisely if inelegantly, as "a festival of Yiddish/Jewish music & culture." Klezmer is only the beginning. Such a hotchpotch of workshops and lectures, concerts and dances, began at a camp in the Catskills of New York. The idea spread: west to California, north to Canada, and as far east as Russia and Ukraine. Some of the better-known musicians and teachers spend a good chunk of each summer hawking their expertise from one klez camp to another. Driving into the parking lot of Camp B'nai Brith, I'd noticed license plates from three Canadian provinces and seven U.S. states. YDSHKT, said a customized plate from Ontario.

With his enviably thick black hair, Netsky, wearing jeans and a striped shirt, looked no older than thirty-five: an illusion. Even so, most of his listeners were a generation older, and a lecture about Holocaust music was bound to raise emotions of the rawest, most painful kind. "There's lots of songs about tragedy in Jewish history," Netsky said, "but there's no other period when tragedy changes everything." Never straying far from a big tape deck, he punctuated his talk with recordings of songs composed by eastern European Jews in the early 1940s — songs written in Yiddish, most of them sung by a single voice. The exuberance of a klezmer band was far removed from the stubborn pathos of these songs. Some people in the audience spoke fluent Yiddish, but others knew little of the language, so Netsky offered his own impromptu translations. "Jews, let's be cheerful . . . Their end is very near . . . Dance, you butchers . . . Jews, let's be cheerful and let them go to hell." The defiant writer of that song, Mordechai Gebirtig of Cracow, was shot by the Gestapo in 1942.

"The Yiddish lullabies of the Holocaust are wonderful," Netsky said. "Some are hopeful. Others are about — reality. My favorite, 'S'dremlen feygl oyf di tsvaygn,' is very severe. Some things are just normal — the birds sleeping in the branches, the child in a cradle — but others are totally incomprehensible. The songs themselves are split. This one was written by Leah Rudnitzky, a teacher in the Vilna ghetto. It's not the mother singing to the child, because the child was abandoned and the mother will never return. So it's a stranger singing. And she tells the child, 'I have seen your father running / under a hail of stones.'"

Netsky ended his talk by playing a couple of songs by Hirsch Glick, another Vilna writer, killed at twenty-three. A love song called "Shtil, di nakht iz oysgeshternt" begins in a conventional fashion — a quiet night, the sky packed with stars — and turns convention upside down: "Do you remember how I taught you to hold a revolver in your hand?" It's the antithesis of schmaltz. Glick addresses the song to a girl in a winter sheepskin and beret. When the night is over, she will creep out of the woods, snowy garlands in her hair, and ambush a convoy of Nazi trucks. At KlezKanada a matronly woman with thick arms and white sneakers was singing along to the music; then she stopped, blinking heavily.

Having introduced the last song, Glick's "Zog nit keyn mol," Netsky

stopped pacing and leaned back against the stage, arms folded. Theodore Bikel's voice filled the theater, accompanied only by an accordion.
A translation might go: "Never say you've reached the end of the road
. . . We survive!" All around me people were singing Yiddish in low
voices. A clinical psychologist from Ottawa, silent until now, joined in,
tears on his cheeks. "I'm putting myself through this," Netsky said, "I'm
putting you through this, but it's very important that we remember."
Jewish culture, in this view, relies on Yiddish memory.

I walked across the wide hall to a room where camp-related merchandise was for sale. English-language translations of Chava Rosenfarb were available, as was a children's book called *Vini-der-Pu*. Outside,
the strains of clarinets and a hammer dulcimer — *tsimbl* in Yiddish —
wafted from outlying cabins among the pine trees. A young man whose
sweatshirt read "Diesel for Successful Living" climbed onto a golf cart
and drove off along a dirt road to fetch one of the camp's senior visitors.
I could have lingered by the lake, but I was already late for lunch.

The dining hall was crowded. Mealtimes provided a noisy chance for
the klezmer players to kibitz with the lecture-going audience. Thanks to
scholarships, about seventy young musicians were here, from across
North America and beyond. I found myself sitting next to a Chicago
doctor named Ira Weiss. Though he is not Hasidic, he had served as
personal physician to the late Menachem Shneerson — the Lubavitcher
rebbe whom many of his fervent followers promoted as the Messiah.
Over his salad Dr. Weiss spoke about the rebbe, a glow in his eyes. "He
had a brilliant mind. Did you know he rode the subway to work every
day for seven years? His job was designing submarines." The rebbe had
been thirty-nine years old when he arrived in New York from a warring
Europe. In his old age his immensely long sermons, broadcast by satellite around the globe, interspersed Yiddish questions with Hebrew answers. I asked if he used to consult his physician in Yiddish. "No, he always spoke to me in English," Dr. Weiss said. "The King's English!"

A class in intermediate Yiddish was about to begin in the library. It
doubles as a synagogue: religious texts rubbed up against Harold Rob-
bins and Stephen King. I had time to finish my coffee and scrutinize the
shelves because the teacher, Peysach Fiszman, was late. Finally he appeared, a small man with a worried expression, glasses, and wispy hair
combed across a balding head. At once he began to speak. He didn't
look like one of the world's most renowned teachers of Yiddish. Yet if I

shut my eyes I could imagine a youthful man beside the tall windows; Fiszman's voice seemed half a century younger than his face.

His aim was to coax long-forgotten words and idioms out of the mouths of his students. Their level varied, of course. A man from Toronto could understand some Yiddish but felt unable to speak it; his North Carolina neighbor could say a few things but had trouble understanding anyone else. Fiszman scoffed at such minor troubles. He told jokes and stories. He welcomed questions. He asked the class to talk about the foods of Rosh Hashanah. And he showed no trace of self-consciousness — trying to get the students to remember *adler,* the Yiddish word for eagle, he flapped his arms like a rickety scarecrow. The more the class spoke, the more animated he became. After an hour and a half of teaching, he looked a lot less tired than when he had walked into the room.

Fiszman grew up on a farm near Buenos Aires. Moving to New York, he became a professor of Yiddish at Columbia University. Officially retired, he continues to teach. "It's a disease," he told me after the class. "I can't stop. Or it's a gift. God gave it to me." Mazel tov!

Yiddish hasn't always been taught in so perky a manner. I remember one account, written by a daughter of Holocaust survivors, that sounds like a recipe for language execution. Growing up in Montreal in the 1950s, she went to school in English. Twice a week she attended a Yiddish program in the shabby basement of a community center. The books were torn and gray. Their stories held no excitement. As the teacher droned on, the pupils would gaze longingly through the basement window at other kids playing in the street. Yiddish was a joyless duty. We know what children think of joyless duties.

Some children of Holocaust survivors continue to speak Yiddish, at least on occasion. I already knew Rivka Augenfeld before visiting Klez-Kanada — she's respected in Montreal as an activist and advocate for refugees from all over the world. As a girl Rivka sang Yiddish songs at a Jewish summer camp (now defunct); at university she helped found a Yiddish youth magazine (also defunct). She still gives occasional poetry recitals in Yiddish, "but my problem is, I've lost a lot of my vocabulary. I don't read Yiddish novels anymore. I in fact haven't read Yiddish for fun in a long time." Pessimism about the language would seem only natural, but Rivka refuses it. Look at the young people who flock to KlezKanada! Think of the value Yiddish carries, the idealism it still attracts! "People shouldn't be too quick to predict the demise of any-thing," she said, glancing at me with a trace of suspicion in case demise was on the tip of my tongue.

It wasn't. Still, I couldn't help wondering if many of the people at-tending KlezKanada saw Yiddish with the same fervor and gave it the same significance that it has for Rivka. Her parents, both partisans in the Second World War, are still alive, and to them she always speaks Yiddish. She has also used the language in her professional life. "When we started getting people from the Soviet Union in the seventies," she told me,

> you could establish a different relationship with them in Yiddish than in Russian. The people from Kiev and Odessa — if you scratched a little bit, even the younger ones had some Yiddish. One of the jobs I loved best was going to the airport and meeting the new arrivals. We used to have a deal with Immigration, they'd let us go behind the scenes, and I would meet the people in Yiddish. It would freak them out! "You're speaking Yid-dish in this public place? You're speaking Yiddish in front of government officials?" It did more than anything else to show them they were in a dif-ferent place.

The epilogue to this story, however, is that very few of those Russian Jews have made space for Yiddish in their North American lives.

Peysach Fiszman had been serious in his teaching. But some of the men and women in the library-cum-synagogue were not so serious in their learning. Yiddish for them was no more than a summer pastime. Its passionate adherents face the same sort of problem that Phil Gawne and Brian Stowell have run up against on the Isle of Man: while the lan-guage now benefits from lashings of sympathy, what it needs is less compassion and more everyday use. For the sake of Yiddish (or Manx), one irascible, bloody-minded, language-speaking son of a bitch is worth a few dozen well-meaning hobbyists.

As evening approached, I seized the chance to talk to Hy Goldman, who founded the KlezKanada festival six years ago and still keeps a close hand on the reins. At seventy-four, he continues to work full-time at the Montreal Children's Hospital — an endocrinologist, he treats dia-betic children. Talking to him was a frustrating experience, because every couple of minutes his cell phone would ring or a passerby would arrive with some trivial or urgent question. Dr. Goldman's patience seemed to be wearing thin.

"What I'm trying to do is swim upstream," he admitted between the interruptions. "In our publicity I say 'Yiddish/Jewish' because some members of our community, for whatever reason, turn away when you just say 'Yiddish.' I don't believe myself that there could be a very significant increase in the use of Yiddish. But now that globalization is making everything the same, I feel very strongly about the need to maintain some form of identity in the face of homogenization. And this is one way to do it. We're using Yiddish not simply to try and keep it alive, but to get through a sense of Jewish identification." Call it language as cultural sustenance.

In parts of Europe, Jewish culture is in vogue — Berlin alone has about twenty klezmer groups, almost entirely made up of goyim. Some Jews resent this as cultural appropriation of an unusually offensive kind. "But I have no problem with it," Dr. Goldman said. "There are Jews who play jazz. It's a fair exchange." What alarms him is the prospect that without Yiddish to serve as a bulwark against the North American mainstream, "Jews will simply become part of the faceless mass. We will be sucked into the vortex of mass culture. If we have Yiddish as a means to justify continuation as a people, we should use it. It provides us with something to hold on to. This is trying to put a finger in the dike. It may be quixotic. But I don't think so."

He gave a rare half-smile. "We will persist," he said. Then his cell phone rang again.

I was sitting near the back of Peysach Fiszman's class, feeling like a lazy no-goodnik, when a woman turned around and asked almost exactly the question I'd heard from my eager neighbor at *The Great Houdini*. But there was a crucial difference in her wording. She looked me in the eye and said: "Do you understand some Jewish?"

In Yiddish, "Yiddish" means Jewish. Yiddish words are the words of Jews — if language and identity are one and the same. To Dr. Goldman, the link remains strong. Yet in the minds of other Jews, even some who are fluent in Yiddish, the link is suspect. To them, the language today can make a meager claim on a Jewish identity.

On a bright Saturday afternoon in Montreal I drove to an unassuming hotel just east of the downtown core. East, that is, of St. Lawrence Boulevard, also called Boulevard Saint-Laurent, otherwise known as the Main — a narrow south-north artery that once divided the wealthy English-speaking neighborhoods to the west from the impoverished

French-speaking quarters to the east. The Yiddish theater used to mount its plays in a grandiose building here. Restaurants along the Main still serve some of the best nosh in town. The hotel was the discreet venue of Blue Metropolis/Métropole Bleu, a bilingual literary festival that attempts to bridge French- and English-language writing in a city where bilingualism is a huge advantage and (in the minds of some apprehensive French speakers) a threat.

I wanted to meet Ruth Wisse, an ex-Montrealer who is now a professor of Yiddish and comparative literature at Harvard University. Dressed in a gray-green cardigan, wearing glasses beneath her dark, graying hair, she had a motherly appearance, veering toward grandmotherly, that was entirely deceptive — her intellect is razor-sharp and merciless. Wisse has written many books, notably *The Modern Jewish Canon: A Journey Through Language and Culture.* Loving the Yiddish language, she refuses to be sentimental about it. For her, nostalgia about its fate is a sign of intellectual weakness.

Wisse's central point is that "the real vitality of the language — and more than that, the *purpose* of the language — had to do with the Jews of central and eastern Europe. They created the legacy. Yiddish was a necessity for them, a repository for their way of life." But for all of Dovid Katz's searching, that repository ended in the death camps. The secular Jewish culture that survived in North America and blossomed in the new state of Israel had other priorities. Jews could forge a full, rich, and coherent identity in English and Hebrew. They did not require the language of shtetls and death camps. They needed strength, not weakness.

Weakness is one of Wisse's overarching themes. Its great literary manifestation is humor, whether in the hollow laughter of Kafka or in the self-deprecating jokes of so many Yiddish-language authors. "The classic expression of Yiddish irony," she has written, "is the saying: '*Ato bokhartonu mikol hoamim — vos hostu gevolt fun dayn folk yisroel?*' 'Thou hast chosen us from among the nations — why did you have to pick on the Jews?'" No translation can convey the full meaning. What reinforces the speaker's complaint is that the scriptural, exalted Hebrew of the first line gets shoved aside by Yiddish in the second.

In the Europe where Yiddish once flourished, anti-Semitism flourished too. In North America today, anti-Semitism still exists, yet it's uncommon, covert, and socially unacceptable. "One dare not discredit what English has achieved in its hegemony," Wisse stressed: "to form a society in which everyone can dream of achieving what everyone else can. I have said in the Jewish community, and you can imagine how popular it makes me, that the greatest gift we owe to North America is assimilation. 'You want to stay separate? You may. But you can't feel nostalgia for discrimination. You can't deny other children the advantages you take for granted.'" Saul Bellow, she mentioned, is one of the finest Yiddish speakers she knows, and in his novels he draws continually on Yiddish rhythms. But he feels no need to write in the language. While Bellow is assimilated, he is not devoiced.

At the end of her talk Wisse accepted questions. The first few were bland. Then a French-Canadian man put up his hand. He was from Ontario, he said in French, but had moved to Montreal thirty years ago. He quoted Albert Camus: "Ma patrie, c'est la langue française." Why, the man asked, have Jews been so unsympathetic to the struggles of French-speaking Quebec?

Wisse stiffened. She understood the question, but she chose to reply in English. "Of course the sympathy is there," she said. "And one understands the fear, the anguish, the commitment of French Canadians. To the extent that one wants to do anything through schooling and taxation for French Canadians to learn and keep their national language, I'd be in favor of it. But to impose a punitive law against English, and to contrast the language negatively with something else, you change the civilization. You become defensive. You become frightened. You teach your children, 'Be careful! Stay in!' And that has a tremendous price." Shaking his head, the questioner wanted to interrupt. Wisse carried on.

"Here's where the difference lies. People say to me, 'Yiddish has to be maintained at all costs.' And even though this is my life, I don't agree. Language is never the sum total of a people. The Jewish people has been absolutely ruthless in terms of its own languages. What has mattered, since the beginning of time, is their religious civilization. In North America, Jews began to leave the Yiddish language. Here there are no walls, not even subtle ones, to keep out our children. When you think of the alternative, you realize what a gift it is. So I cannot give myself over to the absolutism of Yiddish."

I spoke to the French-Canadian man a few minutes later. He was puzzled. How, he asked, could Wisse fail to see that without laws to protect the French language in Quebec, French would become folkloric, a

fading language used less and less outside the home — that it would suffer, in short, the fate of Yiddish?

But modern Quebec no longer has a religious civilization. Its largest
city, Montreal — a place where, Mark Twain once quipped, you can't
throw a brick without breaking a church window — is rapidly convert-
ing its churches into condos, libraries, and colleges. Quebec's birthrate
is low; to pay the pensions of its graying population, it relies on immigrants of many colors. Less and less distinguishes Quebec from the
mainstream of North America. Except for French.

Look at the reclusive, bearded, black-clad Hasidim, Wisse told me, "and
you can see why Yiddish was necessary in the first place. Why did Yiddish form among German-speaking peoples? It formed because the way
of life of the Jews was so different that it generated a language with its
own specific characteristics. Now you can see the same thing in reverse.
The Hasidim value separateness so highly that they speak the language
in order to preserve that separateness. Their purpose is not maintaining
the Yiddish language; their purpose is speaking a language that represents their desire. Yiddish is for them the same thing that it was for
the language's original speakers: the language of the Talmudic way of
life."

The Hasidim and Ultra-Orthodox comprise a small minority of the
world's Jews, but a large and ever growing percentage of those who
speak Yiddish on a daily basis. It's one of fate's twists. For centuries Yiddish was regarded as a secular language, even a profane one. Now its future appears to rest in the hands of an insular group whose adherents
devote themselves to the worship of God — men and women who shun
Isaac Bashevis Singer, I. L. Peretz, and other classic Yiddish authors out
of fear that their stories might infect the purity of Jewish spiritual life.
"Our mother tongue has grown old," Singer wrote in 1986. "The mother
is already a grandmother and a great-grandmother . . . She remembers
what happened fifty years ago better and more clearly than what happened this morning." True, for his own readers. True, for many of the
Holocaust survivors who had escaped a ruined Europe. But not at all
true for the Hasidim, who assiduously follow the biblical edict to go
forth and multiply. Young and not so young Hasidic women endure
pregnancy and labor with such astonishing frequency that, in Montreal,
about seventy percent of their community members are under twenty-
five. Poverty is common.

Most of the city's Hasidim live in Mile End and lower Outremont, multicultural areas once popular among secular Jews. Half a century ago, when Rivka Augenfeld lived here as a little girl and Chava Rosenfarb as a young woman, secular Jews began to move out to greener and grander suburbs, and a welter of other minorities moved in: Greek, Latin American, Portuguese. Many of the neighborhood's brick houses now have small tiles by the front door showing the Holy Family or the Virgin of Fatima. Pavillon La Fontaine of the Collège Français has not yet erased an old brick sign on its front wall: JEWISH PEOPLE'S SCHOOLS. Mile End is a district where languages twine and interlace. I noticed a sign in a politician's office window: BIENVENUE AUX NOUVEAUX MILENDOIS ET MILENDOISES! Don't bother looking those nouns up in a dictionary. You can buy samosas from a nearby Indian-run corner store — an Indian-run "dépanneur," even English-speaking Montrealers would say. Egg cream sodas, half sour pickles, and karnatzel are still on the menu at Moe Wilensky's delicatessen, founded in 1932. But whereas Moe's was once a centerpiece of a Jewish neighborhood, today it stands forlornly on the same street as a Greek pastry shop, a Latino supermarket, and a chic restaurant called Berlin.

Years ago this was my neighborhood too. Then I moved out to a suburb where the air is fresh, the trees outnumber the cars, and there are no samosas or half sour pickles within a ten-minute drive. Nostalgia is an ever present danger. I like to return in the fall, during the Jewish festival of Succoth. In the non-Hasidic gardens, brown-eyed susans and purple asters bloom in the narrow spaces between a sidewalk and a front door. The Hasidim are not gardeners. But outside their homes, temporary structures, like tall playhouses, sprout on the balconies. The makeshift dwellings have coverings made of plywood or pine boughs, through which the stars must be visible. During Succoth the Hasidim eat in these outdoor booths. They commemorate resting places on the escape from Egypt thousands of years ago. As long as the festival lasts, Hasidic homes stand out as clearly as Hasidic businesses — the kosher bakeries and butchers' shops; the tiny stores with "Magical Mitzvah Park" and other religious games in a window.

But of course I have the luxury of seeing the Hasidim as picturesque. To me, they pose no threat. If I were Jewish, their refusal to engage in mainstream society — their absolute rejection of the rest of the world — might provoke in me other feelings.

About seven thousand Hasidim ("pious ones," in Hebrew) live in this neighborhood. Very easy to spot, they are very hard to know. They avoid conversation with outsiders. It's almost impossible to make eye contact. The reason goes much deeper than differences of clothing and hairstyle: it's a question of priorities, of identity, of meaning, of language. All aspects of their daily life are grounded in the 613 commandments of the Torah. On the Sabbath, Hasidim will not use a car or a telephone, nor switch on an electric light. No matter what the day of the week, a Hasidic woman will never touch a man in public — to hold her husband's hand is out of the question.

Even though I live and work in Montreal, was it easy for me to meet a Hasidic man? Don't ask. (To meet a Hasidic woman would have been even harder.) Three rabbis and a teacher turned me down. In 1997 a freelance journalist had spent a week in Montreal with the family of another Hasidic rabbi and written a long article for the *Ottawa Citizen* about the experience. The journalist claimed it was a friendly portrait, but the rabbi was outraged. In a letter to the editor he used the words "grossly misrepresented," "distorted," "negative stereotype," "trivialized," "biased," "preconceived agenda," and "insulting." It may be years before the city's Hasidim open up again to writers.

Alex Werzberger, whom I finally met, is the president of a Hasidic community group called COHO. A heavyset, silver-bearded man in his early sixties, he invited me into his office, discreetly set back from the street. The office was sparsely decorated: I remember little except the computer, the black phone, the big French dictionary, and the incongruous pink Crayola that Alex kept fiddling with. "Most people are reticent," he said. "I'm a little bit freer. I speak a good English, a passable French. But our first language is Yiddish. A child is born, the mother and father speak Yiddish. Then he learns what we call the holy language. Then, at six or seven, he speaks English or French."

The holy language is the one that counts. Only among the Hasidim and Ultra-Orthodox does an old Yiddish saying still hold true: "If you don't know Hebrew, you're an ignoramus. If you don't know Yiddish, you're a goy." Unlike most people in the world — except for the colonized, that is — Alex has a low opinion of his mother tongue. "Yiddish is not a language," he told me. "Yiddish really is a jargon, a *joual*. It's a bastardized version of German. Hebrew and Yiddish are not even third cousins." *Joual* is a term applied in Montreal to working-class street French, riddled with anglicisms, contractions, and slang; some Quebec writers have celebrated it in their novels and plays, but many educated French speakers recoil from its nasal twang and dubious vocabulary. By applying the term to Yiddish, and also by denying Yiddish even the most distant family resemblance to Hebrew, Alex signaled his distaste for the language of his home. Calling it a "jargon," he echoed European Jews of the past — assimilationist Jews like Daniel Nayfeld, who hoped the language would die. Would you ever pray in Yiddish? I asked. "No. You speak to God in the proper language."

So why do the Hasidim persist in using Yiddish? "Why do you speak English?" he retorted. "Because your parents spoke it to you. You don't think about it. That is the first answer. But also, it is a tool or something to keep the community together." When Alex travels on business to Paris or Hong Kong and meets a Jew — "I mean a religious, traditional Jew" — he can strike up a Yiddish conversation. Young men from this part of Montreal often head off to study in New York. In Williamsburg or Crown Heights, they can go on living in Yiddish. Young men from the Hasidic neighborhoods of New York often settle in Montreal. The national border is irrelevant, because the secular world is not entirely real.

"Have you ever studied the Bible?" Alex asked. "When the Jews were in Egypt, they were recognizable." He quoted a verse I failed to recognize and a Talmudic commentary on it. "Five thousand years ago, they had their own names, their own dress, their own language. This is what binds us. It's the glue." To keep the glue from drying out, so to speak, most Hasidim do not watch television. Some homes, including his, have a radio. Every Sunday a multicultural station in Montreal broadcasts a ninety-minute show that mingles Yiddish, Hebrew, and English, and Alex listens regularly. He also tunes in to mainstream English stations. "But ten o'clock at night on Sunday, I'm embarrassed to put it on — gays, sex . . . I get *Time* magazine every week and before I put it on the table, sometimes I tear out a page or two. Fifty years ago we would have called it pornography."

Time is acceptable, more or less, but the writer Sholom Aleichem is not. "Forbidden. Sholom Aleichem, his principal theme is making fun of religious figures. The schlemiel's always a religious guy. So we don't read them and we don't bring them into the home. It's out." Alex is no fool. He must have realized that this inevitably raised the issue of how he could condemn a writer he's not supposed to have read, because after a moment's silence he added: "Sometimes on the radio I listen to him. But an eight- or ten-year-old will listen and say, 'What am I growing up to be? A harmless idiot?'" Yiddish was once a means of getting around walls. The Hasidim have made it a wall. Even their spellings are unlike the spellings of secular Yiddish speakers, the irony being that the Hasidic system retains a few features of German that other Jews have discarded.

Alex was born soon after the Second World War began. He lived in a town near the border of Romania and Hungary — one of two towns, he says, that Nazi soldiers never reached. He remembers hiding in a basement as bombs fell on the town. In 1950 he arrived in Montreal. Some years later, when he was studying in New York, he and a few of his friends wanted to buy train tickets to another city, so they could go and hear a visiting rabbi. They found they didn't have enough money for the fare. But a ticket agent asked, "Are you Amish?" Alex said yes — in Yiddish, *amish* means "among us." They got the tickets. Only later did he realize why.

I asked if English was creeping into the Yiddish of Hasidic homes. "It's not creeping in. It's there. Is there a language in the world that doesn't import foreign expressions?" The Hasidim of Outremont and Mile End belong to eight groups or "courts" — not including the rebbe-loving Lubavitchers, who live a few dozen streets to the west. In the Lubavitch court, too, men dress in black, wear skullcaps or hats, and refrain from shaving their beards. But the Lubavitchers believe they have a mission to reconvert Jews whose families have strayed into the secular world. So they use a lot of English, even at home, and purists would see their Yiddish as a mangled mishmash.

Alex is a member of the Satmar court. Among his people the girls and women usually speak better English than the boys and men. "Men, from when they're born till the age of twenty or when they get married, are in an insular community. They don't get out as much as the women do. The women do more of the shopping. Sometimes they speak to friends in English. They just use it more often." (A Jewish woman who has taught Hasidic girls later told me that while Hasidic women always speak Yiddish to their husbands and sons, they prefer English with their daughters.) As for the boys, Alex said, "Very few are growing up that don't speak English. But when they go out, their accent is lousy, people laugh at them — so they're almost forced to speak Yiddish."

I couldn't tell what he thought about this. Nor did I believe that a fear of outsiders' laughter was truly the main reason Hasidic boys are brought up in Yiddish. Alex's tone was neutral. His face gave nothing away. Did he regret the lousy accent and the scorn? Or was he happy that Yiddish endures? This was the traditional language of Jewish women — the *mama-loshen* of tenderness and endearment. Its final stronghold is Hasidic men.

"The proverb says that hope is the mother of fools," Chava Rosenfarb has written. "But who knows, perhaps the fate of the Yiddish language is like the fate of the Jewish people. Defying annihilation, Yiddish might still rise from the ashes like a phoenix."

One morning in the early fall of 2001, some weeks before I met Alex Werzberger, I sat at my computer composing an e-mail to a Hasidic rabbi. Yonassan Gershom lives not in Brooklyn, Montreal, or Jerusalem but in the midwestern United States, where he maintains a Hasidic Web site full of choice quotations, arcane facts, and occasional polemics. I wanted to ask him how essential it is that Hasidic communities should go on speaking Yiddish. Is there some basic correlation, I wondered, between the Hasidic spirit of life and the Yiddish language — or is the relationship between the two just a historical accident? I sent the e-mail and drove off to do some research at the Jewish Public Library. On the highway I flicked the dial to CBC Radio. It was the middle of the morning, and a live news program had preempted regular broadcasting — something about hijacked planes in Lower Manhattan; something about collapsing towers . . .

I didn't hear back from Rabbi Gershom for more than two months. I almost forgot that I'd written. But when he did reply, his answer was so succinct, so apt, and so (God forbid, am I saying this?) Jewish that I'll quote it at length:

You want that on one foot? Yes, I think Yiddish is important to Hasidic identity, and yes, we would be less Hasidic if we lost the language. Hebrew is a harsher, more abrupt language. It does not have the same "feel" as Yiddish. In fact, it has long been my contention that if Yiddish, and not Hebrew, were the national language of Israel, the whole feel of the country would be different. The founders of Israel . . . wanted to go back to the more militant Biblical Hebrew of King David. In doing so, the softer, gentler, non-violent aspects of Jewishness were lost in Israel.

As for English, it is so filled with Protestantisms that to talk religion in it is to lose the uniquely Jewish flavour of many concepts. *Daven* (Yiddish) is specifically Jewish prayer with all the swaying, etc.; "prayer" brings to mind folded hands in church. *Riboinoi shel oilam* is a name of God; "Master of the Universe" is a cartoon show. Get my point????

Oy.

Revival

So, THE ODDS against reviving a language are long. So, the obstacles are many. So, the archives of history are filled with ghostly voices. Is that any reason to give up the struggle?

I don't think so. But I happen to be a native speaker of English, and hope costs me nothing. If I have to eat crow, the feathers won't be dangling from some other tongue. I'm not required to make the agonizing choices that speakers of a threatened language face every day. As we've seen, languages can die for many reasons: genocide, oppression, slow assimilation . . . Maggie Marsey and Henry Washburn are trying their best, but the forces pushing Yuchi toward the grave appear too strong to overcome. When a language fades from common use, can any revival succeed?

What I heard among the Manx, the Mohawks, and the speakers of Yiddish may provide some clues. What I was to discover in Wales would offer a few more. For the moment, let's concentrate on three languages that have defied the odds, picking up speakers and confidence alike. Each of these languages has gained in vigor and grown in vocabulary. Hebrew is the most famous example of language revival; the stories of Faroese and Hixkaryana are less familiar. Together they show that extinction can be an option, not an inevitable fate.

In 1880 no child in the world spoke Hebrew as a mother tongue. It was a language dependent on religious belief, a language whose emotional content was redolent with holiness. Throughout their diaspora, Jews had kept Hebrew alive as a sacred language of prayer and recitation, and to a very small degree as a means of communication between men who shared no other idiom — a Yiddish speaker and a Ladino speaker, for example. Hebrew still possessed a rich vocabulary — it could easily articulate concepts like "noisome pestilence," "glittering sword," and "stout lion's whelps" — but it lacked a host of essential modern words. You could not ride a Hebrew "bicycle," eat Hebrew "ice cream," send a Hebrew "telegram," or fire a Hebrew "rifle." Many of its best speakers were Orthodox Jews who despised the thought of profaning the language by using it in the street or the home. All in all, the idea of making it a medium of everyday speech appeared quixotic, perhaps even ridiculous. It was a mission impossible that would become, within a single long generation, a mission accomplished.

The man who came to symbolize the Hebrew revival was born in Lithuania in 1858. His name was Eliezer Perelman. As a boy he attended both a yeshiva and a Russian high school; at twenty he went off to Paris to study at the Sorbonne. In Paris he chose to speak Hebrew to every Jew he met, beginning, legend has it, with a conversation in an artists' café in Montmartre. Three years later, in 1881, he boarded ship for Palestine, at that time a neglected fragment of the decaying Ottoman Empire. No such thing as a Zionist congress had yet been convened, though thousands of settlers had anticipated the formal birth of Zionism by moving to the Holy Land. The young Perelman was convinced that Jews needed to gather in their ancestral home — and having gathered there, he decided, they needed to speak their ancestral tongue. He adopted a Hebrew name, Eliezer Ben-Yehuda, and took a wife named Dvora to whom, as he explained on the vessel bearing them across the Mediterranean, he would speak only in Hebrew once they had landed in Palestine. Dvora understood little Hebrew and spoke less. Ben-Yehuda didn't care: he had higher things on his mind than marital bliss.

The couple settled near the Temple Mount in Jerusalem, where their first child, Ittamar Ben-Avi, was born in 1882. Ben-Yehuda intended his home to be a microcosm of a Hebrew society; he vowed that his infant son should hear Hebrew words and no others. The vow denied the child playmates, for they would have contaminated the linguistic purity of the home. His mother couldn't say much to him, either. Until Ittamar was three or four years old he remained silent, refusing to attempt a word. His chief exposure to language consisted of his father reading Bible passages aloud beside his crib. If the silence of the mother was the price that had to be paid for the son's eventual eloquence in Hebrew, so be it.

In his memoirs Ittamar Ben-Avi recalled — and even if his memory was defective or selective, the story has great symbolic value — that a family friend advised Dvora to speak to her mute son. Deprived of normal language use, might the child not become mentally defective? Dvora started singing Russian lullabies to the boy in her husband's absence. One day Ben-Yehuda came home unexpectedly and caught her at it. "What have you done?" he shouted. "All that we've built in the first Hebrew household, you've destroyed in a day." He pounded his fist so hard on a little table that it shattered. "There is no forgiveness for this, Dvora!" he yelled. Dvora sobbed and whimpered. Only the little boy found a way to calm the atmosphere. "I suddenly understood everything that was happening in this house," Ittamar wrote, "stood straight up before my father with the will of a boy defending his mother . . . and screamed, 'Father!'"

Shock and fear forced out a Hebrew word. From then on, language flowed from the boy's lips. Eliezer and Dvora had four other children before her early death in 1891. At one of the deliveries, Eliezer refused to allow her the attentions of a midwife until he had given the woman a quick lesson in Hebrew. Later he was to say, "I do not take care in this matter to abide by the laws of common respect or courtesy toward women. I act in this with great rudeness." The word "fanatical" springs to mind. For the sake of his children's grasp of Hebrew gender, Eliezer made sure that the household's two pets, a dog and a cat, were of different sexes. When Ittamar grew up, he too became a partisan for Hebrew — a gentler one than his father. In a 1928 essay, "The Hebrew Tongue on Women's Lips," he wrote: "It is precisely this that is lacking in our language — womanhood! Childhood!"

Palestine, when Eliezer Ben-Yehuda arrived, had only about twenty thousand Jews. They spoke a variety of languages, including Yiddish, Russian, German, French, and Arabic. Outside the family home, as well as inside, Ben-Yehuda promoted Hebrew: he combined the energy of youth with the passion of a true believer. He taught Hebrew in an Alliance School in Jerusalem. He launched a newspaper, *Hatzvi,* which reported the events of the day while improving the verbal skills of its struggling readers. In 1890 he helped create the Hebrew Language Council — the forerunner of the Hebrew Language Academy, still active in Israel today. The council's members made up words for a range of daily terms, and they advised on a standard pronunciation; Jewish men arriving from Russia and Yemen, for example, spoke the language in dissimilar ways. Theodor Herzl could hardly have chosen Hebrew as the language of a new Zion if not for the work already done by Ben-Yehuda and his friends.

Ben-Yehuda worked longest and hardest as a lexicographer: not a harmless drudge, as Samuel Johnson had it, but a salesman, inventor, and bodyguard of language. In 1922, the year of his death, his *Complete Dictionary of Ancient and Modern Hebrew* comprised six volumes. By the time his successors finished the job, it had run to seventeen — a measure of the language's growth. Not all of Ben-Yehuda's coinages have lasted. Only in his immediate family was a tomato ever a *badura;* the pure Hebrew of *sach-rachok* would give way to the internationally obvious *telefon.* Yet many of his minted expressions remain in daily use. The Israeli journalist Sam Orbaum once asked Ben-Yehuda's daughter Dola, by then a very old lady, if her father had shown a sense of humor when he created words. "Definitely!" she replied. "There are many examples of whimsy in his choice." Orbaum pressed for an example, and Dola obliged: "Clitoris. He decided on *dagdegan,* from the root *l'dagdeg,* to tickle."

When Dola was a little girl, her father would gather the children about him in the evening and tell them the words he had just invented or rediscovered. The children then had the job of passing those terms around. Ben-Yehuda would send a child to the grocer to buy some rice, insisting that the child ask for *orez.* The puzzled grocer would reply in Yiddish: *Vus?* The child would point to the rice and say *orez.* Word by word, the language spread. When Dola fell in love, her choice of bridegroom was a German Christian. Ben-Yehuda didn't fret about the man's religion, but he insisted that the young couple should remain in Palestine and speak only Hebrew. The marriage lasted. The promise was kept.

By no means all the credit for reviving Hebrew should go to Eliezer Ben-Yehuda. His experiment succeeded only because of the enthusiasm of many other Jews whose names history has overlooked. Beyond a commitment to the language itself, they shared a belief in what Hebrew represented: a chance for Jews to overcome the insecurities and weaknesses of exile by reveling in a language of their own. Some of them even created a vigilante group, the Brigade for the Defense of the Language. Arabic was never the prime enemy; Yiddish was.

The growth of Hebrew, slow at first, sped up after 1905, when thousands of eastern European Jews began to pour into the Holy Land. Escaping massacres at home, these immigrants chose to forgo the glamour of America in favor of the sunbaked hardships of Palestine. German and Yiddish had their partisans among the new arrivals. But having turned their backs on Europe, most of the immigrants were ready to embrace a non-European language. By November 1922 Hebrew was so widely spoken that Britain (which had replaced the Ottoman Turks as the ruling authority) recognized it as the official language of Jews in Palestine. Its amazing twentieth-century growth relied on the groundwork that Ben-Yehuda and his family had so feverishly laid. "Before Ben-Yehuda," the saying goes, "Jews *could* speak Hebrew; after him, they *did*." More than five million now do so every day.

As an independent state, Israel has maintained the primacy of Hebrew (initially at the cost of repressing Yiddish). The triumph of Hebrew makes Israel a worldwide model for other small language groups. Delegations of Welsh, Catalans, and Maoris have all visited Israel — indeed the Welsh word *ulpan,* meaning a class where immigrants learn the language, derives from Hebrew. In the 1990s Jewish Agency officials in Georgia and Azerbaijan, dispatched with the mission of teaching Hebrew to potential immigrants, ended up advising the new countries on restoring their national languages after decades of Soviet rule.

With zeal and luck, languages can be resilient. A couple of centuries ago, nobody would have given the Faroese language any more of a chance than Hebrew. Faroese had neither literature nor religious belief on its side. All it had was sheep, fish, poetry, and ring-dancing. As it turned out, that would be enough.

Faroese is a descendant of Old Norse, the language bellowed by the Vikings across most of Scandinavia and the North Atlantic; and the Faeroe Islands, a bunch of hardscrabble rocks northwest of Scotland, were one of the places where Vikings washed ashore and stayed. Since 1380 the Faeroes have been governed by Denmark. So barren are they, so tough a place to wrest a living from, that at the beginning of the nineteenth century they supported barely five thousand people. Among themselves, rural islanders talked an unwritten language passed down from their marauding ancestors and intermixed with words of Germanic and even Gaelic origin — almost nothing had ever been printed in Faroese. The politics, the commerce, and the preaching belonged to Danish. In the capital village of Tórshavn, the everyday spoken lan-

guage was a mixture of Danish and Faroese. Surely the shepherds'
tongue was doomed?

Jens Christian Svabo thought so. He believed that Faroese should be
supplanted by Danish, and when he set out in 1781 to collect "the ruins
of the language" his intentions were scientific. Still, Svabo went to great
lengths to gather the traditional folktales and poems of his homeland.
There were an astounding number for him to find. (The definitive ballad collection would run to eighteen volumes, almost nine thousand
pages, and about seventy thousand stanzas — all this, remember, from a
few thousand people.) Some words endured because of their appearance in one of the ring dances: lengthy songs, chanted by dancers with
linked arms and stomping feet, that date back to the Middle Ages and
underpin Faroese identity even today. While many of the islanders were
proud of such a heritage, they also feared their language was but a corrupt dialect of Danish, worthless in the eyes of government and God.
The Gospel of Saint Matthew appeared in Faroese in 1823, only the second book to be published in the language — and met such a hostile reaction from its intended audience that no further attempt at scripture
translation would occur for more than a century.

Just as the universities, bars, churches, and cafés of London and Paris
later served as seedbeds for independence movements in tropical colo-
nies, so did the student dens of Copenhagen nourish and perhaps even
create the nationalist movements of the Faeroes and Iceland (another
of Denmark's windblown properties). Most Danes looked down on the
Faroese as yokels in a frigid backwater, hundreds of miles away from
civilization. Faroese students, meanwhile, were beginning to feel they
belonged to a distinct people — indeed, a micro-nation. Svabo's successors among the ballad hunters felt pride, not regret, in their language.
One of them, the grandly named Venceslaus Ulricus Hammershaimb,
was a theology student in Copenhagen when, in 1846, he invented an alphabet for Faroese.

The alphabet looked weird to many of his countrymen. He meant it
to do so, because his alphabet was also a polemic, a manifesto. To represent one of the sounds that English conveys by *th*, Hammershaimb introduced a letter — lower-case *ð* or capital *Đ* — that does not exist in
Danish. It does exist, however, in Icelandic. That was Hammershaimb's
point. So as to create a safe distance between Faroese and Danish, he
wanted to drag Faroese closer to Icelandic (and, ultimately, to the
mother or grandmother language of them all, Old Norse). It pleased

him that this written language conformed to nobody's spoken dialect —
as it stood at a distance from all the minuscule dialects, everyone could
accept it on an equal footing.

The alphabet, and the wealth of traditional literature that was waiting to be recorded in it, made Faroese respectable. Yet the battle to save
it would be long and arduous. The islands' first newspaper appeared in
Danish; within a few years it had a rival, printed in Faroese. The government opened a school in every community, announcing that instruction would be given in Danish because Faroese lacked any teaching materials; soon a primer, a basic reader, and a literary anthology were
published in Faroese. In one domain after another — education, law, religion, government — Faroese was fought for. The late nineteenth and
early twentieth centuries marked the heyday of this battle. The language
campaigners were also working to win a national holiday, a national
flag, a national museum, and a national costume. They were inventing
tradition. In *No Nation Is an Island,* a study of language and identity in
the Faeroes, Tom Nauerby uses their struggle to support a striking
claim: "National languages were actually the exact opposite of what nationalist mythology supposed them to be: they were not the primordial
foundations of nations, but the more or less artificial products of the
nation-building process itself." Nauerby, it should be said, is a Dane.

After the Second World War, Denmark granted the Faeroes a high
degree of autonomy. Except for foreign affairs and defense, the islanders
could now run their own affairs. This meant that the Faroese language
at last acquired official standing. The successes of antibiotics and deep-
sea fishing help account for the rise in population (today about forty-
five thousand people live on the islands). But despite home rule, the
Faroese language is not home free. One summer, a dozen students faced
a delay in graduating from high school because they insisted on writing
their final exams in Faroese. The biology exam that year asked for "an
ecological description of a Danish forest" and posed questions on "the
frog in Denmark" — although the Faeroes have neither frogs nor forests. Other students resent Faroese: intending to move on to mainland
universities, they want teachers to use Danish in the classroom.

All minority languages are now challenged by new technology, with
its insatiable demand for fresh words. The Faroese are accustomed to
making words: nationalists did so in the nineteenth century, scrounging
among the medieval ballads in search of half-remembered, non-Danish
terms. Their inheritors established a Faroese Language Committee in

1985. It fights linguistic slippage through continual invention. Danish has adopted the English term "computer," for example, and in the early 1980s most Faroese were saying *computari*. But Jóhan Poulsen, the chair of the language committee, created the noun *telda* from a Faroese verb meaning "to compute." And today *telda* is said to be in daily use. When it came to "television," islanders had to choose from among three terms whose origins lay in Danish, English, and Icelandic. The local TV station adopted the Icelandic-derived *sjónvarp* — and that word, it appears, has also become a fixture in Faroese.

Telda and *sjónvarp* notwithstanding, the danger is that children and teenagers may start to see Faroese as embodying the past, Danish the present, and English the future. Word coiners and language campaigners risk being scorned as purists, hopelessly out of touch with the mobile, world-enamored young. In the early 1990s an official attempt to replace *kompaktdisk* with a Faroese term, *ljómfloga*, did not succeed. Yet enough people of all ages still care about the language — truly, madly, deeply — that Faroese continues to thrive. "There is no question it is a living language," the Montreal writer Cleo Paskal told me; having married a Faroese musician, she was in a position to know. "Everyone speaks it. It is the language of the parliament, the newspapers, neighborhood gossip, football chants, the church, love. There are many people who speak nothing else. It is their language, pure and simple." Faroese has always had farmers; now it has milk cartons, on which the dairy company publishes advice about the proper use of words. It has always had dancers and poets; now it has Web sites, too.

The case of Hixkaryana is very different, and not just because it belongs to one of the world's steamier corners. Hixkaryana is a Carib language spoken in five villages along the Nhamundá River in northern Brazil. It's related to some of the languages Alexander von Humboldt would have heard in his wanderings along the Orinoco. Even in Brazil, the language and its speakers are obscure to the general public. Yet among linguists Hixkaryana is famous. They recognize it as the first proven example of a language whose structure was widely believed to be impossible: the verbal equivalent of a bird with gills. Linguistic theories that prevailed as late as the mid-1970s held that Hixkaryana was inconceivable. Until it was shown to exist, it was known not to exist.

The reason lies in its underlying shape. Most languages, including English, stick a subject at the front of a typical sentence. The basic structure of an ordinary English sentence is Subject — Verb — Object (or SVO for short: "you open a book"). Tibetan and Turkish are among the many languages that delay the verb until the end (SOV: "you a book open"); and a fair number, including Arabic and Manx, introduce a sentence with the verb (VSO: "open you a book"). These three patterns account for the vast majority of the world's languages. Much rarer are languages in which the object turns up before the subject. Malagasy — the predominant language on the island of Madagascar — is one of the very few with a VOS order ("open a book you"). "The other two logically possible orders, OSV and OVS, do not occur at all," wrote Geoffrey Pullum, a distinguished British linguist, in 1977.

His article appeared in the journal *Syntax and Semantics*. While the journal was in press, Pullum expounded this proposition to a graduate class at the University of London. One of the students, Des Derbyshire, put up his hand. "Excuse me, sir," he said, "but I *speak* an object-initial language."

Since January 1959 Derbyshire and his wife, Grace, had been living among the Hixkaryana, providing them with basic medical care and working on a translation of the New Testament. He knew that when the Hixkaryana say *toto yahoslye kamara* ("man grabbed jaguar"), they're not talking about a feat of extraordinary heroism or stupidity. What they mean is "the jaguar grabbed the man." They just say it — from an English standpoint — backward. Almost everything backward say they. To them, of course, we're the backward ones.

Hixkaryana is now believed to have a handful of relatives in the Carib family that share an OVS pattern. Two other languages in the Amazon region, and possibly one in Australia, prefer OSV ("man jaguar grabbed"). None of these languages is widespread. Yet Hixkaryana is far healthier today than it was half a century ago, thanks in good measure to the Derbyshires' intervention. When they first traveled up the Nhamundá River they found about 120 villagers. Few were young. Children had been falling prey to measles and other Western illnesses without the benefit of Western medicine. The care and the new medicines quickly improved the rate of survival. As the years passed the Hixkaryana started to intermarry with a neighboring people, the Wai Wai, who speak a related Carib language (still with the subject at the rear of a sentence, though often with the verb in the lead). Both groups flourished. By May 2001, according to Des Derbyshire, the five Hixkaryana villages along the Nhamundá contained 804 people.

The Derbyshires' work in Brazil has been paid for by a controversial organization called SIL International — formerly the Summer Institute of Linguistics. Based in Dallas, Texas, SIL is among the largest employers of linguists in the field — linguists, that is, who actually study the world's languages rather than engaging in arcane analysis of the structural underpinnings of speech. Every few years SIL publishes an updated version of *Ethnologue,* an invaluable catalogue of each of the world's languages along with its dialects, its family relationships, an estimate of its speakers' numbers, and the principal countries where they live. The institute has long done terrific work. Yet its motives are open to question. SIL is part of the Wycliffe Bible network — a group of Protestant missionary societies, drawing their inspiration from a verse in Matthew and a few more in Revelation: "After this I beheld, and, lo, a great multitude, which no man could number, of all nations, and kindreds, and people, and tongues, stood before the throne, and before the Lamb, clothed with white robes, and palms in their hands; And cried with a loud voice . . ." Christian praise must be uttered in every human language — or so goes one interpretation of the text — for only then can the world come to an end.

You could say, in brief, that SIL is in the business of saving languages so that they will all disappear. Its founder, "Uncle Cam" Townsend, peddled Bibles in Guatemala before the Second World War. He insisted that Summer Institute fieldworkers affirm their faith in such hard-line Protestant doctrines as the divine inspiration of all biblical texts and the moral depravity of man. The tradition continues. Wycliffe organizations still proclaim the "authority of the whole canonical Scriptures" and "the eternal punishment of the lost." A French linguist, Jon Landabaru, has criticized the implicit Wycliffe dogma that "the Indian has the form, the missionary has the content. The missionary has the truth, the Indian provides the form of expression. What the Indian is accustomed to express in this form, what the language reveals, what the Indian thinks is not important: it is ignorance and darkness." Today SIL is active in dozens of countries. Some of its members still deploy the languages of native people as weapons against traditional religious beliefs.

I don't mean to cast aspersions on the work of Des and Grace Derbyshire. SIL may be right to claim on their Web site that the Hixkaryana have grown in number not only because of medical care and intermarriage but also because of "increased self-confidence . . . since the New Testament was translated into their language. The message of a God who loves them and regards them as of great worth has been a significant factor in raising their confidence levels, both in self-worth and in dealing with outsiders." As well as a church, the Hixkaryana now have a school, a nut-gathering industry, and a clinic run by FUNAI, Brazil's Indian agency. They had none of these things before the Derbyshires arrived.

Grounded in their own culture, the Hixkaryana are attempting a difficult, delicate passage into the contemporary world. In the riverine villages, Derbyshire reports, "all the people speak Hixkaryana." More than two hundred school-age children are growing up in the language. If the horizon is clouded, it's only because the future of all indigenous peoples in Brazil is clouded. They account for but 0.2 percent of the country's population — and if the Wild West is dead, no one told the settlers cascading into Amazonia. Clashes between native peoples and lawless gold miners not far from Hixkaryana territory have left dead on both sides. Derbyshire admits that "there has been a lot more contact with Brazilian society in the last twenty years, especially by the men, so there are some who speak Portuguese." The guardians of language and culture are often women — present-day Yiddish being an exception that proves the rule.

For the moment, the Hixkaryana language continues to prosper. Such a thing in 1959 could have expected few.

Together, the tales of Hebrew, Faroese, and Hixkaryana show the sloppiness of a despairing fatalism about rare languages. For it's possible to avert extinction. If most of the speakers of an endangered language trust their own culture — if they regard their language as vital to their livelihood and well-being — they may flout the odds. Hebrew flourishes in Israel, not just because a few dedicated Zionists set out to revive the language, but because they made it central to their ambition of building a Jewish society in the Holy Land. Faroese prospers in the North Atlantic because a handful of islanders, seeing in their homeland something more than just a saltwater outpost of Denmark, promoted an independent culture faithful to its ancient roots. Hixkaryana remains vibrant in Brazil because its speakers were able to distinguish the kind of novelty that saves a people from the kind of novelty that destroys. In each case, a language nourished popular desire.

Reviving languages depend on a shared commitment. Every word is a fresh hope. Every hope is a fresh word.

The Iron of Language

WELSH

I HAD SEEN ENOUGH last-ditch struggles. I had heard enough whistling in the dark. Now I wanted to visit a country where a minority language flourishes: a culture whose strength and endurance show that small languages are not necessarily doomed. And despite the alarming statistics of language loss, there are many places I could have chosen. Israel, the Faeroe Islands, and the Nhamundá River in Brazil are among them; so are small nation-states like Armenia, Slovenia, and Iceland; so is New Zealand, where determined efforts are being made to keep Maori alive and well. In the end, though, I opted for Wales. Ruled, often overruled, by its powerful next-door neighbor for more than seven centuries, Wales has managed to sustain a Celtic language of its own. Speakers of that language have always refused the overwhelming embrace of English.

Besides, Wales and I have a history.

I grew up in western Canada, the only child of immigrants from England. Their words were my words: when I was a boy, I swam in the English language as in a river of clear water. I found it only natural that simple terms — *crow, dough, foe, no, oh, owe, sew, whoa* — could look so mismatched yet sound so alike. Like most North Americans, though unlike the majority of people elsewhere in the world, I considered it normal to speak one language alone.

"Immigrants from England": that's the story I was told. My parents had worked in the industrial city of Coventry, and my birthplace was a nearby town at the heart of the Midlands. It was not what my parents said; it was what they did not say. What my father, in particular, usually avoided mentioning was that he and my mother had been born and raised in Wales.

Admittedly their home lay in a border county, Radnorshire, where few people spoke Welsh, the English language having muscled over the hills generations ago. For my parents, both England and Canada were lands of opportunity. I thought of them as English, and of myself as Canadian. I failed to grasp that having grown up in Radnorshire — having spent their first couple of decades going to schools and churches, farms and villages, social and sporting events in Wales — my parents weren't as English as they said.

When I was eleven we traveled back to Britain for a summer vacation. For a few days we stayed in Knighton — Tref-y-Clawdd, to use its Welsh name — the town where my father used to live and where my mother's brother worked on the railway. Uncle Jim was exotic to a prairie child: tall and kindly but with working-class manners, a hard-to-decipher accent, and an incomprehensible belief that my parents belonged in Knighton. Perhaps I belonged there too — a notion that would have seemed threatening if it hadn't also seemed laughable. I remember walking up from his terraced home toward a new housing estate. Uncle Jim glowered and fumed at the sight. "Birmingham folk," he complained. "Not from these parts." The people living there might well have moved to Radnorshire before I was born; no matter, in my uncle's eyes they would never belong, never be at home. Only when I was older did I learn of the Welsh valleys entombed by reservoirs, the villages drowned by England's thirst for water. Later still, my uncle dead of heart disease, I began to interpret his temper in terms of the bittersweet history of Wales.

After our days in Knighton my father drove west to Aberystwyth. I think my parents wanted me to have a seaside holiday in a place they had enjoyed in the past. The Welsh names, so troublesome for outsiders, rolled off my mother's lips — Dolgellau, Machynlleth, Llangollen . . . (To approximate the famous Welsh *ll*, stick your tongue behind your top teeth and push your breath out through the corners of your mouth.) My Aberystwyth was an English-speaking guesthouse, a few cafés, and a beach. I had no idea it was also a university town overlooked from a hill by the National Library of Wales and inhabited by thousands of people who called that library Llyfrgell Genedlaethol Cymru.

Even on the beach, my father seemed keen to leave Wales. It was the land of his own father, and he wanted no part of it. He spoke bitterly of Knighton, "the last place on earth." I was baffled. Better to bury my feet in the sand as the waves rolled in from the bay. Perhaps, even then, his rejection of his homeland had begun to provoke in me a kind of hunger.

My father was an organist and choirmaster. Back in Canada, the hymn tunes he chose for a Sunday morning often had Welsh names: Hyfrydol, Rhosymedre, Cwm Rhondda. (Thanks to that hymn, I grew accustomed to the notion that *w* could be a vowel.) But the rousing words were English: "Bread of heaven, Bread of heaven, / Feed me till I want no more." After the service, my father's favorite meal was roast lamb. At the time I never realized that this fondness was, like so much else in my childhood, characteristically Welsh. Each December my mother hoped that CBC Radio would broadcast Dylan Thomas's own reading of *A Child's Christmas in Wales,* and usually she got her wish. I loved the tipsy aunts beside a carol-singing sea. Years later I grew to love Thomas's poetry too. Instinctively I felt at home in its bird-busy, light-filled landscapes. Yet there was something, I began to suspect, that the critics never quite explained about his use of language — a mystery in his "psalms and shadows among the pincered sandcrabs prancing."

Wales, too, remained a mystery. In high school I took part in model United Nations assemblies, where Rotarians sponsored young wind-bags like me to wax eloquent on behalf of faraway regimes. A boy or girl played the role of Ireland at such ritual gatherings; no one spoke up for Wales. But if Wales was not a proper country, why did it have its own stamps and coins? And why did it compete so ferociously in international rugby and soccer matches? If its sports teams could tackle the English and Irish, why could Wales not join the United Nations? The heir to Canada's throne was the Prince of Wales. So why did he live in central London?

At last I came to see the sheer survival of Wales and of its language as a linked pair of achievements. I learned that of the six Celtic languages, Welsh is by far the healthiest. Even apart from Manx and the unfortunate Cornish, its fortunes have far outstripped those of Irish and Scottish Gaelic, which endured — until a recent and still tenuous revival — mainly in coastal outports and second-language classes. At least five hundred thousand people call Welsh their mother tongue — more native speakers than these other tongues combined. A century ago its younger cousin Breton, the only Celtic language left on the European mainland, had more than a million speakers. But a tide of French has drowned out most Breton voices since. Today Breton may be spoken by less than half the number of people who use Welsh. Somehow, shoved up against English, Welsh has resisted fate.

Likewise its motherland remains more than a region. With a history, culture, and language distinct from anywhere else in the British Isles, Wales is a nation. Less than a fifth of the nation's three million residents are fluent in Welsh; yet the numbers are apparently on the rise. Even in the post-industrial belt of south Wales, where English has long been dominant, many people agree that the future of the nation and the future of its language go hand in hand. Thinking again about my father, I realized finally that he would not have identified so strongly with England if he had spoken Welsh.

The language has borrowed hundreds of words from English. It preserves some lost English meanings (*sad* has the sense of firm), even some lost English words (*barclod,* meaning apron). Yet to linguists, Welsh and English are far apart. Although they both belong to the vast Indo-European family, they perch on separate branches of the family tree. It's not just a question of vocabulary; it's also a matter of syntax, how the language functions in the mind. Most Welsh sentences start with a verb. Even the alphabet is distinct. Welsh has no use for *j, k, q, v, x,* or *z.* But it treats *ch, dd, ff, ll, ng, ph, rh,* and *th* as letters in their own right, pronouncing some of them in ways no English speaker would recognize.

Welsh entered the twenty-first century in style. It is taught in schools and universities, used in businesses and courts of law, heard on TV and radio, and spoken by some politicians in the young Welsh Assembly. It even survives among a few hundred residents of Patagonia, near the wind-smacked tip of South America, the descendants of hardy Methodists who sailed away in the 1860s. The language is robust. At first glance, it looks secure.

I drove through the Cheshire plains, eyeing the flooded fields. November, and Britain was suffering a long cold bath. *Crow, foe, owe:* English might have been alone in the world until *whoa,* a sign appeared by the highway's edge: CROESO I GYMRU. And below it: WELCOME TO

WALES. Farewell, England, in the rearview mirror. Linguistically, I'd crossed into a pair of overlapping worlds. If these green, soggy meadows belonged to the Wales I thought I knew, they also existed in a land that was largely strange to me: Cymru (pronounced "CUM-ree" except when spelt "Gymru," *c* being one of nine Welsh consonants that mutate). "Cymru" comes from a Celtic word for compatriot, "Wales" from a Saxon word for foreign. Foreignness is in the eye of the beholder.

From the border on, names are doubled, as if superimposed on each other: what you see depends on what you speak. The first sizable town has the English name of Mold. It may sound more appealing in Welsh — Yr Wyddgrug — but not being a Welsh speaker, I can't be sure. Unless you grow up amid Welsh, the language looks intimidating. Academic grammar texts are little help: they offer such bleak advice as "An interjection may be the predicate in a noun predicate sentence" or "The diphthong in which an obscure *y* occurs must be a rising diphthong." Welsh is full of what the grammarians call tensed embeddings, passive adjectives, and unreality endings. Traditionally, it also lacked a simple way of saying "yes" or "no." I once came across a 321-page tome entitled *Mutations in Welsh* that had sections fit for a physiology journal ("Airflow investigation of the nasal mutation") if not a physics text ("Zero triggers and the pre-sentential particle system").

A small part of the trouble for outsiders is that while some nouns take more than one plural form — among them key terms like "cat," "lover," "author," and "vineyard" — other nouns have a dual meaning in the singular but not in the plural. Only by checking the context can you learn if *bron* means a breast or a hillside, *asen* a rib or a female donkey. But context doesn't help when it comes to the mutations. A dog is normally *ci*, but your dog is *gi*, my dog is *nghi*, and her dog is *chi*. In her book *The Welsh Language*, Janet Davies downplays the challenge of mastering the tongue. Still, she admits that "the variety of Welsh plural forms can appear wilfully multifarious." To make a noun go plural, you either alter its vowel, add one of twelve possible endings, alter the vowel *and* add an ending, drop the singular ending, or alter the vowel *and* drop the ending. Not to forget the unruly irregulars: *chwaer* becoming *chwiorydd* (sisters), *ci* becoming *cwn* (dogs), *blwyddyn* becoming *blynyddoedd* (years) . . .

I knew from the Isle of Man that Celtic languages mutate. But Welsh mutates more than any of the others. "Mother will make tea" — a useful notion in Wales — would normally be said *Fe wneith Mam de.* The verb *wneith* mutates because of the particle ahead of it, but that would happen in Breton or Gaelic too. Only in Welsh does the sentence's object also mutate, so that *te* turns into *de*. Someone learning the language could get the idea across without the mutations, but a fluent Welsh speaker would hear the result as wrong, not just ugly. Learners also have to grasp that the language employs three sounds — "voiceless nasals," in phonetic parlance — only in the mutations. They don't appear, that is, in the dictionary form of any word.

The farther the English border receded, the stronger the mutating language grew around me. In demographic terms, northwest Wales is the language's heartland. Yet often, even here, Welsh remains hidden. Businesses that cater to visitors have little motive to adopt bilingualism. Stopping at a roadside café a few miles from Rhuddlan Castle — where, in 1284, the English king Edward I signed a statute relegating Welsh to the rank of a casual, unofficial language — I saw that the abysmal menu was in English only. So were the ads in the men's room, where a machine held condoms "vibrantly coloured for extra fun." Welsh and other small languages find that Eros in all his forms often arrives in English packaging.

I crossed a bridge over the Menai Strait, which divides the mainland from the island of Anglesey — "Ynys Môn," to a slim majority of its residents. For a few nights I would be staying with a Welsh-speaking family in a Welsh-speaking village. The inner reaches of Anglesey, where Medwen and her sisters live, are a bastion against the swirl of English; a region never occupied by Saxons. I noticed an item in the weekly *Holyhead & Anglesey Mail*:

> Wales is the land of song as they say and it certainly was last weekend when the voices of young farmers echoed through the island.
>
> The Anglesey Young Farmers held their annual Eisteddfod at Ysgol David Hughes, Menai Bridge.
>
> Entertaining solos, comic duets about Adam and Eve, songs about Tecwyn the Tractor mingled with sketches and reciting of the highest degree . . .

You wouldn't find young farmers in Canada carrying on like that. Although the newspaper was in English, those songs and recitations had sprung to life in Welsh alone. Offstage, too, the language echoes through the island. What does it sound like? One sympathetic outsider — the novelist J.R.R. Tolkien — described the pleasure he took in the

Welsh "fondness for nasal consonants, especially the much-favoured *n*, and the frequency with which word-patterns are made with the soft and less sonorous *w* and the voiced spirants *f* and *dd* contrasted with the nasals." In English terms, those last two letters are pronounced *v* and *th*. Thanks to reforms in the last few decades that would have shocked Edward I, Welsh spirants and other sounds can now be voiced at work by lawyers, college teachers, and civil servants. Medwen writes her checks and pays her taxes in Welsh; rummaging in a kitchen drawer, she produced brochures from the Royal Mail, the U.K. Department of the Environment, and the Energy Efficiency Advice Centre, all of them bilingual.

A blessing, surely. Yet for a minority language, bilingualism can also be a danger. Except for the youngest children, all speakers of Welsh are bilingual. When Medwen was chatting away in Welsh on the phone for two or three minutes, I heard her say "okay," "well," "sorry," "protest," "phone number," and "great." English words just kept slipping out. In the nearby market town of Llangefni, unglamorously Welsh to the core, the concert posters were not in the townspeople's usual language, and many shops had unilingual English names — assuming a phrase like "Kwik Save" qualifies as English. It's as though the big language is waiting, hovering at the margins of thought. Attrition is a perpetual risk.

But Welsh has weapons against attrition, among them a network of publicly funded schools whose teachers are resolved to pass the language on. It's a quiet revolution from the long decades when pupils caught speaking Welsh wore a strap around their necks with a heavy piece of wood attached: a badge of dishonor, the infamous "Welsh Not." My parents never had a chance to study Welsh in the classroom. Now, whatever their family background, children throughout the country learn the basics of the language — Welsh lessons, long forbidden, have become compulsory. Many of the children go to schools in which Welsh is the dominant language of instruction.

One day I drove back onto the mainland to visit a school in a slate-quarrying village called Tregarth. The winding road up to the village provided glimpses of snowcapped mountains above shining fields. But the houses, as usual in north Wales, were the color of rain-soaked pavements. My appointment was at Ysgol Gynradd Tregarth, where 130 or so children between the ages of three and eleven are educated in Welsh. It's the only school in town. I had no trouble finding the building — it flanks the main road — but finding the headmistress was a puzzle. I didn't want Miss Mai Parry, and I didn't want Miss Gwen Parry, either; I wanted Mrs. Meriel Parry. The culture has not produced a wealth of surnames.

Like many Welsh speakers, Mrs. Parry uses English with flair. "When the children come in," she told me, "we drown them in Welsh. Some of the three- and four-year-olds know only Welsh. But even the three-year-olds, because they watch television, have a lot of English vocabulary. The nursery class is only half a day. In that half day, we get them to be as fluent as possible in Welsh."

She showed me around the school. On walls and doors, every word was in Welsh. Mrs. Parry glared at a mural left over from her predecessor's time: Henry VIII, full-sized and big-bellied, encircled by portraits of his wives' heads. He belonged to the Tudor dynasty, and the Tudors were originally Welsh, but Mrs. Parry shook her head. "I mean to change that soon," she said. "I don't like him, and I don't think it reflects our heritage." A poster in the nursery room, the realm of the smallest children, showed cartoonlike people and animals hoisting balloons and cramming into a sausage-shaped car. PWY SYDD YN Y CAR GYDA SALI MALI? Sali Mali was a girl: plump, black-haired, and, Mrs. Parry said, "lovable. Lots of children learn to read through Sali Mali." Videos, TV shows, and beginners' books make her a homegrown Barney or Spot — the Welsh create their culture, they don't just import it. One of the Miss Parrys on staff has written a picture book of her own, although I doubt if *Bili Broga a'r Peli Bach Duon* (Billy Broga and His Frogspawn) poses a threat to Sali Mali.

Tregarth lies in Gwynedd, the most Welsh-speaking county. Its policy is that by the age of eleven all children should be nimbly bilingual. So, after that abrupt Welsh immersion, the school begins to deliver history and geography in English — though it continues to teach math and science in Welsh. As they grow older, some of the children like to shout English in the playground. "They play football," the headmistress said, "and you hear 'Shoot! Score! Pass the ball!' Then you get clusters of children, and all you want is one who's not so fluent in Welsh for the whole dynamic to change. It's a constant battle."

Yet it's not out of mere obstinacy that Mrs. Parry answers the office phone in Welsh; it's out of a belief that her language is something valuable for the people of Tregarth. She and her staff teach Welsh not just for the sake of the language, but for the sake of the children too. It validates their identity; it grounds them in their community; it ensures that most of them will be able to communicate with their families in the families' first language. Above and beyond all this, evidence from several countries shows that children in solid bilingual programs enjoy greater flexibility of mind than their unilingual counterparts. By mastering the complex grammar and rich vocabulary of Welsh, young children don't corrupt their English — they enhance it.

Some of the pupils at Ysgol Gynradd Tregarth have English parents. Mrs. Parry introduced me to a four-year-old girl who had arrived a few months earlier; already she could sing and carry on a basic conversation in Welsh. I walked into the classroom of the ten- and eleven-year-olds — they had just been using English to e-mail students in Jerusalem — and answered their questions about Canada. "Is it hot where you live?" "Do you believe in aliens?" Some of the inquiries were disconcerting. "Do the houses in Canada have slate roofs?" "What color jersey does the Canadian rugby team wear?" Wales is a nation with many divisions; rugby transcends them all.

In return, I asked the children to tell me the best thing about learning Welsh. Replies came thick and fast. "It's a very old language with lots of history." "It's easier to spell than English." (This seems improbable — but unlike English, Welsh has no silent letters and few exceptions to its rules.) "I like Welsh, it's a really strange language," said a ginger-haired waif called Sam with a heavy pair of glasses across his freckled nose. An *X-Files* fan, he was the boy with aliens on his mind. He was also a native speaker of English. A couple of years ago Sam and his family moved to Tregarth from "outside." "In Welsh you can say the same thing in different ways," he added, "a lot more than in English."

In the past, children like Sam would seldom have had the chance to say anything at all in Welsh. Foreigners (and some Welsh people) saw the language as a hindrance or worse. The success of schools like Ysgol Gynradd Tregarth is that while stabilizing the language among its native speakers, they also spread it to immigrants. They help Welsh survive as a robust community language, not just a private idiom of scattered homes. In south Wales, where mother-tongue speakers are sparse, schools may be taking a mother's place and giving the language a future.

Outside a school's doorways, the competition swoops in. You hear it yelled in sports fields, spoken at cash registers, sung on the radio. You see it on the Internet. You face it, above all, on TV. Michael Krauss, the founder of the Alaska Native Languages Center, once wrote, "The battle of the living room will be fought with what I call 'cultural nerve gas' — insidious, painless and fatal." This is one more battle that speakers of Welsh intend to win.

It's one of the rare minority languages — languages, let's say, which are spoken by fewer than a million people, and which don't have an independent state behind them — that enjoy a substantial presence on TV. Through the 1960s and 1970s Welsh-language shows were meager, sporadic, and much resented because they broke up regular programming in a country that had just three channels. Activists kept pressing for a channel dedicated to Welsh, and under its new leader, Margaret Thatcher, Britain's Conservative opposition promised to comply. Once in power, she changed her tune. But in 1980 Gwynfor Evans, the president of the nationalist party Plaid Cymru, declared that he would launch a hunger strike to the death unless she kept her promise. Unusually, Thatcher caved in.

Sianel Pedwar Cymru — S4C for short — began broadcasting in 1982. On weekdays during the late afternoon and evening, and for longer spells on the weekend, S4C is an exclusively Welsh-language channel, providing a mix of news, sports, music, and comedy. It also features original dramas, true to local experience. The best-known series is *Pobol y Cwm,* a long-running soap about families in a south Welsh valley: a Celtic counterpart to *Coronation Street.* But an equally crucial show may be *Rownd a Rownd,* which is aimed at young adolescents — the age when kids are most likely to look on Welsh as drastically unhip. Each week the show has two fifteen-minute episodes (rebroadcast together on the weekend) centering on a bunch of young people who deliver newspapers. Jump-cutting from work to home, from school to leisure time, *Rownd a Rownd* presents a slice of life without moralizing. The only moral is implicit from the start: teenagers can have jobs, have friends, have fun, and have sex in Welsh.

It's filmed in the Anglesey town of Menai Bridge, also known as Porthaethwy, a slightly scruffy place not yet gentrified into submission. The studios occupy a row of shops near the bus station, and I walked right past them without realizing what they were. Morton's newsagent, K-Kabs taxis, Fanna beauty salon, and Scram café are all unreal, which is conceivably why they look so authentic. A bilingual sign explains:

THIS IS A FILM SET!
"ROWND A ROWND"
A DRAMA SERIES FOR S4C BY NANT FILMS

"We bought the place in '95," said Robin Evans, one of the show's producers, "and gutted it in ten weeks. Initially it was a garage for motor repairs. Then it was a timber merchant's yard, and then a double-glazing showroom. But we still get people walking in and saying, 'Can I have a *Western Mail* and twenty Marlboro Lights?'"

Robin grew up in Pwllheli, a town in northwestern Wales, not speaking an English sentence until he was seven. His partner, Sue Waters, comes from the southeastern part of the country, the daughter of English-speaking parents who sent her to school in Welsh. That's a perfect combination for *Rownd a Rownd,* which is watched by about seventy thousand people a week — over ten percent of the language's users. *Rownd a Rownd* clubs have sprung up, and in weeks without filming, Nant Films takes school parties on guided tours of the set. "We've done hundreds of episodes," Sue told me. "And they remember every single detail."

She and her partner debate the vocabulary in each script. "I read it," she said, "and I think, 'Would I have known that word?' If I say no, I take it out." Robin didn't miss a beat: "But I still say, 'We should use that word occasionally. Otherwise people will never know it.'" Sometimes they resolve the issue by finding the right context to slip in an uncommon word. In everyday speech a lot of Welsh terms have lost ground to their English equivalents — *madarch,* the word for mushroom, is a case in point. But in a recent episode, a girl who had been doing a school project on forests came home and asked her mum, "Have you got any *madarch?*" "What?" the woman replied. "Oh, mushrooms, you mean." The child teaches her mother, the show teaches the nation, and if mushrooms appear on *Rownd a Rownd* again, *madarch* won't need to be explained.

"The worst words," Sue said, "are 'okay,' 'right,' 'so,' and 'anyway.' We never put them into a script. But during filming they creep in."

Filming was about to start on a set that uses every inch of space to simulate many fragments of a community. "Because of the zap factor," Robin whispered in the makeup room, "we try to get about twenty scenes into a fifteen-minute episode." I went upstairs to the producers' offices and watched an earlier show on video. The opening scene involved twin girls whose father works on a construction site — like most British movies and TV programs, *Rownd a Rownd* uses sets and props that are far more true to life than North America's sanitized shows. There was grime in a little kitchen, brown sauce on the table, and plastic chairs in a hall. No daily newspaper is published in Welsh, and so — irony of ironies — the children in *Rownd a Rownd* deliver English-language papers. Sue smiled when a pair of lowlifes entered the picture: they run the taxi business when they're not selling drugs. "There isn't any subject we won't touch," she said. "But we're story-led, not issue-led. Entertainment is number one — we do education if we can."

Onscreen, I noticed, a boy of about nine was shouting "You snob!" in English. Robin nodded sadly: "The Welsh word is *crachach*, but a child that age wouldn't know it. So we let him use the English. Otherwise it wouldn't be realistic." A slightly older girl spiced up a conversation by saying what sounded like "hunk." "*Hync*," Sue confirmed. "We Welshen the English name. Up to a point, that's okay. You see, we haven't got a Welsh word for 'hunk.'" Centuries of Calvinism have taken their toll. But *crachach* can come later; for now, the presence of a *hync* or two reinforces the message that Welsh belongs outside the classroom.

One of the keys to the show's long success is the work of Cefin Roberts, who writes the story lines for each episode (other writers then flesh out his plot). A veteran actor, he has a shrewd grasp of what the young performers can do — many of them take weekend or evening classes at Ysgol Glanaethwy, a private performing-arts school that he and his wife direct. It's located on the edge of the city of Bangor. Children travel up to two hours each way for a session of theater, music, or dance.

Cefin's professional charm doesn't quite hide his flinty determination. I met him one evening after he'd taught an acting class of twelve-to fifteen-year-olds. A crowd of them emerged bubbling into the hallway, still caught up in the spirit of the class, not speaking a word of English. Cefin — a wiry man wearing a gray, short-sleeved shirt and a silver chain around his neck — had every right to be tired, but he ushered me into his office and began to talk. An hour and a half later, he was still talking.

"Our professional theater is only forty years old," he said, "and TV is even younger, yet we have to compete with English standards. We tend to copy everything we see, and we haven't evolved a recognizable national style yet. Diction, projection, the enunciation of words, the whole feel of language, the *songlines* if you like: it all comes from within. But it needs proper training. What we do in Wales is send our best to London for training, and when they come back they tend to be lost." Or, at least, confused — uncertain which voice is their own.

When Welsh people speak English, outsiders sometimes praise and sometimes mock them for the songlike quality of their voices. Instead of remaining on a single note, their sentences rise and fall in pitch. It's a phenomenon that goes back, linguists say, to changes that occurred in the Welsh language during the early Middle Ages. A thousand years ago, the stress and the pitch of a word both rose on the final syllable. Then the stress moved to the second-to-last syllable, while the pitch remained highest on the last. Finally this became a feature, not just of long words, but of entire phrases. The resulting "pitch peak" was carried into English, creating a verbal music whose charms are all too easy to parody.

Cefin gave me a tour of the building, by now empty. In one room a tribute by the Welsh baritone Bryn Terfel hung on display: "I would have given my right foot to be a member of Ysgol Glanaethwy when I was in school, and I used to score penalties with my right foot." To the annoyance of some local people, who complain that regular schools don't have a hope, Ysgol Glanaethwy scoops up most of the prizes in regional arts competitions. And Welsh culture is famously competitive.

The largest competition of all is the National Eisteddfod, a weeklong outpouring of pride and joy in Welsh. It's renowned as a festival of singing and poetry, bulging with tents where apparently sane people dress like Druids — one of those "ancient" traditions that was, in large measure, dreamed up in the nineteenth century. But the Eisteddfod means a lot more than flowing costumes and grandiose rhetoric. As well as honoring actors, filmmakers, visual artists, and musicians, it embraces science. Recently it offered a prize for the finest essay on either global climate change or discoveries in genetics. Another award went to the designer of a Web site explaining science to young children. The Web site, like the essay, the poems, and the songs, had to be in Welsh.

Cefin wants Welsh speakers to transcend the old inwardness of their culture. That doesn't mean backing down and giving in. "Sometimes you feel so *minority*," he admitted with a disarming smile. "It's an ongoing battle. You can still find yourself put to the test. If you're in a pub speaking Welsh, you will get, even now, an Englishman saying, 'Are you speaking about me?' And it brings out the worst in you — a desire to say, 'Shut up!' Then you find yourself saying, 'I'm sorry.' And *then* you ask, 'Why am I apologizing?'"

His story reminded me of the meanings the English language ascribes to the verb "welsh": to cheat, to swindle, to abscond without paying. The mistrust runs deep. Yet as many as thirty percent of Cefin's students come from English-speaking backgrounds. No matter what their origin, the young actors need to master Welsh dialects and accents distinct from their own — the language has intricacies apart from its primordial north-south divide. Depending on where you come from, the word you say to mean "young girl" can be any of six terms. The idiom of the northwest enjoys the highest prestige; some of its speakers still look down their noses at other dialects.

Disputes involving the language are often intense. A few nights before I met him, Cefin had been standing among a dripping crowd of protestors outside the Bangor studios of BBC Radio Cymru. The station broadcasts eighteen hours a day in Welsh, but much of the music it plays is American or English, and its disc jockeys favor a colloquial, no-nonsense Welsh, jam-packed with slang. Cefin led some of his students in singing "Yma O Hyd" (We're Still Here), an unofficial anthem for Welsh nationalists. "Then we walked down to University Hall," he said, "and some bards and playwrights got us going."

Why should bards and playwrights join the fray? Because, as Cefin explained, the argument dealt with the quality of language. "The BBC is telling us, 'Don't be so paranoid about the standard of Welsh of our presenters. Let them be natural!' Okay, fine. But if you had presenters in English with that standard, they would not be allowed on the radio. One day I was listening to this awful presenter, 'Jonesey,' who prides himself on not speaking perfect Welsh. An eight-year-old boy phoned in, wanting to speak — he was obviously a good little talker — and he said, '*Dwi'n cefnogi, Manceinion Unedig.*' And Jonesey answered, 'Manchester United, you mean!' Now that's completely wrong. It's putting the boy down. And it's saying, 'Don't speak such proper Welsh!'"

Radio Cymru made no commitment to purify its speech. But Welsh nationalists are astute at picking their campaigns; they seldom waste energy on battles they can't win. A recent victory involved one of the main hotels on the west coast, the Celtic Royal in the largely Welsh-speaking town of Caernarfon. Fearing that the sound of Welsh would irritate customers, the owner had forbidden his staff to speak their language within earshot of a guest. Nationalists picketed the hotel; the media leapt on the story; local people began to boycott the place. Eventually the owner backed down.

What gives this tale a certain edge is that the hotel's owner isn't Welsh. He isn't English, either. The owner of the Celtic Royal, James White, comes from Donegal, a stronghold of Gaelic. Indeed, he's a former member of the Irish parliament. He owns a dozen other hotels, all of them in Ireland, and he told a BBC reporter that Welsh speakers ought to change their tune — the tourist industry in his own country had not flourished by being anti-English. White calls his properties, including the one in Wales, the Traditional Ireland Hotel Group. "Tradition" is a word with many meanings, or none.

Advocates of Welsh like to look south — past the language's struggling cousin in Brittany, all the way to northern Spain. There, in the Basque country and Catalonia, minority languages are thriving, fostered by serious money from regional governments. ("We're like the Catalans," Sue Waters had said, "but ten or fifteen years behind.") Among the living languages of Europe, only Basque — unique, isolated, craggy, unrelated to any Indo-European form of speech — is older than Welsh. They're a pair of survivors, having endured centuries of encroachment by youthful upstarts like Latin and Anglo-Saxon. Both Basque and Welsh belong to peoples enclosed by a larger state; both contain dialects that are now starting to dissolve into a shared speech. No doubt the British government has had moments of fear that Wales might develop a guerrilla force as ruthless as the Basque terrorist movement, ETA.

Something more. In the twentieth century Basque and Welsh each enjoyed a literary and political renaissance that owed an incalculable amount to a writer — a writer who converted to the language.

ETA was founded in 1952 — its initials stand for Euzkadi Ta Askatasuna (Basqueland and liberty) — not, initially, as a terrorist group but as a movement of cultural resistance. Among the founders was a young man named José Luis Alvarez. His mother was Basque, his father Spanish, and he grew up in his father's tongue. Alvarez learned Basque secretly as a teenager, when General Franco's regime was grinding its boots on the language. He took the pen name Txillardegi and in 1957, only a decade after mastering Basque, published *Leturiaren egunkari ezkutua* (The Secret Diary of Leturia), an unorthodox novel that opened up the language to modern fiction. Txillardegi became a linguistics professor. He also wrote a host of poems, novels, and essays, tirelessly promoting Basque as a literary medium. After ETA's other leaders forced him out in the 1960s, the movement turned increasingly violent.

His Welsh counterpart was born in Wallasey, on England's Wirral peninsula, in 1893. Saunders Lewis's father worked as a Welsh-language minister in the nearby city of Liverpool. The boy went to school in Wallasey, studied English at university in Liverpool, and married a woman from the city's big Irish community. Yet after a nationalist conversion, Lewis switched over from English, the language of his first books, to write plays, novels, and poems in Welsh. In the 1920s he helped found a nationalist party that soon took the name Plaid Cymru (the party of Wales); for many years he served as its president.

These were radical gestures. Just as Txillardegi was to choose a Basque identity, Lewis chose a Welsh one. A few years before his birth, an editorial in the *Times* — the voice of imperial authority — had declared: "The Welsh language is the curse of Wales. Its prevalence and the ignorance of English have excluded, and even now exclude, the Welsh people from the civilisation, the improvement and the material prosperity of their English neighbours . . . Their antiquated semi-barbarous language, in short, shrouds them in darkness."

By 1936 Lewis was teaching Welsh at University College of Wales in Swansea. In that year the British government, seeing war on the horizon, decided to create a bombing range to train Royal Air Force pilots. It proposed a few options in England, notably the ancient monastic site of Holy Island; local opposition scuttled them all. The choice settled on Penyberth, in the distant Lleyn Peninsula: the most staunchly Welsh area in all of Wales. The government didn't know — or didn't care — that the farmhouse at Penyberth was no ordinary building. Praised in medieval poetry, it had been a resting place on the pilgrims' route to Ynys Enlli, still a holy island to many people in Wales. Ardent opposition rang out through the nation, and it went unheeded: the RAF demolished what Lewis called "a thing of hallowed and secular majesty." A pile of old timber was left.

On 8 September 1936, Saunders Lewis and two other men — a schoolteacher and a Baptist minister — set fire to the bombing school. They promptly went to a police station and turned themselves in. In October they were tried at Caernarfon for "arson and malicious damage to the King's property." The men pleaded not guilty, at first in Welsh. But the judge obliged them to speak English. He was in Caernarfon, he said, to administer "the law of England."

Lewis based his defense on morality, not statutes. "If the moral law counts for anything," he told the jury, "the people who ought to be in this dock are the people responsible for the destruction of Penyberth farmhouse." His words drew loud applause, at which the judge ordered everyone in the courtroom to keep quiet. Lewis went on to argue that "the development of the bombing range in Lleyn into the inevitable arsenal it will become will destroy this essential home of Welsh culture, idiom and literature. It will shatter the spiritual basis of the Welsh nation."

The jury could not agree on a verdict. But the Crown refused to let the men go free. For the first time in centuries, it transferred a criminal case from Wales to England. At the Old Bailey in 1937, a London jury showed no sympathy for the spiritual basis of the Welsh nation. Sentenced to nine months in prison, Lewis and his friends served their time at the suitably named Wormwood Scrubs prison. They came home as heroes.

But Lewis found himself a hero without a job: the university fired him. Embittered, scrounging for freelance work, he took a harder and harder political line against England. He saw the Second World War as a clash of imperial powers, and asked the Welsh to stay neutral. On this score he had few listeners. The war had been over for seven years before he was offered an academic job again, this time in the Welsh capital, Cardiff. He could have faded into decent obscurity, and he did no such thing. In 1962, invited to lecture on BBC Radio in Wales, he delivered "Tynged yr Iaith" (The Fate of the Language), a lucid and devastating analysis of the future of Welsh — or, as Lewis feared, its lack of a future.

His tone was angry. "The whole economic tendency in Great Britain," he said, "is to drive the Welsh language into a corner, ready to be thrown, like a worthless rag, on the dung-heap." Lewis saw the language "as the English government has always seen it: as a political matter." He warned that "Welsh will end as a living language, should the present trend continue, about the beginning of the twenty-first century." Census figures showed the number of Welsh speakers to be in free fall (from 977,000 in 1911, the total would drop as low as 508,000 in 1981). The language's position was not yet hopeless. But hope would be justified, Lewis said, only if Welsh speakers engaged in civil disobedience and ushered in "a period of hatred, persecution and controversy . . . It will be nothing less than a revolution to restore the Welsh language."

The impact of the lecture was astonishing. Suddenly, nationalism was alive and well among the young people of Lewis's adopted country. In response to his talk, some of them founded Cymdeithas yr Iaith Gymraeg, the Welsh language society. Its members fought for bilingual road signs, and for the right to speak Welsh in courts and post offices. These campaigns were successful — although, as Lewis had predicted, acts of civil disobedience meant that many enthusiasts spent time in prison.

He died in 1985, a time when housing costs were rising dramatically. Across much of rural Wales, English people kept buying up the properties. The Welsh, it appeared, were being priced out of their own country. Then an underground group, Meibion Glyndŵr (Sons of Glendower), firebombed some holiday cottages, and prices started to tumble. Meibion Glyndŵr also inspired a young Phil Gawne on the Isle of Man. As in 1936, nobody was killed or injured in the Welsh fires. But half a century later, nobody turned himself in. Some of the modern-day arsonists have never been caught.

Nothing could restore Penyberth. But a few miles from the bombing range, nationalists took over Nant Gwrtheyrn, a deserted quarrying village on the Lleyn Peninsula, and in 1978 they transformed it into a year-round center for the learning of Welsh.

When Saunders Lewis embraced Welsh, he was not forsaking the civilized traditions of Europe for some marginal, semi-barbarous language. On the contrary, he was entering a culture of remarkable age and grace. Lewis made English translations of Taliesin, the earliest major Welsh-language poet, whose work probably dates back to the sixth century — the "Dark Ages," we say. The Roman Empire was a fresh memory, the English language yet unborn. Its first great poet, Geoffrey Chaucer, would compose the *Canterbury Tales* in the late fourteenth century, a period that now seems inconceivably remote. Yet Chaucer is closer in time to Steven Spielberg than to Taliesin.

The language Taliesin spoke evolved over time, as all languages do, shrinking in territory but acquiring an aristocratic prestige that stood in contrast to the peasant reputation of Early Middle English. Occasionally Welsh influenced its younger neighbor. A three-word phrase like "I am traveling" has no counterpart in German or French, where *ich reise* or *je voyage;* the English structure may well derive from Welsh.

So do a handful of our words, such as "car," "flannel," and "gull." But after the bardic order collapsed, Welsh-language literature sank into a long depression. For centuries most of its texts were dourly Protestant. The translation of the Bible, more than four hundred years ago, did much to fortify the language — its majestic cadences and bleak admonitions echoed through the homes of people from all walks of life. Still, the secular generation that heard Lewis's lecture in 1962 needed more than bardic or biblical models. It needed to create a tradition of its own.

It was raining again as I drove to the one-street village of Talybont, halfway down the coast of Wales. I was looking for Y Lolfa, a publishing firm that started life in 1967 in a mood of exuberant protest. Its founder was a young nationalist named Robat Gruffudd ("Robert Griffith" by my spelling) who launched the satirical magazine *Lol* (Nonsense). He bought a press and became the unofficial printer for the fledgling Cymdeithas yr Iaith Gymraeg — the Welsh-language society — turning out posters and manifestos as well as magazines and books. A few decades and a few hundred books later, Y Lolfa's roots are sturdy.

"My father wanted to do something for the language. And he was lucky, I think, because there was a gap for this." I was listening to Lefi Gruffudd, a young man with round glasses who has assumed the helm of Y Lolfa as general editor. "What we provided," he added, "was quite shocking." Robat occasionally paid for his audacity — a book entitled *Police Conspiracy* cost Y Lolfa a fat bill for libel. Years later, the company's offices take up Talybont's former police station, with a bucolic view over grassy hills and a river of clear water. Y Lolfa continues to publish books in English, either to spur the nationalist cause or to subsidize literature in Welsh. But some of its Welsh-language fiction sounds eminently profitable. "Four horror stories in the style of Stephen King." "A fast-moving thriller set in depressed south Wales." "A sex-crazed American visits Wales on holiday. The first-ever Welsh-language erotic novel." Not, I imagine, the last.

One novel absent from Y Lolfa's list is *The Lord of the Rings*. Yet its author, J.R.R. Tolkien, happily plundered the Welsh language as he composed his saga. Tolkien, a specialist in Old English at Oxford University, was an extraordinary linguist — the languages he invented became his inspirations for character. For the Riders of Rohan he drew on Old English, for the dwarves he turned to Old Norse, and for the elves he used his favorite human languages, Finnish and Welsh. Having poured what he most loved about human languages into Elvish, Tolkien had to grant the elves a nobility and grandeur to match their speech. Elvish names like Lothlórien, Galadriel, and Legolas echo the liquidity of Welsh names (Arwen, in fact, *is* a Welsh name). "The names of persons and places in this story," Tolkien wrote, "were mainly composed on patterns deliberately modelled on those of Welsh . . . This element in the tale has given perhaps more pleasure to more readers than anything else in it." Mutations in Elvish also have their origin in Welsh, the author admitted shortly before his death. Tolkien had kept such matters private, convinced "they would have been passed over, or have been felt unintelligible and tiresome, by practically all readers, since that is the normal attitude of the English to Welsh."

Despite its populist leanings, Y Lolfa can have trouble making its books visible. A well-known bookseller in Aberystwyth stocks but a handful of volumes in Welsh, relegating them to a shelf marked "Local Interest." "It's a disgrace, really," Lefi said with a shrug. I remembered a W. H. Smith chain store in the center of Caernarfon. I'd wandered in, my ears ringing with the Welsh I'd heard in the walled streets below the castle, and glanced at a magazine rack labeled "Ffordd O Fyw/Lifestyle." The sign's bilingualism proved nothing: the sixty or so magazines were all in English.

Y Lolfa may seem remote, but at least it's on a main road. Unearthing the studios of Sain, the leading music company in Wales, is a harder task. You need to head south from Caernarfon toward the deep countryside of the Lleyn Peninsula, then take an abrupt turn onto a lane that twines through a drowsy village called Llandwog. Have faith: the single track will widen, slightly, and the lane will bring you somewhere other than a stone church, a barking collie, and sheep-filled, breast-shaped hillsides. Turn right onto another lane, passing an unkempt yard full of boats and used cars, and you'll arrive unexpectedly at the pebblestone building that houses Sain. Decades ago it belonged to the Royal Air Force. Subtle revenge by the Welsh.

Sain, like Y Lolfa, has its origin in the nationalist upheavals of the 1960s. The company's founders, Huw Jones and Dafydd Iwan, were young singers at the time. Jones went on to run S4C; Iwan became one of the leading singer-songwriters in Wales. Today he serves as Sain's managing director of music. His firm has diversified — it produces a DVD of world rugby and a Welsh-language CD-ROM of *Peter Rabbit* — but it remains a music company at heart.

"Americans and Canadians think that Welsh music is very traditional," Manna Medi said, "mostly harps and choirs. And the expats from Wales support that." A tall woman in a pale green sweater, she seemed to be speaking on behalf of a cause, not just a corporation. "But we've got our rock tradition, our middle-of-the-road tradition, our country tradition — all in Welsh. Within Wales, country is the favorite." The harps still flourish: we were talking just after a festival of *cerdd dant* — solo folk singing to a harp's accompaniment — that drew twenty-three hundred competitors. Sain has put out dozens of CDs by choirs and *cerdd dant* musicians. But the company welcomes rawer sounds, too. Bands like Super Furry Animals, Catatonia, and Gorky's Zygotic Mynci (say "monkey") sing in Welsh as well as English.

Manna's sister teaches in a Welsh-medium school in Treorchy, high up the Rhondda — a mining valley in the south where the language has been weak for decades — and the children graduate fluent in Welsh. Her mother lives in Bala, amid the rugged splendor of the north, and "she never hears a word of English spoken from one day to the next." At Sain, Welsh is the everyday language. Manna is proud of all this. "If you read all the books that are published in Welsh," she said, "there wouldn't be one single minute of the day left over." Broadcasting, music, and publishing have given the old language a new status, even a fitful glamour. Yet Manna's bets are hedged.

She began to talk about immigration, saying that "poor families are sent here by English councils. Problem families. And they anglicize the area. So do the English people who buy Welsh houses. It's a great shame that we've got so many immigrants still coming here who think they own the place. And they change the rules, because they're the people who always go on committees." Her voice had feeling in it now, a feeling that had not been audible when she reeled off the statistics of Sain's overseas sales. Incongruous though it seemed — the furnishings were gracious, the twenty-four-track studio just a few steps away — I had a memory flash of my Uncle Jim, stuffing salted lettuce between his dentures and railing against Midlanders in his Knighton kitchen.

"They've got more guts than the Welsh have," Manna said with something close to hatred, or self-hatred. "We're very shy. We shy away from the limelight. So our voices don't get heard. That's what gets under my skin. And in the end, it'll go English."

Manna's sour prediction was official policy four and a half centuries ago. Henry VIII, a Welshman's son, was on the throne of England in

1536 when the parliament in London passed an Act of Union. "Act of takeover" might be a better phrase: "No person or persons that use the Welsh speech or language shall have or enjoy any manor, office or fees within the realm of England, Wales or other the king's dominions upon pain of forfeiting the same offices or fees unless he or they use and exercise the speech or language of English." Welsh resistance was quiet yet constant. In *Wild Wales,* the English author George Borrow — one of the great travelers of Victorian days — noted that "all conquered people are suspicious of their conquerors. The English have forgot that they ever conquered the Welsh, but some ages will elapse before the Welsh forget that the English have conquered them."

Perhaps memory is the mother of suspicion. Pressured by nationalist agitation, Britain passed Welsh Language Acts in 1967 and 1993. The first gave Welsh a somewhat ambiguous legal footing; the second went further. It created a Welsh Language Board with a mandate to promote the language, politely but firmly. As the new century dawned, Wales had its first national assembly since the brief rebellious heyday of Owain Glyndŵr, six hundred years earlier. That's not all. Thanks to Britain's membership in the European Union, the Welsh could begin to bypass London, taking their proud place in a continent of regions while forging partnerships with other minorities. Official Europe is no longer made up just of nation-states; it also recognizes the Catalans, the Frisians, the Sardinians, and so on.

Is the long battle over? Some Welsh speakers think it's safe to relax. The hard-liners in Cymdeithas yr Iaith Gymraeg disagree. Its offices lie in the resort and university town of Aberystwyth, in a seafront building I must have scampered past as a sandcastle boy. I remembered the view from the beach: mountains emerging like burly ghosts to the northwest and sinking into a salt horizon. Outside the tourist season, the sands were empty. An American-style entertainment complex now dominates the harbor: Pizza Royal, Inn on the Pier, Pier Pressure . . . In the global market of fast food, lamb and leeks don't stand a chance.

Dafydd Morgan Lewis, who runs the campaigns Cymdeithas wages, was hiding behind his computer screen. That was my impression, at least. A shy man with thick glasses and tangled, bushy hair, he seemed happy to answer my questions as long as I didn't get too close. The office was in dramatic need of cleaning, its floor half hidden by old envelopes, rubber bands, index cards, and other debris. A black-and-white photograph of a protesting crowd recalled the glory days of Cymdeithas, when most of its members had the joyful single-mindedness of youth. Dafydd said nothing about himself. By chance, I later found out that in 1984 he was one of three people who broke into Conservative headquarters in Cardiff, causing five thousand pounds' damage to equipment, files, furniture, and a portrait of Margaret Thatcher.

He trotted through the society's demands. It's time for a new radio station to supplement Radio Cymru: "We've noticed that they've got more than one waveband in Basque and Catalan." As for the young, "we're placing a special emphasis on further education colleges, and for people to be able to do vocational training through the medium of Welsh." The word "education" rolled off his lips heavily: ed-dew-cay-shun, its four thick syllables each given due weight. When native Welsh speakers speak English, they often sound as if their tongues are non-plussed at being so underemployed in the mouth.

"Forty years ago," Dafydd said, "many people didn't believe the language was worth fighting for. We have actually made Welsh people take pride in their culture. We have made the language into a serious political issue." At present Cymdeithas has a mailing list of two thousand names, but its active members are fewer. When I suggested that the group was afflicted by apathy, he half agreed: "But I'd use the word 'complacent' rather than 'apathetic.' Nobody who lives in Welsh-speaking areas would think the battle's won, not by a long shot."

Dubious logic, I see now. At the time I merely asked for reasons, and Dafydd threw up his hands as though not knowing where to begin. Farmers can't make ends meet; families are too poor to buy homes; businesses don't take the language seriously; users of mobile phones can't get service in Welsh . . . Some Cymdeithas members had lately clambered up mobile-phone towers to press the point. "But we take responsibility for our actions," Dafydd said, "and we always confine our action to something that is in no way a threat to human life." Except their own, possibly. I didn't like to imagine Dafydd Morgan Lewis, with his generous torso and thick spectacles, perched in the sky.

He did not expound the extreme position, associated with the late poet and priest R. S. Thomas, that only Welsh speakers qualify as truly Welsh. "If you take a common history, a common territory, and a common language," Dafydd said, leaning back alarmingly far toward the wall, "sometimes you can achieve identity with only two out of three. It's not easy to define what Welshness is. But if the Welsh language was to die, everyone's Welsh identity would suffer, even if they didn't speak it."

I left the Cymdeithas offices and strolled along the seafront. By Welsh standards Aberystwyth displays an almost tropical frivolity: houses rising from the slate pavements are painted white, yellow, green, even pink. I noticed a pair of fading words on a wall in the shopping district: MEIBION GLYNDŴr. Arsonist graffiti, still visible. Above the town center stand the magnificent National Library and a campus of the University of Wales. (Charles Windsor spent a few months here in the late 1960s, attempting to wrap his tongue around Welsh before his investiture as Prince of Wales; he has seldom returned.) I climbed the hill, tore myself away from the view, and set off to find Dylan Phillips, a research fellow with the Centre for Advanced Welsh and Celtic Studies. His hair close-cropped, his tall frame in jeans, a denim shirt, and work boots, he seemed to embody the "Cool Cymru" look of a generation that seeks its fulfillments outside politics, a generation that prefers a good party to a good demonstration. In fact, though, he joined Cymdeithas yr Iaith Gymraeg when he was only sixteen.

"Cymdeithas is a victim of its own success," Dylan argued. "Since the society started off, interest in the language has skyrocketed and the official status of Welsh has vastly improved. That has made it difficult to convince people to carry on with other campaigns. But the *need* is not less at all. Because although things look better now for Welsh, the erosion of the language isn't that much less." A recent survey, for instance, showed that almost half the adults who speak decent Welsh never use it on the job. Keeping Welsh vibrant entails ensuring that it's uttered in factories, shops, and offices — not just in kitchens and chapels.

Dylan's current work as a social historian is on the impact of mass tourism in Welsh-speaking regions: what Gwynfor Evans once called "the determined effort to convert the homeland of an ancient nation into a lovely park and dormitory for the people of England." Tourism brings in money and jobs. But it also leads to immigration — many of the English fall in love with the place — so that residents, Dylan said, "are priced out of the housing market. And in summer, there are areas where the Welsh speakers are just drowned." In parts of west Wales, summer visitors outnumber the locals by more than four to one. Children brought up there, seeing tourists full of wealth and confidence, start to aspire to the tourists' values and culture. And language.

Later, walking down from the university toward Royal Pier Tandoori in the lit-up town, I realized that the longer Dylan had talked, the more bitter he had sounded. "When Welsh speakers have their backs against the wall, they tend to be quite militant. Otherwise the vast majority are apathetic. Look at the 2001 census. The powers that be decided to have a box where you could tick off that you were Scottish, Irish, or British — but they omitted one for Welsh. The absolute disgust of a sizable number of people has been very revealing. But it's always the same. The Welsh come out of their shells only when they have to, and maybe when it's too late."

Of course, it's hard to stay vigilant all the time. And even though Welsh is less secure than most of the politicians or Welsh Language Board members admit, it's important to add that the language continues to inspire passionate defenders. People like Cefin Roberts, Dafydd Morgan Lewis, and Dylan Phillips are well aware of the mistakes made across the Irish Sea early in the twentieth century, when a newly independent Ireland entrenched the status of Gaelic. The Irish institutionalized their language, requiring it on official documents and making knowledge of it compulsory for anybody wanting to enter the civil service. They turned Gaelic into a civic duty, overlain with a hint of ancestor worship. Somehow they forgot the passion. As an everyday language Gaelic came close to death in Dublin. It subsisted in the far west, a turf of nostalgia self-consciously remote from the modern age. No wonder the young in Ireland turned against it, pouring their creativity into the English language. No wonder the Welsh are resolved to do things differently.

I was driving south from Aberystwyth when something dawned on me: the significance of those famous campaigns in the 1960s for bilingual road signs. Welsh place names often bear no resemblance to their English counterparts — Holyhead is "Caergybi," Barmouth is "Abermaw," and even the Welsh-sounding town of Carmarthen is also "Caerfyrddin." It's not just a question of slight variations on a theme, as you find with Bruxelles (Brussels) or Wien (Vienna, Vienne). If the absence of names like Caergybi and Abermaw was a mark of impotence, their re-emergence came as proud confirmation that the Welsh really are still here.

Carmarthen, or Caerfyrddin, stands near a shifting, invisible frontier: the line that divides a region of everyday bilingualism from a region where English is the bread-and-butter language and the public use of Welsh is rare. Merlin is rumored to have lived here, and an impressive gallery bears his name: Oriel Myrddin. The show that morning featured luminous watercolors of Welsh landscapes. I spoke to Sian Conti, an artist and designer. Slim, elegant, clothed in black, she deflected questions with an offhand flick. "I think people just carry on speaking their own language, don't they?" "People do live their daily life in Welsh, don't they?" I wondered if this was a tensed embedding or an unreality ending. "We do hear a lot of Welsh in Carmarthen": I half expected her to add "Don't we?" Reluctantly she admitted that many English people migrate to the area, that the gallery's working language is English, and that "Welsh artists, a lot of them are born and bred here, but they won't necessarily speak Welsh." I took this as proof that Dylan Phillips was right to complain about erosion.

In 2001 anxieties about erosion led to the founding of a new pressure group: Cymuned (Community). Its members looked on the bilingual road signs and even the establishment of S4C as largely symbolic victories, won at a time when Welsh-speaking communities were starting to decline — a decline that accelerated through the 1990s. To maintain and restore the status of Welsh as the main language in its traditional heartlands must therefore become a critical goal in the new century. That goal is made more elusive by the absence of any restrictions on English people buying up rural Wales, where property values have again jumped beyond the reach of most Welsh people.

When it appeared before the National Assembly's culture committee in November 2001, Cymuned published the testimony of seventy-two people, almost all of them from villages and small towns. The pattern they described was grim. Let Ieuan Evans of Llanbedrog stand as typical. "Until the 1960s," he wrote, "Llanbedrog was a village full of life and activity, but today there isn't a single Welsh society left except for some half dozen members in the three chapels" — in each of the three chapels, one hopes. "Two-thirds of the village are holiday homes or houses of in-migrants from England, and the prices of those houses are over £100,000 for a two-bedroomed property . . . There's no work here so the local youngsters leave for Cardiff and the south." In Cardiff they may still speak Welsh, some of the time at least. But what will they find if they go back? "If nothing is done," Evans warned, "Llanbedrog will be a completely dead village for eight months of the year." And a living one, the rest of the time, in English.

From the bilingual bustle of Carmarthen it's but a short drive to the south coast. I wanted to visit Swansea, the second-largest city in Wales, where the poet Dylan Thomas grew up. Having satirized his homeland in English, having spent much of his short career in England, and having been a scandalous drinker by anybody's standards, Thomas is not universally revered in Wales. He grew up in a Victorian semidetached house, brick above, gray pebbledash below, facing a park on a steep hill. The boy would have had a wonderful view down to Swansea Bay: "the two-tongued sea." Perhaps by that phrase he meant its ebb and flow, its calms and storms; or perhaps he meant Welsh and English. Whatever their language, the city's people have tended to shy away from the world. The *South Wales Evening Post* once ran a story with the immortal headline "Swansea Man Weds Swansea Woman in Swansea."

Lefi Gruffudd of Y Lolfa had said I must meet his distinguished uncle there. But as I waited on a drizzling evening for a car to pick me up, I wasn't sure which Heini Gruffudd to expect. There seemed so many possibilities: the lecturer at the University of Wales; the editor of *Wilia,* a monthly newspaper for the city's Welsh speakers; the national chair of Rhieni dros Addysg Gymraeg, a pressure group of parents whose children go to school in Welsh; or the tireless author of such books as *Get By in Welsh, The Welsh Learner's Dictionary,* and (his all-time bestseller) *Welsh Is Fun!* Legend has it that the devil struggled for seven years to learn Basque — and then gave up. Thanks to Heini Gruffudd, he'd have an easier time with Welsh.

But the rumpled, diffident man at the wheel was none of the above. It was Heini Gruffudd the bartender.

"We all take a turn behind the bar," he said, maneuvering toward Tŷ Tawr, the clubhouse of Swansea's Welsh-language speakers. The little street was dark, the building darker, and its unmarked side entrance gave no hint that once Heini had unlocked a few doors and turned on a few lights, we'd be standing in a brick-red and yellow room with a vaguely Mediterranean décor. Upstairs are the classrooms in which adults discover if Welsh really is fun. Demand is heavy: the university gives Welsh courses in eight locations around town. Parents of small children now enjoy a choice of fifty-three Welsh-speaking playgroups. Bilingualism, at long last, has become chic.

In Tŷ Tawr, if you talk, you talk Welsh. Heini, making an exception in my honor, remarked, "We've always had a fair number of Welsh speakers in Swansea, but the trouble is we're so outnumbered." In parts of north Wales, despite the tourists and the immigrants, the language still flows naturally; but in south Wales, home to most of the nation's people, Welsh demands a conscious personal commitment. When you're surrounded at every turn by English, each conversation is a modest triumph.

More people began to arrive, surprised to see a new face. Heini told them that my parents came from Radnorshire, a fact that appeared to make my journey understandable. Even more, it made me instantly acceptable. But amid their chosen language and their chosen beer, most of the club's members displayed a certain reticence. They spoke quietly. They even laughed quietly. Heini watered the plants and switched the music from Catatonia to Bryn Terfel.

"The Welsh have been very successful," he said in a respite from gardening and bartending, "in founding institutions to help their cause. Trouble is, they've tended to rely too heavily on those institutions. They've not paid enough attention to the basic need to carry on speaking Welsh in all social circumstances." A key question, then, is not how many people *can* speak Welsh; it is how many people *do*. "There is vast support," Heini added, "for the continuation of Welsh — but the language is getting less and less use."

Walking back to my guesthouse, I passed the open door of the Celtic Pride, a pub where a ska band named Hot 'n Bovverd was performing. Even on the street, the music stung my ears. The pub was full and the dancing looked high-octane. No reticence; no Welsh.

He'd gone to chapel in the morning. On a Sunday afternoon, he still wore a conservative jacket, a discreet tie. A soft-spoken man in his early fifties, he had well-groomed, graying hair. Robat Powell lives in a Victorian house on what the street signs, and most residents, call Vicarage Road. It runs through Morristown, a northern suburb of Swansea. Or does it? Robat also lives on Heol y Ficerdy, in the suburb of Treforys and the city of Abertawe. We sipped tea from china cups in a book-lined dining room — a far cry from the factory town where Robat grew up. "Ah, but he's a brilliant man," I'd been told. In 1985 he won the poetry chair at the National Eisteddfod — the first time in living memory that this, the highest honor in Welsh-language writing, had gone to an author whose mother tongue is English. The chair is no metaphor: it sits in his front room, carved from a pale wood, tall and austere.

The archdruid handed Robat the prize for a long poem called

Cynefin. "An untranslatable term," he said with a faint smile. "It means locality, habitat, where you come from; your square mile, your own patch." The patch in question was Ebbw Vale, a town that is commonly felt to be so depressed, so devoid of interest for outsiders, that it doesn't rate a single mention in the five-hundred-page *Rough Guide to Wales*. When Robat was a boy, the steelworks employed fourteen thousand men and stretched along the valley for miles. "You'd hear the sound of the engines, the whistles, the steam being let off, and you'd go to sleep with the noise. A sort of lullaby, really. Now there are only eight hundred jobs left in the works. If you walk along the main street of Ebbw Vale, every second shop is closed down."

Cynefin is partly about Robat's experience there. But he also wove the distant past and the not-so-distant future into the poem: "The pristine forests of oak and beech, the burning of the forests to make charcoal, and then the opening of the furnaces: how they sucked in people, as if the people were being fed into the furnaces as a sacrifice to industry. Then I look ahead to when the whole works is closed down — we don't want to see this but it's inevitable — with snow over the valley and forests growing there again."

When the mines and furnaces opened during the Industrial Revolution, the first migrants to Ebbw Vale came from rural Wales. But soon the newcomers were overwhelmingly English. Their language, spoken by the bosses, came to dominate the pits and factories, then the newly built schools; gradually, over decades, it won the chapels too. By the end of the nineteenth century, Welsh had died in Ebbw Vale. The pattern held true in most of the coal-dark valleys.

As a boy, Robat knew nobody who spoke the old language. Only when he went off to university in London in 1966 did he meet Welsh speakers his own age. Sunday evenings, after a chapel service, the students would adjourn to a pub "and so there'd be three hours of hymn singing and carousing. It was an immersion in something that was exciting and stimulating. I was a part of it, and yet I wasn't, because I couldn't speak the language. I had a strong emotion of being excluded. It wasn't the students' fault. But the only way to unlock the door was to learn the language." And the learning took over his life. It smacks of a conversion. A conversion — like that of Saunders Lewis — which attests to the abiding power of Welsh.

Robat became a teacher, then an educational researcher. In 1981 he began to write in his adopted tongue. It had taken a decade of everyday use for him to absorb the language's nuances and turn its rhythms his way. The door he had opened and unlocked led not merely to a different language but to a different part of himself. "Only when I started to write in Welsh," Robat said, "could I express what was *in* me and *around* me."

His chosen medium was classical poetry, an art form whose rules are demanding in the extreme. Think of a Shakespearean sonnet, with its fixed number of lines, its formal rhythm, and its regular end-rhymes. Most poets writing in English would scramble to come up with a presentable version. Yet in Welsh a Shakespearean sonnet might almost qualify as free verse. A classical Welsh poem adheres to the laws of *cynghanedd* — another untranslatable term, "the harmonies" being a rough equivalent. In *cynghanedd*, you take an easy matter like line-ending rhyme virtually for granted. The trick comes in coordinating meters, vowel sounds, and internal rhymes, all the while shaping the patterns of repeated consonants — line after line, page after page. *Cynghanedd* was codified in the fourteenth century, Robat told me, "and since then we've had the rules to stick to." Those rules have fired his imagination. He called his first book *Haearn Iaith* (The Iron of Language). In its grip, his mind grew free.

The best way to grasp how *cynghanedd* works is by way of illustration. The iron of the following lines bends a little more than it should. Still, try rolling this around on your tongue:

> Open a pathway through the slow sad sail,
> Throw wide to the wind the gates of the wandering boat
> For my voyage to begin to the end of my wound,
> We heard the sea sound sing, we saw the salt sheet tell.
> Lie still, sleep becalmed, hide the mouth in the throat,
> Or we shall obey, and ride with you through the drowned.

The words are English, but much of their music and phonetic structure comes straight from Welsh. Which is how their author — not Robat Powell but Dylan Thomas — achieved a lot of his effects. Thomas's parents were Welsh speakers; his father even taught the language. In his poetry he made use of an intricate patterning that he borrowed from *cynghanedd*. Its medieval harmonies sounded new in London and Manhattan. Here, then, was an answer to the mystery I'd felt about Thomas's poems long ago: Welsh is their subtext, their undercurrent.

The public Dylan Thomas turned his back on Welsh. The private man made it his muse.

"I could have written *Cynefin* in English," Robat surprised me by saying. "I think you can express the same thoughts in different languages. But they *feel* different. And they're colored differently. One thing I've found in learning Welsh is that the language is interwoven with the environment in a way that English is not. In English, when you say the word 'mountain,' so many things come to mind: Mount Everest, the Peak District, the Alps . . . But when you say *mynydd*, a very clear picture comes to mind: what I can see on the other side of the valley." He gestured toward the dining room window, which looks out beyond the roofs of Morristown toward the bare forbidding heights of the Brecon Beacons. "So if it were in English, the poem wouldn't be so strikingly local."

He looked at me in silence, as though wondering whether to add something more. Finally he did: "I can express myself more fully in Welsh, not because I can't write English, but because English has a coldness about it. Expressing things through Welsh seems to come from the heart — from one's whole being. I work in education, I sit on a lot of committees, and if I go to a meeting in London, I'm aware that the people are very different. They're very nice — but I don't belong there. In Welsh-language committees, there's a feeling of 'We're all in this together.' It's closer. It's warmer. It's less formal. And it's friendlier."

The streets were quiet as I waved farewell: most of the country was watching a rugby international, live on TV in two languages. I don't know if the commentary in English was colder or less heartfelt than that in Welsh. But I do know that lovers of Welsh find it hard to be generous about English. Maybe this will be the future for much of the world: a steady growth in English, a steady growth in hostility to English. That afternoon I slipped onto an empty motorway and headed for the border. Even maps do Wales an injustice: the nation is hemmed in by "Liverpool Bay," the "Irish Sea," and the "Bristol Channel." Some people find the border irrelevant; there are train-besotted commuters who live in south Wales and work in London. Still, national feeling is hard to erase. Globalization may even be heightening it. No one has yet figured out how to be a citizen of the world and only the world. North of the motorway the post-industrial valleys coiled into the distance, but the remaining lights of Ebbw Vale were too far away to see. I missed the last *mynydd* in the darkness.

Will the Welsh language still be vibrant a century from now? I recalled what Dylan Phillips had said in Aberystwyth: "You can have all the goodwill in the world toward the Welsh language, but unless its problems are addressed, it will die off in the end." But I remembered, too, the small children speaking Welsh at Ysgol Gynradd Tregarth and the teenagers in a hallway at Ysgol Glanaethwy, the language pouring from their lips. The demise of Welsh has been predicted for generations. It hasn't happened yet.

Crossing the Wye Valley, I entered the land of my birth. HWYL FAWR CYMRU in the rearview mirror. Road signs were now unilingual, Radio Cymru a distant splutter. I pressed a dial and was alone with my thoughts. *Crow, foe, no, owe* . . . Every mile deepened the silence, a silence that felt like exile. Welsh "rings a bell," J.R.R. Tolkien once observed, "or rather it stirs deep harp-strings in our linguistic nature . . . It is the native language to which in unexplored desire we would still go home."

15

The Face of All the Earth

A
S A SPEAKER," says Tiorahkwáthe, the councilor at Kahnawake responsible for the status of Mohawk, "I envision language as a 1-800 number to my ancestors." His choice of
metaphor is revealing: not a trail, a canoe route, or a smoke
signal, but a toll-free line. Even while minority languages maintain a
priceless link with history, they don't have to be mired in the past. A
message stick off the coast of Australia is replaced by a fax machine, yet
the story that emerges can still be in Tiwi; the medium is not always the
message. Or rather, the message doesn't have to be one of loss and erasure — it can speak of continuance and change. Any living tradition is
also a tradition in flux.

The founders of modern Hebrew in what is now the state of Israel aspired to do more than just preserve a language. They wanted the language to grow. To use a preferred term of sociolinguists, they wanted to
extend its domains, making its presence felt in many spheres of life.
When I visited the offices of Y Lolfa and Sain in rural Wales, I saw that
Welsh has entered realms of the imagination that would have aston-
ished, even scandalized the preachers and hymn writers of the not-so-
distant past. Y Lolfa publishes thrillers and erotic novels. Dafydd Iwan,
the singer-songwriter in charge of Sain, doesn't limit his protest ballads
to English targets like Prince Charles and "Magi Thatcher" — he has recorded songs about Nelson Mandela, Oscar Romero, and Victor Jara,
too. On the Mohawks' side of the Atlantic, it's only right that Brian
Maracle should turn Hootie and the Blowfish into "Hootie and the fish

that has a potential to get bigger." Mohawk and every other minority language have the same potential, or need.

Yet if, in the twenty-first century, more and more of us are aspiring to the freedom of a fluid identity — if we are equating modernity with mobility — then that freedom may be hard to reconcile with the demands of a traditional language. On the Isle of Man, the determined rootedness of Phil Gawne, *Yr Greinneyder,* touched and impressed me. It did not, however, convince me that many of his fellow islanders are likely to emulate him. Phil and his family know where they belong. But if you have any doubts on that score, you won't spend serious time on a language that travels poorly. You're likely to use words that belong everywhere and nowhere. Manx is never going to displace English as English so thoroughly displaced Manx; it will never become an idiom of convenience. One of the tasks facing Phil Gawne and Manx's other stalwarts is to persuade a sufficient number of people that great value, as well as great inconvenience, lies in a language that still baffles most of the islanders.

Their struggle, it should be clear by now, is part of a worldwide battle to prevent language annihilation. But even this larger battle — I ask forgiveness for the metaphor — may be part of a wider war, perhaps the central one of our time: the fight to sustain diversity on a planet where globalizing, assimilating, and eradicating occur on a massive scale. As the eminent sociolinguist Joshua Fishman once observed, a question facing minority cultures is also an issue for everyone living in the contemporary age: "how one can build a home that one can still call one's own and, by cultivating it, find community, comfort, companionship and meaning in a world whose mainstreams are increasingly unable to provide the basic ingredients for their own members." Home is a place where knowledge resonates with meaning. Home is where the tongue is — or was.

Through the pages of this book, I have proposed various analogies to the condition of threatened tongues: locally run stores, confronted by a Wal-Mart invasion; small nations, bordered by aggressive neighbors; rare species of animals and plants, their living space depleted or overrun by intruders. The biological analogy may be the most pertinent — "linguistic ecology" is now a recognized field of study, not just a figure of speech. What dialects are to languages, subspecies are to species. Chain saws and invaders menace them indiscriminately. Yet in the end, all these parallels are imperfect.

None of the analogies quite matches the predicament of threatened languages, and the most basic reason lies in language's very nature. A struggling business provides merchandise or services; it has tangible assets. A beleaguered nation owns a great variety of assets, from buildings and weaponry to radio stations and banknotes. An endangered species consists of bones and blood, feathers or scales or fur. But a language is intangible. Unless it's written down, a language is nothing more than structured mouthfuls (or handfuls) of air. Its lexicon, its underlying rules, and its patterns of sound exist only as long as people use them. If all the speakers of Welsh woke up one day and, instead of muttering *Bore da,* turned to each other with "Good morning," Welsh would be over — it would require the past tense.

For the moment, Welsh remains vibrant. I realize that sentence risks a logical flaw — the speakers, not the language, are the vibrant ones; Welsh is merely spoken, or not spoken. Yet to persist in associating Welsh or any other language with the passive mode, to deny it any independent power, goes against the grain. It feels intuitively wrong. Something about language insists on the active voice. If we are the ones who decide what words to use at any given moment, our languages guide and constrain every choice we make. And so we are thrown back on metaphor. In the words of the Scottish poet W. S. Graham, "What is the language using us for?"

My answer would be this: to articulate a vision of the world, a vision that shapes us even as we shape it. To express what is common to all of us, along with what is different for many of us. Only by noticing the differences can we fully grasp the commonalities. Otherwise we are restricted to the path of thinking and imagining that a single language lays down. Had I not come across *A Descriptive Analysis of the Boro Language,* I would never have felt *gabkhron:* to be afraid of witnessing an adventure. I would never have discerned *onsra:* to love for the last time.

This is not a self-help book for languages in trouble. I don't have a scorecard or a checklist; I can't offer you a six-point recovery plan. True, we can distinguish some challenges that are shared by almost all the cultures described in earlier chapters: passing on the language to children; keeping it alive among teenagers; using it at work; seeing and hearing it in the mass media; resisting the innumerable demands and blandishments of a majority tongue. The strategies that meet those challenges will often overlap — the Faroese, the Maoris, and the Welsh are doing many of the same things. But to proffer a single set of remedies would not only be futile; it would go against a central premise of this book, which is that differences matter.

"Differences are extremely fecund," wrote the great anthropologist Claude Lévi-Strauss in 1978. "It is only through difference that progress has been made. What threatens us right now is probably what we may call over-communication — that is, the tendency to know exactly in one point of the world what is going on in all other parts of the world." In terms of computer technology, of course, 1978 counts as the Dark Ages. Before the World Wide Web, before search engines and e-mail, before PCs themselves — how could such a world be considered overcommunicative? And what adjective could possibly describe our own?

"In order for a culture to be really itself and to produce something," Lévi-Strauss went on, "the culture and its members must be convinced of their originality . . . It is only under conditions of under-communication that it can produce anything." That sense of originality may well be an illusion. Many ancient cultures felt they enjoyed a unique relationship with the divine, a peerless grasp of spiritual truth, and one at most can have been right. But as Lévi-Strauss explained, the illusion was perhaps necessary; it's something we have shed at a price. "We are now threatened with the prospect of our being only consumers, able to consume anything from any point in the world and from every culture, but of losing all originality." No longer does every culture have a self-created pantheon; every culture has Julia Roberts.

All right, I'm exaggerating. Yet before the consumer age, small languages were not so obviously in danger. In the nineteenth century much of Europe rode a wave of Romanticism, which exalted national and cultural differences. The Victorian philosopher John Stuart Mill was among those who deplored the trend. "Nobody," he declared, "can suppose that it is not more beneficial to a Breton or a Basque . . . to be a member of the French nationality, admitted on equal terms to all the privileges of French citizenship . . . than to sulk on his own rocks, the half-savage relic of past times, revolving in his own little mental orbit, without participation or interest in the general movement of the world." I wonder, given his low opinion of Bretons and Basques, if Mill ever stopped to ask them about their degree of interest in the outside world, or tried to measure their mental orbits. If their chief pursuit was their own culture, they were sulking; if they declined the beguilements of Paris, they were uncivilized. With the arrogance of empire behind him, Mill also assumed his argument could not be answered.

Few people any longer stand up and say they want languages to die out. "Progress" is so clearly winning the day, such a wish would seem like pleading for the inevitable. But occasionally polemics still appear in praise of uniformity. The trend is "worth celebrating," John J. Miller wrote in the *Wall Street Journal* in March 2002. "A growing number of people are speaking a smaller number of languages, meaning that age-old obstacles to communication are collapsing. Surely this is a good thing." History suggests it isn't. The ravaged nations of Somalia and Rwanda have a greater uniformity of language than almost anywhere else in sub-Saharan Africa. When Yugoslavia disintegrated in the early 1990s, its feuding Serbs, Croats, and Bosnians all spoke a common tongue: what used to be called "Serbo-Croat." (Today, in the aftermath of civil war, Serbian, Croatian, and Bosnian have begun to split apart.) The presence of a common language in a divided country brings no guarantee of peace. Protestants and Catholics in northern Ireland understand each other clearly — all too clearly.

But for those with an agenda to push, multiple languages can indeed be an obstacle. Far easier to deal with uniformity, as long as the uniform in question is your own. In 1868 a federal commission on Indian affairs in the United States released a report urging that rapid steps be taken to abolish Indian languages: "Through sameness of language is produced sameness of sentiment and thought." Therefore the Indians' "barbarous dialect should be blotted out and the English language substituted." The report paid implicit tribute to the power of language — though it failed to recognize that many dozens of native languages existed. Indeed the Indians were not even granted the dignity of speaking language; to the commissioners, all they had was a dialect, and a barbarous one at that. As soon as they talked the same as other Americans, Indians would feel and think the same too. Difference was a possible ambush, an arrow in the back of the neck.

Even now, in large parts of northern Canada, there are tens of thousands of people who show by their ancestral languages how differently they see the world. They speak Algonquian languages like Cree, Innu, Ojibwa, and Mi'kmaq. In these languages, the grammatical first person is not "I" or "me," "we" or "us." The first person is "you." The Innu way of saying "You see me" is what linguists call the "direct form": *tshi-ua:pam-in*. To say "I see you" is more complex, requiring an extra syllable: *tshi-ua:pam-it-in.* Linguists call this the "inverse form": in our terms, roughly, "You are seen by me." Evidence from many languages shows that direct forms of speech are the oldest and deepest; they precede all elaborations and complications. Those who are fluent in Algonquian languages confirm the rank of "you." Speakers of these languages, writes the Quebec linguist Danielle Cyr, "often request that linguists who prepare descriptive grammars place 'you' forms at the head of verbal paradigms . . . When asked what is more natural to them when listing verbal forms, my informants say that if they have to start with 'I,' their tongue 'trips' because it feels stupid."

To speak properly, in an Algonquian language, is to be aware of the identities and interrelationships of all the people you address. You express yourself most fully when you are most aware of your listeners. As Cyr warns, "When we teach Algonquian schoolchildren that 'I' comes first, we somehow pervert one of the social functions that language is supposed to perform. By imposing our notion of truth, we increase the assimilation pressure on endangered cultures." And yet mainstream grammars take it for granted that the "I" form of speech is the most basic, the most essential. It worked for the Greeks and Romans, and it works for us. "I" is the true ground of our being. It is not everyone else's.

What the survival of threatened languages means, perhaps, is the endurance of dozens, hundreds, thousands of subtly different notions of truth. With our astonishing powers of technology, it's easy for us in the West to believe we have all the answers. Perhaps we do — to the questions we have asked. But what if some questions elude our capacity to ask? What if certain ideas cannot be fully articulated in our words? "There are amazing things about Aboriginal languages," Michael Christie told me when I visited his office at Northern Territory University in Darwin. "Their concepts of time and agency, for example. They go right against our ideology of linear time — past, present, and future. I reckon they'd completely revolutionize Western philosophy, if only we knew more about them."

Western linguists tend to analyze any language as though it were a machine functioning in response to precise commands. Yet machines are only one model for understanding language. In a trenchant, subversive essay entitled "Yolngu Linguistics," Michael suggested that "language abides in the structures of what we have learnt to be real." Having learned that expression is a private act, we select words to embody our individual perceptions. But the Yolngu of Arnhem Land, like the speakers of Algonquian languages in northern Canada, have learned to regard expression as a social event. For the Yolngu, the continuance of a language does not just mark the survival of a unique set of words and rules. It marks the survival of a unique form of singing. We perceive vocabulary. The Yolngu perceive music.

There was a time, so the story goes, when the floodwaters had receded from Mount Ararat and the moist plain below had begun to swarm with people. The wives of Ham and Shem and Japheth have borne children at a heroic rate; generations are becoming nations. But as yet, "the whole Earth was of one language, and one speech." Enterprising, ambitious, its naked apes have discovered the use of bricks and mortar. They have settled in the land of Shinar, where, hungry to make a name for themselves, they decide to build "a city and a tower, whose top may reach unto heaven." Nobody asks the Lord's opinion. Does he want a cloud-capped ziggurat pushing up through his basement? At this early point in a long narrative he still takes a lively interest in his creation, and he comes down to take a close look. His reaction, even by his own notoriously unpredictable standards, is odd.

"Behold, the people is one," the Lord observes, "and they have all one language; and this they begin to do; and now nothing will be restrained from them, which they have imagined to do." We don't know what else the people have in mind. Perhaps they don't know, either. Presumably they believe the tower will be glorious in the Lord's sight — proof of their strength and unity, their wondrous capacity to dream. Have they not enameled its bricks in blue as brilliant as the sky? All we know is God's response.

He fails to see the glory. Yet he refrains from wrecking the building, nor does he flatten the city — this isn't Sodom or Gomorrah. To stop the eager citizens from fulfilling their desire, all the Lord needs to do is to "confound their language, that they may not understand one another's speech." Having done so, he proceeds to "scatter them abroad upon the face of all the earth." That's why the people stop working on the tower; that's why they abandon the city. "Therefore" — it's one of the Bible's innumerable weird therefores — "is the name of it called Babel."

Usually this passage of Genesis is seen as a divine curse. Why are there so many languages in the world? Because God, wanting to punish human pride, toppled the Tower of Babel. The reason we can't understand one another is that in our overarching vanity we tried to force an entry into heaven. But heaven is forbidden territory, and now we endure the shame of multilingualism. Dust that we are, we remain doomed to roam the earth, bewildered by exile, always running into people who are saying urgent things we fail to grasp. Thanks to Babel, they end up gesticulating wildly, speaking abnormally slowly, and raising their voices in frustration at our ignorance. Or we do the same to them. Babel is the mother of confusion. That's the common interpretation.

I prefer to read the passage in a different way. It goes like this: Having almost wiped out the human race by water, God made a covenant with Noah, the ancestor of these workaholic bricklayers. Promising Noah that he would never again resort to the drowning of flesh, the Lord urged the ark-builder and his sons to "be fruitful, and multiply, and replenish the earth." In accordance with the divine command, Shinar is beginning to suffer a population explosion. Yet in their devotion to a towering city the builders have neglected to carry out the third of God's injunctions. The city teems with workers, their gaze turned up to the sky. Most of the world is empty and silent.

Viewed in this light, the dispersal from Babel serves as a means to replenish. It enables cultures to be fruitful and multiply in a host of landscapes and climates, not just on a plain in Iraq. It is a gift as well as a restraining order. As for the tower, let it be. God knows it will come to grief.

The Lord is aware that without some stern measures of restraint, anything human beings imagine is liable to become real. And that must never happen. That would be the true disaster — God understands what people are like. The speakers of a unified tongue would have too much power for comfort, their own and also God's. So, feeling partly bitter, expressing his anger by a sidelong glance, he mixes up their language. And the mixing is a blessing, not a curse.

Thanks to this blessing, Noah's heirs are free to play and work and worship in a multitude of voices. Now, being made in God's image, they will carry that image as far as the Timor Sea and the Orinoco River, Baffin Island and the Isle of Man, dreaming the world into being as they go. The Lord's behavior requires them to gain a new skill: translation.

They pause occasionally to lament a lost and primal unity, but they don't really miss it; they have outgrown it. It's something they pretend to love. It belongs to the world's early childhood.

The divine confounding and scattering offer languages, like their speakers, an opportunity to fill the earth. Valleys from the Himalayas to the Ozarks can be exalted in songs of their own. The diversity of human speech will give rise to a shimmering, ever changing balance, as the stories belonging to any one nation run up against the songlines of all the others. After Babel, the human race will be rid of uniformity. After Babel, the Lord won't need to worry about how the world might unravel if people spoke a single language. After Babel, the Lord can relax.

I mean, he didn't need to worry. I mean, he could relax.

SOURCES

ACKNOWLEDGMENTS

INDEX

Sources

The fate of endangered languages is central to David Crystal's *Language Death* (Cambridge: Cambridge University Press, 2000); Daniel Nettle and Suzanne Romaine's *Vanishing Voices: The Extinction of the World's Languages* (Oxford: Oxford University Press, 2000); Claude Hagège's *Halte à la mort des langues!* (Paris: Odile Jacob, 2000); and Andrew Dalby's *Language in Danger: How Language Loss Threatens Our Future* (London: Penguin, 2002). Language loss emerges as a theme of John McWhorter's *The Power of Babel: A Natural History of Language* (New York: Times Books, 2001). See also UNESCO's *Atlas of the World's Languages in Danger of Disappearing* (Paris, 2d ed., 2001) and the somewhat technical *Endangered Languages: Current Issues and Future Prospects*, ed. Lenore A. Grenoble and Lindsay J. Whaley (Cambridge, 1998). A more hopeful volume is *The Green Book of Language Revitalization in Practice*, ed. Leanne Hinton and Ken Hale (San Diego: Academic Press, 2001).

Two outstanding Web sites, as of February 2003, are www.sil.org and www.terralingua.org; the former contains the electronic version of *Ethnologue*, a catalogue of the world's languages. The information given there should, if possible, always be cross-checked with other sources. For a good introduction to language in general, see the *Cambridge Encyclopedia of Language*, ed. David Crystal (2d ed., 1997).

1. PATRICK'S LANGUAGE

For Mati Ke, I relied on the resources of the Wadeye Aboriginal Languages Centre, including its 2001 calendar. See also the "Top End" chapter of Lonely Planet's *Australian Phrasebook* (Melbourne, 2d ed., 1998) — a section written by Denise Angelo, Carolyn Coleman, and Melanie Wilkinson. Virtually all Australian languages have been spelled and classified in different styles. For the spelling of Mati Ke I follow Mark Crocombe and the Lonely Planet phrasebook — while nervously observing that the language is spelled "Marti-Ke" on Wadeye's community Web site and "Marri Ke," "Magadige," and "Magadi Ge" in other sources. In much of Australia, the term "homeland center" is used instead of "outstation," but around Wadeye, where people living in the bush are not necessarily in their traditional homeland, "outstation" is preferred.

I quote George Steiner's *After Babel: Aspects of Language and Translation* (Oxford: Oxford University Press, 1975). Steiner added: "Often, cultures seem to expend on their vocabulary and syntax acquisitive energies and ostentations entirely lacking in their material lives."

Edward Sapir wrote about Nootka in "Language and Environment" and "Abnormal Types of Speech in Nootka," both in *Collected Works of Edward Sapir* (Berlin: Mouton de Gruyter, 1989 et seq.). For Whorf's comments on Nootka see "Languages and Logic," in *Language, Thought and Reality* (Cambridge, Mass.: MIT Press, 1956). On Abkhaz, see Z. K. Khiba, "A Contribution to Abkhaz Lexicography: The Secret Language of the Hunters," *Bedi Karthlisa* (Paris) 38 (1980).

On Lardil and Damin, my principal source was David McKnight's *People, Countries and the Rainbow Serpent* (Oxford, 1999). I also used Ken Hale's excellent essay "On Endangered Languages and the Importance of Linguistic Diversity," in Grenoble and Whaley's *Endangered Languages;* and Ken Hale and David Nash, "Damin and Lardil Phonotactics," in *Boundary Rider: Essays in Honour of Geoffrey O'Grady,* ed. Darrell Tryon and Michael Walsh (Canberra: Pacific Linguistics, C-136, 1997).

2. DREAMERS: LANGUAGES IN NORTHERN AUSTRALIA

I used Annette Schmidt's *The Loss of Australia's Aboriginal Language Heritage* (Canberra: Aboriginal Studies Press, 1990) and R.M.W. Dixon's *The Languages of Australia* (Cambridge, 1980). Dixon's *Australian Languages* (Cambridge, 2002) appeared too late for me to do more than consult at high speed. In it Dixon suggests a total of about 240 precontact languages for the continent; my figure of 270 comes from Paul Black. (Dixon excludes Tasmania, about whose extinct languages little can be known.) By contrast, Stephen A. Wurm, the editor of UNESCO's *Atlas,* puts the Australian total at "around 400 or more."

Robert Hughes's study of early colonization in Australia, *The Fatal Shore* (New York: Knopf, 1987), and Michael Walsh and Colin Yallop's collection, *Language and Culture in Aboriginal Australia* (Aboriginal Studies Press, 1993), were helpful to me. Walsh's "Classifying the World in an Aboriginal Language" deals largely with Murrinh-Patha. I also used Chester S. Street's *An Introduc-*

tion to the Language and Culture of the Murrinh-Patha (Darwin: Summer Institute of Linguistics, Australian Aborigines Branch, 1987).

On Tiwi, I used Teresa A. Ward's *Towards an Understanding of the Tiwi Language/Culture Context: A Handbook for Non-Tiwi Teachers* (Nguiu: Nguiu Nginingawila Literature Production Centre, 1990). Easier to find are Jennifer Lee's *Tiwi-English Dictionary* (Summer Institute of Linguistics, 1993) and her *Tiwi Today: A Study of Language Change in a Contact Situation* (Pacific Linguistics, C-96, 1987). See also C.M.W. Hart, Arnold Pilling, and Jane Goodale, *The Tiwi of North Australia* (New York: Holt, Rinehart and Winston, 3d ed., 1988); and Eric Venbrux, *A Death in the Tiwi Islands* (Cambridge, 1995).

A profoundly affecting book is Richard Trudgen's *Why Warriors Lie Down and Die* (Darwin: Aboriginal Resource and Development Services 2000). The final chapter consists of "Five Steps to a Yolngu-Friendly Environment." The first step: "Take the people's language seriously."

Michael Christie and his colleagues at Northern Territory University have disseminated a good deal of material about Yolngu languages. Christie's work heavily influenced my understanding of the Dreamtime; see especially his "Yolngu Linguistics," in *Ngoonjook: A Journal of Australian Indigenous Issues,* June 1993, and "Grounded and Ex-Centric Knowledge: Exploring Aboriginal Alternatives to Western Thinking," in *Thinking: International Interdisciplinary Perspectives,* ed. John Edwards (Melbourne: Hawker Brownlow Education, 1994).

For Kriol, I used the essays by John Harris and Mari Rhydwen in Walsh and Yallop's *Language and Culture in Aboriginal Australia,* as well as Harris's *Northern Territory Pidgins and the Origin of Kriol* (Pacific Linguistics, C-89, 1986). On Juba Arabic and other developing languages, see Mark Sebba, *Contact Languages: Pidgins and Creoles* (New York: St. Martin's, 1997).

On the languages described in the Halls Creek section, see William McGregor, *Handbook of Kimberley Languages,* vol. 1 (Pacific Linguistics, C-105, 1988). My few lines about Pama-Nyungan agree with McGregor, Dixon (1980), and most other linguists; but Dixon (2002) now denies the validity of the entire Pama-Nyungan grouping. *Ngaapa Wangka Wangkajunga* was published in 2000 by the Kimberley Language Resource Centre. On the significance of ears in Jaru, see Tasaku Tsunoda, *The Djaru Language of Kimberley, Western Australia* (Pacific Linguistics, B-78, 1981). On the forcible removal of Aboriginal children, see Robert Manne, "In Denial: The Stolen Generations and the Right," *Australian Quarterly Essay* 1 (2001).

A further source was Thomas Keneally's *Outback* (London: Hodder and Stoughton, 1983). The quote about Tasmanians is from F. G. Clarke's *The Land of Contrarieties* (Melbourne University Press, 1977).

The Kimberley Language Resource Centre and the Wadeye Aboriginal Languages Centre have many counterparts across Australia. The Aboriginal and

Torres Strait Islanders Commission — accessible via the Internet — should be able to provide a list.

3. Constructing the World

Jorge Luis Borges's "Poem Written in a Copy of Beowulf," trans. Alastair Reid, is available in several editions. I found the quotations from Mather and Thoreau in Joshua David Bellin's *The Demon of the Continent* (Philadelphia: University of Pennsylvania Press, 2001).

The most accessible discussion of language from a Chomskyan perspective is Steven Pinker's *The Language Instinct* (New York: William Morrow, 1994). Despite his hostility to the Sapir-Whorf hypothesis, Pinker wrote, "Speakers of different languages have to pay attention to different aspects of reality simply to put words together into grammatical sentences." In his later book *The Blank Slate: The Modern Denial of Human Nature* (New York: Viking, 2002), Pinker called generative grammar "a kind of software." It's a suggestive metaphor — as long as it remains a metaphor.

An early but useful study is John Lyons, *Chomsky* (London: Fontana, 1970). And see the responses to and by Chomsky in George Steiner's *Extraterritorial: Papers on Literature and the Language Revolution* (London: Faber and Faber, 1972). Chomsky's thinking has evolved over the decades. See John Maher, *Introducing Chomsky* (New York: Totem Books, 1996); and Neil Smith, *Noam Chomsky: Ideas and Ideals* (Cambridge, 1999). The latest version of Chomsky's theories is laid out in his *New Horizons in the Study of Language and Mind* (Cambridge, 2001). See the review essay by John Searle, *New York Review of Books,* 28 Feb. 2002, and Searle's exchange with Chomsky, ibid., 18 July 2002.

On the legacy of Sapir see, e.g., *Language Diversity and Cognitive Representation,* ed. Catherine Fuchs and Stéphane Robert (Amsterdam: John Benjamins, 1999). Dell Hymes's remarks, from *Daedalus* (1973), are quoted in Steiner's *After Babel.* Sake'j Youngblood Henderson is a key influence on both Rupert Ross's *Returning to the Teachings: Exploring Aboriginal Justice* (Toronto: Penguin, 1996) and F. David Peat's *Blackfoot Physics: A Journey into the Native American Universe* (London: Fourth Estate, 1995).

On visual and linguistic relativity, see J. Davidoff et al., "Colour Categories in a Stone-Age Tribe," *Nature* 398 (1999). As for fuzzy sets and dynamic typology, see Rik Pinxten et al., *Anthropology of Space: Explorations into the Natural Philosophy and Semantics of the Navajo* (University of Pennsylvania Press, 1983). And see John A. Lucy, *Language Diversity and Thought* (Oxford, 1992), and Alison Motluk, "You Are What You Speak," *New Scientist,* 30 Nov. 2002.

The Inuktitut words for knowledge are taken from Lucien Schneider, *Ulirnaisigutiit,* "An Inuktitut-English Dictionary of Northern Quebec, Labrador and Eastern Arctic Dialects" (Les Presses de l'Université Laval, 1985). Pronunciations and spellings of Inuktitut are notoriously variable.

For illustrations of the pain that language shift can evoke, see the work of the Cree playwright and novelist Tomson Highway — especially the monologue of Simon Starblanket near the end of Highway's play *Dry Lips Oughta Move to Kapuskasing* (Saskatoon: Fifth House, 1989).

On the joys of Michif see Peter Bakker, *A Language of Our Own* (Oxford, 1997). An alternative view, given in vol. 17 of the *Handbook of North American Indians* (Washington: Smithsonian Institution, 1996), is that Michif represents "one of the most bizarre instances of language contamination."

4. Unseen and Unheard: Yuchi

The prime source for Yuchi is now Mary Linn's "A Grammar of Euchee" (Ph.D. diss., University of Kansas, 2001). Günter Wagner published *Yuchi Tales* (New York: G. E. Stechert, 1931) and *Yuchi* (New York: Columbia University Press, 1934). *A Creek Source Book,* ed. William C. Sturtevant (New York: Garland, 1987), reprints early items about the Yuchis as well as the Creeks. W. L. Ballard and James M. Crawford have also published work on the Yuchi language.

I consulted Muriel H. Wright's *A Guide to the Indian Tribes of Oklahoma* (Norman: University of Oklahoma Press, 1951); Carolyn T. Foreman's "The Yuchi: Children of the Sun," *Chronicles of Oklahoma* 37 (1959–60); and Rennard Strickland's *The Indians in Oklahoma* (University of Oklahoma Press, 1980). Yuchi made the front page of the *Washington Post* in an article by Guy Gugliotta on 9 Aug. 1999. And see Richard Grounds, "The Yuchi Community and the Human Genome Diversity Project," *Cultural Survival Quarterly,* Summer 1996.

On the indigenous languages of the United States, see, e.g., Burkhard Bilger, "Keeping Our Words," *The Sciences,* Sept.–Oct. 1994; and Earl Shorris, "The Last Word," *Harper's,* Aug. 2000. I highly recommend *Coming to Light: Contemporary Translations of the Native Literatures of North America,* ed. Brian Swann (New York: Random House, 1995).

I quote N. Scott Momaday's *The Man Made of Words* (St. Martin's, 1997). Momaday also wrote: "One who has only an oral tradition thinks of language in this way: my words exist at the level of my voice. If I do not speak with care, my words are wasted. If I do not listen with care, words are lost. If I do not remember carefully, the very purpose of words is frustrated. This respect for words suggests an inherent morality in man's understanding and use of language."

Bilingualism among children is a vexed issue in the United States. Start with Kenji Hakuta's *Mirror of Language: The Debate on Bilingualism* (New York: Basic Books, 1996). Jay P. Greene's "Meta-Analysis of the Effectiveness of Bilingual Education" (1998) is available on line, as is Stephen D. Krashen's response. In Greene's words, "An unbiased reading of the scholarly research suggests that bilingual education helps children who are learning English." See also Carla

Meskill et al., "Bilingualism, Cognitive Flexibility, and Electronic Literacy," *Bilingual Research Journal* 23, nos. 2–3 (1999); and Judy Foreman, "Two Tongues Better Than One," *Boston Globe,* 10 Sept. 2002. Research in Montreal on the benefits of bilingual education is associated particularly with the work of Fred Genesee, e.g. his *Learning Through Two Languages: Studies of Immersion and Bilingual Education* (Cambridge, Mass.: Newbury House, 1987).

I quote Simon Jenkins's column "The Triumph of English," *Times* (London), 25 Feb. 1995. The "mushing parson" is discussed by Michael Krauss in *Alaska Native Languages: Past, Present and Future* (Fairbanks: Alaska Native Language Center, 1980). J.D.C. Atkins's report is widely available on line.

For Burushaski, see E. O. Lorimer's delightful *Language Hunting in the Karakoram* (London: George Allen and Unwin, 1939), and the work of David Lorimer and, more recently, Étienne Tiffou and Dick Grune. On Lokele, see John F. Carrington's "The Talking Drums of Africa," *Scientific American,* Dec. 1971. Yishai Tobin's *Phonology as Human Behavior* appeared from Duke University Press (Durham, N.C., 1997).

5. Dont Vori, Bi Khepi

On the spread of English, see David Crystal, *English as a Global Language* (Cambridge, 1997), and his later, darker *Language Death.* See also "Christmas Special: The Triumph of English," *Economist,* 22 Dec. 2001. On cultural globalization, see *Le Monde Diplomatique*'s special issue of Sept. 1993, *L'Agonie de la culture?* For a skeptical view, see Barbara Wallraff, "What Global Language?" *Atlantic Monthly,* Nov. 2000.

In this chapter I have acted even more like a magpie than usual, pecking away here and there at will. Besides the sources cited here, I drew on articles from the *New York Times,* the *Guardian,* the *Toronto Globe and Mail,* the *Los Angeles Times,* the *Times* (London), the *Daily Telegraph,* and the *Observer.*

A principal source was the magazine *English Today,* published by Cambridge University Press. See the April 1986 issue entitled "Is English Killing Off Other Languages?" and the April 1997 feature on the Language Rights Movement, as well as Paul Christopherson, "A Bilingual Denmark" (July 1991), and John Dougill, "English as a Decorative Language" (Oct. 1987).

On Louise Beaudoin, see Nicolas van Praet, "Beaudoin Questions Francophonie's English," *Montreal Gazette,* 10 July 2001. On Claude Duneton, see Kevin Dougherty, "France in Throes of English Invasion," *Montreal Gazette,* 29 Apr. 2000. Nathalie Petrowski's column appeared in *La Presse,* 29 Nov. 2001.

Junior is published by Asian Readers in Kuala Lumpur; my examples are taken from vol. 32, 2002. I quote Ngũgĩ wa Thiong'o's "What Is African Literature?" *New Left Review,* no. 150 (Mar.–Apr. 1985). The *Far Eastern Economic Review* article by William McGurn is dated 21 Mar. 1996. On East Timor see "Le casse-tête de la langue nationale," *Courrier Internationale,* 18–24 Apr. 2002. Li

Yang and his Crazy English have been featured on many Web sites. And see Hal Cohen, "A Farewell to Esperanto?" *Lingua Franca,* May–June 2000.

6. Leaving the Grave: Manx

A Short History of the Manx Language, a booklet by Brian Stowell and Diarmuid Ó Bréasláin (Belfast: An Clochán, 1996), is worth searching out. And see George Broderick's three-volume *Handbook of Late Spoken Manx* (Tübingen: Max Niemeyer Verlag, 1984–1986). The mere title of Broderick's *Language Death in the Isle of Man* (Max Niemeyer Verlag, 1999) aroused serious annoyance on the island. Ned Maddrell's photograph appears in Nettle and Romaine's *Vanishing Voices;* a caption calls him the "last speaker of Manx."

Phil Kelly maintains a fine Web site on Manx; as of December 2002 its address was homepages.enterprise.net/kelly. The publications and Web sites of the Celtic League and the Celtic Congress contain news about Manx, Welsh, and the other Celtic languages.

Language in the British Isles, ed. Peter Trudgill (Cambridge, 1984), includes chapters relating to Manx by R. L. Thomson and Michael V. Barry. The "Survey of Manx Speakers and Learners" was jointly issued by Manx National Heritage and the Manx Heritage Foundation in Dec. 1999. The Manx National Heritage Library contains a wealth of material; its mailing address is Manx National Heritage, Douglas, Isle of Man, IM1 3LY.

I quote T. F. Ó Rahilly's *Irish Dialects Past and Present* (Dublin: Institute for Advanced Studies, 1972). On Irish Gaelic in Belfast, see Gabrielle Maguire, *Our Own Language: An Irish Initiative* (Clevedon: Multilingual Matters, 1991). Flann O'Brien's novel *The Poor Mouth* was published in Gaelic in 1941; an English translation appeared in 1973.

7. The Verbs of Boro

Needless to say, my prime source was Pramod Chandra Bhattacharya, *A Descriptive Analysis of the Boro Language* (Gauhati: Gauhati University Press, 1977). I hope it is clear that the fun I poke at this book is gentle; I hold it in considerable esteem. For an overview of the region's languages see *Tibeto-Burman Languages of the Himalayas,* ed. David Bradley (Pacific Linguistics, 1997).

For a counterpart to Boro, see D. N. Shankara Bhat, *Tankhur Naga Vocabulary* (Poona: Deccan College, 1969). Tankhur Naga is also a Tibeto-Burman language spoken in the hills of northeastern India. The language is built up from monosyllabic roots. One root forms the base of Tankhur Naga's words for water, honey, tears, curry, starch, tank, marshy place, sugarcane juice, diarrhea, sweat coming after death, and the Milky Way.

I quote Rupert Ross's *Returning to the Teachings* and George Steiner's *Extraterritorial.* Ken Hale's comparison between the extinction of languages and the destruction of the Louvre has taken on a life of its own, with an assortment of words being put in Hale's mouth (the oral tradition at its finest?); I first came across it in Burkhard Bilger's "Keeping Our Words," *The Sciences,* Sept.–Oct. 1994.

I found the "Unreached Peoples Prayer Profiles" at www.bethany.com.

C. R. Hopgood's *A Practical Introduction to Tonga* appeared in London in 1953 from Longmans, Green. A second edition, using an alternative name of the language, "Chitonga," was published by the Zambia Educational Publishing House in Lusaka in 1992.

8. The Lion's Tongue: Provençal

As if to illustrate the confusion about this language (or dialect), UNESCO's *Atlas of the World's Languages in Danger of Disappearing* (2001) makes no mention of Occitan, but lists Alpine Provençal, Auvergnat, Francoprovençal, Gascon, Languedocian, Limousin, and Provençal as separate languages — all of them "seriously endangered." "La France, combien de langues?" is one of the articles collected in *Courrier International,* 24 Mar. 2000, under the title *SOS: Langues en péril.*

On the family of languages to which Provençal belongs, see, e.g., W. D. Elcock's *The Romance Languages* (Faber and Faber, 1964); and Rebecca Posner's two books by that title, one published in 1966 (New York: Anchor Books), the other in 1996 (Cambridge). In 1966 she used the term "Provençal"; three decades later she preferred "Occitan," even when referring to the troubadours. And see *Latin and the Romance Languages in the Early Middle Ages,* ed. Roger Wright (London and New York: Routledge, 1991).

The fate of French — and of France's regional languages — is the theme of *L'Histoire,* no. 248 (Nov. 2000). On the political ramifications of Occitan, see Marya DuMont, "Minority Sociolinguistics in Europe: The Occitan Language vs. the French State" (M.A. thesis, University of Chicago, 1996).

Most of Mistral's work is unavailable in English and difficult to find in French. My main biographical source was Tudor Edwards's *The Lion of Arles: A Portrait of Mistral and His Circle* (New York: Fordham University Press, 1964). See also Richard Aldington's *Introduction to Mistral* (London: Heinemann, 1956). *The Memoirs of Frédéric Mistral,* trans. George Wickes, appeared from New Directions (New York, 1986). And see "Les félibres en accusation," in *Archives de Provence,* ed. Jacques Borgé and Nicolas Viasnoff (Paris: Ed. Michèle Trinckvel, 1994).

If you follow Mistral, then the grammar of the language is properly set out in Xavier de Fourvières's *Grammaire Provençal* (1899, but available in newer editions). Pierre Bec's *Manuel pratique d'Occitan moderne* (Paris: Picard, 1973) gives a grammar for those who want nothing to do with Mistral's version of the tongue. The French-Provençal dictionary was edited by Jules Coupier (Marseille: Association Dictionnaire Français-Provençal, 1995).

On language in the Nazi era, see Christopher M. Hutton's *Linguistics and the Third Reich: Mother-Tongue Fascism, Race and the Science of Language* (Routledge, 1999). I quote Lawrence Durrell's *Caesar's Vast Ghost: Aspects of Provence* (Faber and Faber, 1990). See also Alphonse Roche's *Provençal Regionalism* (Evanston, Ill.: Northwestern University Press, 1954). Anyone tempted to idealize French education in the past need only read René Grosso's *En Vaucluse: Notre école au bon vieux temps* (Lyon: Ed. Horvath, 1993) to be disabused. I discovered the rhyme about flea-ridden cushions in *Récits et contes populaires de Provence*, vol. 2 (Paris: Gallimard, 1979), ed. Guy Mathieu. The saying about October weather is from Charles Gautier's *Météorologie populaire dans la France ancienne: La Provence* (Horvath, 1980).

Little work by Sèrgi Bec has been translated into English. One beautiful example of his work in Occitan and French is *Tres balado / Trois ballades* (Aix-en-Provence: Édisud, 1993). *Siéu un païs* appeared from Édisud in 1980.

9. MELTING AT THE EDGES

I learned about Nicaraguan Sign Language from Lawrence Osborne's "A Linguistic Big Bang," *New York Times Magazine,* 24 Oct. 1999. On Huron, see the writings of John Steckley.

On the Inuit and their language, see the work of Hugh Brody, notably *Living Arctic: Hunters of the Canadian North* (Faber and Faber, 1987) and *The Other Side of Eden: Hunters, Farmers and the Shaping of the World* (Vancouver: Douglas and McIntyre, 2000); and Derek Rasmussen's "Dissolving Inuit Society Through Education and Money," *Interculture,* no. 139 (Oct. 2000). On Inuktitut in a region outside Nunavut, see Donald M. Taylor's *Carving a New Inuit Identity: The Role of Language in the Education of Inuit Children in Arctic Quebec* (Kativik School Board, 1990).

As for Nunavut, the best source is *The Nunavut Handbook,* published in Iqaluit by Nortext Multimedia and updated regularly. My 1998 edition includes an essay on Inuktitut by Ann Meekitjuk Hanson. An excellent introduction to Inuktitut, "Our Language, Our Selves," by Alexina Kublu and Mick Mallon, is or was available at www.nunavut.com/nunavut99/english/our.html.

Inuktitut has been written in a Roman alphabet with Danish influence (in Greenland), a Roman alphabet with Moravian German influence (in Labrador), a Roman alphabet with French influence (in Quebec), a Roman alphabet with American and British influence (in Alaska and much of northern Canada), a syllabic alphabet (in other parts of northern Canada), and a Cyrillic alphabet with Russian influence (in Siberia). One consequence is that no two English-Inuktitut dictionaries agree on very much.

10. The Words That Come Before All Else: Mohawk

Brian Maracle's *Back on the Rez: Finding the Way Home* (Viking, 1996) is a superb introduction to Mohawk culture. On Iroquois tradition, see the works of William Fenton as well as Daniel K. Richter's *The Ordeal of the Longhouse: The Peoples of the Iroquois League in the Era of European Colonization* (Chapel Hill: University of North Carolina Press, 1992). For an outsider's portrait of contemporary Mohawk life see Ann Charney's "The Last Indian War," in *Defiance in Their Eyes: True Stories from the Margins* (Montreal: Véhicule Press, 1995). For an insider's view, see the writings of Dan David, notably "All My Relations," in *Taking Risks: Literary Journalism from the Edge*, ed. Barbara Moon and Don Obe (Banff: Banff Centre Press, 1998).

On the thorny details of Mohawk, I consulted the following works: Gunther Michelson's *1000 Words of Mohawk* (Ottawa: National Museum of Man, 1973); Nancy Bonvillain's *A Grammar of Akwesasne Mohawk* (National Museum of Man, 1973); several of David Maracle's works, notably *Mohawk Language Dictionary* (Belleville, Ont.: Mika, 1990) and *One Thousand Useful Mohawk Words* and *More Than One Thousand Mohawk Verbs* (London, Ont.: University of Western Ontario, 1992 and 1993); Nora Deering and Helga Delisle's *Mohawk: A Teaching Grammar* (Kahnawake: Thunderbird Press, 1976); and the conference report of the Mohawk Language Standardisation Project (Toronto: Ontario Ministry of Education and Training, 1997). I have tended to use Maracle's spellings.

Information about the cultures of the Six Nations is available in *Wadrihwa*, the newsletter of the Woodland Cultural Centre in Brantford, Ontario. Most Mohawk communities have Web sites of their own. For example, www.kahnawake.com includes a link to the Web site of the community newspaper, the *Eastern Door*. The *Eastern Door* published the provisions of the Kahnawake language law on 15 Oct. 1999, with further comments on 14 Jan. 2000. The controversy about Mohawk street names appeared in the editions of Jan. 2002. I also used Gerald Taiaiake Alfred's "Culture Change and the Founding of Kahnawake," (15 May 1992) and "The Unconscious Influence of the Seven Nations in Kahnawake" by Teyowisonte (21 Dec. 2001).

The Association du développement durable in Montreal co-sponsored a report by Mélanie Dantonel on Mohawk place names, "Tiohtiake: Cartographie des noms des lieux et des villages des Premières Nations" (2001). The former Egyptian diplomat Omar Z. Ghobashy wrote *The Caughnawaga Indians and the St. Lawrence Seaway* (New York: Devin-Adair, 1961). The talkative otter appears in *Tyendinaga Tales*, collected by Rona Rustige (Montreal: McGill-Queen's University Press, 1988). I quote J. B. Mackenzie's *The Six-Nations Indians in Canada* (Toronto: Hunter, Rose, 1896). Joseph Mitchell's *New Yorker* article "The Mohawks in High Steel" reappeared in Edmund Wilson's *Apologies to the Iroquois* (New York: Farrar, Straus and Cudahy, 1960).

Several versions of the Thanksgiving address can be read on line, in English and in Iroquois languages. Bear in mind that these texts, even if accurate, would not be accepted by all Iroquois people. It's not just that spelling is a bone of contention; it's also that written versions can give a false impression of authority and finality, while the oral tradition requires a certain flexibility.

Three essays in Grenoble and Whaley's *Endangered Languages* discuss Mohawk: those by Marianne Mithun, Christopher Jocks, and Kaia'titahkhe Annette Jacobs. I quote from the first two.

On Canadian indigenous languages in general, see Basil H. Johnston's "One Generation from Extinction," in *Native Writers and Canadian Writing,* ed. W. H. New (Vancouver: University of British Columbia Press, 1990). The proposals of the Royal Commission on Aboriginal Peoples appear in the "Arts and Heritage" chapter of vol. 3 of its complete report (1996). An important earlier survey was *"You Took My Talk": Aboriginal Literacy and Empowerment* (Ottawa: Standing Committee on Aboriginal Affairs, 1990).

11. HUMBOLDT'S PARROT

Parks Canada provides information about the Banff Springs snail at www .parkscanada.gc.ca. The Queensland Museum does the same for the northern hairy-nosed wombat and other endangered wildlife; see www.qmuseum.qld .gov.au and follow the link to "endangered species."

Chelonian Conservation and Biology: International Journal of Turtle and Tortoise Research published the first scientific description of *Chelodina burrungandjii* in Nov. 2000. I'm tempted to say, "I read 'em all"; this would not, however, be true.

An ecological theory of language shift is associated especially with Peter Mühlhäusler; see, e.g., *Linguistic Ecology: Language Change and Linguistic Imperialism in the Pacific Region* (Routledge, 1996). Edward O. Wilson, in *Consilience: The Unity of Knowledge* (Knopf, 1998), links environmental awareness to many other forms of knowledge, including linguistic. *Time* published Wilson's "Vanishing Before Our Eyes" in Apr. 2000. See also the work of the Terralingua organization.

On the relationship between cultural and biological diversity, see the work of Wade Davis, notably *Light at the Edge of the World* (Douglas and McIntyre, 2001); Beth Ann Fennelly's "Fruits We'll Never Taste," *Utne Reader,* Mar.–Apr. 2002; and Thomas Homer-Dixon's "We Need a Forest of Tongues," *Toronto Globe and Mail,* 7 July 2001.

I found the Wilhelm von Humboldt quotation, which dates from 1836, in Umberto Eco's *Search for the Perfect Language* (Oxford: Blackwell, 1995); the Haida word for alum root in *Recherches amérindiennes au Québec* 27, nos. 3–4 (1997); and the Halkomelem word for wild ginger in Taras Grescoe's "Leaving Ourselves Speehless," *Imperial Oil Review,* Autumn 1996. *Ngaapa Wangka*

Wangkajunga appeared in 2000 from the Kimberley Language Resource Centre in Halls Creek, Western Australia. See Helena Norberg-Hodge's *Ancient Futures: Learning from Ladakh* (San Francisco: Sierra Club Books, 1991) and Tony Juniper's *Spix's Macaw: The Race to Save the World's Rarest Bird* (Fourth Estate, 2002).

As for Alexander von Humboldt, I spent some happy hours searching out the parrot, the mosquitoes, and the resinous bones in a multivolume English translation, published in the nineteenth century, of his *Personal Narrative of Travels to the Equinoctial Regions of the New Continent During the Years 1799 to 1804.* Humboldt's remarkable life and work deserve to be much better known. This is, after all, a man of whom Charles Darwin wrote, "I shall never forget that my whole course of life is due to having read and reread as a youth his Personal Narrative."

12. Ways of Escape: Yiddish

See Dovid Katz's *Grammar of the Yiddish Language* (London: Gerald Duckworth, 1987), and, on a lighter note, Leo Rosten's *The Joys of Yiddish* (New York: Simon and Schuster, 1968). Also see Joshua Fishman's *Yiddish: Turning to Life* (Philadelphia: John Benjamins, 1991), and Benjamin Harshaw's polemical *The Meaning of Yiddish* (Berkeley: University of California Press, 1990).

On the history of Yiddish, see Max Weinreich's *History of the Yiddish Language,* trans. Shlomo Noble (University of Chicago Press, 1980); Sol Steinmetz's *Yiddish and English: A Century of Yiddish in America* (Tuscaloosa: University of Alabama Press, 1986); Sol Liptzin's *A History of Yiddish Literature* (New York: Jonathan David, 1985); George Johnson's "Scholars Debate Roots of Yiddish, Migration of Jews," *New York Times,* 29 Oct. 1996; and Emanuel S. Goldsmith's *Modern Yiddish Culture: The Story of the Yiddish Language Movement* (Fordham University Press, expanded ed., 1997).

Scholars, speakers, and friends of Yiddish have their own on-line forum, Mendele by name. I read Abraham Brumberg's "Yiddish and Hebrew — End of a Feud?" at www.haruth.com/YiddishHebrew.html.

Chava Rosenfarb's trilogy *Der boim fun leib* has not yet appeared in English. Her own translations of some of her other fiction, *Bociany* and *Of Lodz and Love,* were published by Syracuse University Press in 2000. See also her "Writing in Language Foreign to Nearly All," *Montreal Gazette,* 14 Aug. 1999. She was the subject of a documentary by Elaine Kalman Naves broadcast in 2001 on CBC Radio's *Ideas.*

The title of Ruth Wisse's "Yiddish: Past, Present, Imperfect," *Commentary,* Jan. 1997, echoes Lucy S. Dawidowicz's "Yiddish: Past, Present, and Perfect," *Commentary,* May 1962. And see Wisse's *The Modern Jewish Canon: A Journey Through Language and Culture* (New York: Free Press, 2000).

The long article in the *Ottawa Citizen,* Leonard Stern's "The Pious Ones," appeared on 20 Apr. 1997; Rabbi Ronnie Fine's reply ran on 11 May 1997. The relationship between Hasidim and Québécois in Outremont was explored in 1991 in *Bonjour Shalom,* a documentary film directed by Garry Beitel. See COHO's *Survey of the Hasidic and Ultra-Orthodox Communities in Outremont and Surrounding Areas* (Montreal: Coalition of Outremont Hasidic Organizations, 1997). The description of Yiddish teaching in Montreal in the 1950s is from Grace Feuerverger's *Oasis of Dreams: Teaching and Learning Peace in a Jewish-Palestinian Village in Israel* (New York: Routledge Falmer, 2001).

I learned of Miriam Weinstein's *Yiddish: A Nation of Words* (South Royalton, Vt.: Steerforth Press, 2001) too late to incorporate any of its insights into this chapter.

13. Revival

On modern Hebrew, see, e.g., Robert St. John's *Tongue of the Prophets* (North Hollywood: Wilshire Books, 1952) and Bernard Spolsky and Elana Shohamy's *The Languages of Israel: Policy, Ideology and Practice* (Multilingual Matters, 1999). More generally, see Martin Gilbert's *Israel: A History* (London: Doubleday, 1998). For a feminist view, see Naomi Seidman's *A Marriage Made in Heaven: The Sexual Politics of Hebrew and Yiddish* (University of California Press, 1997). Sam Orbaum's article on Ben-Yehuda's daughter appeared in the *Jerusalem Post,* 30 Apr. 2000. See also Jack Fellman's "Eliezer Ben-Yehuda and the Revival of Hebrew," at www.us-israel.org/jsource/biography/ben_yehuda .html.

On Faroese culture see Tom Nauerby's *No Nation Is an Island: Language, Culture, and National Identity in the Faroe Islands* (Aarhus: SNAI — North Atlantic Publications, 1996). See also *Minority Languages in Scandinavia, Britain and Ireland,* ed. Ailbhe Ó Corráin and Séamus Mac Mathúna (Uppsala University, 1999); John F. West, *Faroe: The Emergence of a Nation* (London: G. Hurst, 1972); and Jonathan Wylie and David Margolin, *The Ring of Dancers: Images of Faroese Culture* (University of Pennsylvania Press, 1981).

I quote Geoffrey Pullum from *Syntax and Semantics* 8 (1977). I first learned about Hixkaryana by reading Michael Cahill's "From Endangered to Less Endangered: Case Histories from Brazil and Papua New Guinea" at www.sil.org.

For a critical view of the Summer Institute of Linguistics (to use its old name), see David Stoll's *Fishers of Men or Founders of Empire? The Wycliffe Bible Translators in Latin America* (London: Zed Press and Cultural Survival, 1982). SIL's own Web site gives a much more secular view of the organization than does www.wycliffe.org. In July 2002 the Wycliffe site said: "Pray for the SIL training sessions going on in North Dakota and Oregon. Pray that God will enable each student to learn the basics of linguistic analysis. Pray too that God will burden the students' hearts for Bible translation." See also Lowell Weiss, "Speaking in Tongues," *Atlantic Monthly,* June 1995.

14. THE IRON OF LANGUAGE: WELSH

Janet Davies's *The Welsh Language* (Cardiff: University of Wales Press, 1999) is a good place to begin. In the same Pocket Guide series is Dafydd Johnston's *The Literature of Wales* (1994). And see Pamela Petro's *Travels in an Old Tongue* (London: Flamingo, 1998). Those with a lively knowledge of linguistics might consult *Welsh Phonology,* ed. Martin Bell and Glyn Jones (University of Wales Press, 1994), or Stephen J. Williams's *A Welsh Grammar* (University of Wales Press, 1980). I also used *A Most Peculiar People: Quotations About Wales and the Welsh,* ed. Meic Stephens (University of Wales Press, 1992). For eloquent nationalist polemics about Welsh history, see any book by Gwynfor Evans.

On the Web, both Cymuned and Cymdeithas maintain excellent bilingual sites. The Welsh Language Board has a Web site packed with official information.

Heini Gruffudd has written and compiled much material for Welsh learners. He is also a keen analyst of the language situation; see his "The European Year of Languages 2001 — Welsh as an Example of Minority Language Survival" at www.swan.ac.uk/conferences/transcomm/gruffudd.htm.

I quote Michael Krauss's *Alaska Native Languages: Past, Present, and Future.* J.R.R. Tolkien's "English and Welsh" appears in *Angles and Britons* (University of Wales Press, 1963), as does T. H. Parry-Williams's "English-Welsh Loan-Words." See also *The Letters of J.R.R. Tolkien,* ed. Humphrey Carpenter (Boston: Houghton Mifflin, 2000).

Presenting Saunders Lewis, ed. Alun R. Jones and Gwyn Thomas (University of Wales Press, 1973), offers a generous selection of Lewis's work as well as critical assessments of it. See also Bruce Griffiths's *Saunders Lewis* (University of Wales Press, 1979). My main source on Txillardegi was Mark Kurlansky's *The Basque History of the World* (Toronto: Knopf Canada, 1999).

George Borrow's *Wild Wales* (1862) is available in various modern editions. For R. S. Thomas, see his *Selected Prose,* ed. Sandra Anstey (Bridgend: Poetry Wales Press, 1986), and selected editions of his poetry. For a more skeptical view of tradition in general, see *The Invention of Tradition,* ed. Eric Hobsbawm and Terence Ranger (Cambridge, 1983).

Jan Morris has written superbly about Wales on many occasions. Less lyrical and more political than usual is her "Go Home, Englishman," *Spectator,* 31 Aug. 2002. Robat Powell's *Haearn Iaith* was published by Gomer Press (Llandysul, Ceredigion) in 1996. I quote Dylan Thomas's poem "Lie Still, Sleep Becalmed."

For an astute comparison of Welsh and Maori, see Anthony Hubbard's Reuter Foundation Paper for Green College, Oxford, "Language Revitalization: Welsh and Maori" (Dec. 2001). On Maori, see, e.g., the Web site of the Maori Language Commission, and Edward Te Kohu Douglas's "Maori Language Nests," *Journal of Indigenous Studies,* Winter 1992.

15. THE FACE OF ALL THE EARTH

The quote from Tiorahkwáthe in this chapter is from www.kahnawake.com.

I quote Joshua Fishman's "What Is Reversing Language Shift and How Can It Succeed?" in *Fourth International Conference on Minority Languages* (Multilingual Matters, 1989). W. S. Graham's poem "What Is the Language Using Us For?" is in his *Implements in Their Places* (Faber and Faber, 1977). I quote Claude Lévi-Strauss's "'Primitive' Thinking and the 'Civilized' Mind," in *Myth and Meaning* (University of Toronto Press, 1978).

John Stuart Mill's words on Breton and Basque have been used approvingly in at least two articles by Kenan Malik; see *Living Marxism* 88 (Mar. 1996) and the *Montreal Gazette*, 9 Dec. 2000. For the original text, see Ch. 16 of Mill's *Considerations on Representative Government.*

The report of the U.S. "Peace Commission" that in 1868 recommended the abolition of Indian languages has been widely quoted. John J. Miller's "How Do You Say 'Extinct'?" appeared in the *Wall Street Journal*, 8 Mar. 2002.

I quote Danielle Cyr's "La lune est notre grand-mère," *Recherches amérindiennes au Québec* 26, nos. 3–4 (1996), and Michael Christie's "Yolngu Linguistics," *Ngoonjook: A Journal of Australian Indigenous Issues*, June 1993. Cyr's argument about the significance of Algonquian pronouns is supported by another Quebec linguist, José Mailhot.

On the importance of diversity, I am consciously echoing Wade Davis. In the Canadian magazine *Saturday Night*, Dec. 1999, he warned: "All the technological innovations and the wars of this bloodstained century will be wiped away in historical memory by the fact that the 21st century was the era in which we stood by and either actively endorsed or passively accepted the massive loss of both cultural and biological diversity. And that will be the hallmark of the coming century."

Readers who would like to explore the issue of language loss further — and perhaps to contribute some money — may want to join the Foundation for Endangered Languages, based in the United Kingdom. It gives modest grants to individuals and organizations fighting for languages around the world, and its journal *Ogmios* offers much information. Other groups working to save languages include the Endangered Language Fund (United States), International Clearing House for Endangered Languages (Japan), and Gesellschaft für bedrohte Sprachen (Germany). All these organizations have Web sites.

Acknowledgments

What a long strange trip this book has been! The writing of it proved to be far more arduous and time-consuming than I imagined back in a previous millennium when I conceived the idea of a book about language that would also embrace travel, ideas, history, and polemic.

My first thanks go to the speakers of the languages described in *Spoken Here*. Some of them appear in these pages — they know who they are, and so do you. Without their willingness to show me something of their lives, the book could not exist. From time to time, reacting and writing as an English-speaking outsider, I may inadvertently have hurt some feelings. If so, I ask forgiveness. In the end, I trust that people fighting to save threatened languages will understand this book has been written in their honor.

For continual encouragement, terrific suggestions, and gentle criticism at every stage, *diolch* above all to my wife, Ann Beer. Her understanding of the book's subject matter, at an emotional as well as an intellectual level, has been essential. The first reader of almost every page, she made innumerable astute comments. Thanks also to our children, Kate and Megan, for putting up with their father's absence on journeys and obsession at home.

Only Eamon Dolan, my editor at Houghton Mifflin, knows what a huge impact he has had on *Spoken Here*. His merciless attentions sometimes left me bruised and dazed. But when I'd picked myself up off the floor, I usually found he was right. Every writer should have the chance to suffer so devoted and so gifted an editor. Camille Smith provided intelligent manuscript editing. Thanks also to Emily Little, Liz Duvall, Dan O'Connell, and everyone else who worked on the book at Houghton Mifflin.

In Anne Collins, executive editor of Random House Canada, I found an ideal combination of sympathy and discernment. Several chapters are much the better because of her comments, and her confidence in the book has sustained me. My thanks extend to her colleague Pamela Murray for calm and clearheaded practical advice.

I owe a huge debt of gratitude, too, to my agent, Jackie Kaiser. Not only did she skillfully negotiate with editors and publishers, she suggested many key improvements to the manuscript in its early stages. Thanks also to Jan Whitford, who before her retirement as an agent encouraged me to reenter the world of books, and who sold the idea of *Spoken Here* to Random House on the basis of an extraordinarily skimpy proposal. And thanks to Nicole Winstanley for her tireless and skillful work in finding publishers for the book outside North America.

The germ of this book lies in an essay that I wrote in 1997 under the auspices of the Cultural Journalism program at the Banff Centre for the Arts. It is a pleasure to acknowledge the challenging advice of Barbara Moon, Michael Ignatieff, and my seven fellow writers in the Leighton Studios that July. I returned to the Banff program as an editor in July 2000, when I had just begun work on this book. The good counsel and friendly ear of Denis Sampson were important to me then and have been important since.

Thanks to Ray Brassard for granting me an unpaid leave of absence from *The Gazette* so that I could give myself to this book, and for extending the leave a year later. I finished the manuscript in the red; but I might never have been able to finish it at all if not for a nonfiction grant from the Canada Council for the Arts. My thanks to the jury and to the council's hardworking staff.

For her help in arranging some of my journeys in Australia, and for her friendship when I was there, I thank Fran Murray of the Catholic Education Office in Darwin. Even if some of what I have written displeases her, I hope she will accept my gratitude and understand my point of view. My particular thanks in Australia also go to Cath Rouse and Mark Crocombe. Joyce Hudson, Sonia Emery, and Cathy McGinness kindly answered many questions. Rob Amery made two crucial initial contacts for me in Darwin, and Paul Black, Waymamba Gaykamangu, Paul Bubb, Paul Daglish, Jan Pilcher, Ursula Kinthari, Bonnie Deegan, and Bill Young provided insights and assistance in Darwin, Wadeye, and Halls Creek.

My trip to Oklahoma depended on the willing cooperation of Richard Grounds. It will be clear from the chapter on Yuchi how much I am in his debt. Thanks to the leaders of the Euchee Tribe, who agreed to my visit; to Mary Linn, who answered all my questions and sent me a large chunk of her doctoral thesis; and to Patchen Barss, who first alerted me to the existence of the Yuchi language.

My discussion of Manx owes much to Brian Stowell. Long after he had put me in touch with several of his fellow islanders, he patiently replied to my queries about his beloved language. Thanks to Phil Gawne for his e-mail remarks, too. For my meeting with the Crellin sisters I am indebted to Jane Baines —

and for putting me in touch with her, it's agreeable to thank my mother, Mary Abley, who awakened my love of languages and reading.

In Provence, I was fortunate to be the guest of Marianne Ackerman and Gwyn Campbell. Their hospitality, their commitment to cultural diversity, and their lively conversation gave me lasting inspiration. Through them I met Nini Albertini and Patric Choffrut, whom I thank for their helpful correspondence. I'm grateful to Céline Missonnier for the poems and other documents, and to Gustaf Sobin for the discussion about Provençal in an Avignon café.

My trip to Baffin Island took place thanks to the approval of Catherine Wallace and Brian Kappler of *The Gazette*. For help and ideas in Kimmirut, I'm grateful to Saa Pitsiulak, Nalenik Temela, Annie Ikkidluak, Pascale Baillargeon, Pitseolak Michael, Mattoo Michael, and Pierre Obendrauf. Chapter 9 is dedicated to the memory of the Kimmirut artist and teacher Simata Pitsiulak, who died in a plane crash shortly after my visit. He is not described in these pages, but his vision, I hope, informs them. On a wall beside his home computer, I saw his own framed translations of a passage from the *Song of Songs* into Inuktitut syllabics and Canadian English: "The winter is over, the darkness and the cold; in the tundra land the arctic flowers will soon bloom. This is the time for singing; the songs of snowbirds will soon be heard in the hills . . ."

My friend Dan David of Kanehsatake kindly read an early version of my chapter on Mohawk. For candor and generosity at Six Nations, special thanks to Brian Owennatekha Maracle and Audrey Bomberry. For speedy answers to technical and occasionally vapid questions, thanks to David Kanatawakhon Maracle. Timmy Norton of the Mohawk Council of Kahnawake approved my visit to the Kahnawake Language Centre; Barry Lazar, Loreen Pindera, and Dane Lanken shared their excellent contacts; and Salli M. R. Benedict put me in touch with Ernie Benedict of Akwesasne.

I am grateful to Kim Echlin for introducing me to Humboldt's parrot, a bird that makes a cameo appearance in her novel *Dagmar's Daughter*, and to Rod Kennett and Brent Williams for clearing up my misconceptions about long-necked turtles.

The linguist Nick Ukiah may find much in this book insufferably romantic — even so, I thank him for his witty and valuable comments about Yiddish. Irwin Block read a draft of the Yiddish chapter, lent me a copy of the script of Melville Shavelson's play *The Great Houdini*, and made sure I grasped the vital difference between a *nudnick* and a *nudzh*. My dear friend Marcy Kahan put me in touch with Nick Ukiah and sent me a cassette of a BBC Radio show about Dovid Katz. Thanks also to my equally dear friend Nancie Kahan for her help. Elaine Kalman Naves kindly opened my eyes to Chava Rosenfarb's unpublished "Confessions of a Yiddish Writer." I'm indebted to Dr. Hy Goldman for inviting me to come and see KlezKanada for myself.

Thanks to the late Sam Orbaum for his generous insights on Hebrew and Yiddish in Israel, to Cleo Paskal for enlightening me about some aspects of

Faroese, and (especially) to Des Derbyshire for bringing me up to date on Hixkaryana.

As for Welsh, I'm grateful again to Gwyn Campbell, for his useful suggestions and for his eloquent, sometimes angry declarations about his language. His passion for Welsh served as a constant reminder of what is at stake. Special thanks to my mother-in-law, Arabella Beer, for information about Welsh and Cornish, and for putting me in touch with Medwen and John Rhodes, the kindest and best of hosts on Ynys Môn. I am indebted to Helen Jones, who arranged my visit to Tregarth; to Susan Mayse, thanks to whom I contacted Y Lolfa; to Robin Campbell, who discussed Welsh with me during a gale in Swansea; to the Reverend John Gillibrand, for his insights into the learning of Welsh; and to Paul Birt, who directed me to Cymuned. Dylan Phillips (now a senior lecturer at Trinity College, Carmarthen) painstakingly answered my questions; not only did he save me from an absurd spelling of *madarch,* he also sent me his provocative essays about Cymdeithas yr Iaith Gymraeg and about the impact of tourism on the Welsh language.

Much of the research for this book was carried out in the McLennan Library of McGill University; my gratitude to the librarians. Singular thanks go to Dave Pinto of *The Gazette,* who fed me a rich diet of clippings about languages, many of them wonderfully obscure. Who else could have come up with a yellowed obituary from *Le Monde,* mourning a long-forgotten champion of the Breton language, or an essay published in *The Listener* in 1953? He has repeated such favors more times than either of us can count.

For miscellaneous advice, tips, or other help, thanks to Robert Bringhurst, Katherine Berg, Carl Diotte, Calestous Juma, Derek Johns, Charles Foran, Adrian King-Edwards, Alex Norris, John Ryle, Ronald Wright, Robert C. Suggs, Kelly Haggart, Étienne Tiffou, Sujit Attavar, Alex Schultz, Michael Dungan, Emily Urquhart, Joe Fiorito, Barbara Samuels, David Crystal, John M. Miller, Stephen Hume, Alex Lancaster, Douglas Jack, Jeff Heinrich, and Tom Perry.

I want to reiterate my thanks to those fellow writers who allowed me to describe them in this book. Robat Powell, Brian Maracle, Chava Rosenfarb, Sèrgi Bec: such people are all too aware of the distorting power of the word, especially (but not only) in a foreign tongue. No doubt they would have chosen to emphasize different aspects of their work and of their beloved languages. I hope I have not betrayed the faith they placed in me. All credit to them and their struggle.

In spite of all this help, it's inevitable that a book like this will contain some errors. I am, after all, presuming to tell you about languages that are foreign to me. My apologies in advance for whatever mistakes I have perpetrated.

Index